Nozel

Noelle

Nebra

Solid

Black * Clover

YŪKI TABATA **19** SIBLINGS

Characters

Yuno

Member of: The Golden Dawn

Magic: Wind

Asta's best friend, and a good rival who's also been working to become the Wizard King. He controls Sylph, the spirit of wind.

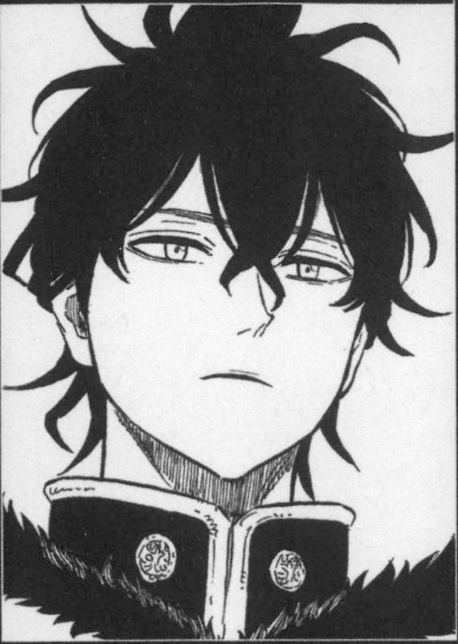

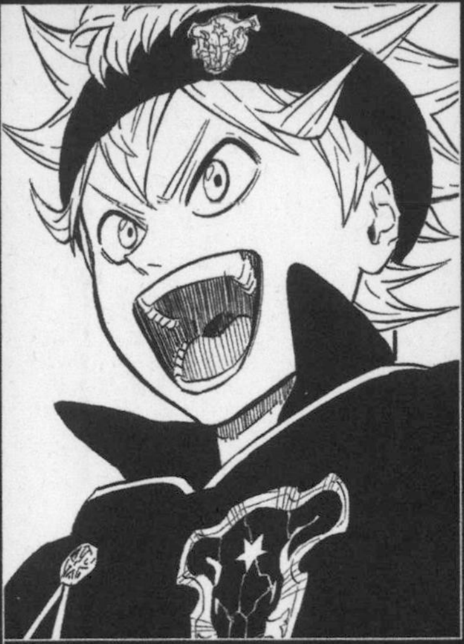

Asta

Member of: The Black Bulls

Magic: None (Anti-Magic)

He has no magic, but he's working to become the Wizard King through sheer guts and his well-trained body. He fights with anti-magic swords.

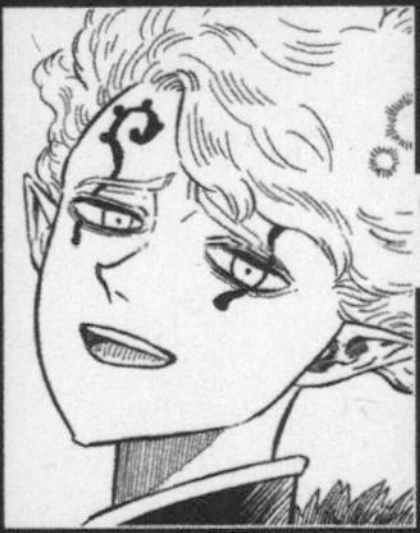

Langris Vaude

Member of: The Golden Dawn

Magic: Spatial

Finral's younger half-brother. His body has been taken over by an elf named Latry, Patry's cousin.

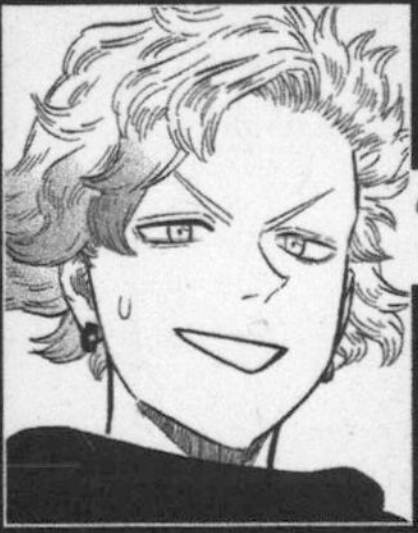

Finral Roulacase

Member of: The Black Bulls

Magic: Spatial

A playboy who immediately chats up any woman he sees. He can't attack, but he has high-level abilities.

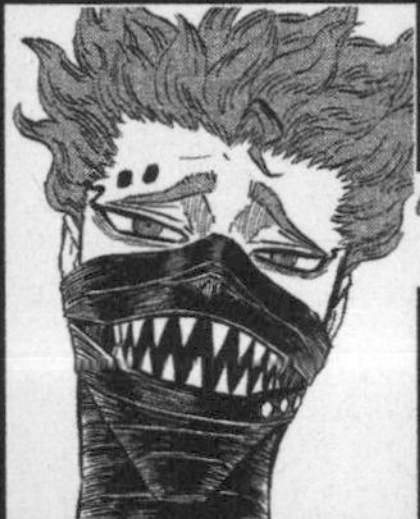

Zora Ideale

Member of: The Black Bulls

Magic: Ash

He idolizes his father, who was a Magic Knight, and he's particularly good at trap spells. Has a cynical personality.

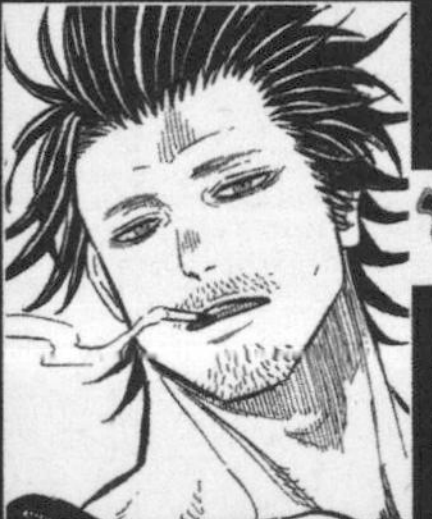

Yami Sukehiro

Member of: The Black Bulls

Magic: Dark

A captain who looks fierce, but is very popular with his brigade, which has a deep-rooted confidence in him. Heavy smoker.

Noelle Silva

Member of:
The Black Bulls
Magic: Water

A royal. She feels inferior to her brilliant siblings. Her latent abilities are an unknown quantity.

Nozel Silva

Member of:
The Silver Eagles
Magic: Mercury

Noelle's older brother. A captain who values his pride as a royal. Considers Fuegoleon a friendly rival.

Raia

Magic: Copy

Once he touches his opponent's grimoire, he's able to copy their magic. He's regained powerful mana through the reincarnation spell.

Mimosa Vermillion

Member of:
The Golden Dawn
Magic: Plant

Noelle's cousin. She's ladylike and a bit of an airhead, but she can be rude. She just might like Asta...

Licht

Magic: Sword

The leader of the elves. He was resurrected by the reincarnation spell, but his mind hasn't returned yet, and he's unstable.

Patry

Magic: Light

He monopolized the body he'd shared with William and completed the reincarnation. His temporary form looks exactly like Licht.

STORY

In a world where magic is everything, Asta and Yuno are both found abandoned on the same day at a church in the remote village of Hage. Both dream of becoming the Wizard King, the highest of all mages, and they spend their days working toward that dream.

The year they turn 15, both receive grimoires, magic books that amplify their bearer's magic. They take the entrance exam for the Magic Knights, nine groups of mages under the direct control of the Wizard King. Yuno, whose magic is strong, joins the Golden Dawn, an elite group, while Asta, who has no magic at all, joins the Black Bulls, a group of misfits. With this, the two finally take their first step toward becoming the Wizard King...

Although the Black Bulls hideout had been nearly destroyed, Henry's magic transforms it into the Raging Black Bull. Asta and friends then board it and head for the capital. Meanwhile, members of the Golden Dawn who've been turned into elves assemble at the royal palace with Yami and Finral hot on their tails.

CONTENTS

BLACK ✿ CLOVER

19

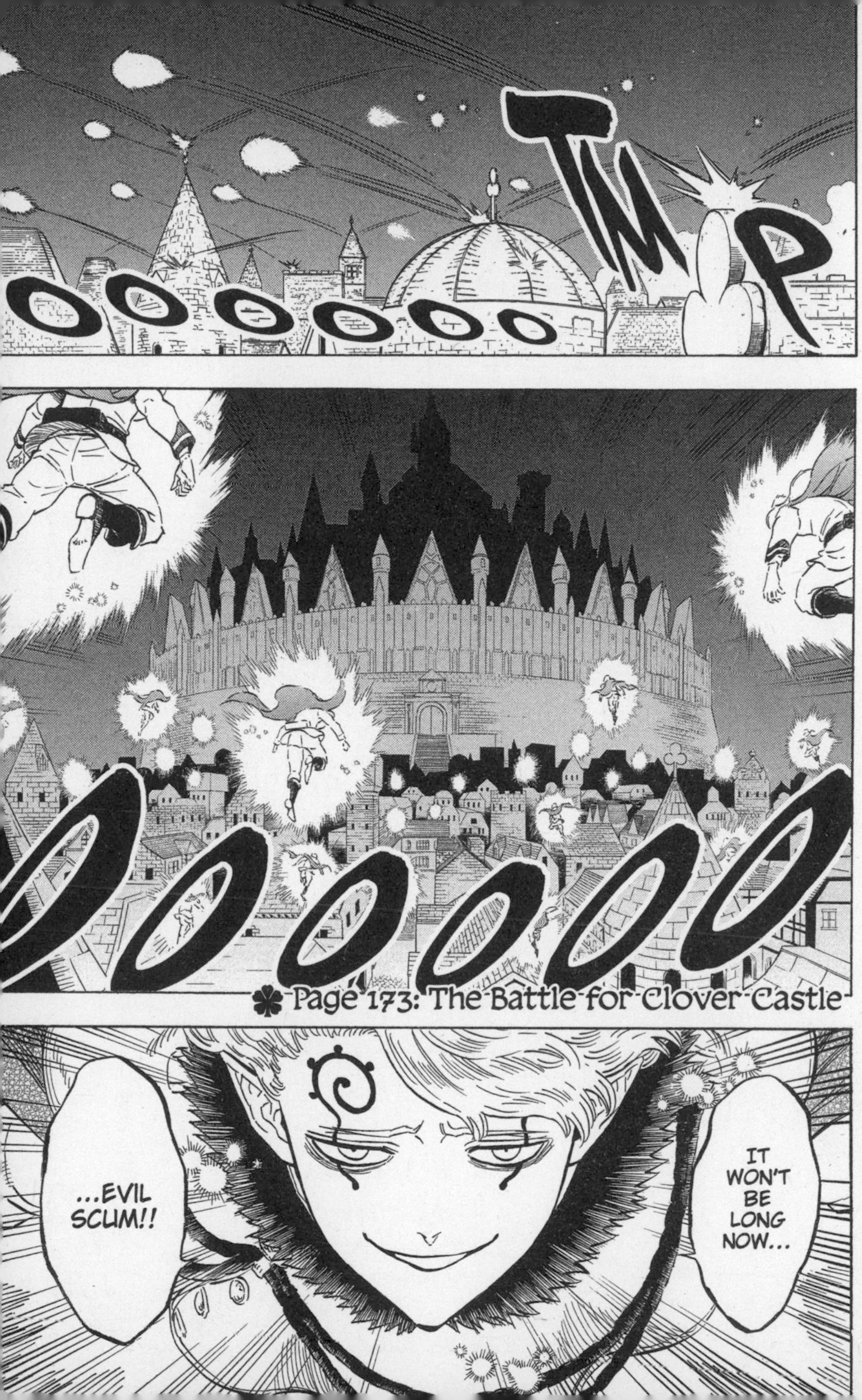
TMP
OOOOOOO
OOOOOOO
Page 173: The Battle for Clover Castle
IT WON'T BE LONG NOW...
...EVIL SCUM!!

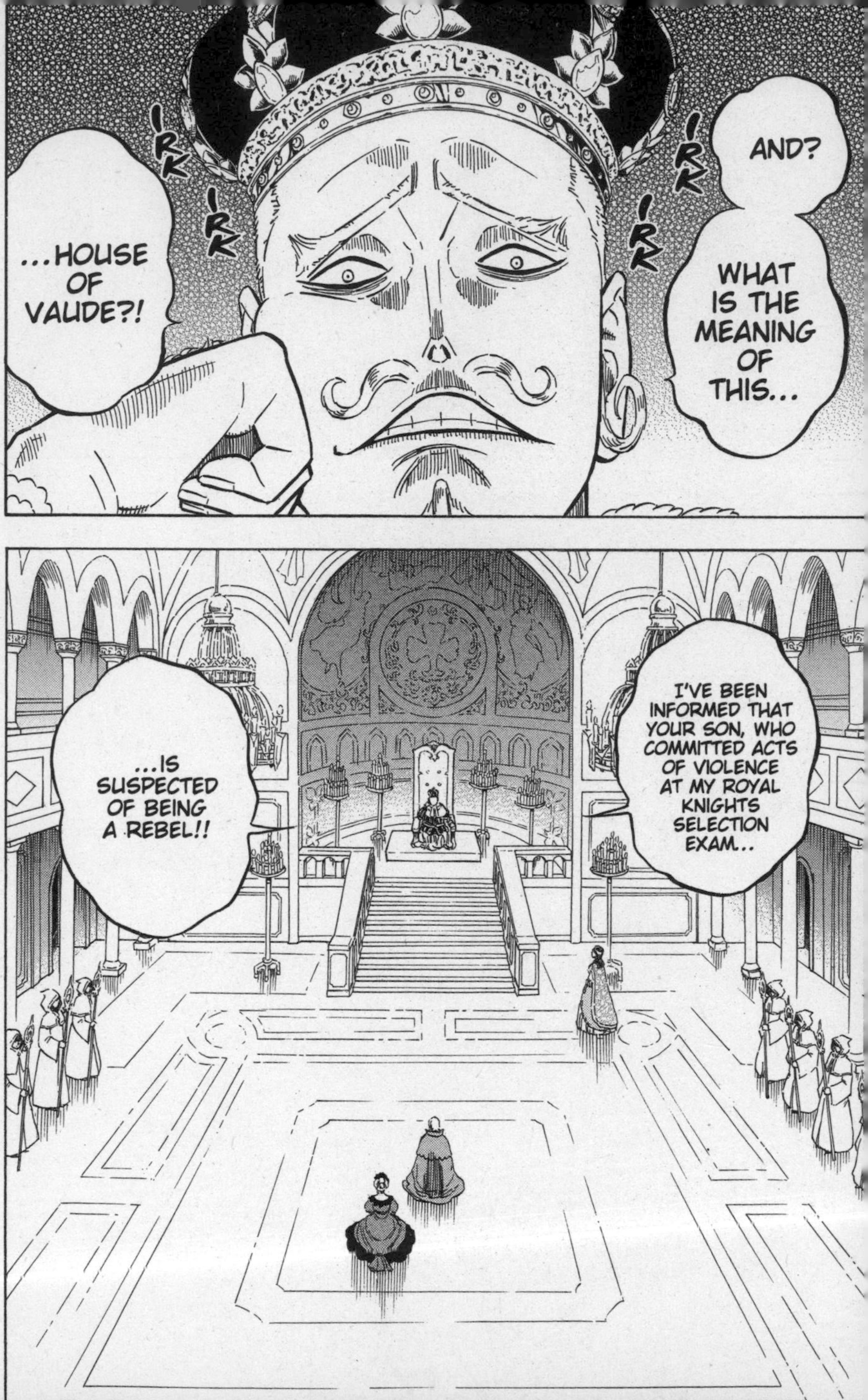
IRK IRK
AND?
WHAT IS THE MEANING OF THIS...
IRK IRK
...HOUSE OF VAUDE?!
I'VE BEEN INFORMED THAT YOUR SON, WHO COMMITTED ACTS OF VIOLENCE AT MY ROYAL KNIGHTS SELECTION EXAM...
...IS SUSPECTED OF BEING A REBEL!!

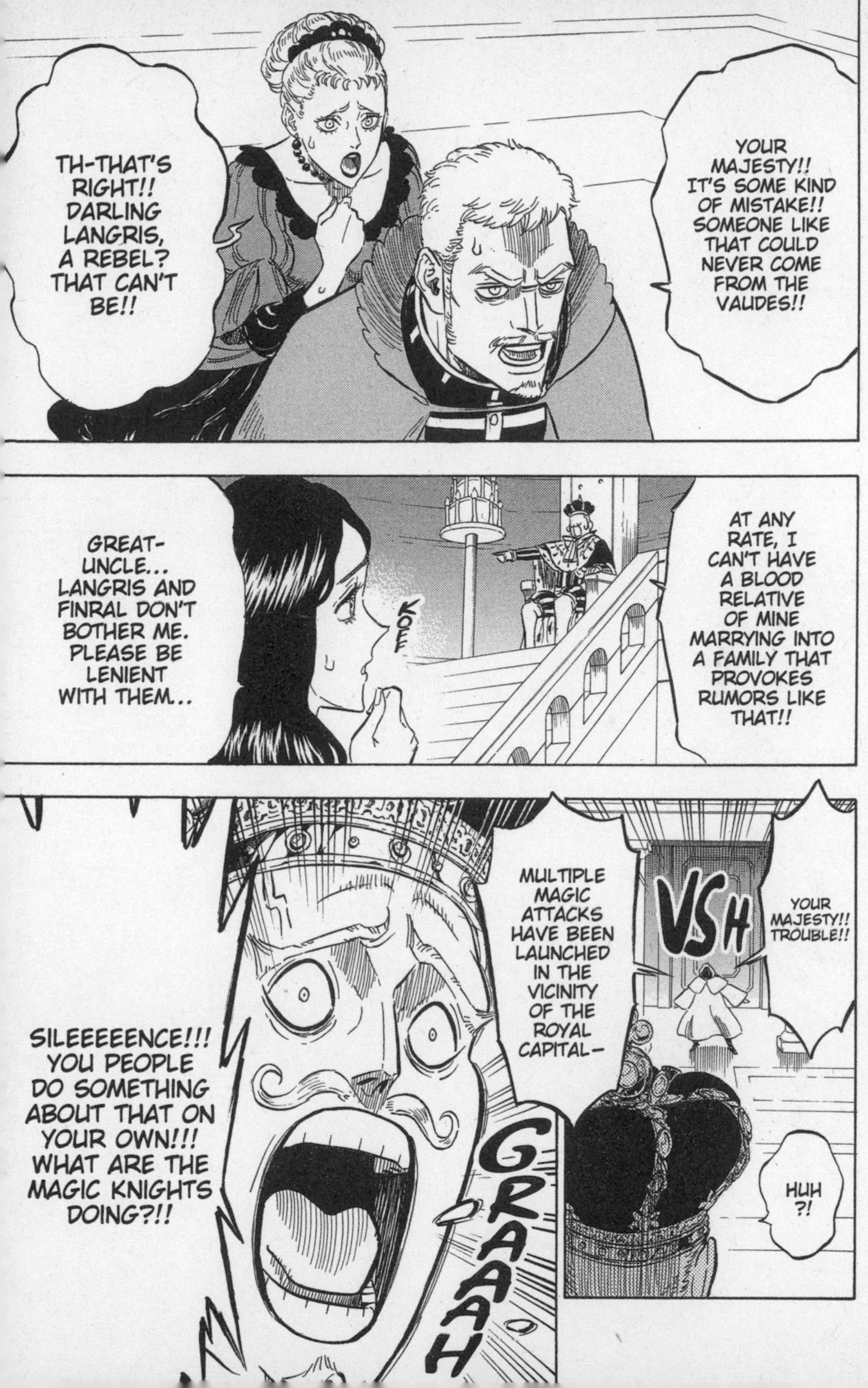
YOUR MAJESTY!! IT'S SOME KIND OF MISTAKE!! SOMEONE LIKE THAT COULD NEVER COME FROM THE VAUDES!!
TH-THAT'S RIGHT!! DARLING LANGRIS, A REBEL? THAT CAN'T BE!!
AT ANY RATE, I CAN'T HAVE A BLOOD RELATIVE OF MINE MARRYING INTO A FAMILY THAT PROVOKES RUMORS LIKE THAT!!
KOFF
GREAT-UNCLE... LANGRIS AND FINRAL DON'T BOTHER ME. PLEASE BE LENIENT WITH THEM...
YOUR MAJESTY!! TROUBLE!!
VSH
MULTIPLE MAGIC ATTACKS HAVE BEEN LAUNCHED IN THE VICINITY OF THE ROYAL CAPITAL—
HUH ?!
SILEEEEENCE!!! YOU PEOPLE DO SOMETHING ABOUT THAT ON YOUR OWN!!! WHAT ARE THE MAGIC KNIGHTS DOING?!!
GRAAAAH

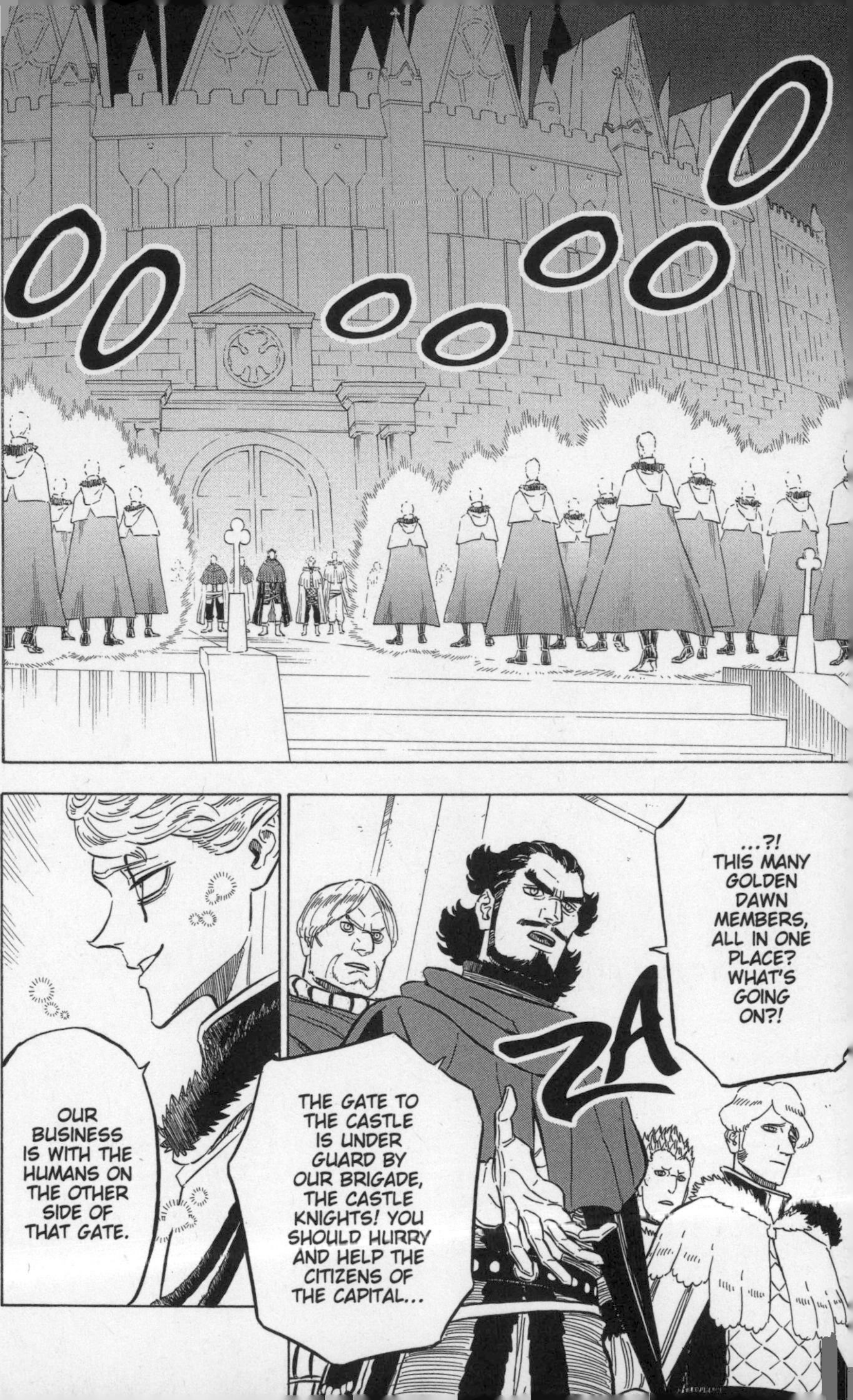
...?! THIS MANY GOLDEN DAWN MEMBERS, ALL IN ONE PLACE? WHAT'S GOING ON?!
ZA
THE GATE TO THE CASTLE IS UNDER GUARD BY OUR BRIGADE, THE CASTLE KNIGHTS! YOU SHOULD HURRY AND HELP THE CITIZENS OF THE CAPITAL...
OUR BUSINESS IS WITH THE HUMANS ON THE OTHER SIDE OF THAT GATE.

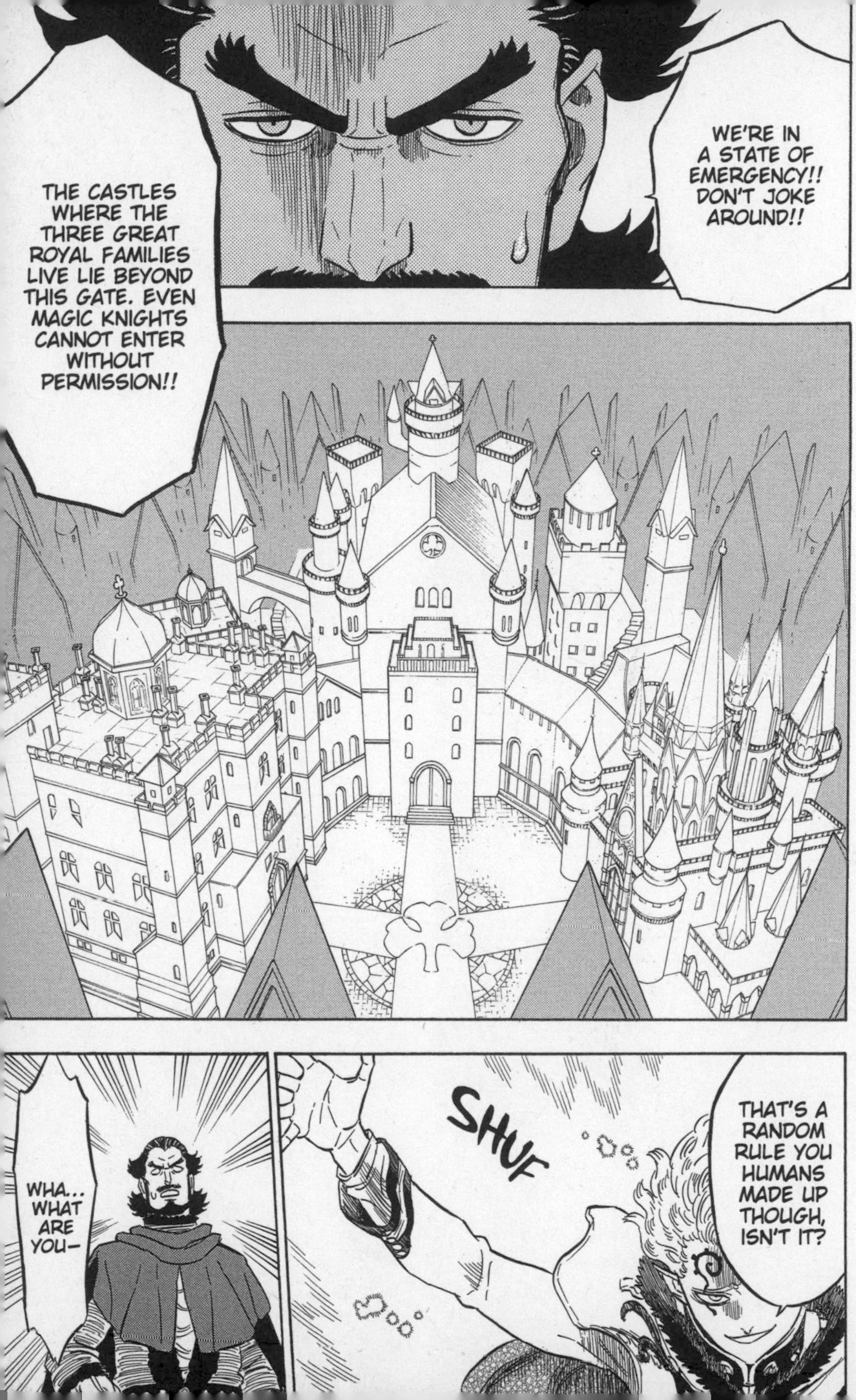
WE'RE IN A STATE OF EMERGENCY!! DON'T JOKE AROUND!!
THE CASTLES WHERE THE THREE GREAT ROYAL FAMILIES LIVE LIE BEYOND THIS GATE. EVEN MAGIC KNIGHTS CANNOT ENTER WITHOUT PERMISSION!!
SHUF
THAT'S A RANDOM RULE YOU HUMANS MADE UP THOUGH, ISN'T IT?
WHA... WHAT ARE YOU-

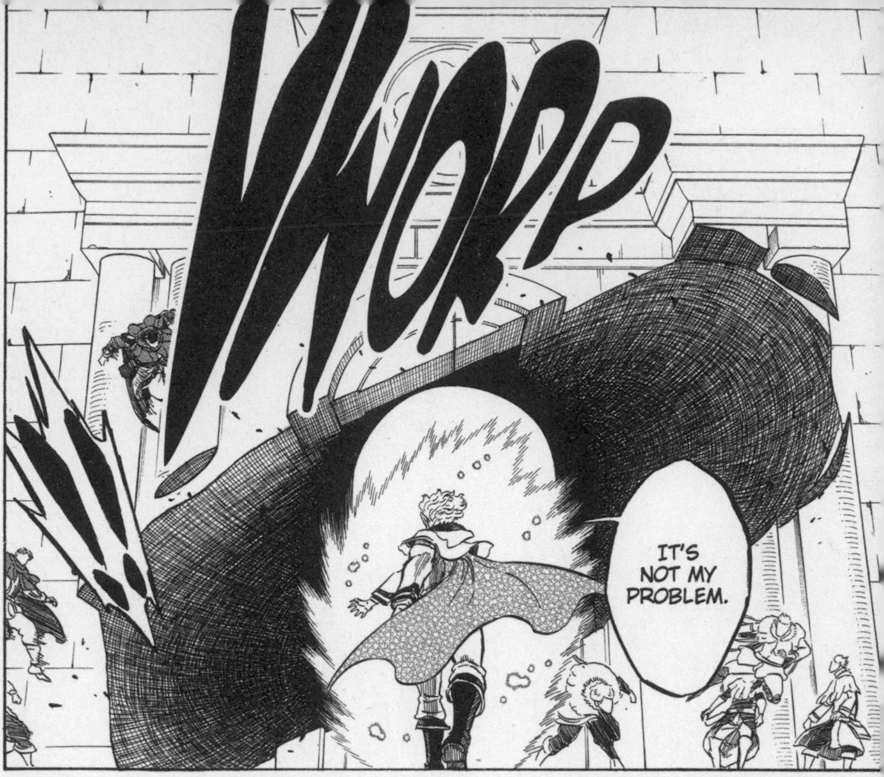
WHOP
IT'S NOT MY PROBLEM.
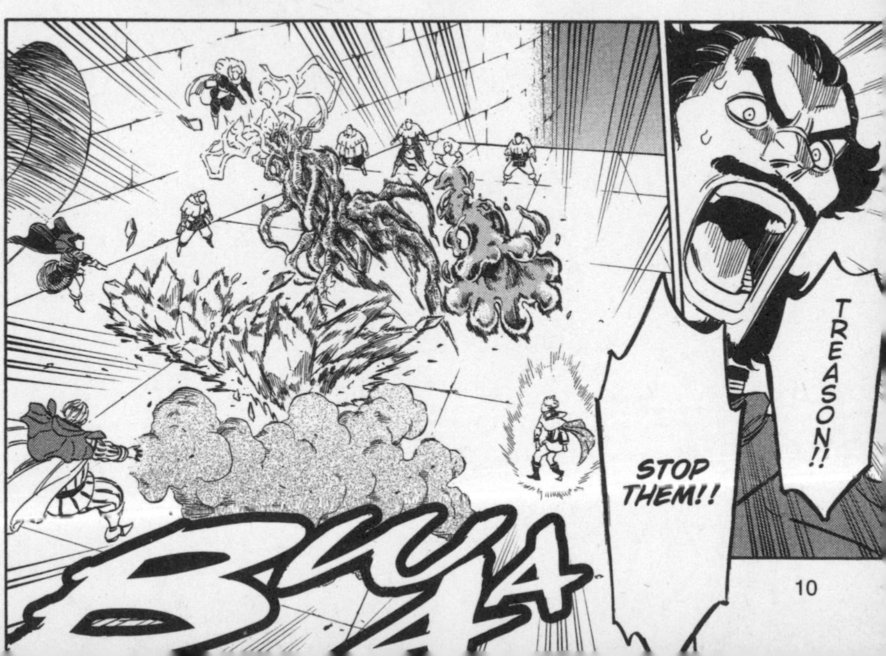
TREASON!!
STOP THEM!!
BAYA

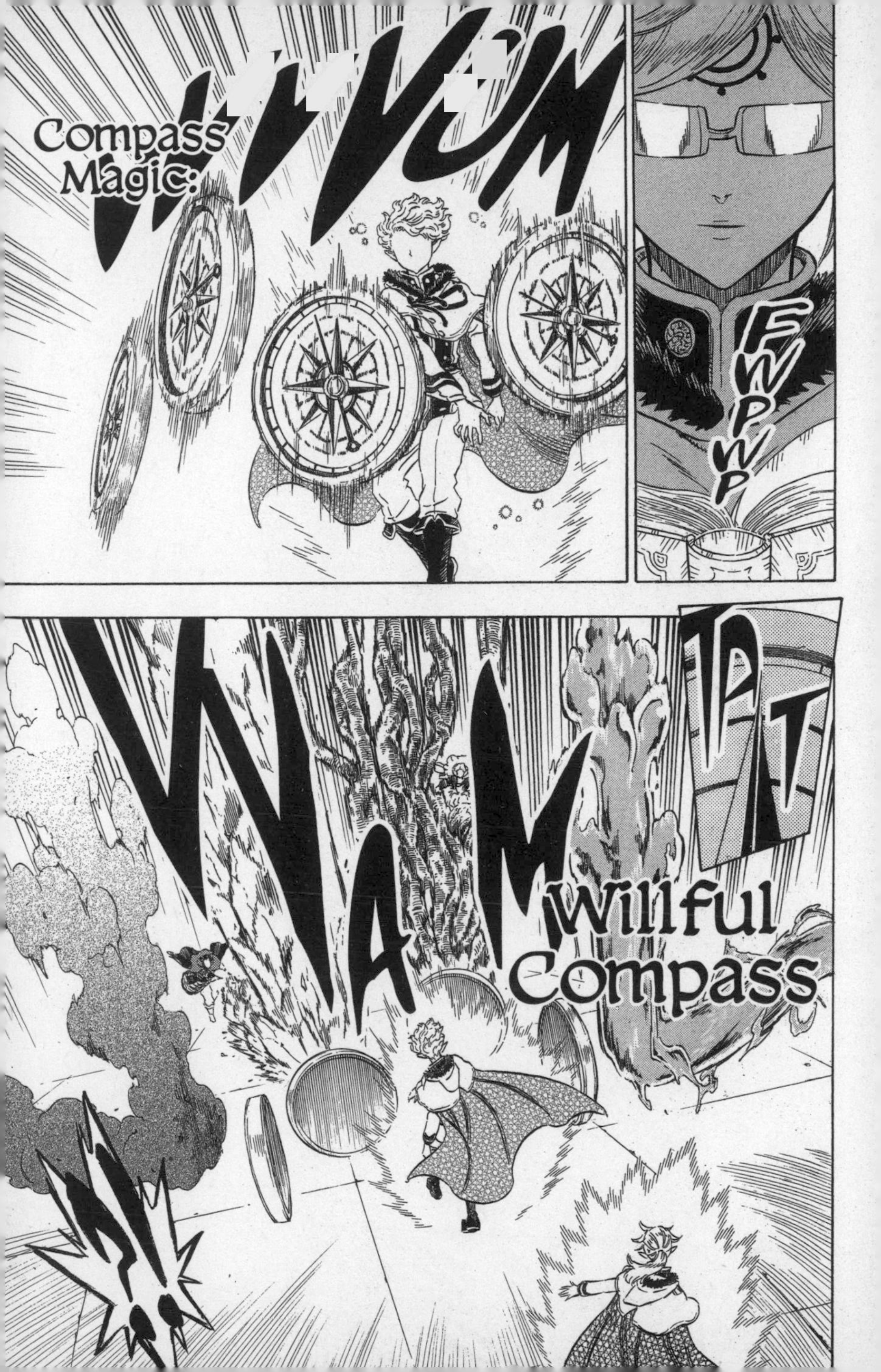
FWPWP
Compass Magic:
TAT
Willful Compass
VWAM

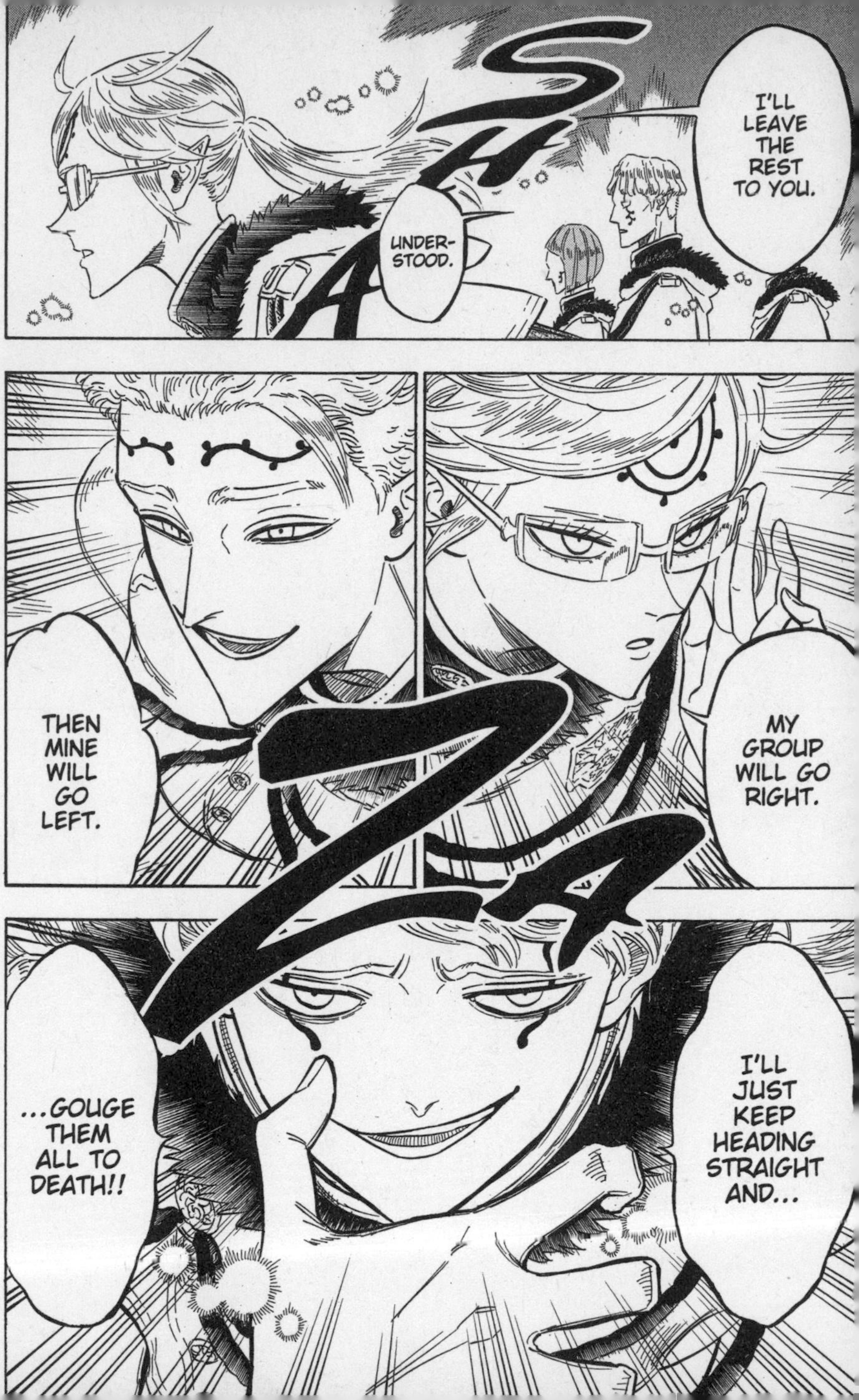
SHA
I'LL LEAVE THE REST TO YOU.
UNDER-STOOD.
MY GROUP WILL GO RIGHT.
THEN MINE WILL GO LEFT.
ZA
I'LL JUST KEEP HEADING STRAIGHT AND...
...GOUGE THEM ALL TO DEATH!!

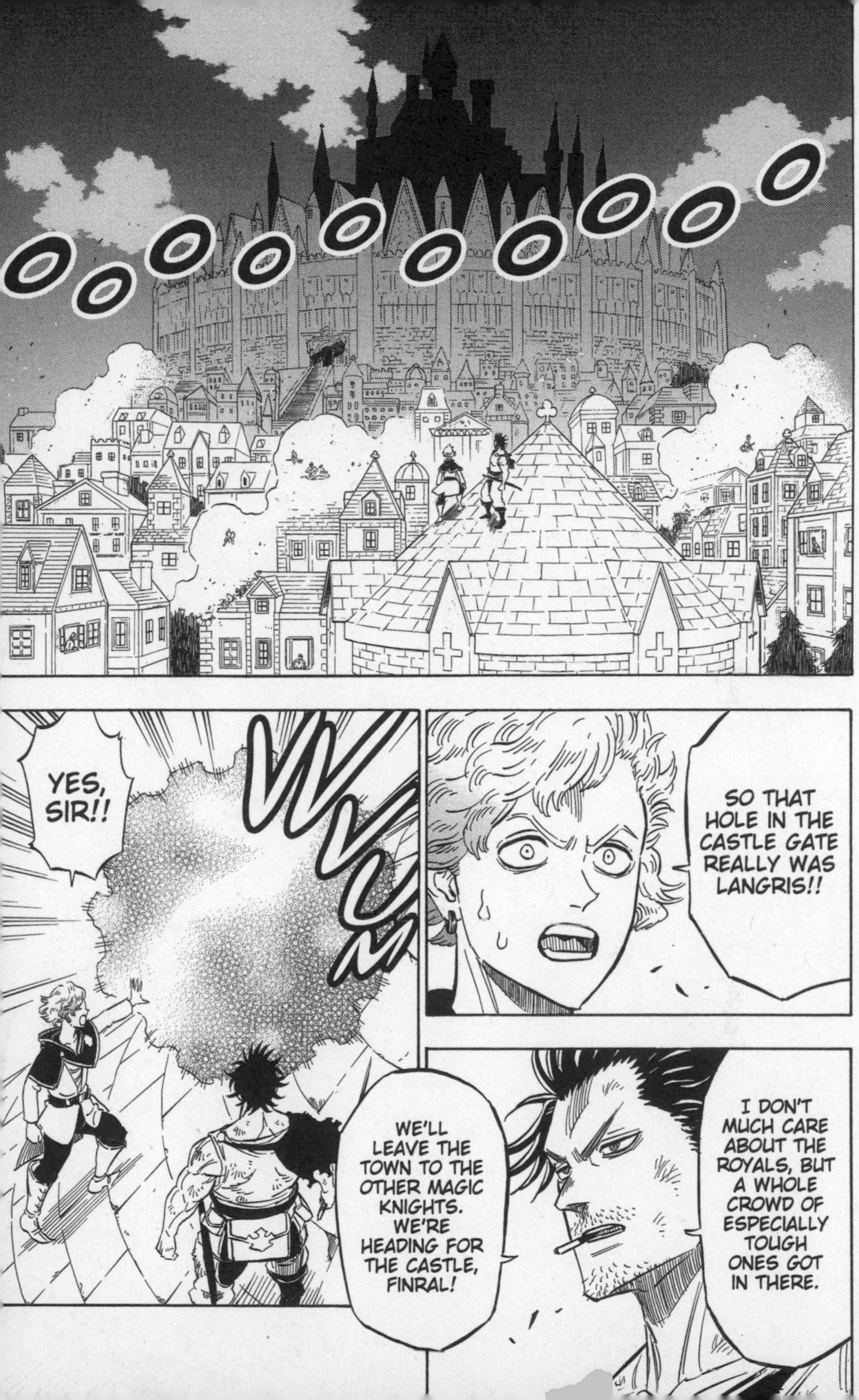
OOOOOOOOOO
SO THAT HOLE IN THE CASTLE GATE REALLY WAS LANGRIS!!
I DON'T MUCH CARE ABOUT THE ROYALS, BUT A WHOLE CROWD OF ESPECIALLY TOUGH ONES GOT IN THERE.
WE'LL LEAVE THE TOWN TO THE OTHER MAGIC KNIGHTS. WE'RE HEADING FOR THE CASTLE, FINRAL!
YES, SIR!!

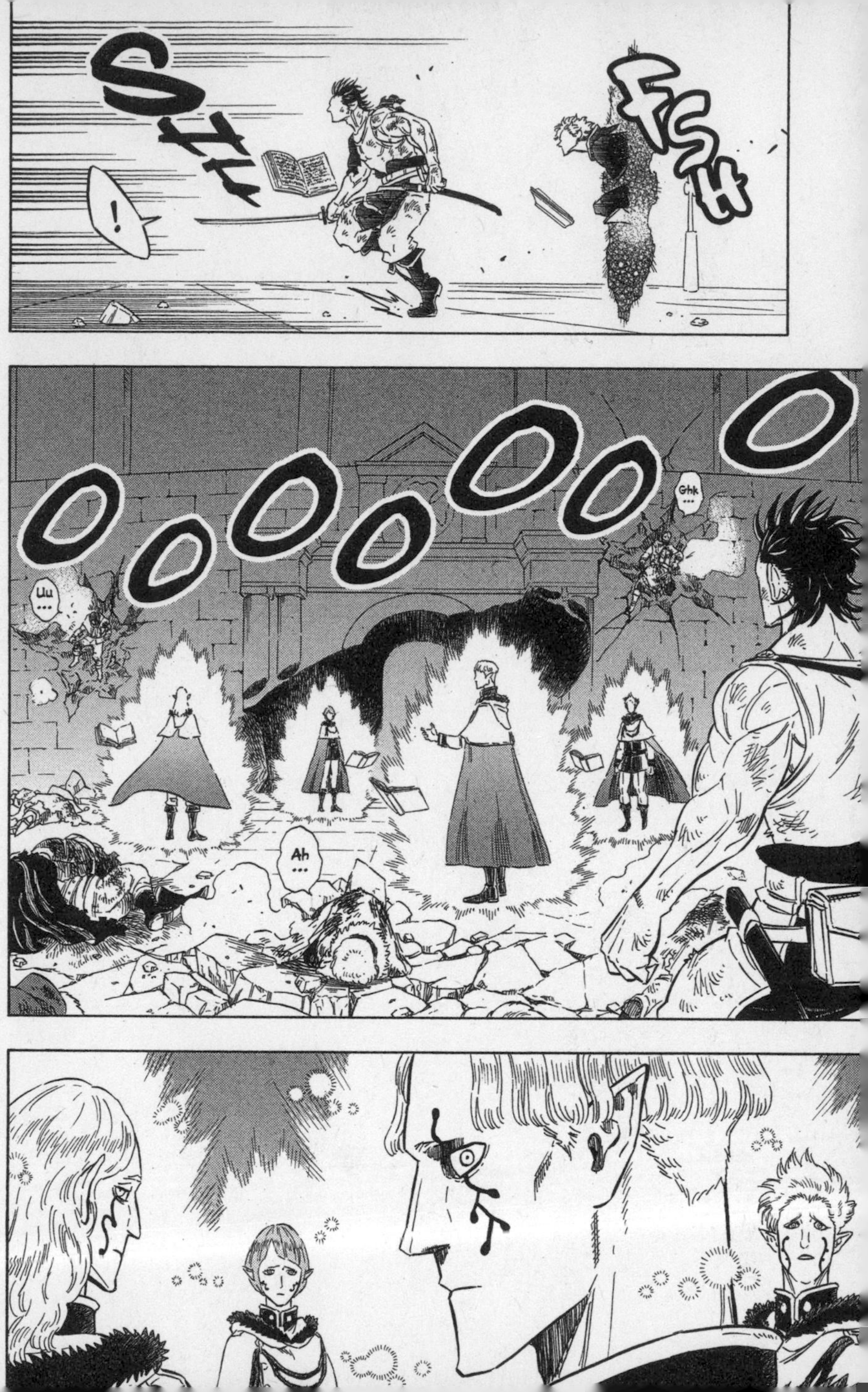

FSH
SZZ
!
Ghk...
OOOOOOOOO
Uu...
Ah...

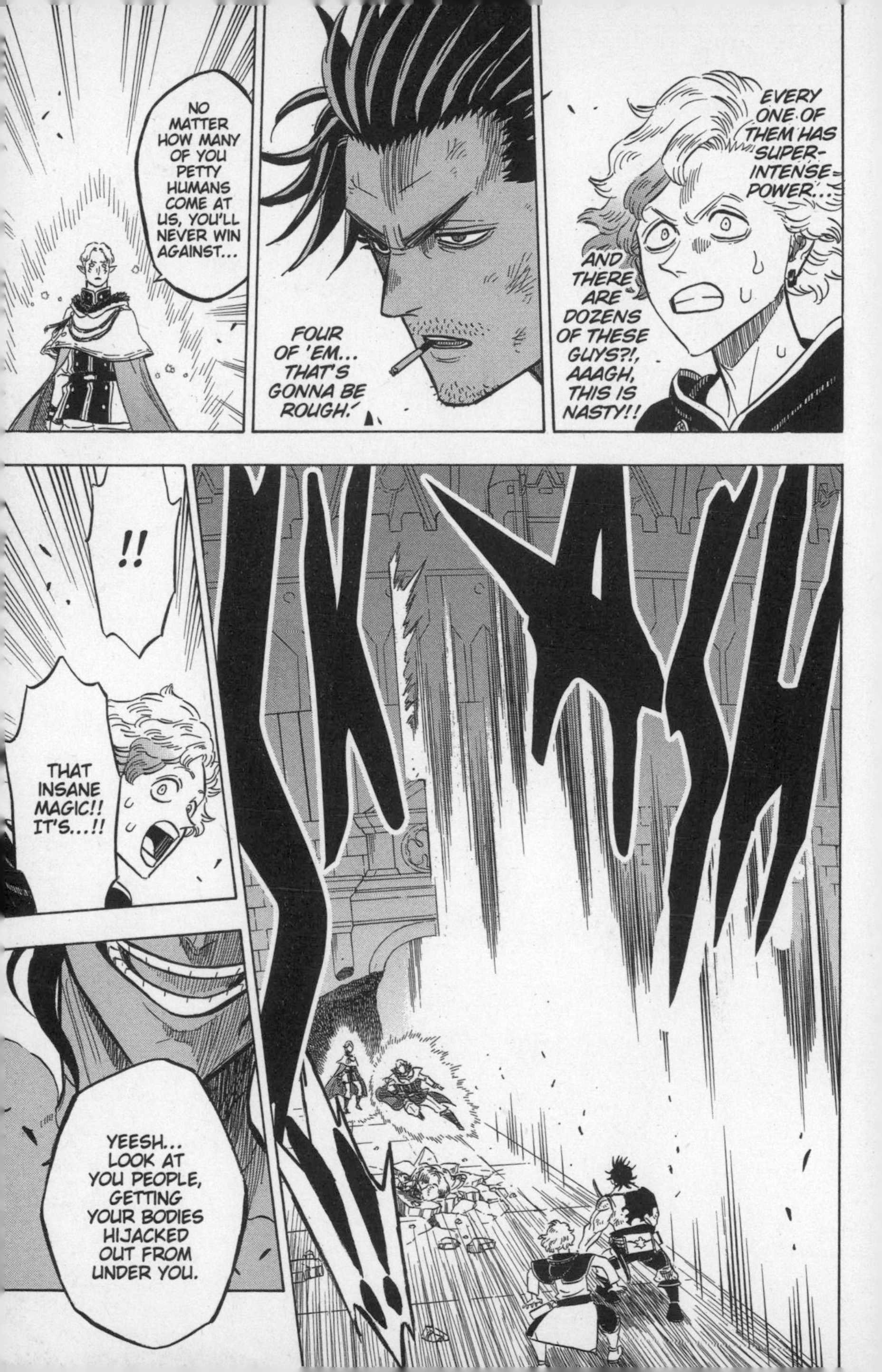
EVERY ONE OF THEM HAS SUPER-INTENSE POWER...
AND THERE ARE DOZENS OF THESE GUYS?!, AAAGH, THIS IS NASTY!!
FOUR OF 'EM... THAT'S GONNA BE ROUGH.
NO MATTER HOW MANY OF YOU PETTY HUMANS COME AT US, YOU'LL NEVER WIN AGAINST...
!!
THAT INSANE MAGIC!! IT'S...!!
YEESH... LOOK AT YOU PEOPLE, GETTING YOUR BODIES HIJACKED OUT FROM UNDER YOU.

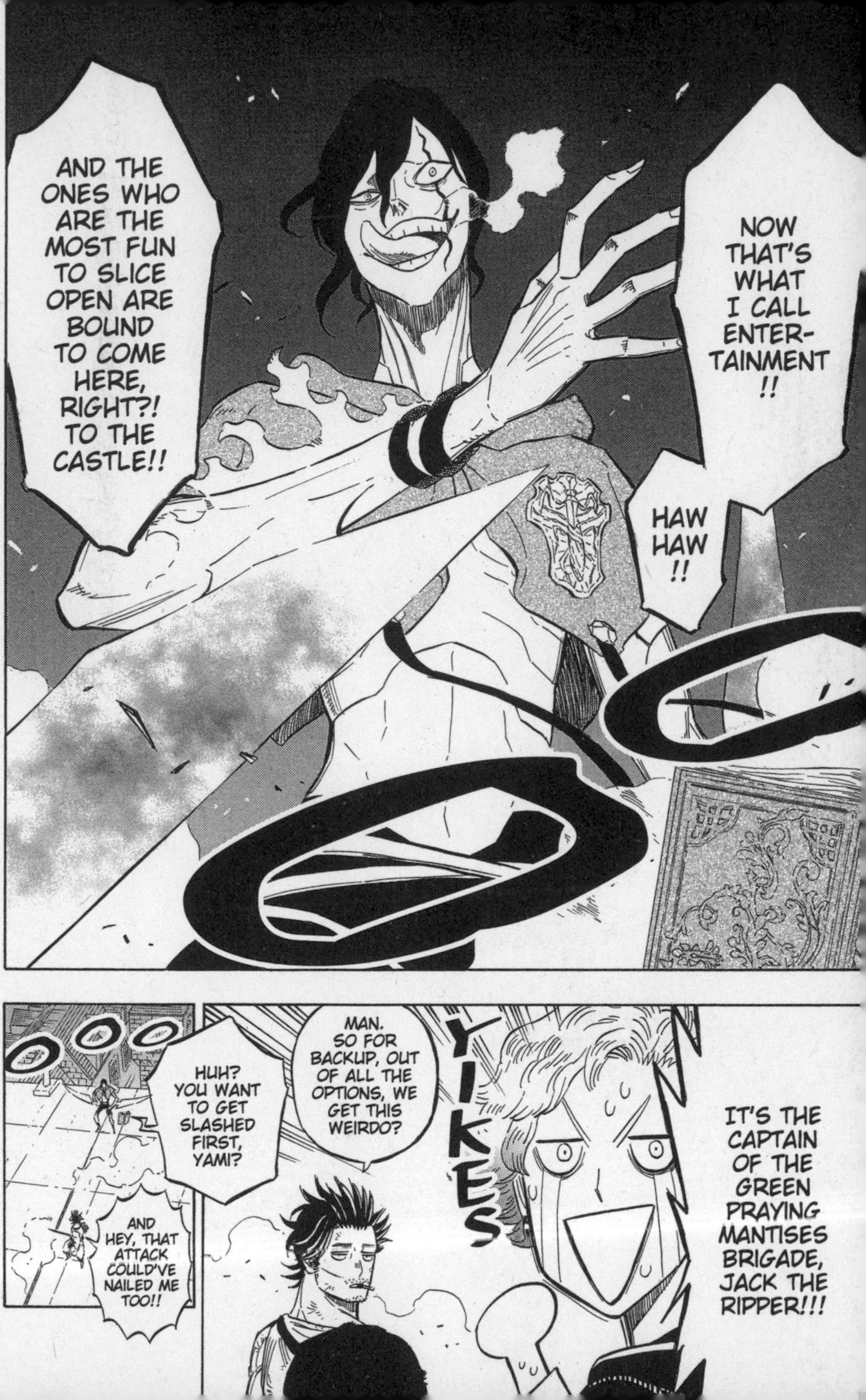
NOW THAT'S WHAT I CALL ENTER-TAINMENT!!
AND THE ONES WHO ARE THE MOST FUN TO SLICE OPEN ARE BOUND TO COME HERE, RIGHT?! TO THE CASTLE!!
HAW HAW!!
IT'S THE CAPTAIN OF THE GREEN PRAYING MANTISES BRIGADE, JACK THE RIPPER!!!
YIKES
MAN. SO FOR BACKUP, OUT OF ALL THE OPTIONS, WE GET THIS WEIRDO?
HUH? YOU WANT TO GET SLASHED FIRST, YAMI?
AND HEY, THAT ATTACK COULD'VE NAILED ME TOO!!

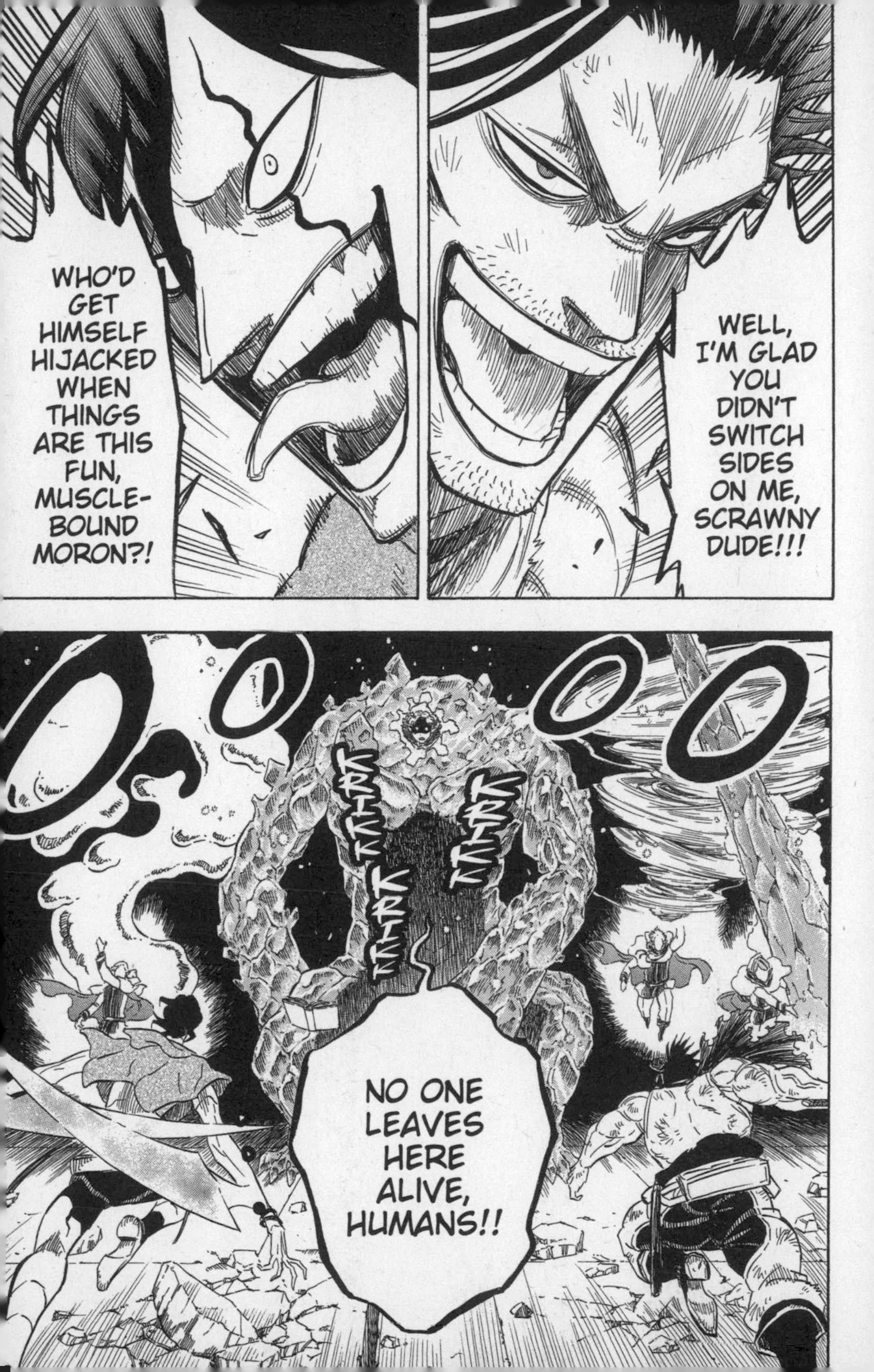
WELL, I'M GLAD YOU DIDN'T SWITCH SIDES ON ME, SCRAWNY DUDE!!!
WHO'D GET HIMSELF HIJACKED WHEN THINGS ARE THIS FUN, MUSCLE-BOUND MORON?!
KRIK
KRIK
KRIK
NO ONE LEAVES HERE ALIVE, HUMANS!!

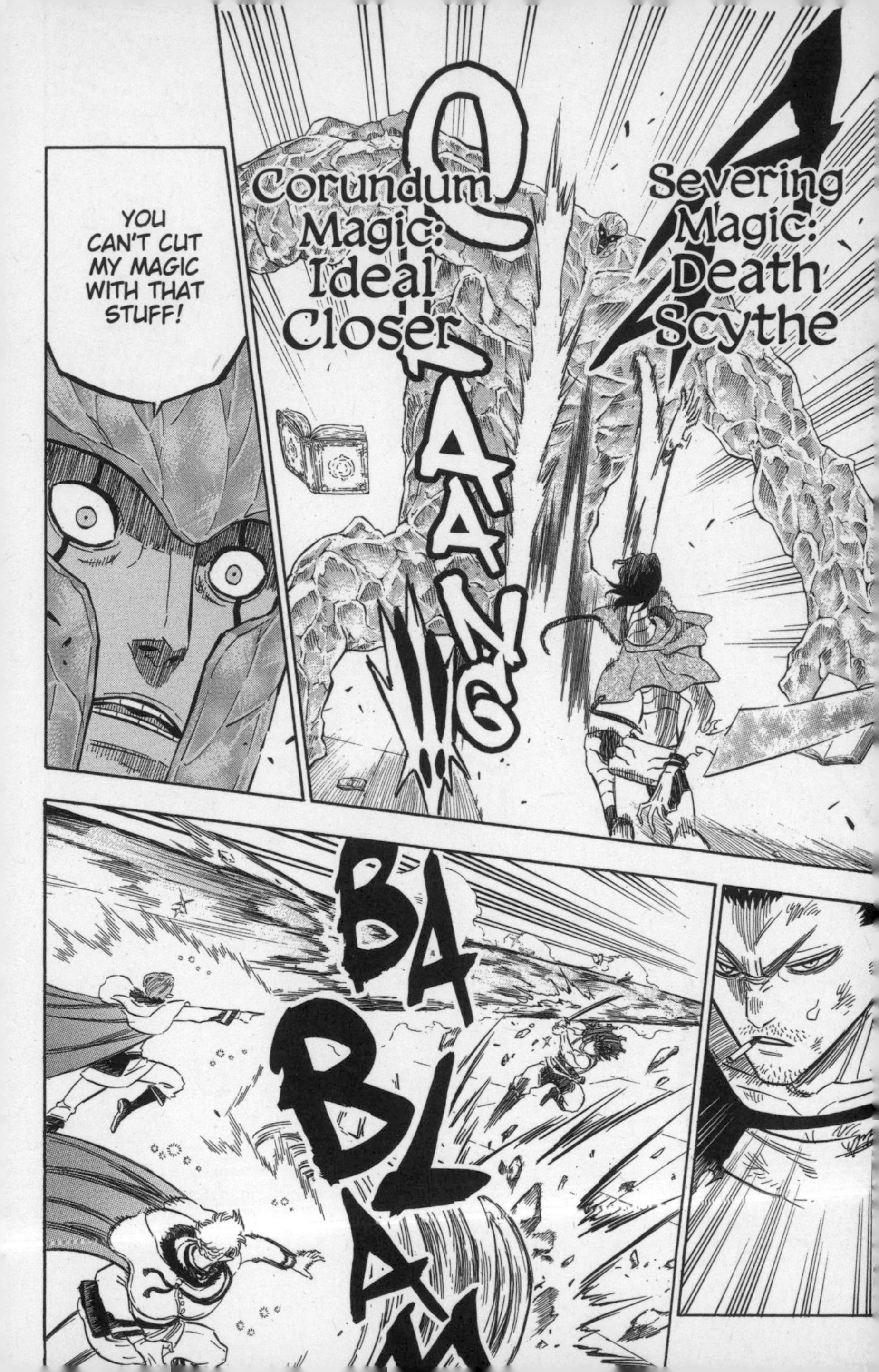
Severing Magic: Death Scythe
Corundum Magic: Ideal Closer
CLAANG!!
YOU CAN'T CUT MY MAGIC WITH THAT STUFF!
BABLAM

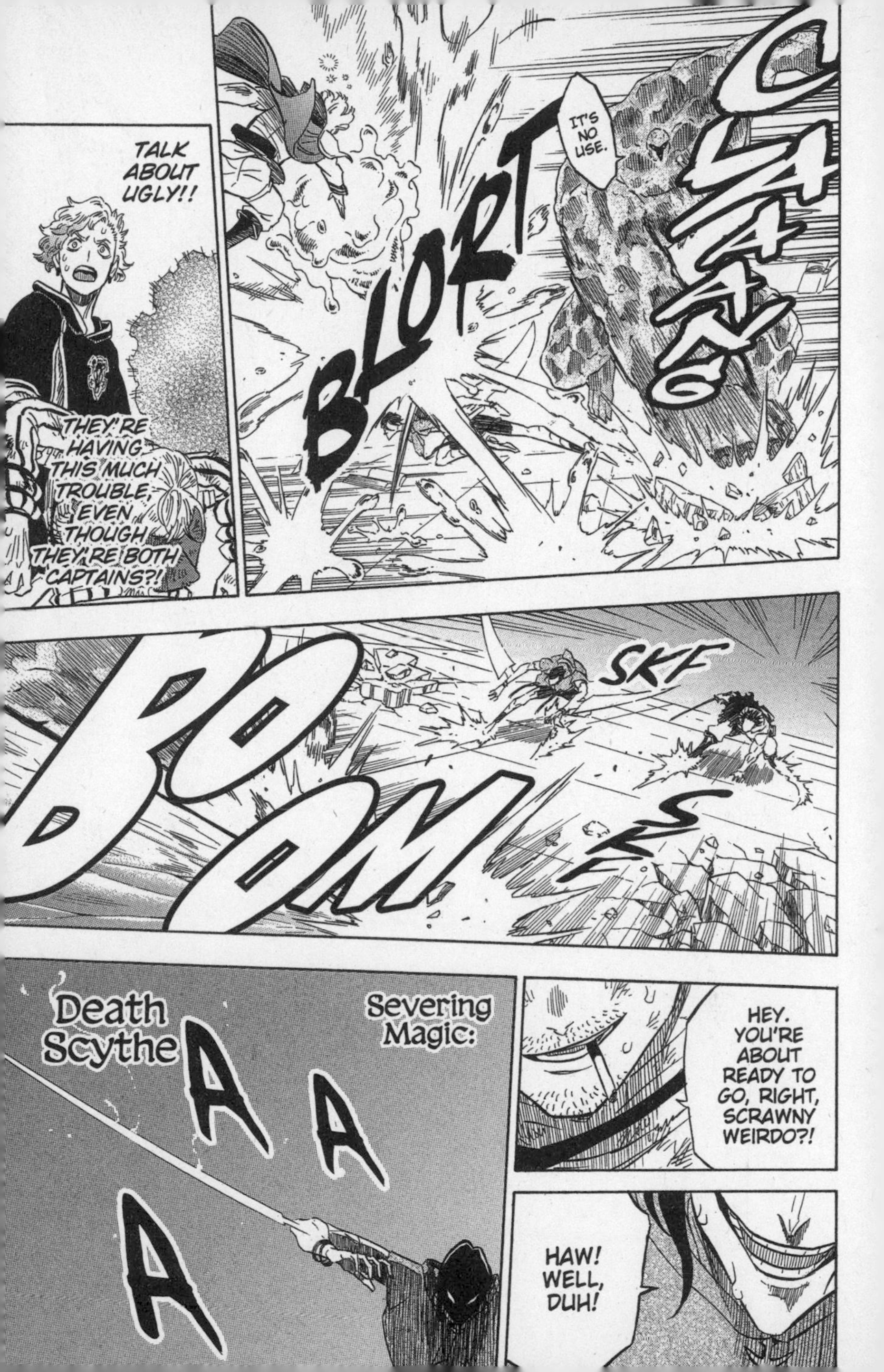
IT'S NO USE.
BLORT
TALK ABOUT UGLY!!
THEY'RE HAVING THIS MUCH TROUBLE, EVEN THOUGH THEY'RE BOTH CAPTAINS?!
SKF
SKF
BOOM
HEY. YOU'RE ABOUT READY TO GO, RIGHT, SCRAWNY WEIRDO?!
HAW! WELL, DUH!
Severing Magic:
Death Scythe
AAAAA

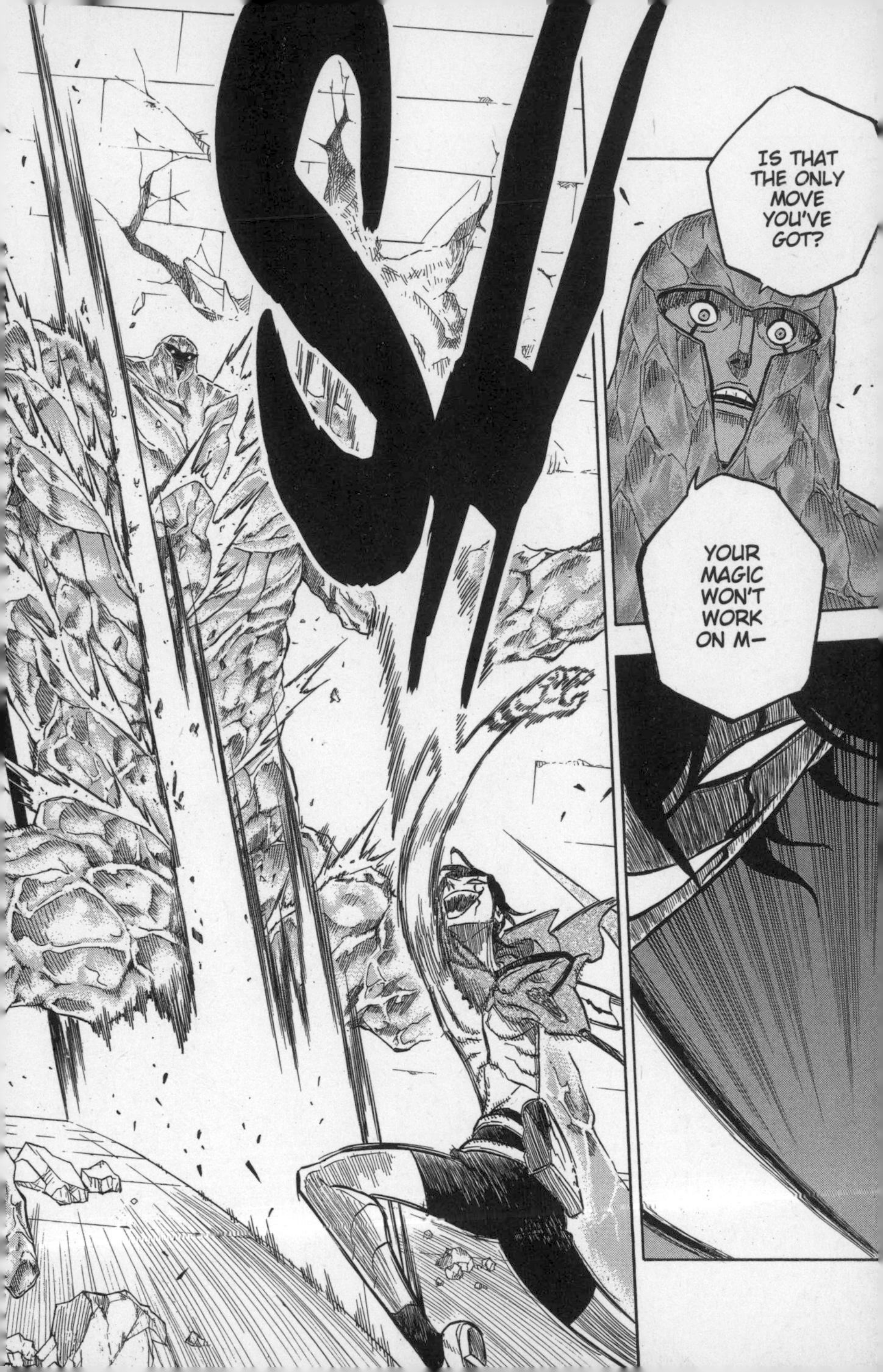
IS THAT THE ONLY MOVE YOU'VE GOT?
YOUR MAGIC WON'T WORK ON M—
SH

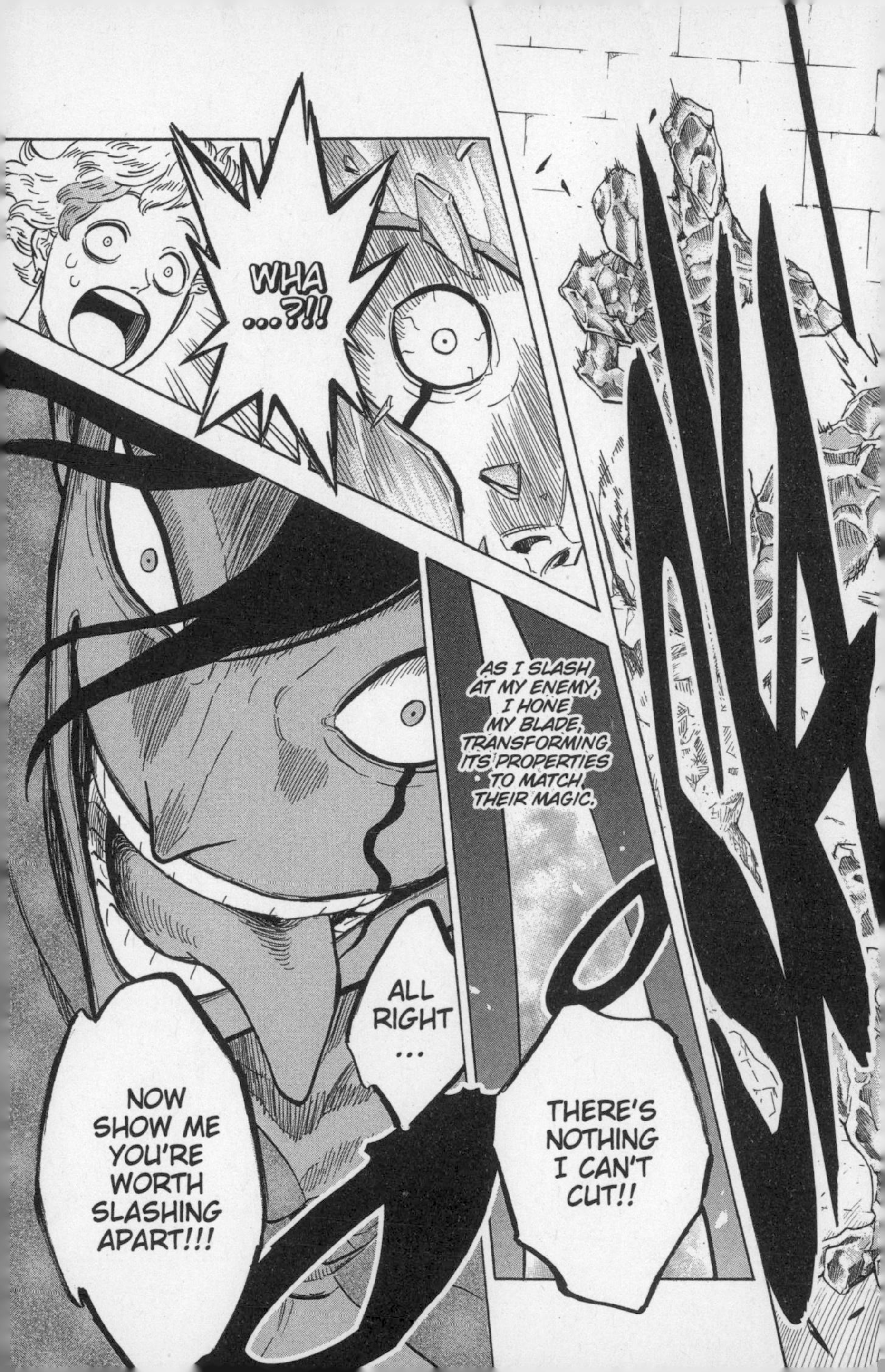
WHA ...?!!
AS I SLASH AT MY ENEMY, I HONE MY BLADE, TRANSFORMING ITS PROPERTIES TO MATCH THEIR MAGIC.
ALL RIGHT ...
THERE'S NOTHING I CAN'T CUT!!
NOW SHOW ME YOU'RE WORTH SLASHING APART!!!

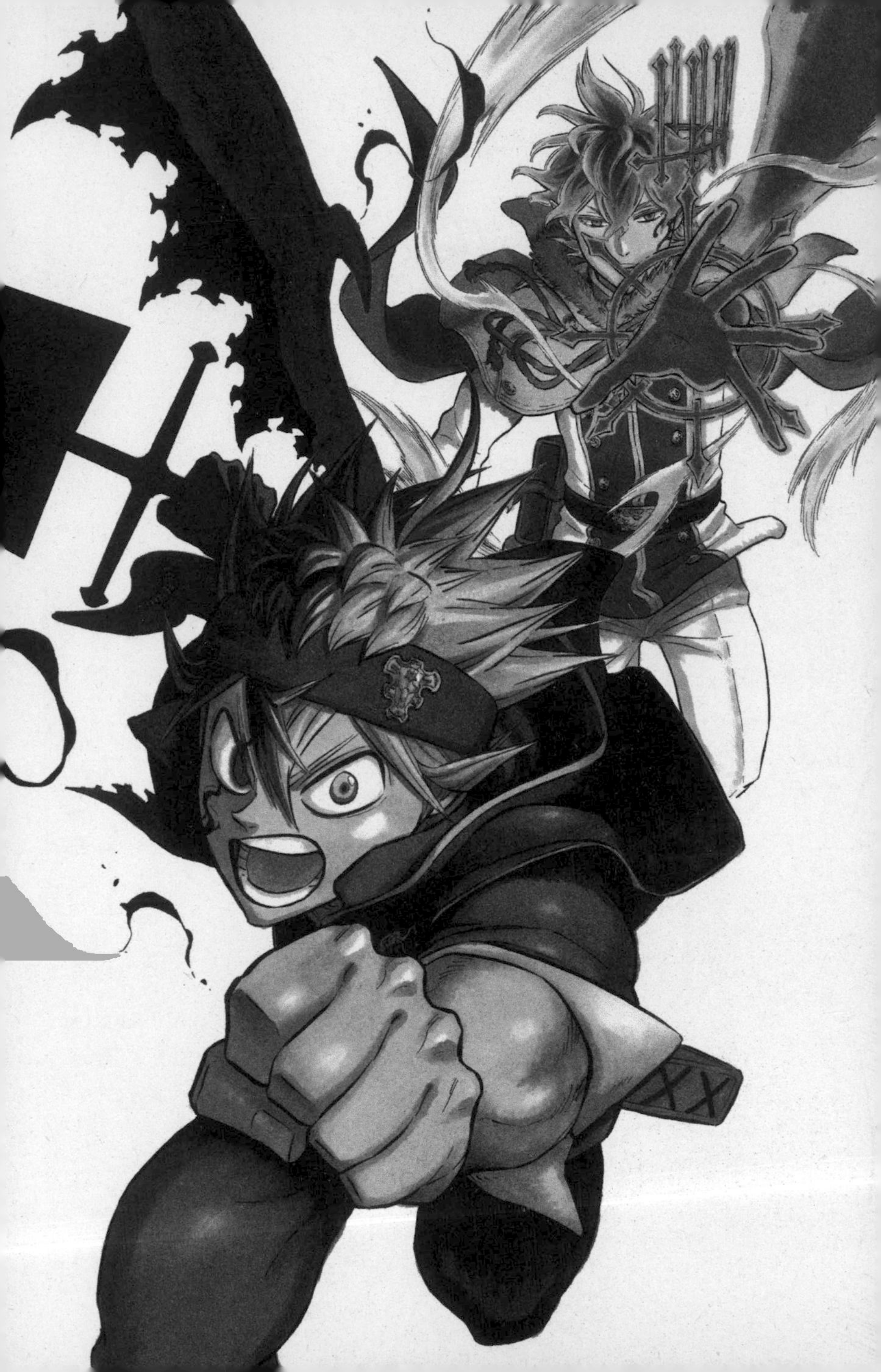

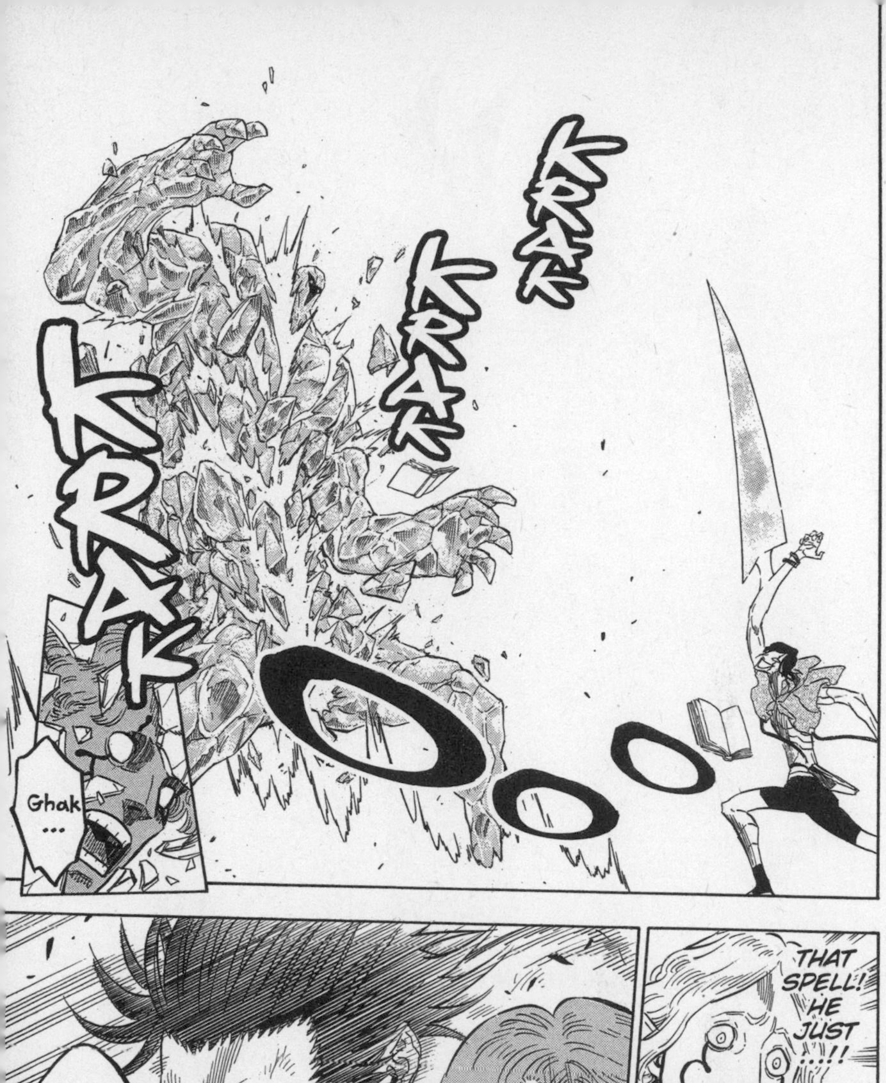
KRAK
KRAK
KRAK
OOOO
Ghak...

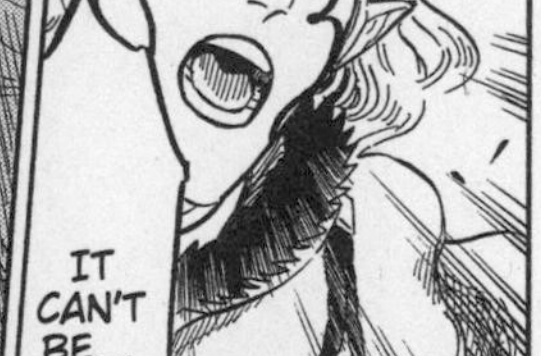
THAT SPELL! HE JUST...!!
IT CAN'T BE...

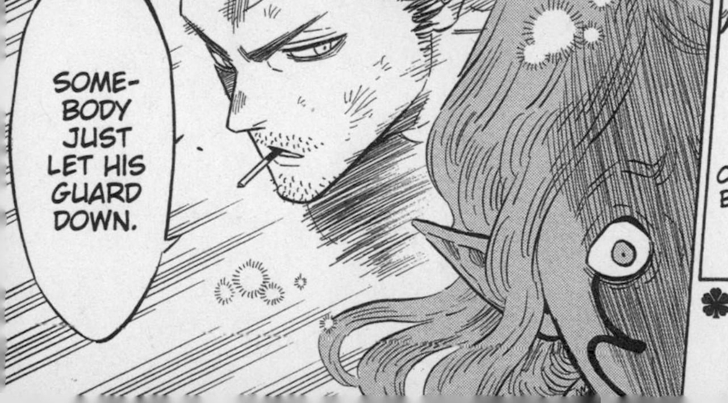
SOMEBODY JUST LET HIS GUARD DOWN.

Page 174: Flying In

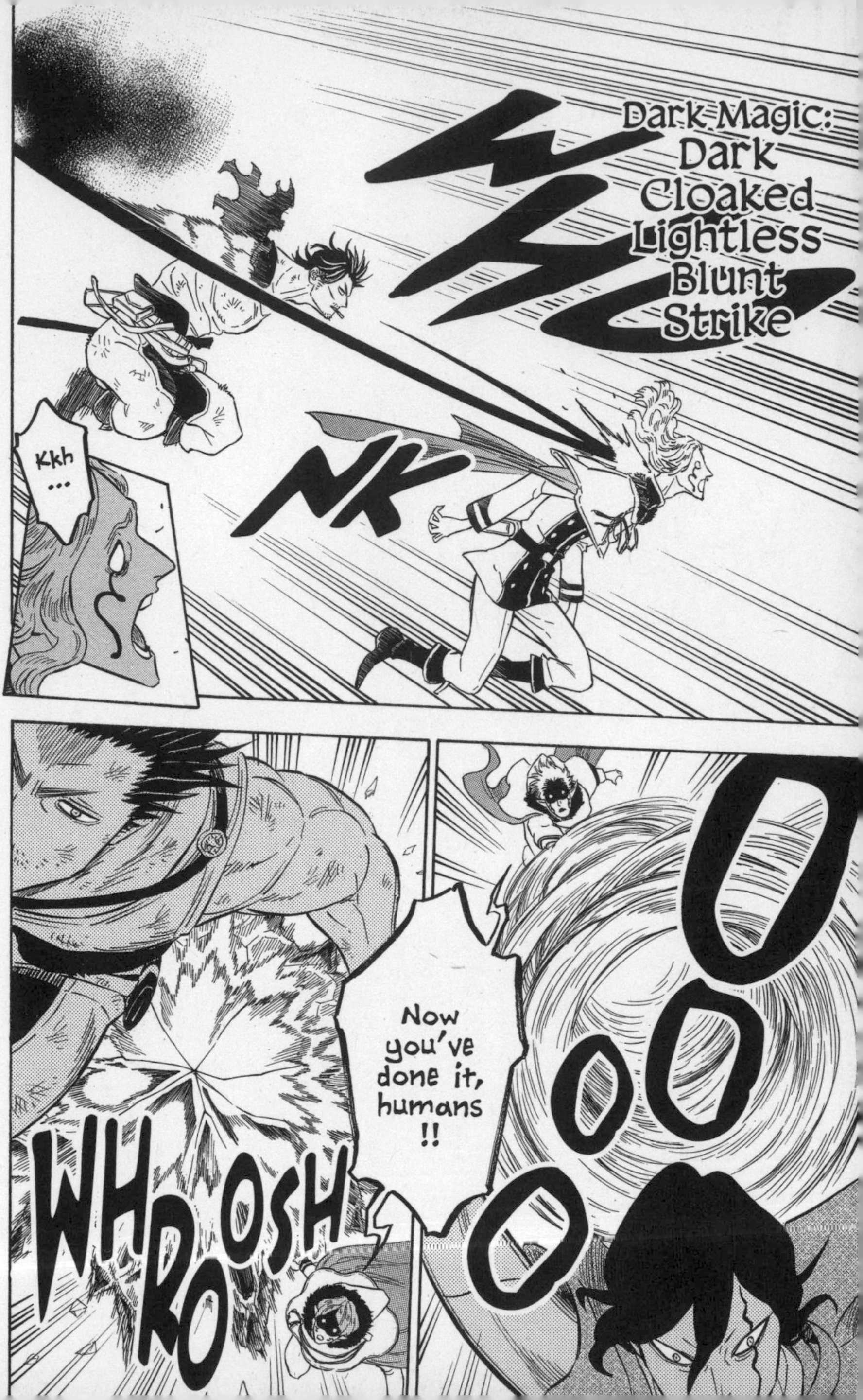
Dark Magic: Dark Cloaked Lightless Blunt Strike
Kkh ...
Now you've done it, humans !!
OOOOO
WHROOSH

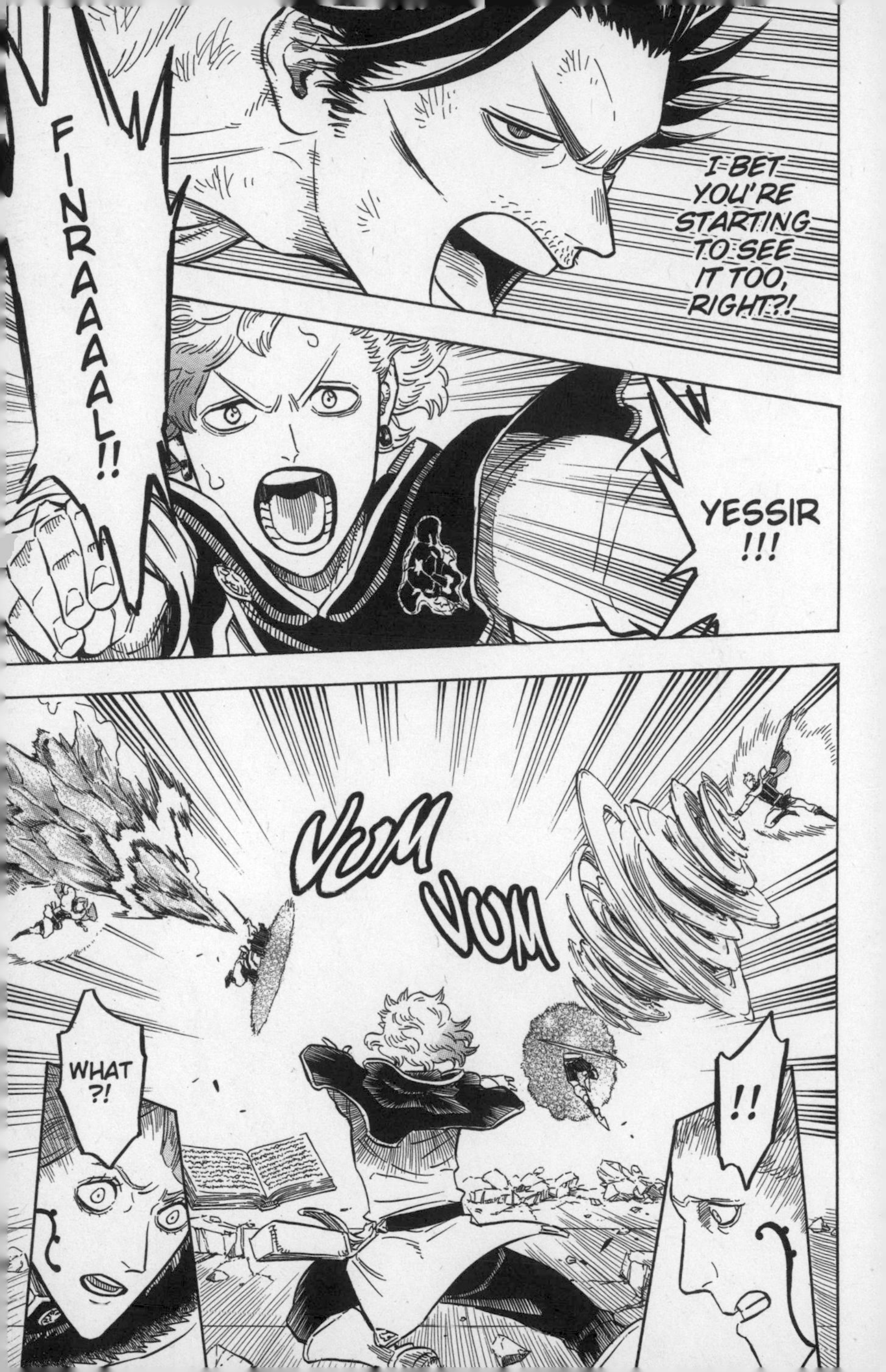
I BET YOU'RE STARTING TO SEE IT TOO, RIGHT?!
YESSIR !!!
FINRAAAAAL!!
VUM
VOM
!!
WHAT ?!

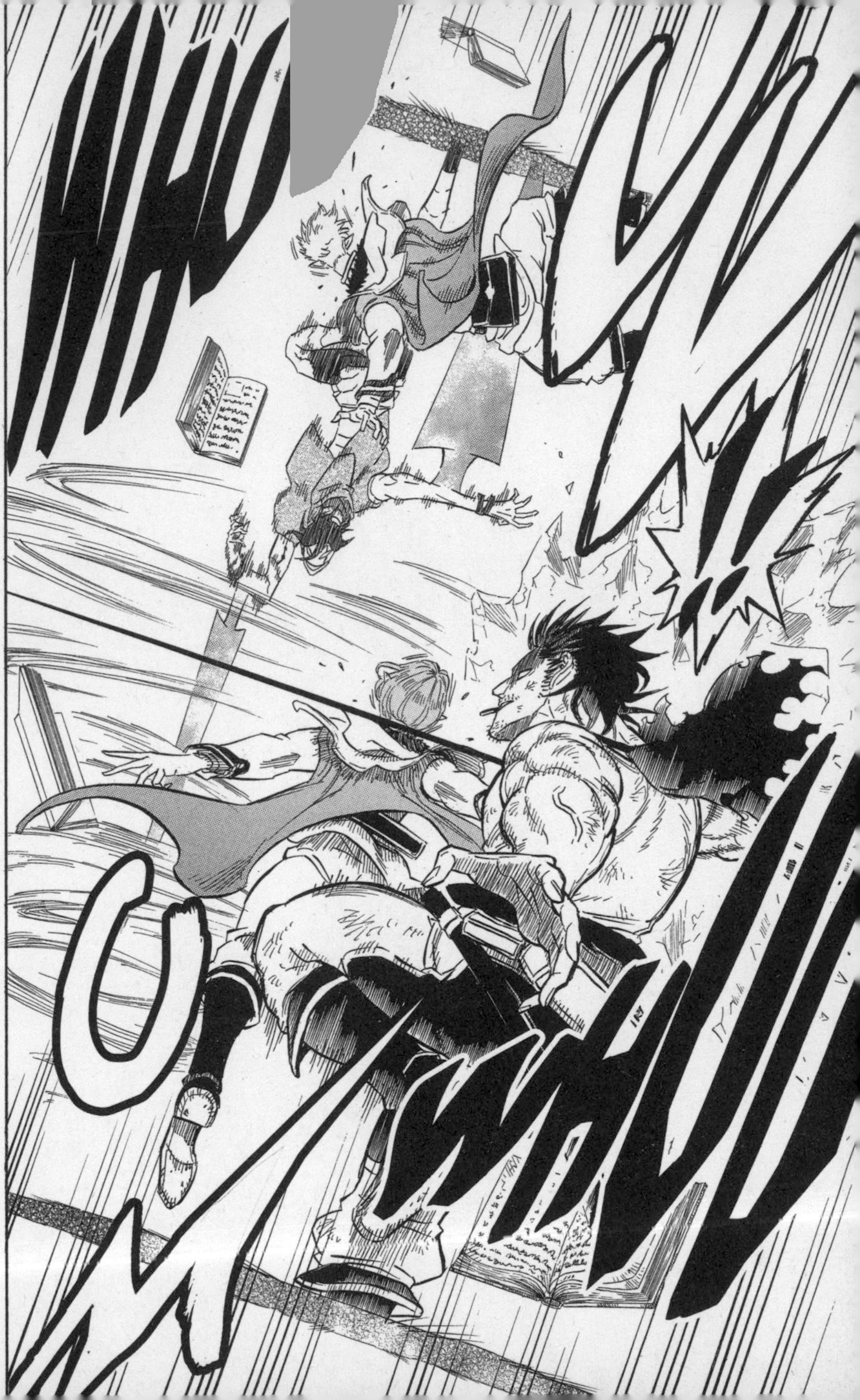

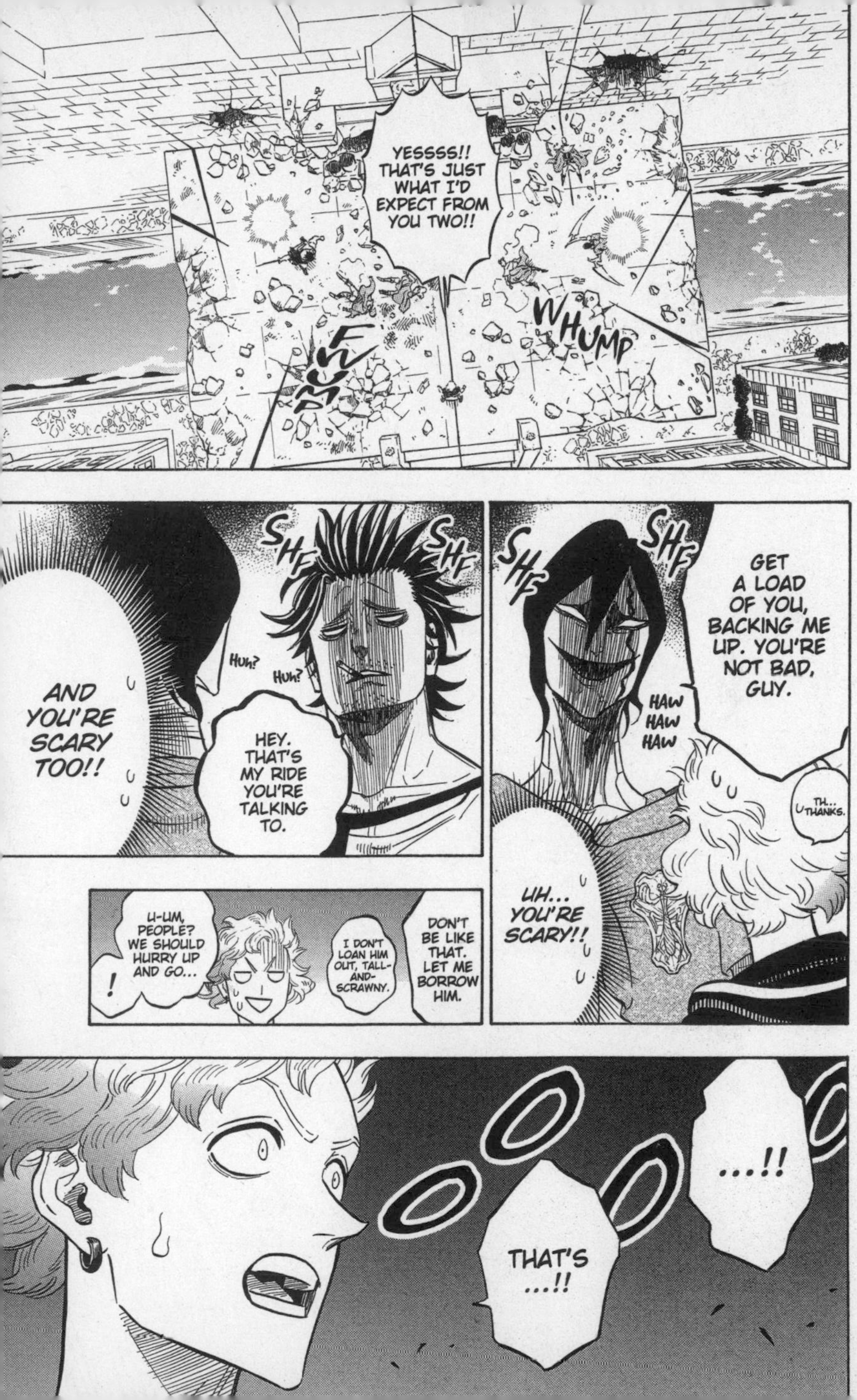
YESSSS!! THAT'S JUST WHAT I'D EXPECT FROM YOU TWO!!
WHUMP
FWUMP
SHF
SHF
GET A LOAD OF YOU, BACKING ME UP. YOU'RE NOT BAD, GUY.
HAW HAW HAW
TH... THANKS.
UH... YOU'RE SCARY!!
SHF
SHF
HEY. THAT'S MY RIDE YOU'RE TALKING TO.
Huh?
Huh?
AND YOU'RE SCARY TOO!!
DON'T BE LIKE THAT. LET ME BORROW HIM.
I DON'T LOAN HIM OUT, TALL-AND-SCRAWNY.
U-UM, PEOPLE? WE SHOULD HURRY UP AND GO...
!
...!!
THAT'S ...!!

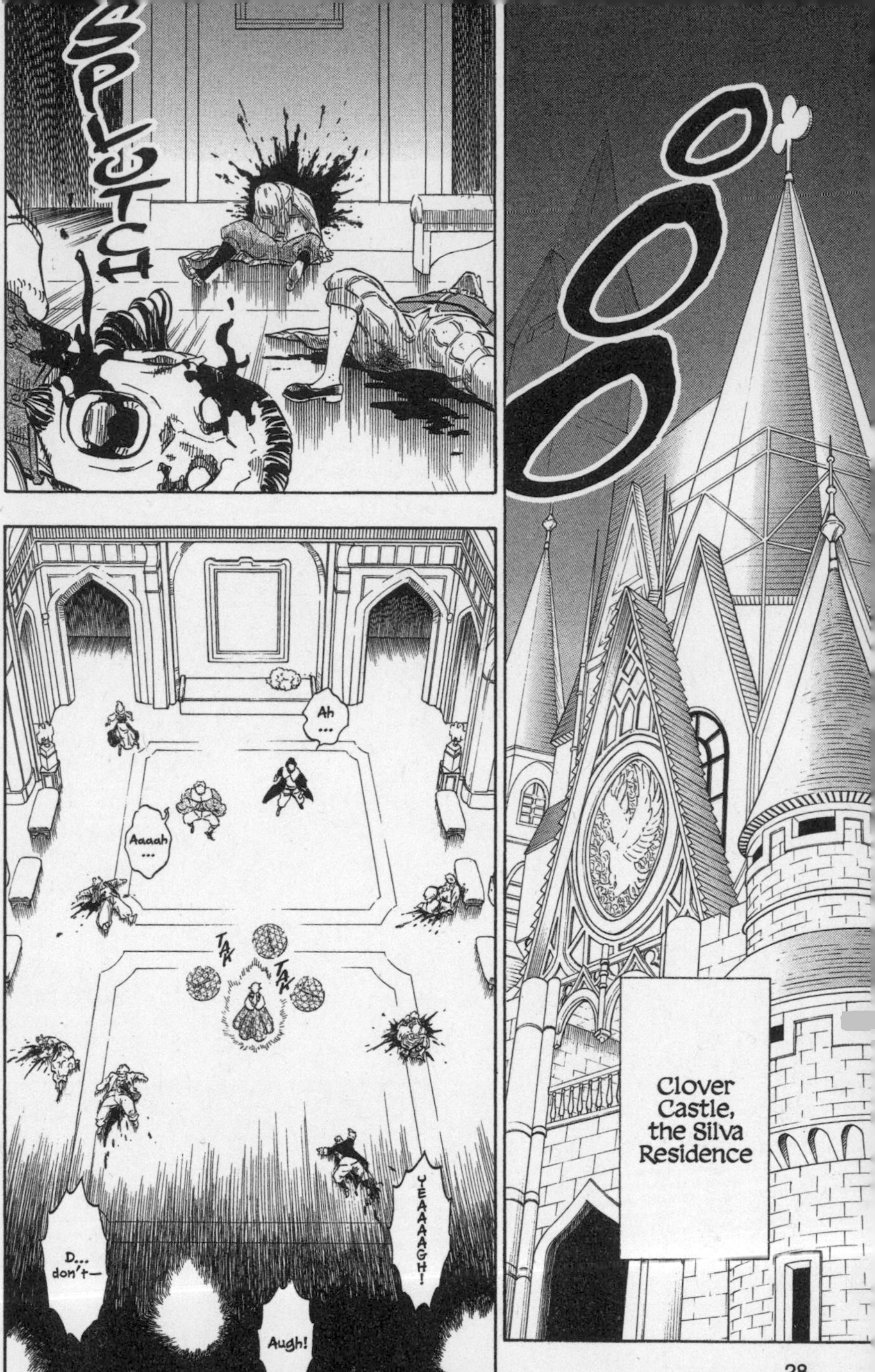
Clover Castle, the Silva Residence
SPLUTCH
Ah...
Aaaah...
TAK
TAK
YEAAAAGH!
D... don't—
Augh!

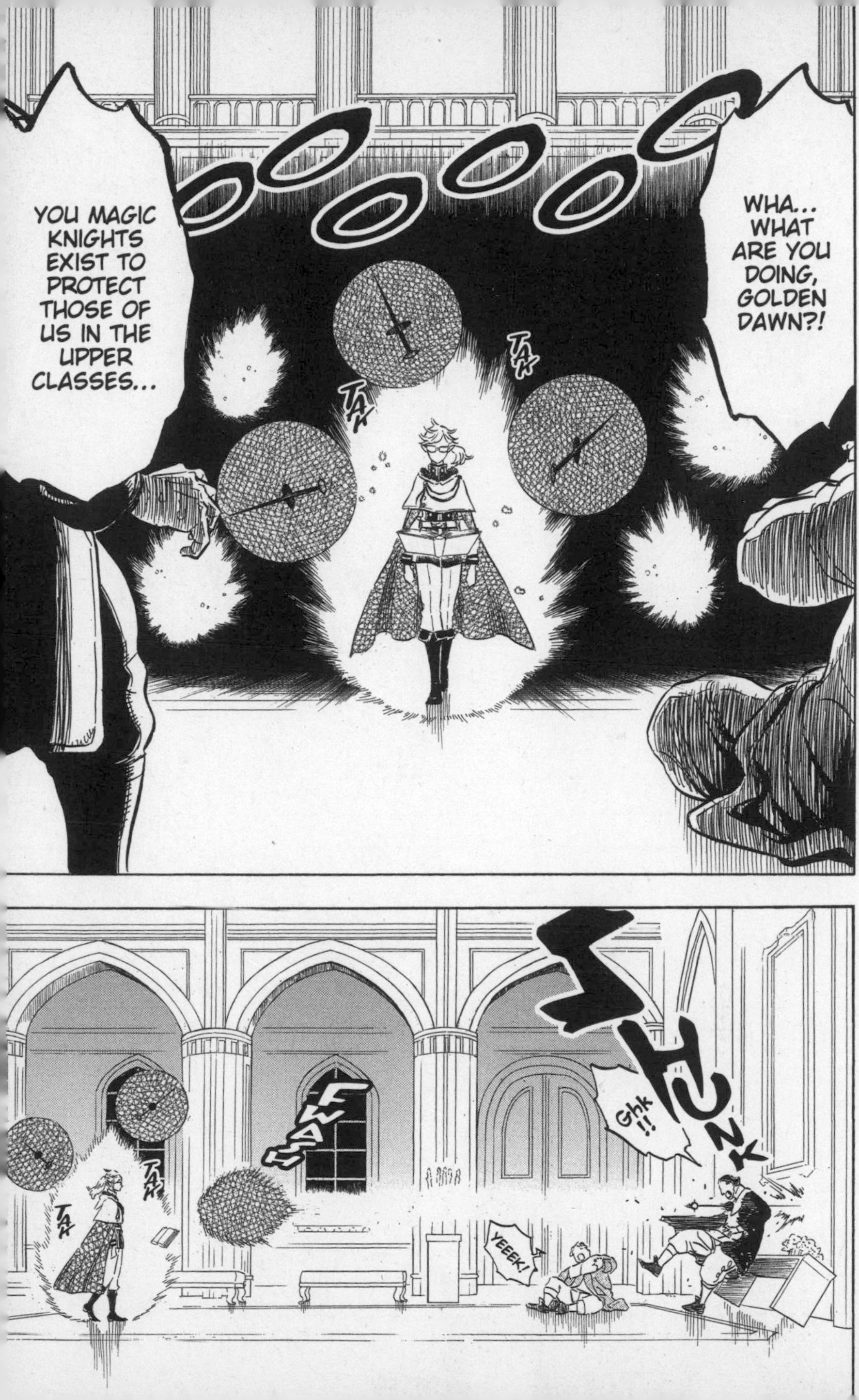
WHA... WHAT ARE YOU DOING, GOLDEN DAWN?!
TAK
YOU MAGIC KNIGHTS EXIST TO PROTECT THOSE OF US IN THE UPPER CLASSES...
TAK
SHUNK
Ghk!!
YEEEK!
FWASH
TAK
TAK

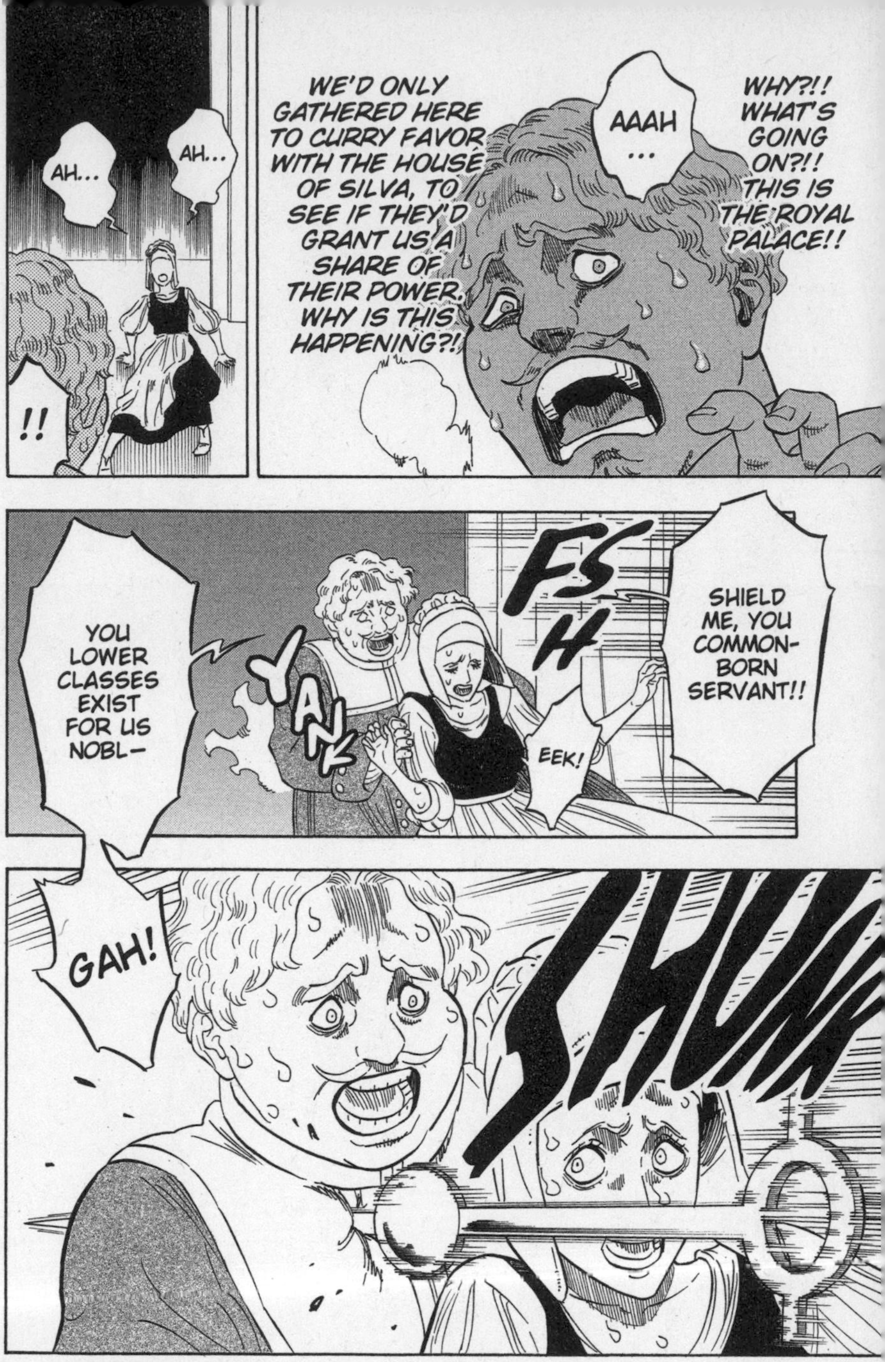
WHY?!! WHAT'S GOING ON?!! THIS IS THE ROYAL PALACE!!
AAAH ...
WE'D ONLY GATHERED HERE TO CURRY FAVOR WITH THE HOUSE OF SILVA, TO SEE IF THEY'D GRANT US A SHARE OF THEIR POWER. WHY IS THIS HAPPENING?!
AH...
AH...
!!
SHIELD ME, YOU COMMON-BORN SERVANT!!
FSSH
EEK!
YANK
YOU LOWER CLASSES EXIST FOR US NOBL-
SHUN
GAH!

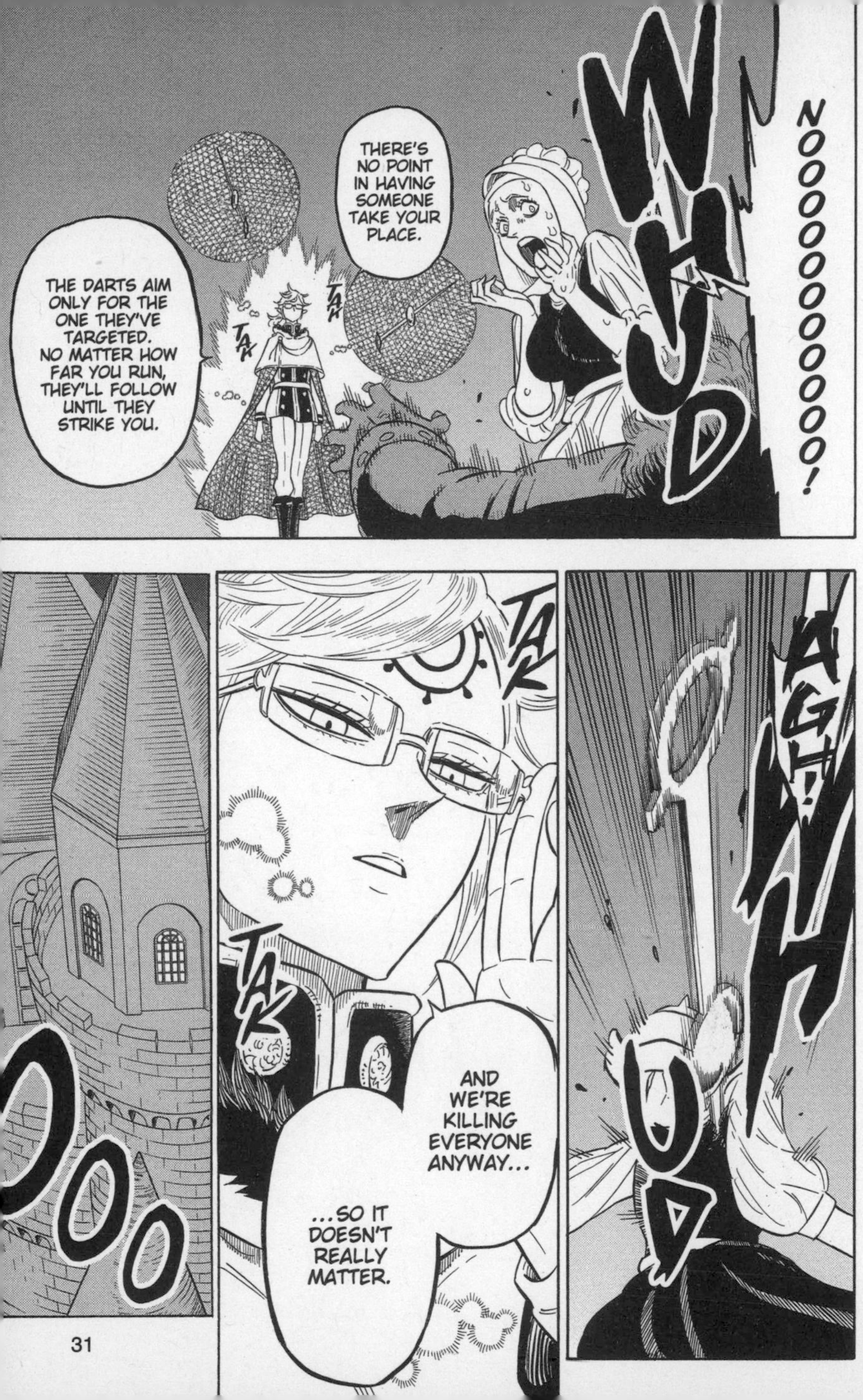
NOOOOOOOOOOOOO!
WHUD
THERE'S NO POINT IN HAVING SOMEONE TAKE YOUR PLACE.
TAK
TAK
THE DARTS AIM ONLY FOR THE ONE THEY'VE TARGETED. NO MATTER HOW FAR YOU RUN, THEY'LL FOLLOW UNTIL THEY STRIKE YOU.
AGH!
TAK
TAK
AND WE'RE KILLING EVERYONE ANYWAY...
...SO IT DOESN'T REALLY MATTER.
OOOO

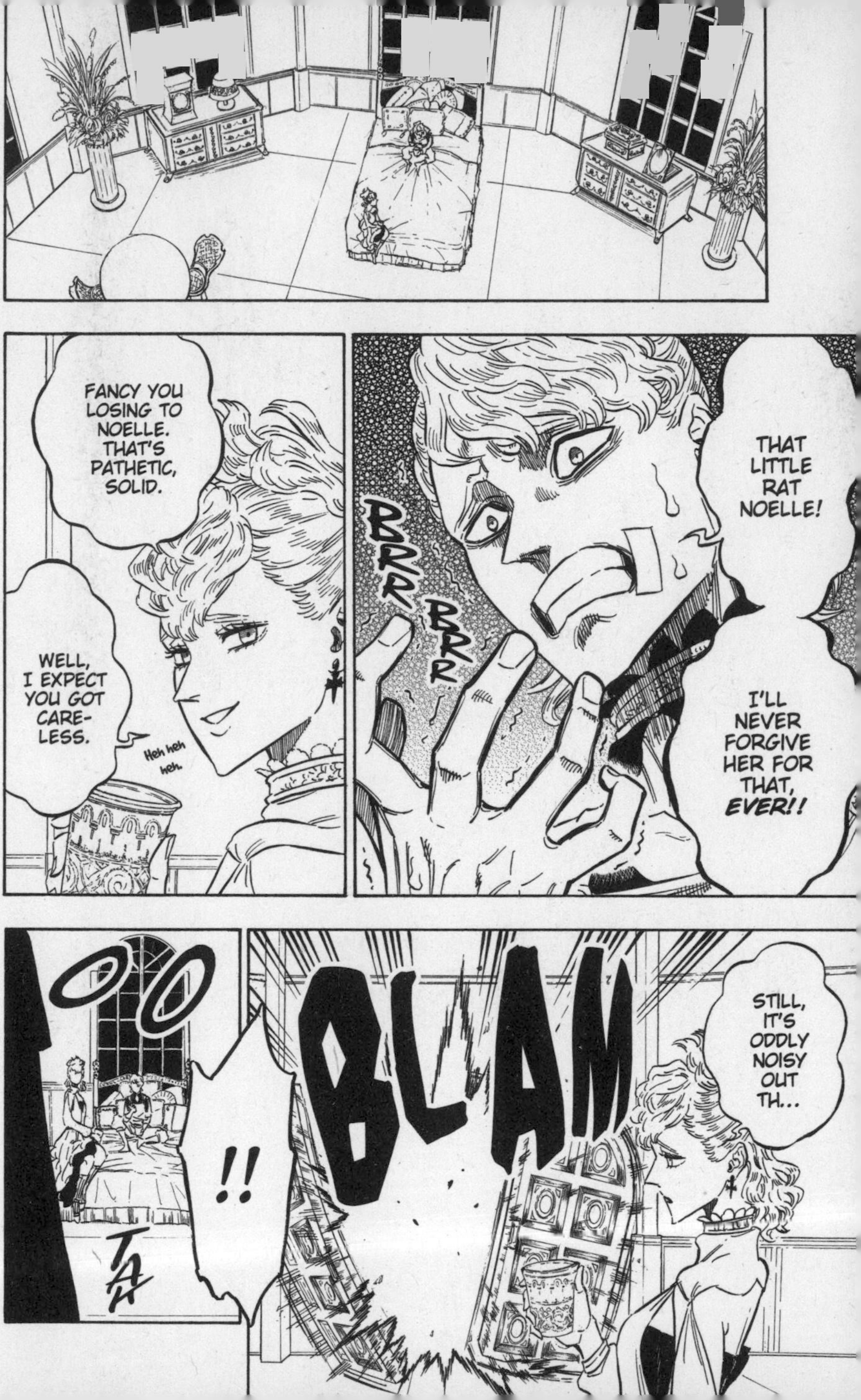
THAT LITTLE RAT NOELLE!
BRRR
BRRR
I'LL NEVER FORGIVE HER FOR THAT, EVER!!
FANCY YOU LOSING TO NOELLE. THAT'S PATHETIC, SOLID.
WELL, I EXPECT YOU GOT CARE-LESS.
Heh heh heh.
STILL, IT'S ODDLY NOISY OUT TH...
BLAM
!!
TA

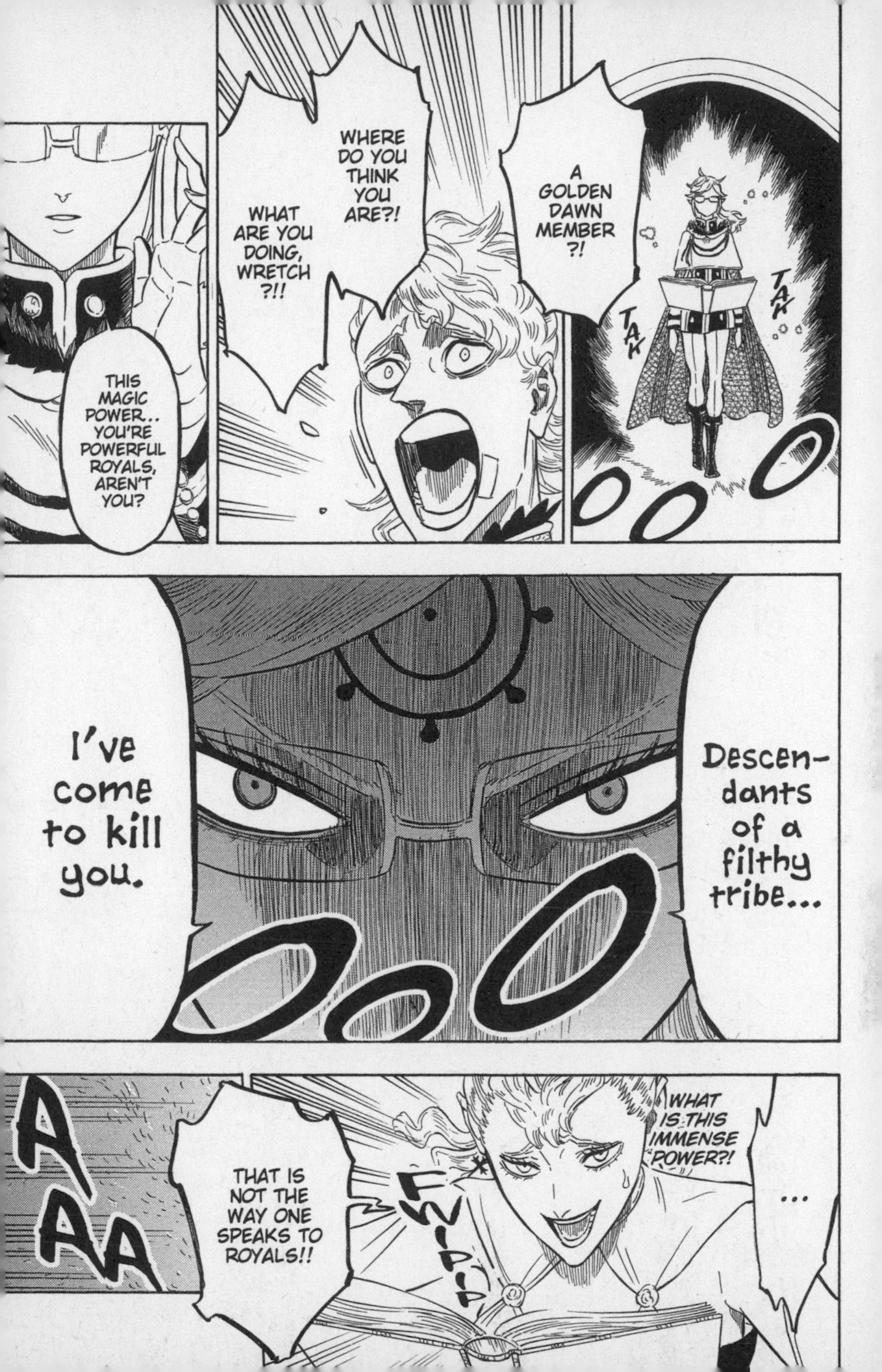
A GOLDEN DAWN MEMBER?!
TAK TAK
WHERE DO YOU THINK YOU ARE?!
WHAT ARE YOU DOING, WRETCH?!!
THIS MAGIC POWER... YOU'RE POWERFUL ROYALS, AREN'T YOU?
Descendants of a filthy tribe...
I've come to kill you.
...
WHAT IS THIS IMMENSE POWER?!
FWIPIP
THAT IS NOT THE WAY ONE SPEAKS TO ROYALS!!
AAA

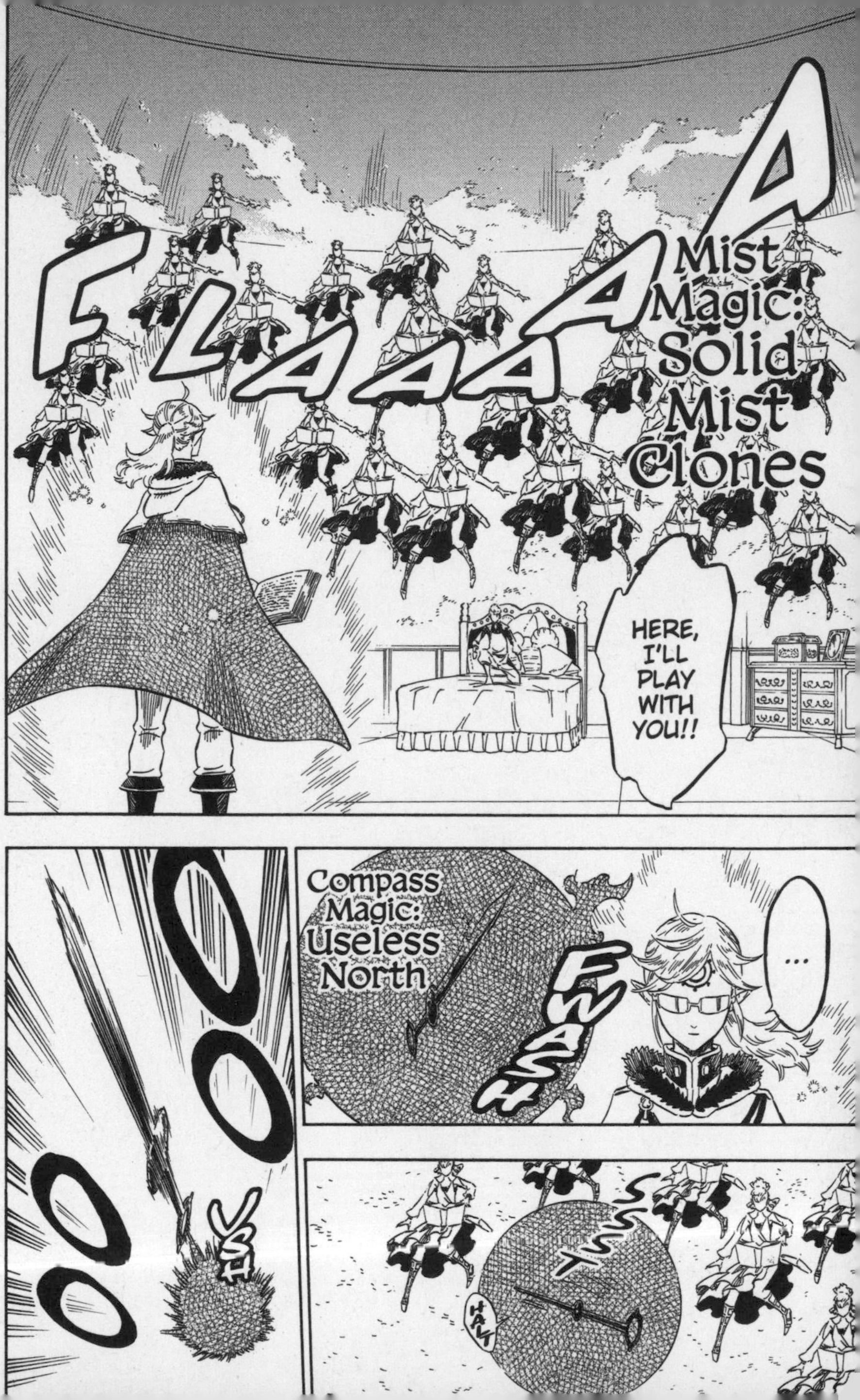
FLAAAAA
Mist Magic: Solid Mist Clones
HERE, I'LL PLAY WITH YOU!!
...
FWASH
Compass Magic: Useless North
SSST
HALT
VSH

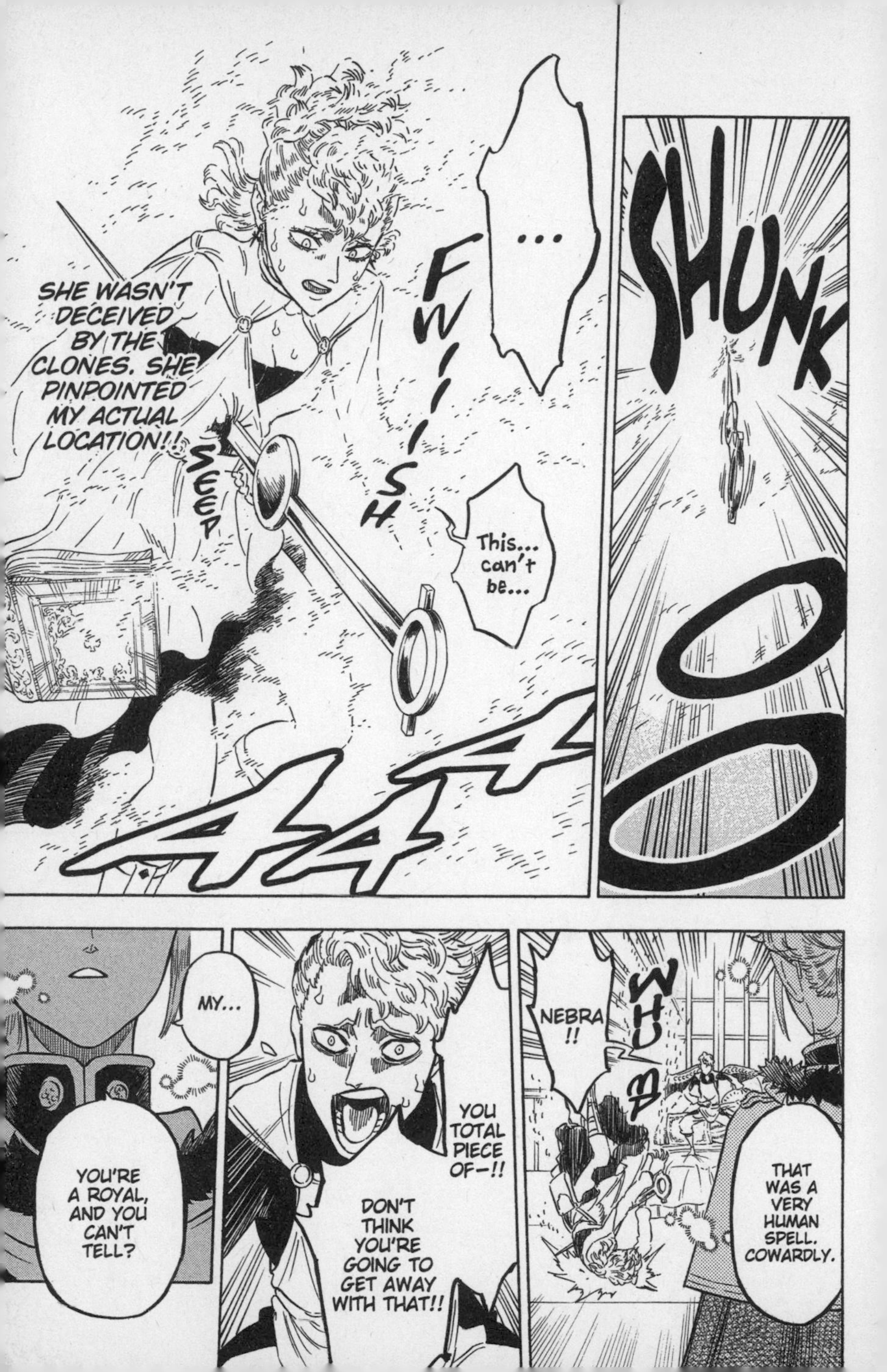
SHUNK
...
FWISH
This... can't be...
SHE WASN'T DECEIVED BY THE CLONES. SHE PINPOINTED MY ACTUAL LOCATION!!
SEEP
WHUM
NEBRA!!
THAT WAS A VERY HUMAN SPELL. COWARDLY.
YOU TOTAL PIECE OF—!!
DON'T THINK YOU'RE GOING TO GET AWAY WITH THAT!!
MY...
YOU'RE A ROYAL, AND YOU CAN'T TELL?

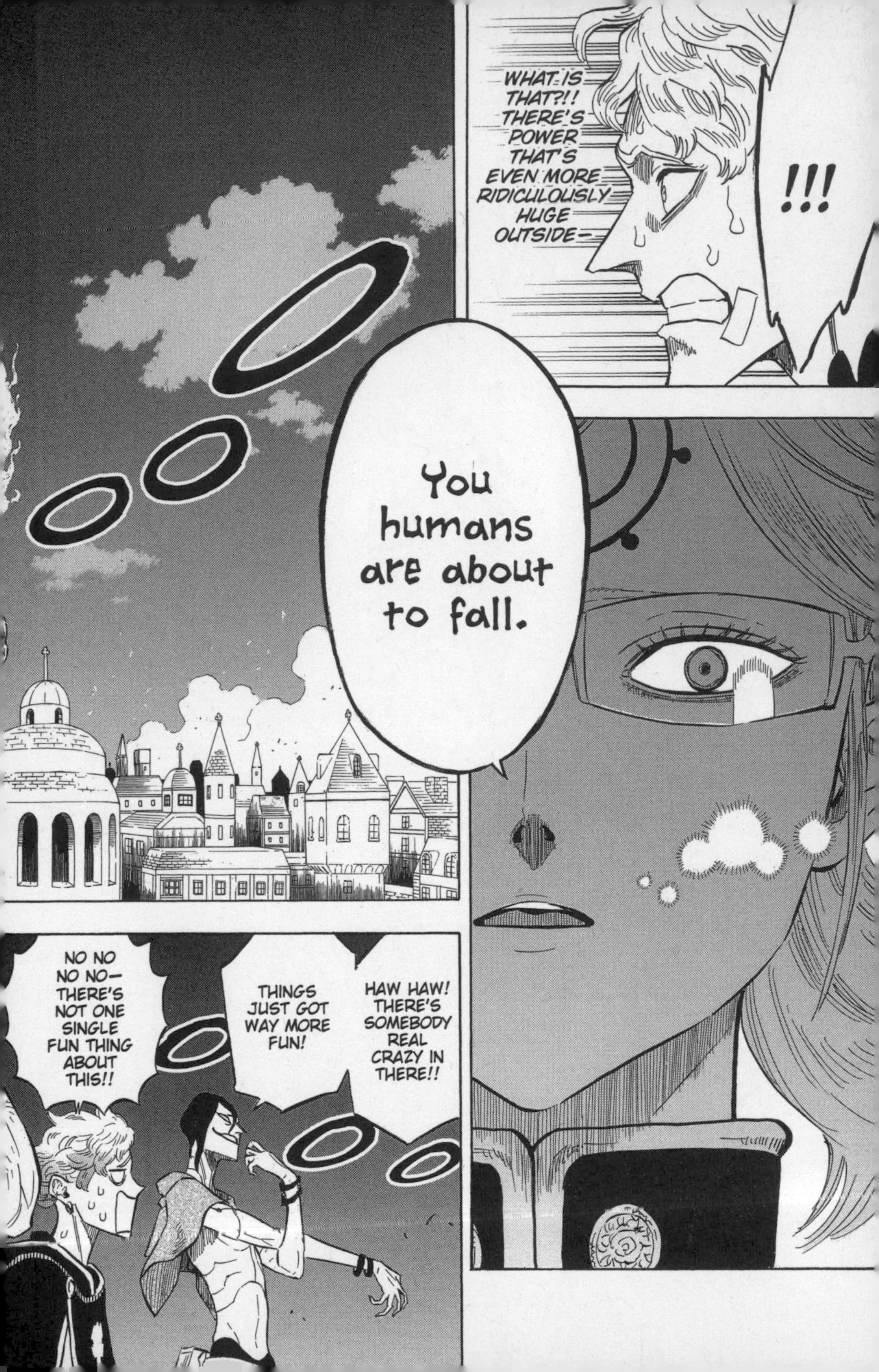
WHAT IS THAT?!! THERE'S POWER THAT'S EVEN MORE RIDICULOUSLY HUGE OUTSIDE—
!!!
You humans are about to fall.
HAW HAW! THERE'S SOMEBODY REAL CRAZY IN THERE!!
THINGS JUST GOT WAY MORE FUN!
NO NO NO NO— THERE'S NOT ONE SINGLE FUN THING ABOUT THIS!!

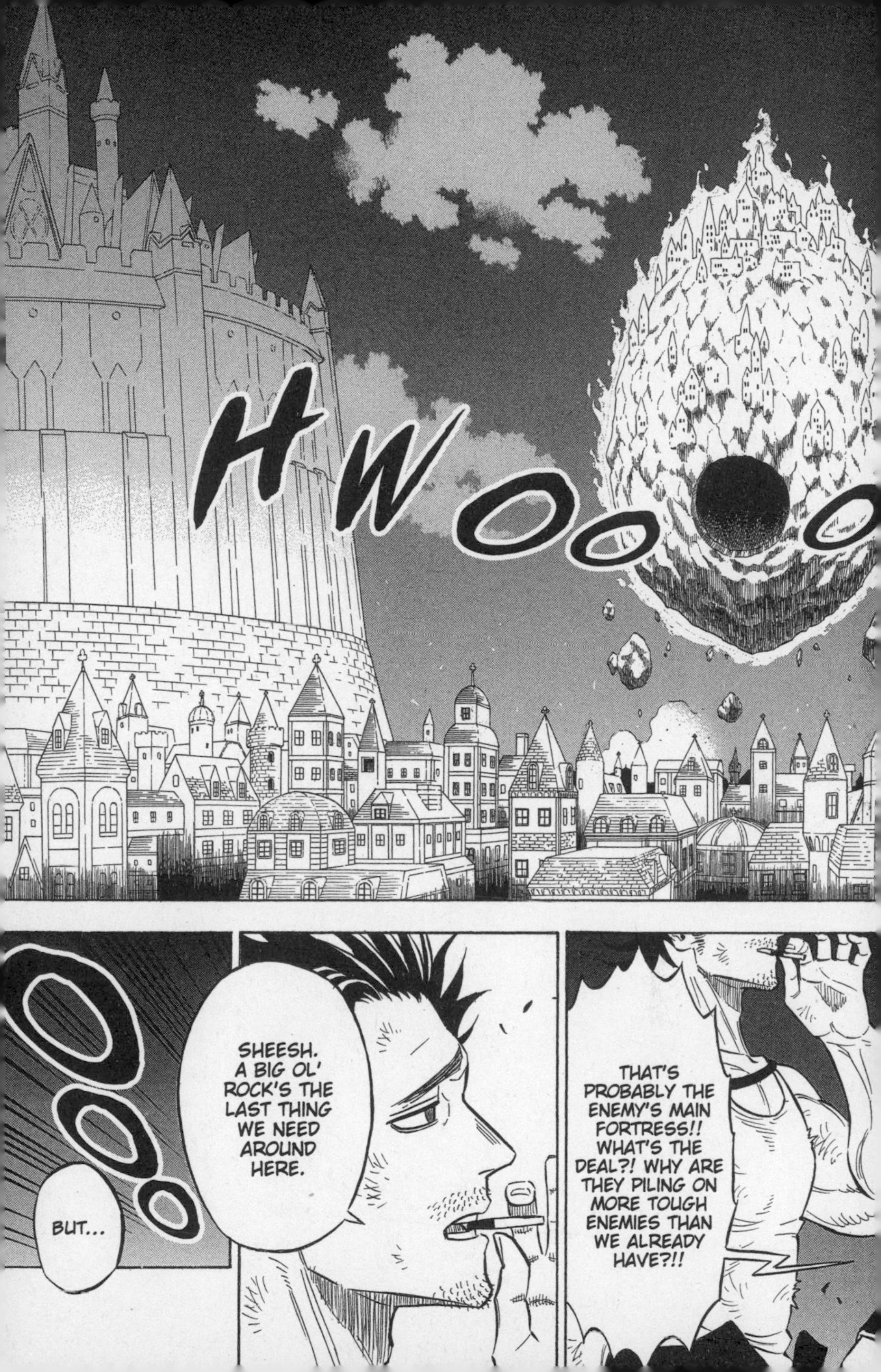
HWOOOO
THAT'S PROBABLY THE ENEMY'S MAIN FORTRESS!! WHAT'S THE DEAL?! WHY ARE THEY PILING ON MORE TOUGH ENEMIES THAN WE ALREADY HAVE?!!
SHEESH. A BIG OL' ROCK'S THE LAST THING WE NEED AROUND HERE.
OOOO
BUT...

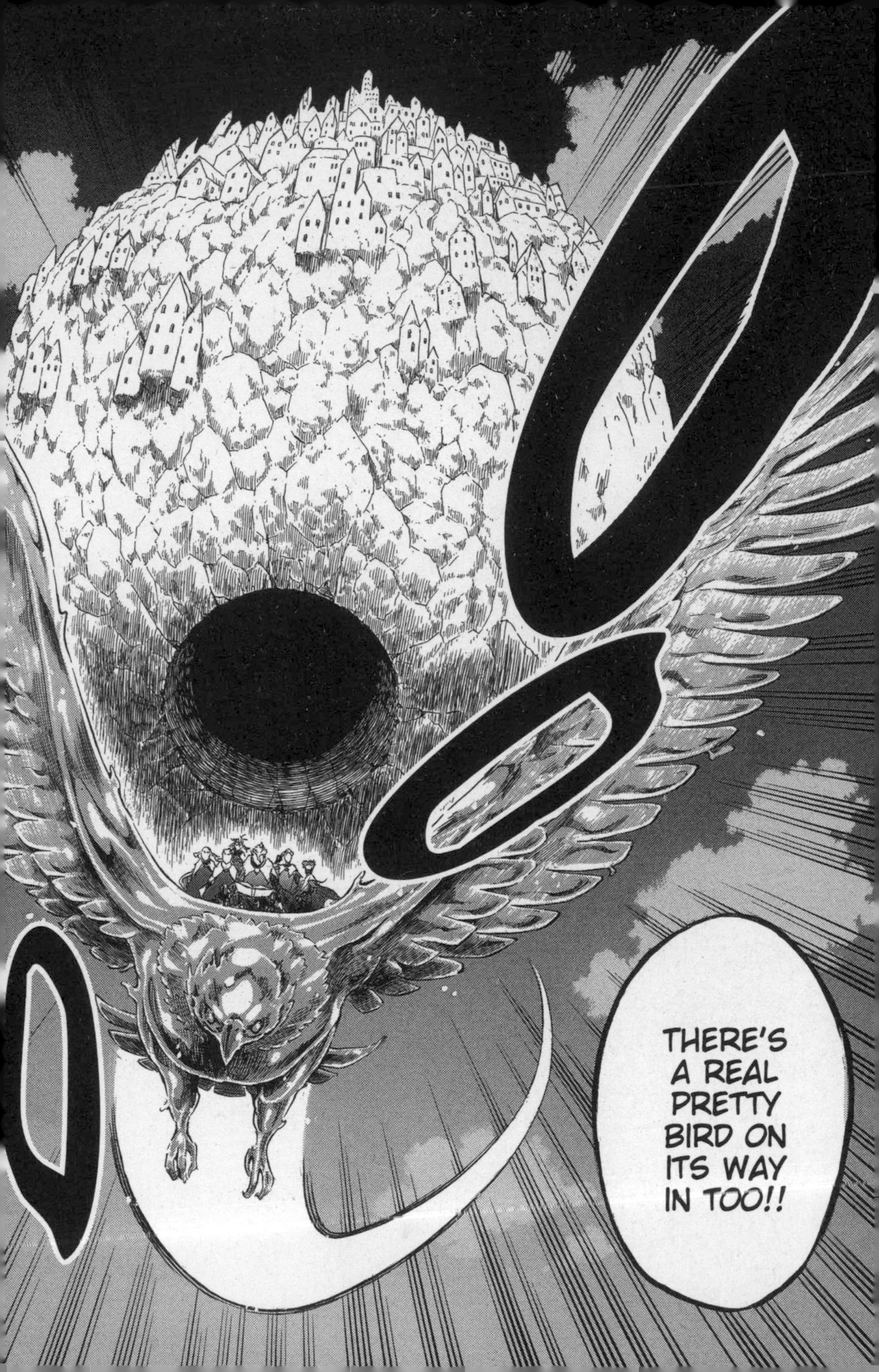
THERE'S A REAL PRETTY BIRD ON ITS WAY IN TOO!!

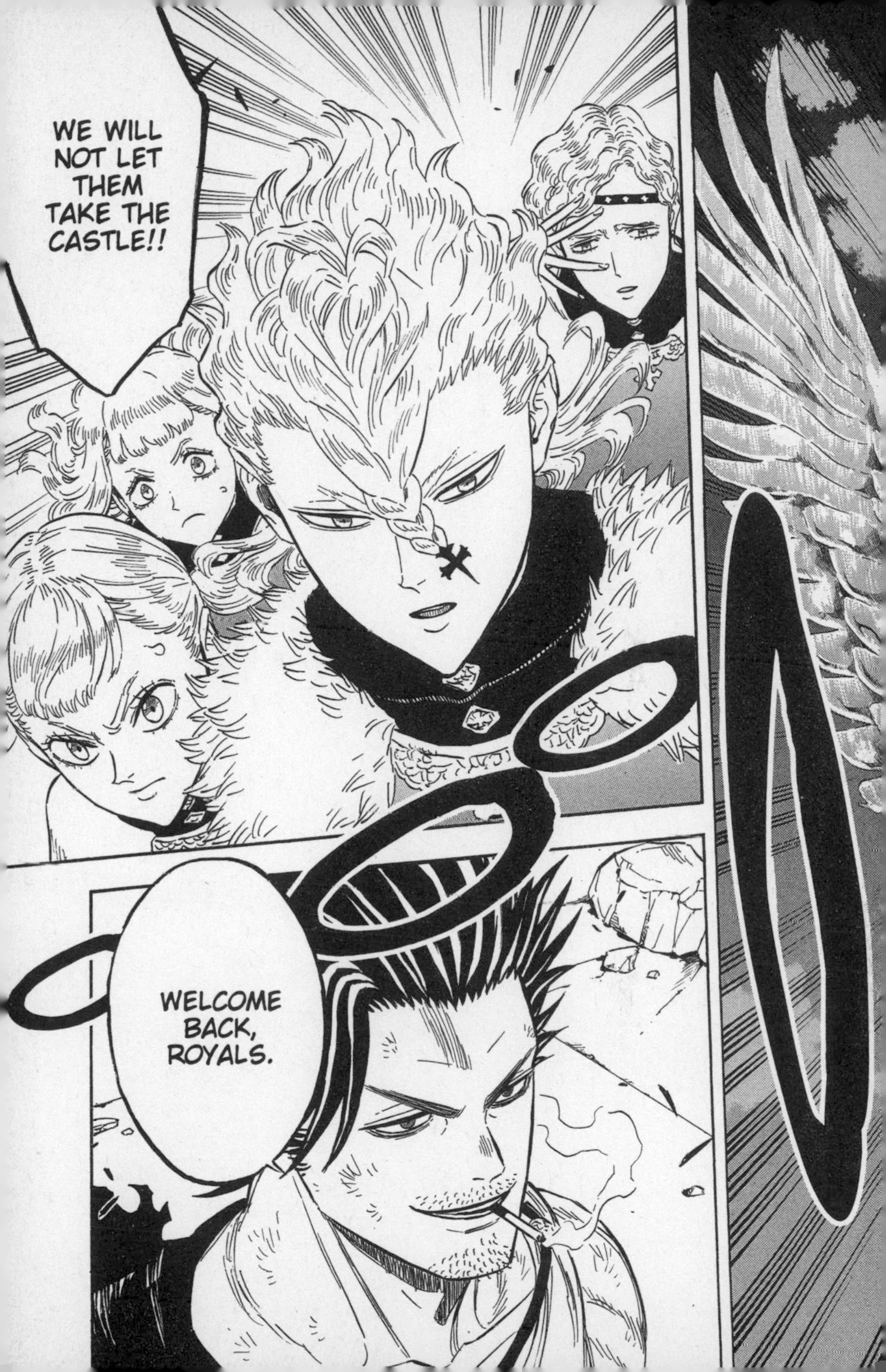
WE WILL NOT LET THEM TAKE THE CASTLE!!
WELCOME BACK, ROYALS.

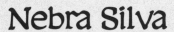

Nebra Silva

Age: 24
Height: 170 cm
Birthday: October 23
Sign: Scorpio
Blood Type: B
Likes: Sautéed pork,
　　　toying with people

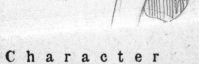

Character Profile

Page 175: The Silvas' Battle

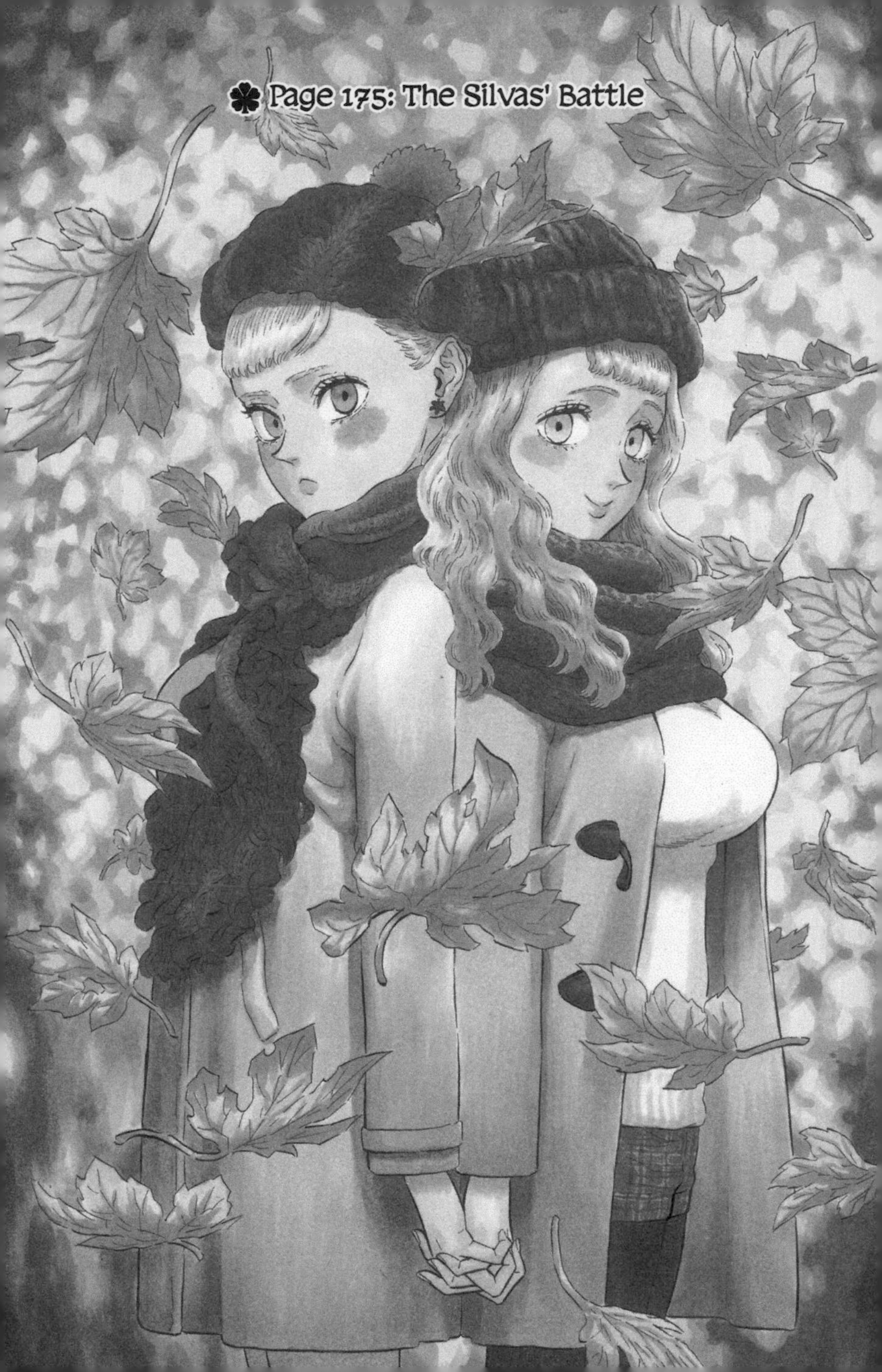

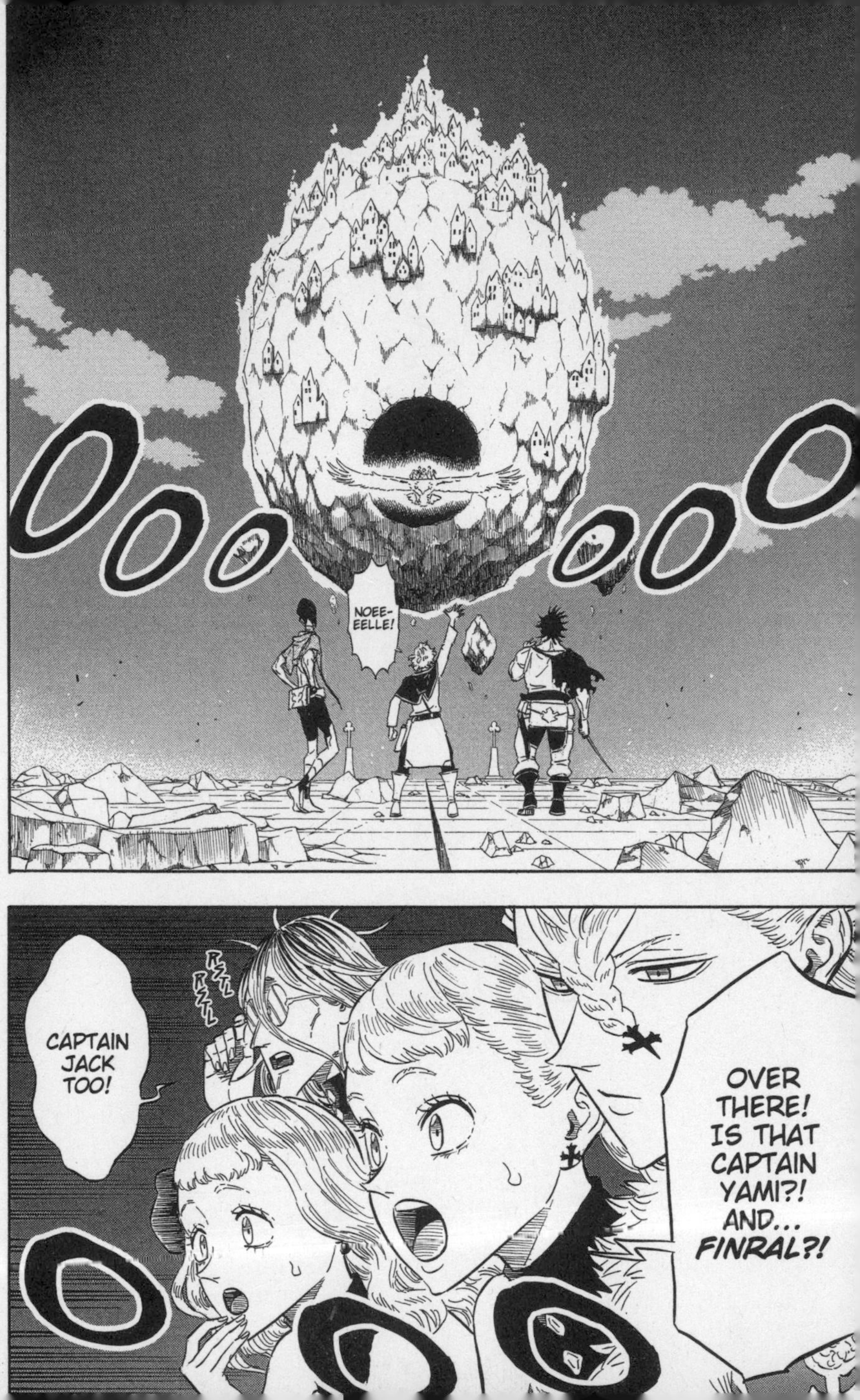
OOOOOOO
NOEEE-ELLE!
OVER THERE! IS THAT CAPTAIN YAMI?! AND... *FINRAL?!*
RSTL RSTL
CAPTAIN JACK TOO!
OOOO

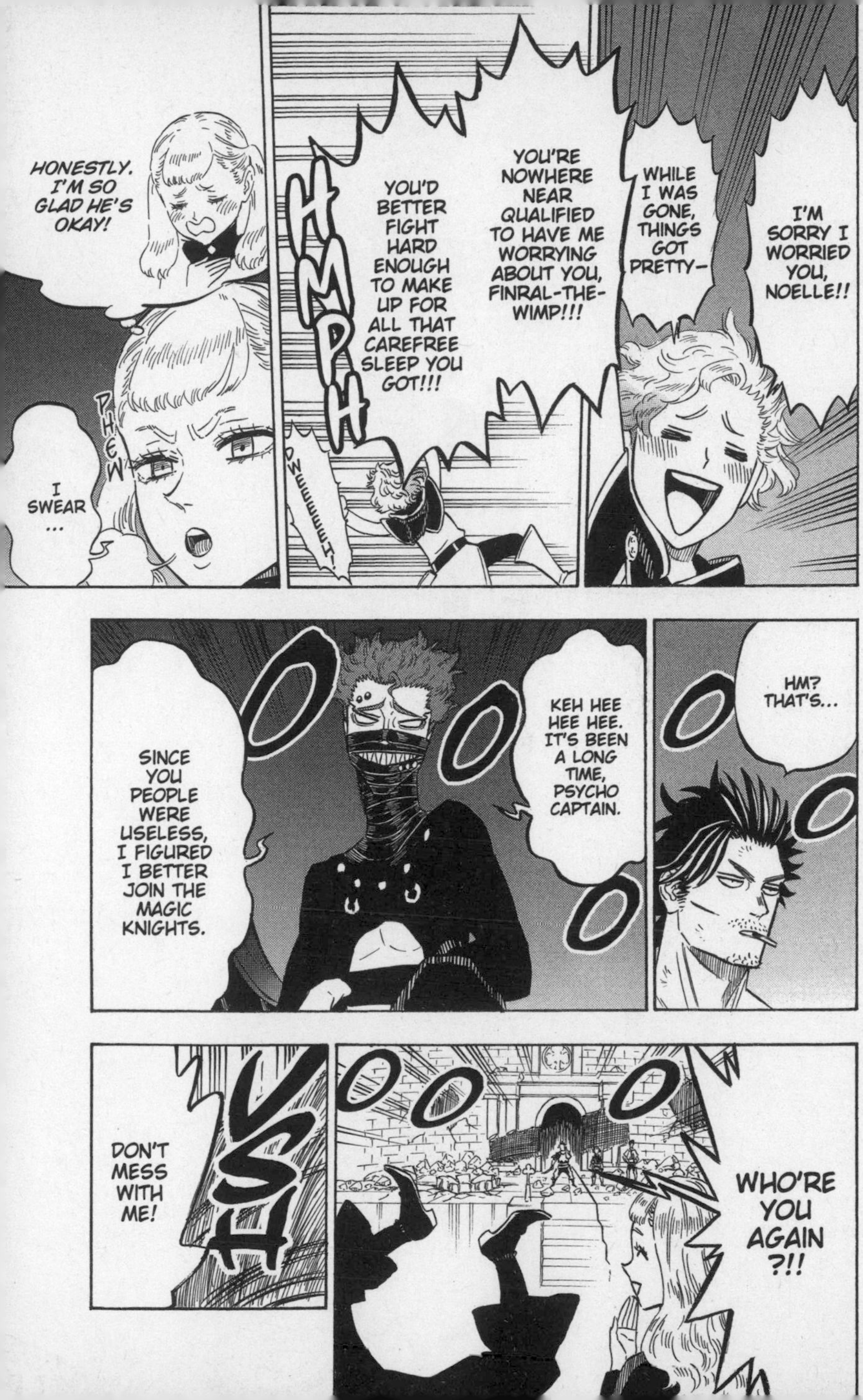
I'M SORRY I WORRIED YOU, NOELLE!!
WHILE I WAS GONE, THINGS GOT PRETTY–
YOU'RE NOWHERE NEAR QUALIFIED TO HAVE ME WORRYING ABOUT YOU, FINRAL-THE-WIMP!!!
YOU'D BETTER FIGHT HARD ENOUGH TO MAKE UP FOR ALL THAT CAREFREE SLEEP YOU GOT!!!
HMMPH
DWEEEEEH!
HONESTLY. I'M SO GLAD HE'S OKAY!
PHEW
I SWEAR...
HM? THAT'S...
KEH HEE HEE HEE. IT'S BEEN A LONG TIME, PSYCHO CAPTAIN.
SINCE YOU PEOPLE WERE USELESS, I FIGURED I BETTER JOIN THE MAGIC KNIGHTS.
WHO'RE YOU AGAIN?!!
VSH
DON'T MESS WITH ME!

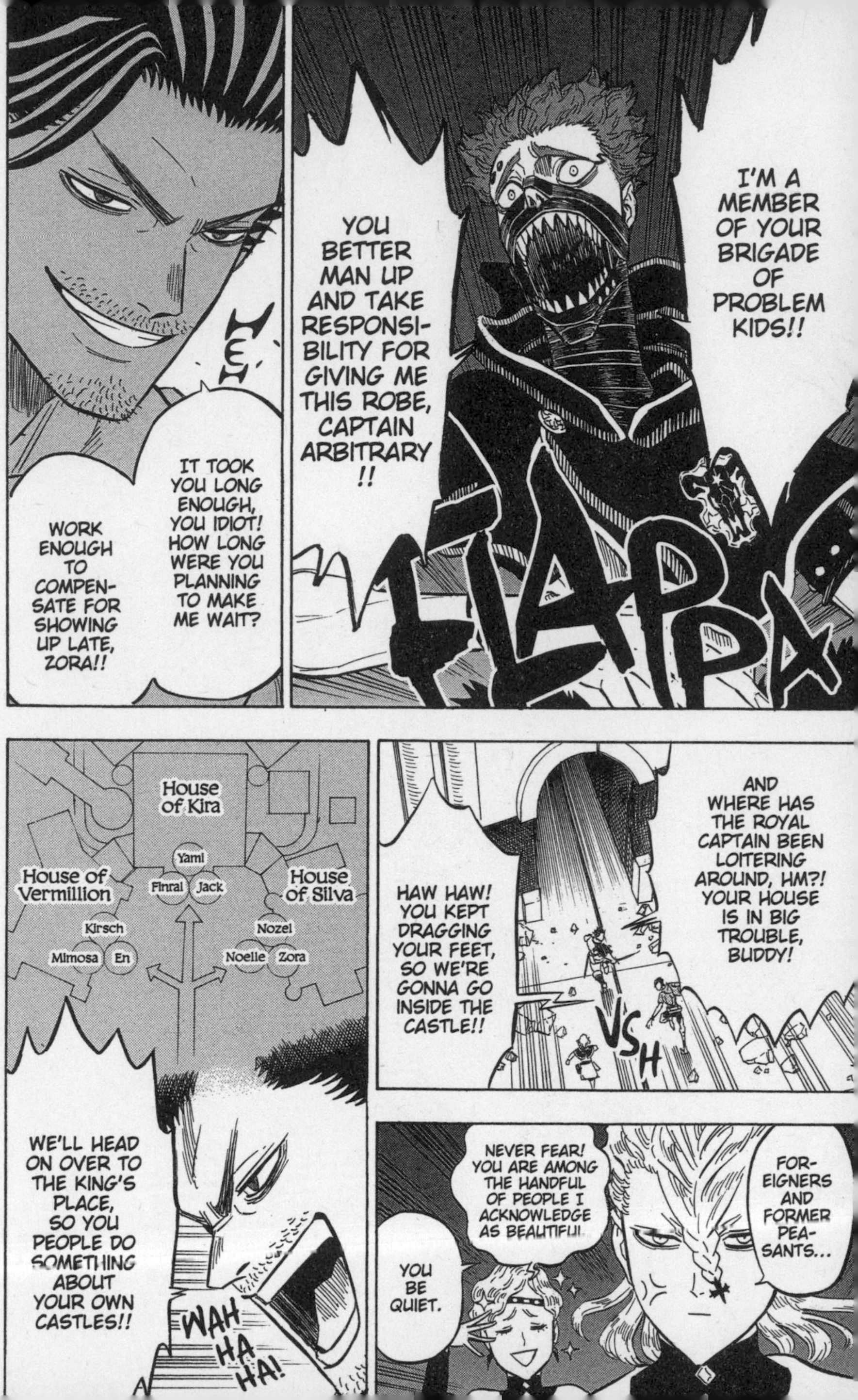
I'M A MEMBER OF YOUR BRIGADE OF PROBLEM KIDS!!
YOU BETTER MAN UP AND TAKE RESPONSI-BILITY FOR GIVING ME THIS ROBE, CAPTAIN ARBITRARY!!
HEH
IT TOOK YOU LONG ENOUGH, YOU IDIOT! HOW LONG WERE YOU PLANNING TO MAKE ME WAIT?
WORK ENOUGH TO COMPEN-SATE FOR SHOWING UP LATE, ZORA!!
AND WHERE HAS THE ROYAL CAPTAIN BEEN LOITERING AROUND, HM?! YOUR HOUSE IS IN BIG TROUBLE, BUDDY!
HAW HAW! YOU KEPT DRAGGING YOUR FEET, SO WE'RE GONNA GO INSIDE THE CASTLE!!
VSH
FOR-EIGNERS AND FORMER PEA-SANTS...
NEVER FEAR! YOU ARE AMONG THE HANDFUL OF PEOPLE I ACKNOWLEDGE AS BEAUTIFUL.
YOU BE QUIET.
House of Kira
Yami
Finral
Jack
House of Vermillion
House of Silva
Kirsch
Mimosa
En
Nozel
Noelle
Zora
WE'LL HEAD ON OVER TO THE KING'S PLACE, SO YOU PEOPLE DO SOMETHING ABOUT YOUR OWN CASTLES!!
WAH HA HA!

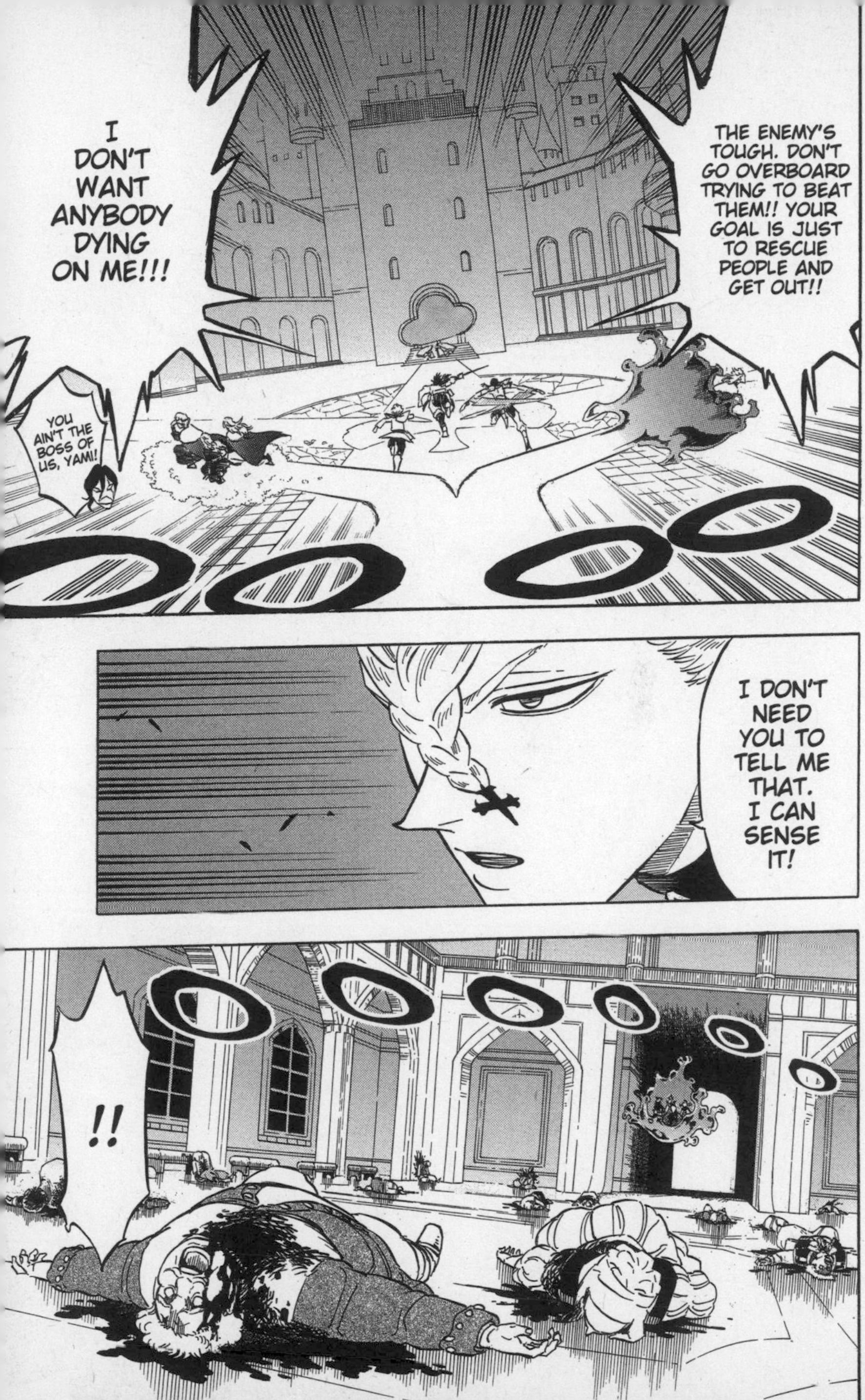
THE ENEMY'S TOUGH. DON'T GO OVERBOARD TRYING TO BEAT THEM!! YOUR GOAL IS JUST TO RESCUE PEOPLE AND GET OUT!!
I DON'T WANT ANYBODY DYING ON ME!!!
YOU AIN'T THE BOSS OF US, YAMI!
I DON'T NEED YOU TO TELL ME THAT. I CAN SENSE IT!
!!

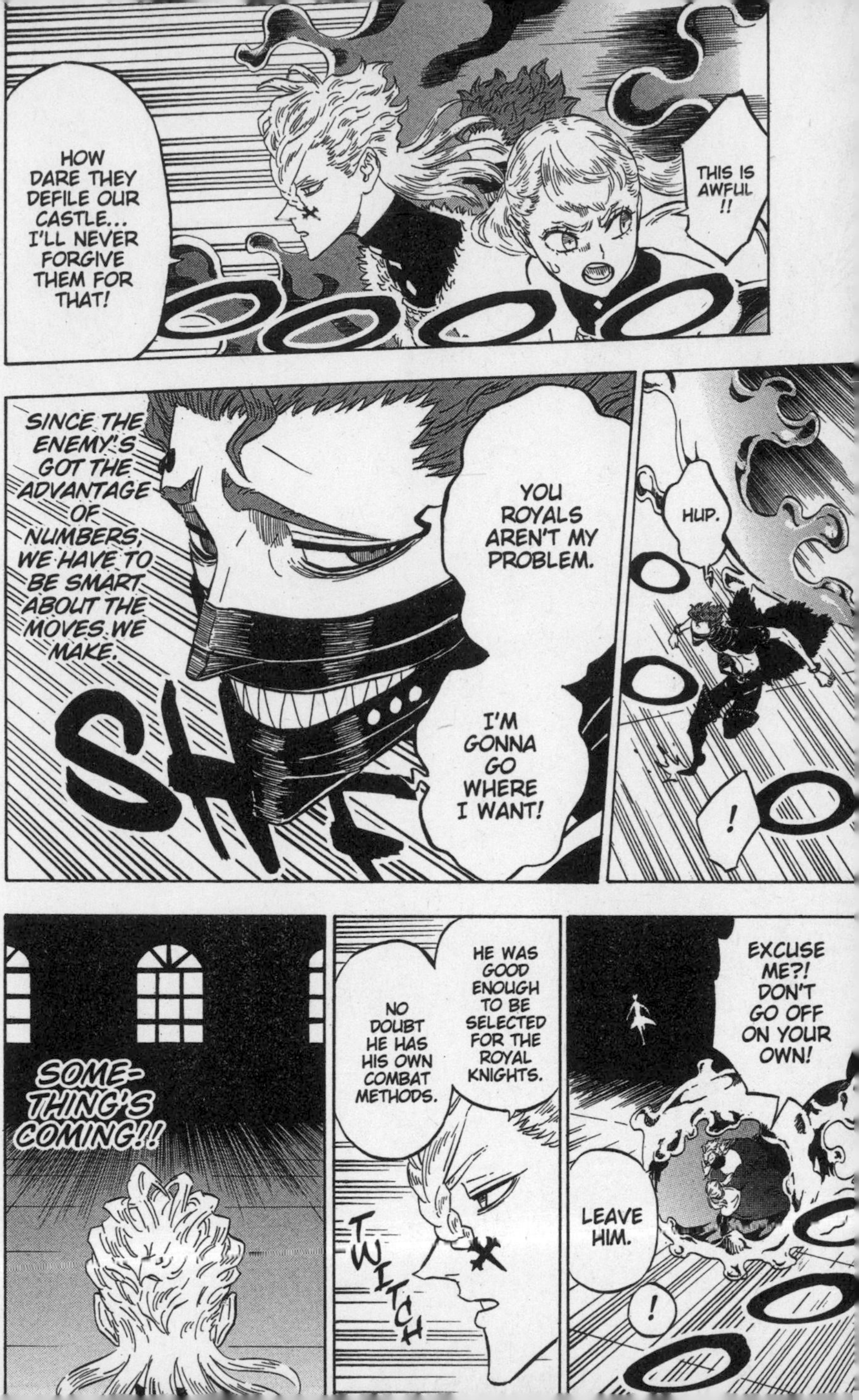
THIS IS AWFUL!!
HOW DARE THEY DEFILE OUR CASTLE... I'LL NEVER FORGIVE THEM FOR THAT!
HUP.
!
YOU ROYALS AREN'T MY PROBLEM.
SINCE THE ENEMY'S GOT THE ADVANTAGE OF NUMBERS, WE HAVE TO BE SMART ABOUT THE MOVES WE MAKE.
I'M GONNA GO WHERE I WANT!
SHF
EXCUSE ME?! DON'T GO OFF ON YOUR OWN!
LEAVE HIM.
!
HE WAS GOOD ENOUGH TO BE SELECTED FOR THE ROYAL KNIGHTS.
NO DOUBT HE HAS HIS OWN COMBAT METHODS.
TWITCH
SOME-THING'S COMING!!

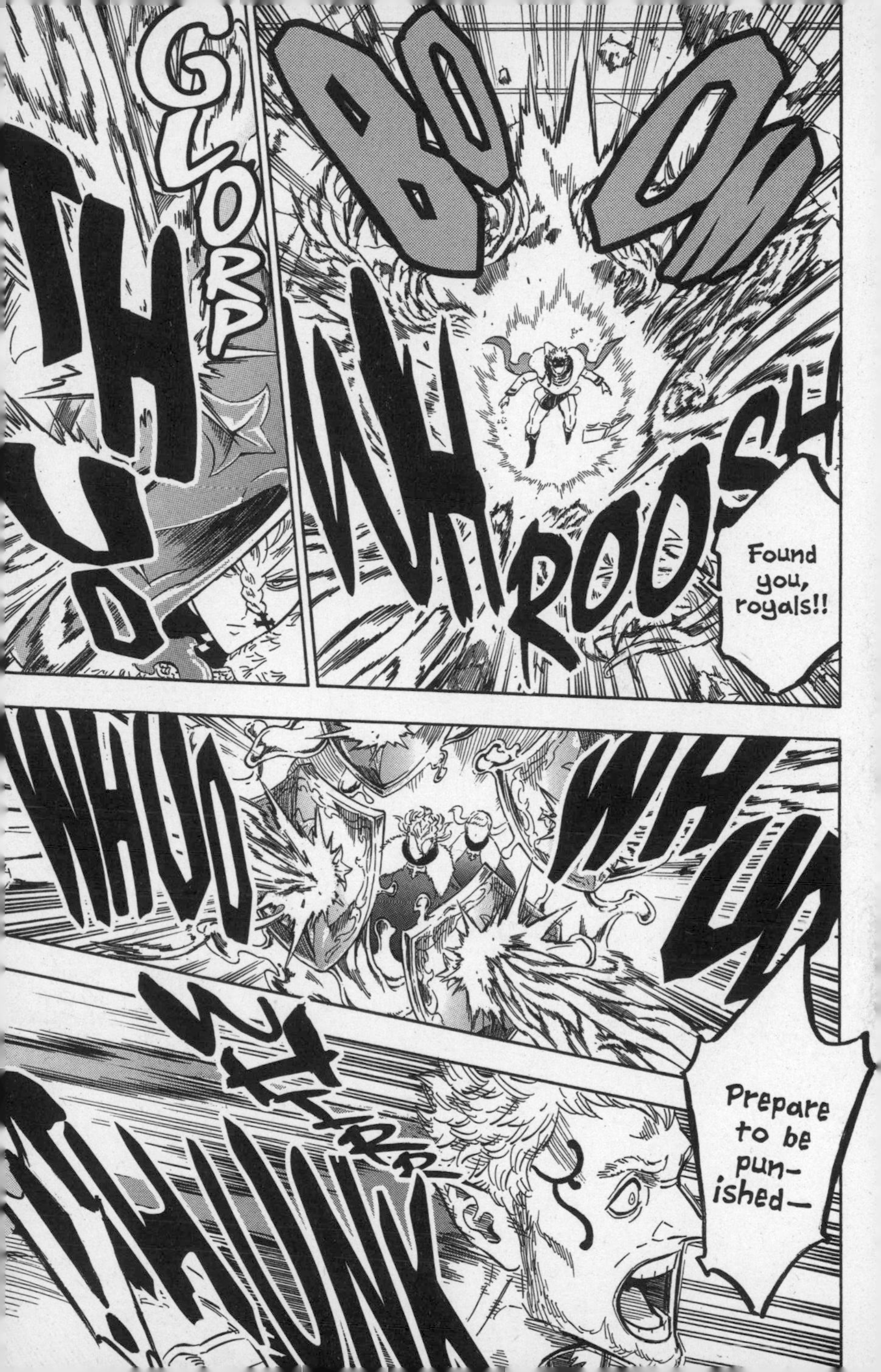
BOOM
WHROOSH
Found you, royals!!
GLORP
WHUD
WHUD
Prepare to be pun-ished—

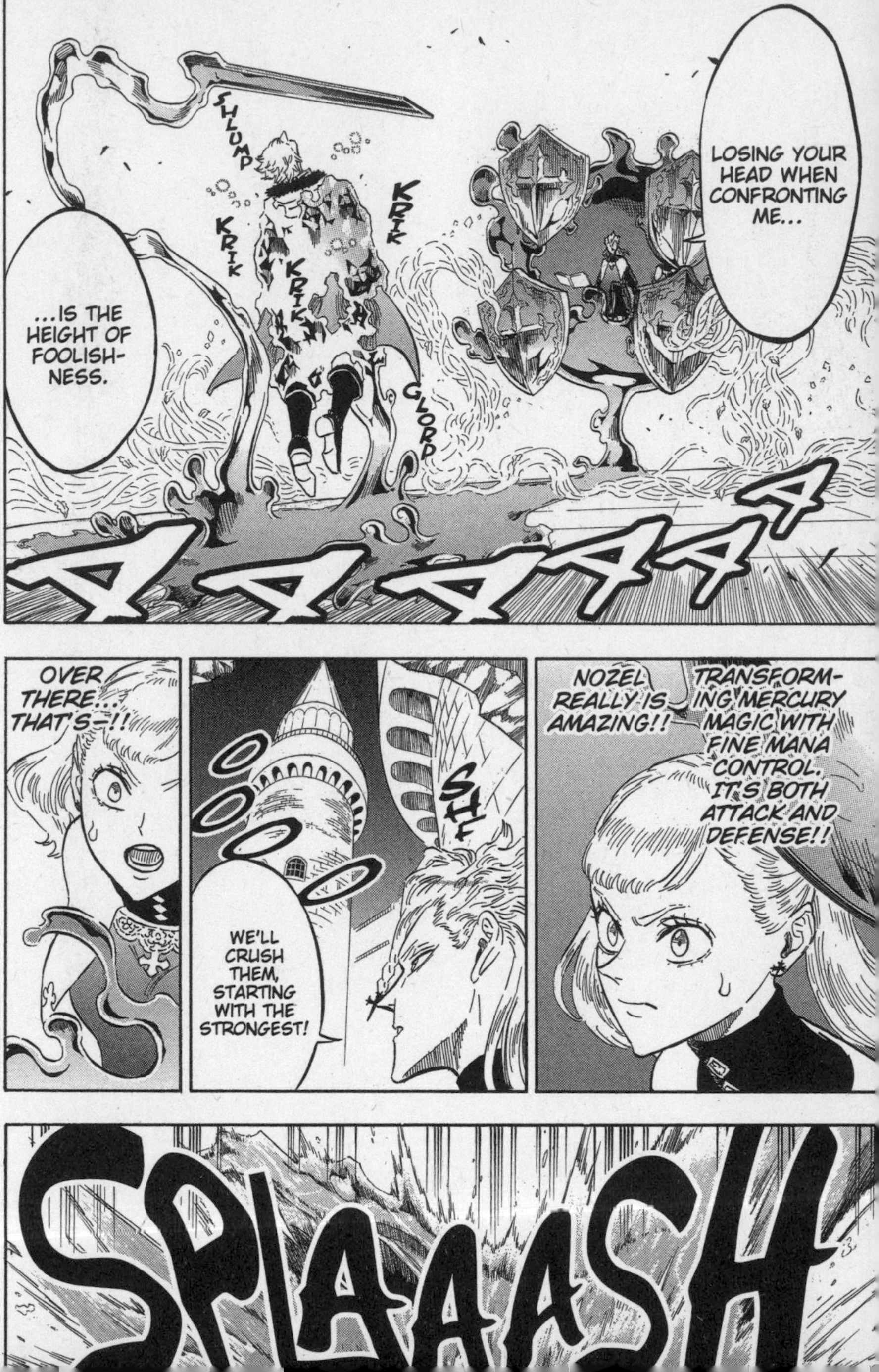

LOSING YOUR HEAD WHEN CONFRONTING ME...
...IS THE HEIGHT OF FOOLISH-NESS.
KRIK
KRIK
KRIK
SHLUMP
GLORP
AAAAA
TRANSFORM-ING MERCURY MAGIC WITH FINE MANA CONTROL. IT'S BOTH ATTACK AND DEFENSE!!
NOZEL REALLY IS AMAZING!!
SHF
WE'LL CRUSH THEM, STARTING WITH THE STRONGEST!
OVER THERE... THAT'S—!!
SPLAASH

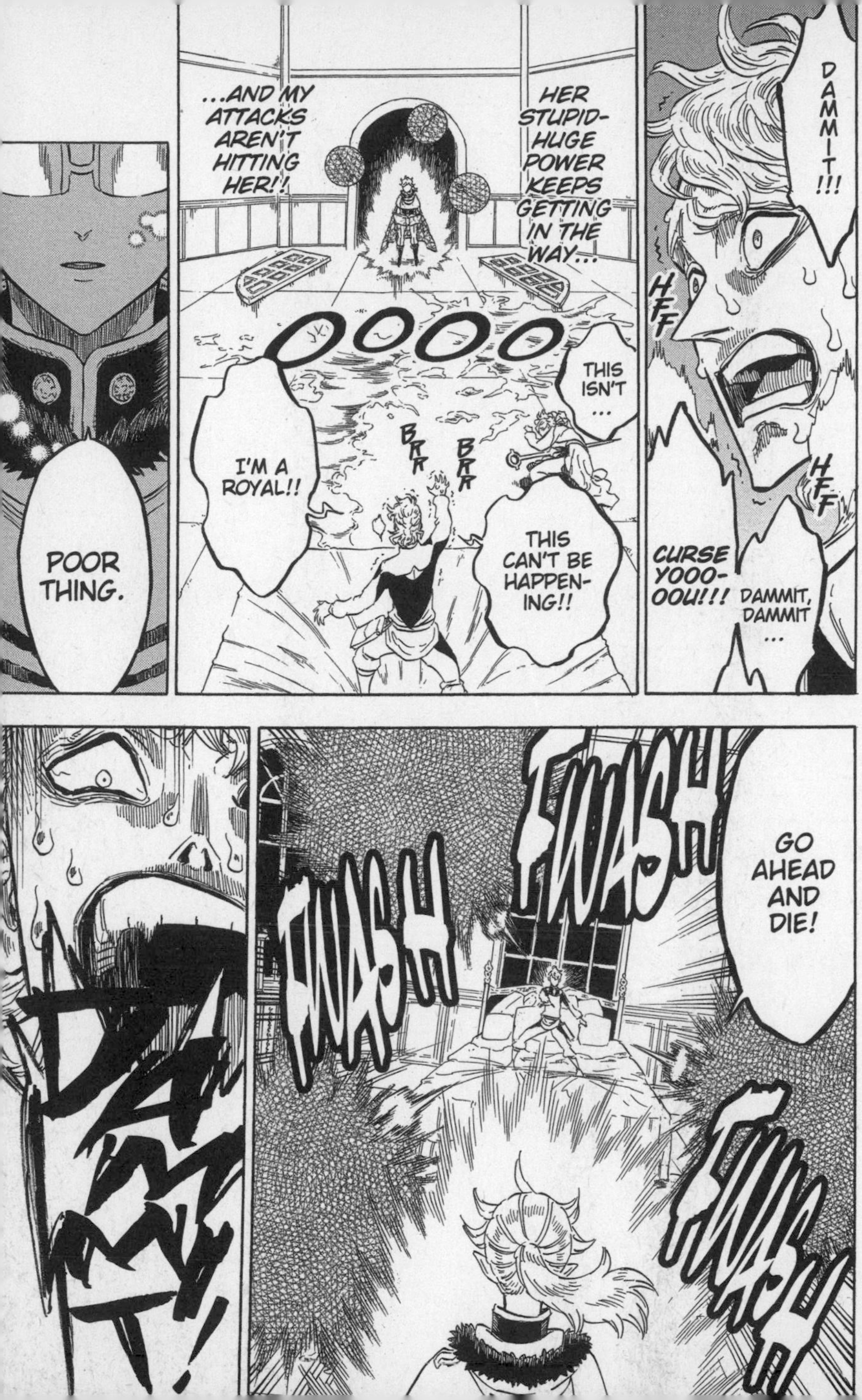
DAMMIT!!!
HFF
HFF
CURSE YOOOOOU!!!
DAMMIT, DAMMIT...
HER STUPID-HUGE POWER KEEPS GETTING IN THE WAY...
...AND MY ATTACKS AREN'T HITTING HER!!
OOOO
THIS ISN'T...
I'M A ROYAL!!
BRR
BRR
THIS CAN'T BE HAPPENING!!
POOR THING.
GO AHEAD AND DIE!
FWASH
FWASH

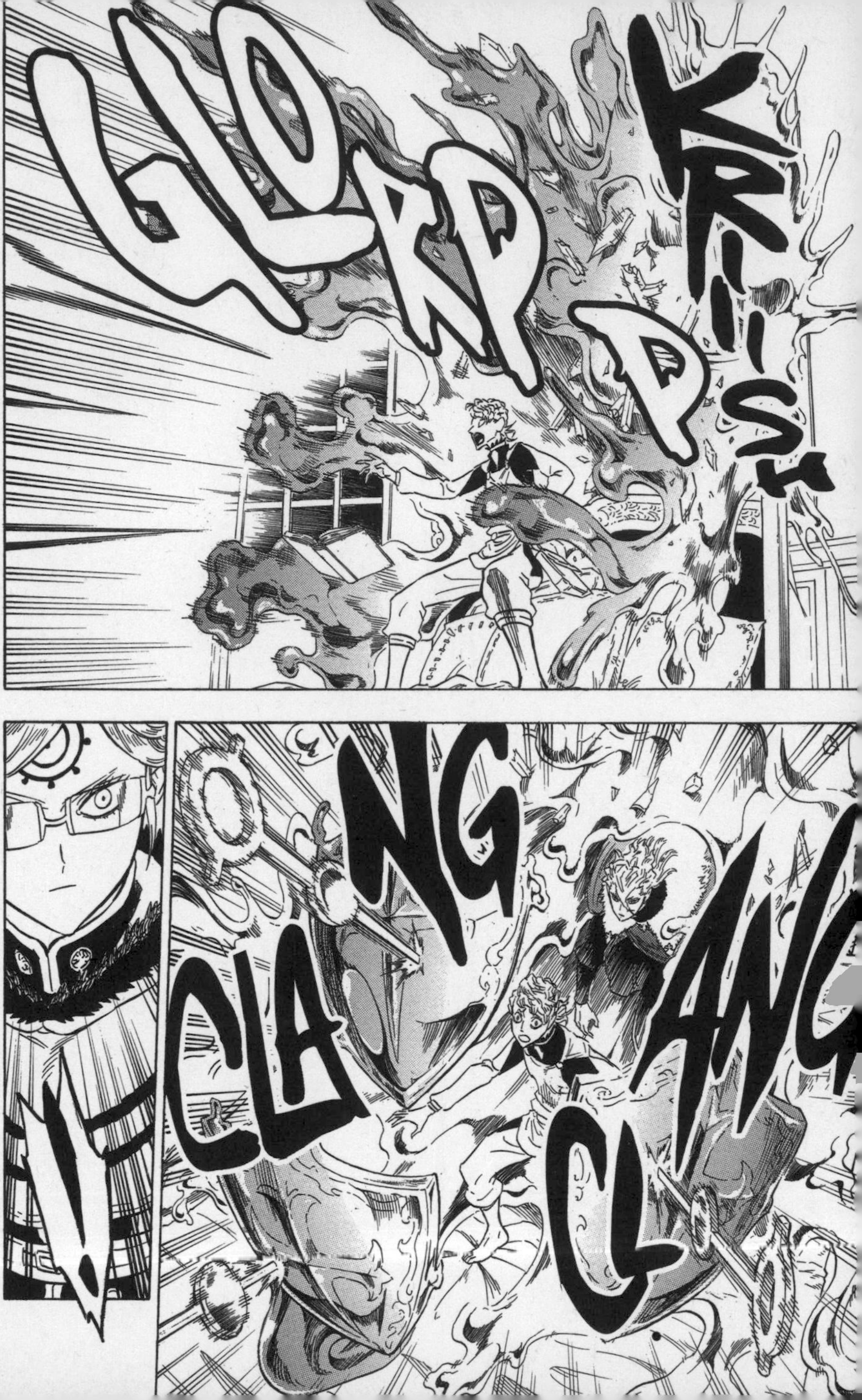
KRISH
GLORP
CLANG
CLANG
!

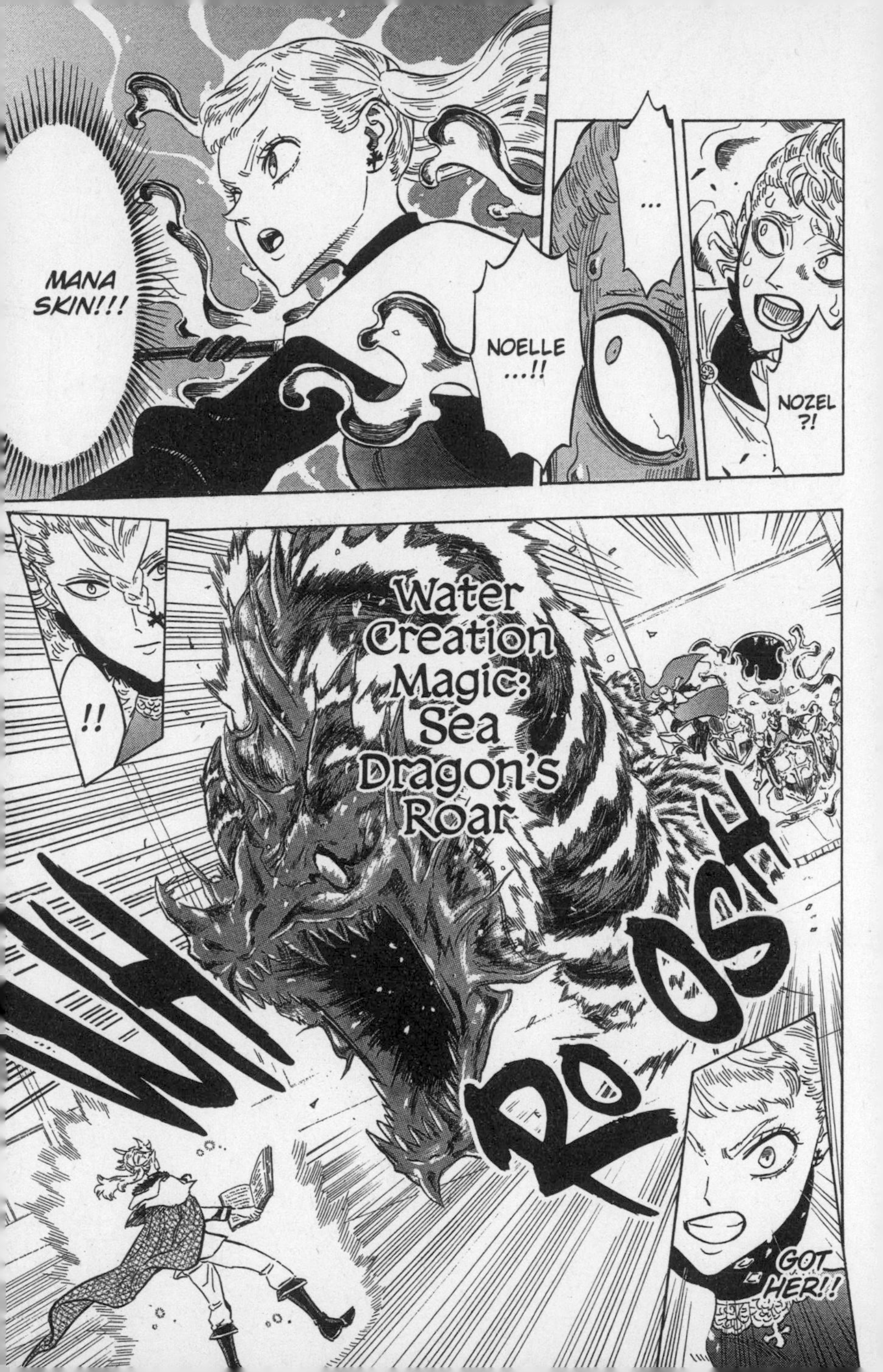
NOZEL ?!
...
NOELLE ...!!
MANA SKIN!!!
Water Creation Magic: Sea Dragon's Roar
!!
ROOSH
WHH
GOT HER!!

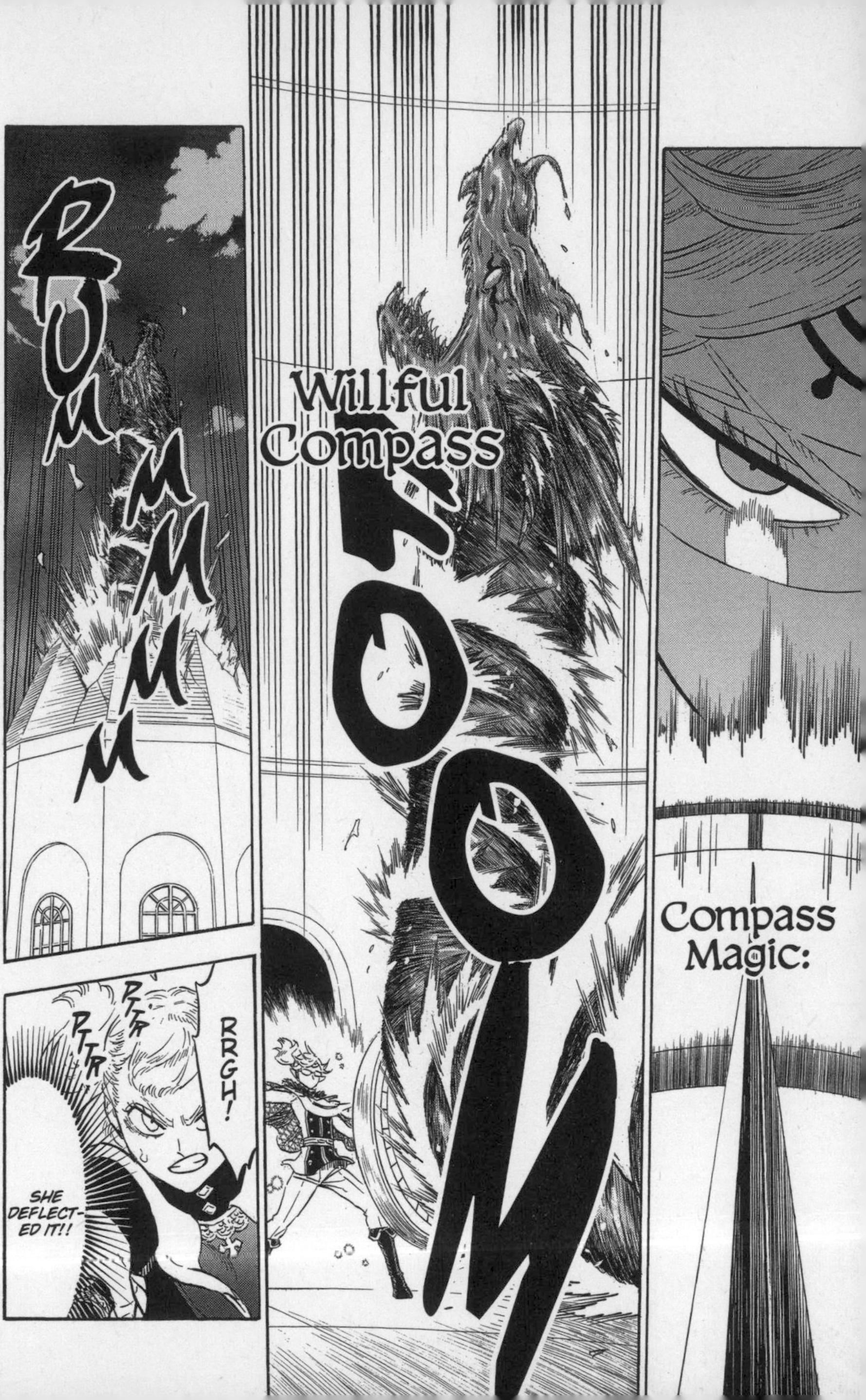
Compass
Magic:
Willful
Compass
BOOOM
RUMMMMM
RRGH!
PTTR
PTTR
SHE
DEFLECT-
ED IT!!

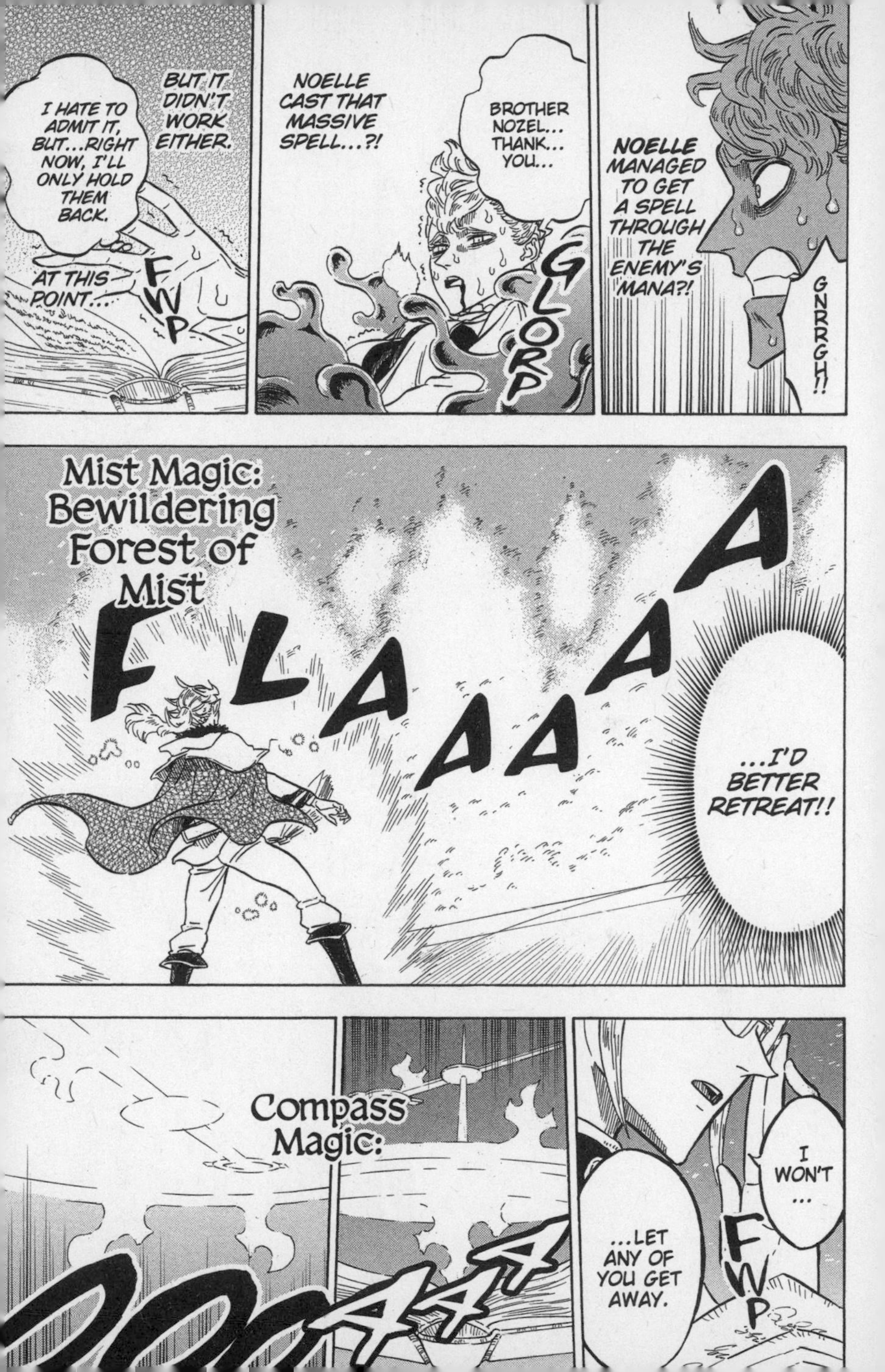
NOELLE MANAGED TO GET A SPELL THROUGH THE ENEMY'S MANA?!
GNRRGH!!
BROTHER NOZEL... THANK... YOU...
NOELLE CAST THAT MASSIVE SPELL...?!
GLORP
BUT IT DIDN'T WORK EITHER.
I HATE TO ADMIT IT, BUT...RIGHT NOW, I'LL ONLY HOLD THEM BACK.
AT THIS POINT...
FWP
...I'D BETTER RETREAT!!
Mist Magic: Bewildering Forest of Mist
FLAAAAA
I WON'T ...
...LET ANY OF YOU GET AWAY.
FWP
Compass Magic:

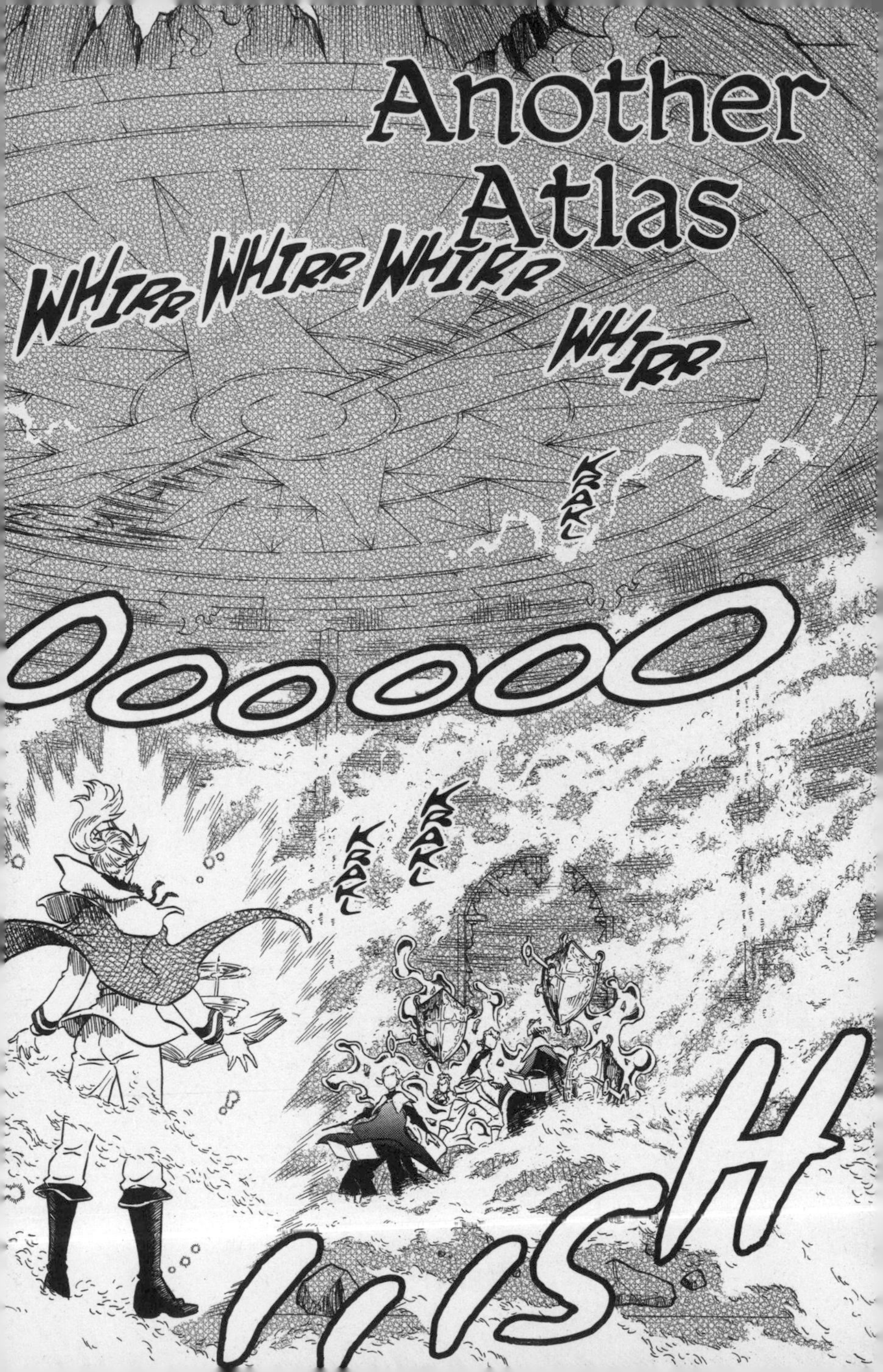
Another Atlas
WHIRR WHIRR WHIRR
WHIRR
KRAK
OOOOOO
KRAK
KRAK

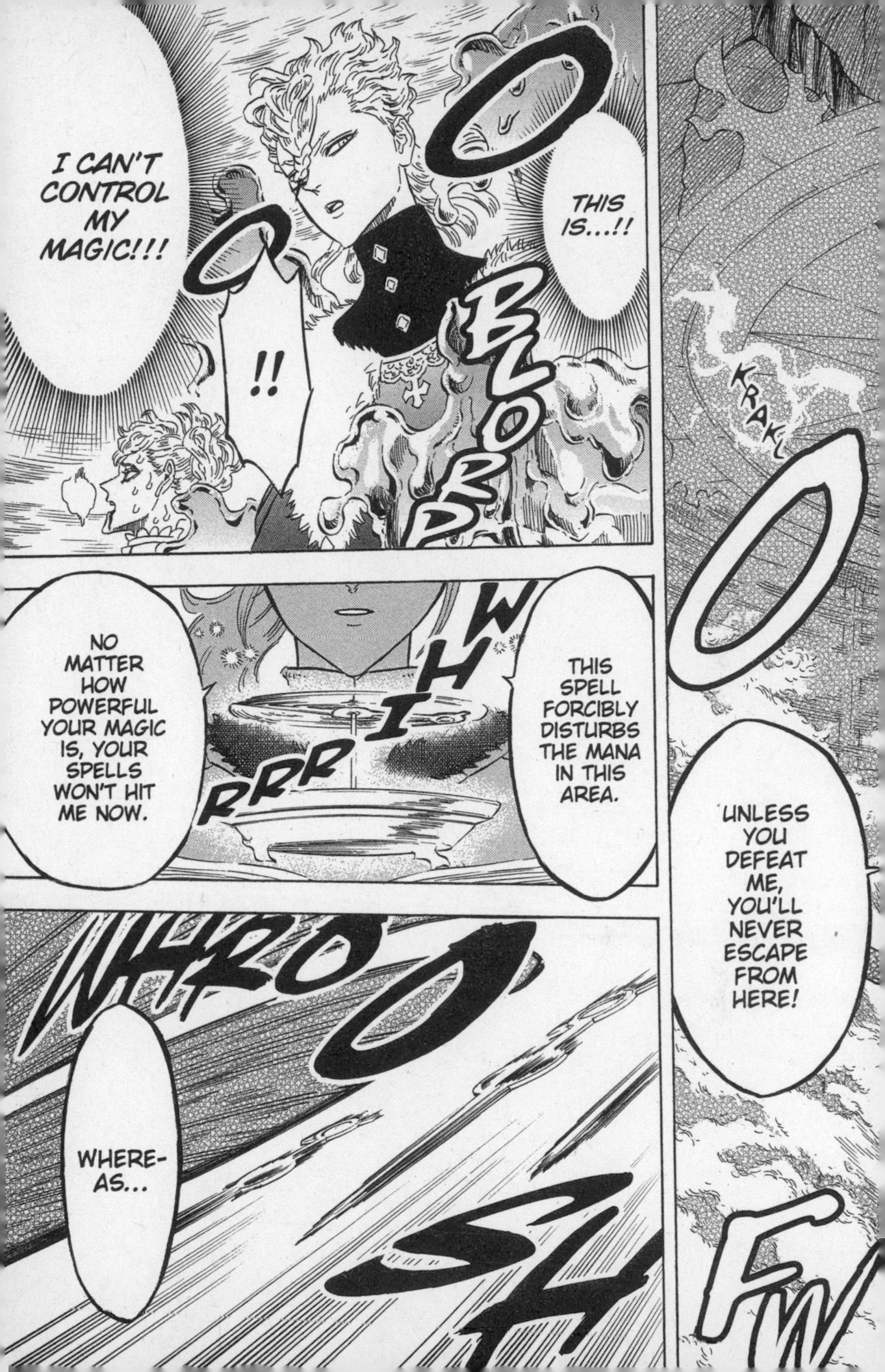

KRAK!
UNLESS YOU DEFEAT ME, YOU'LL NEVER ESCAPE FROM HERE!
FW
THIS IS...!!
BLORP
I CAN'T CONTROL MY MAGIC!!!
!!
THIS SPELL FORCIBLY DISTURBS THE MANA IN THIS AREA.
WHIRRR
NO MATTER HOW POWERFUL YOUR MAGIC IS, YOUR SPELLS WON'T HIT ME NOW.
WHROOSH
WHERE-AS...

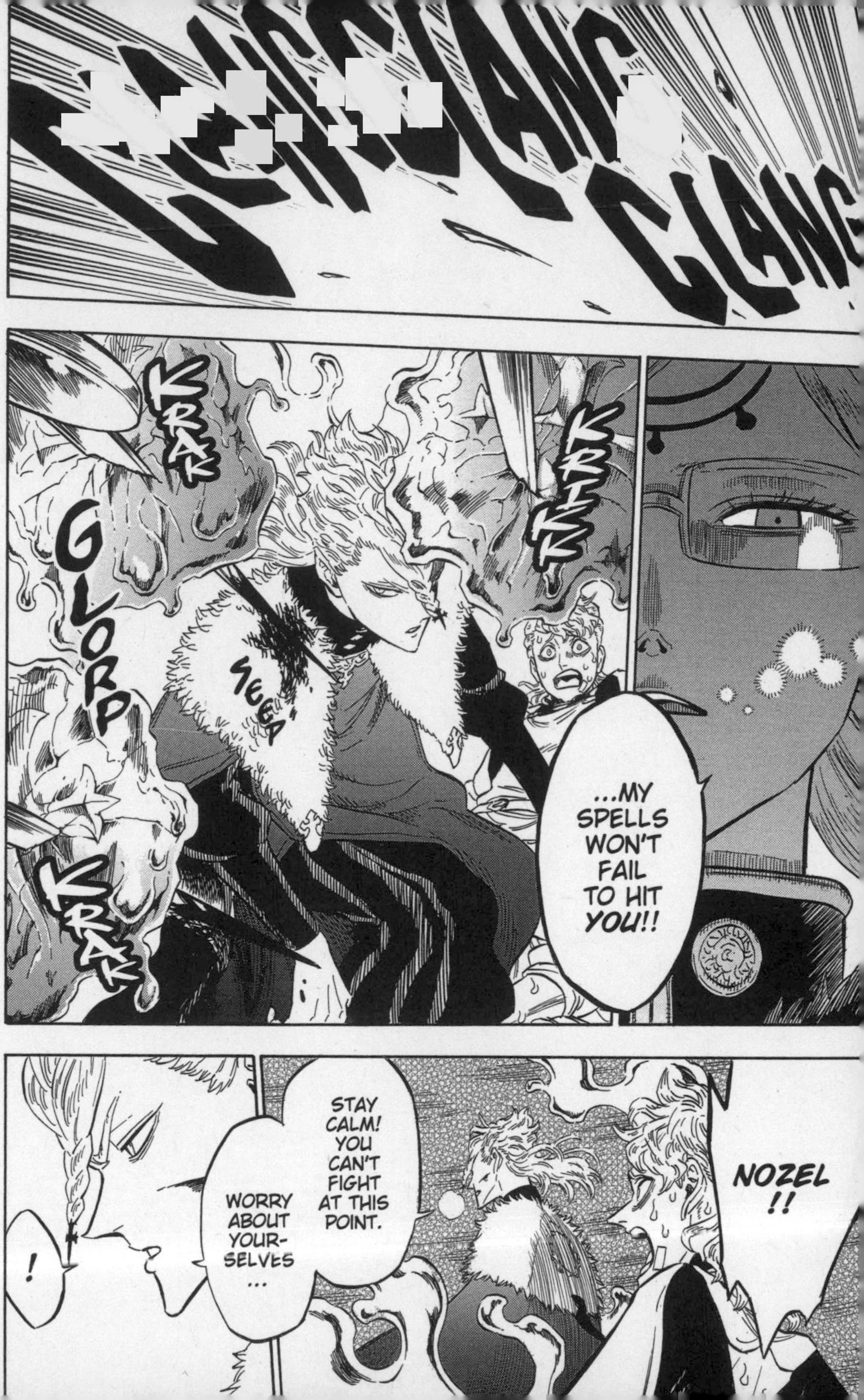
CLANG
...MY SPELLS WON'T FAIL TO HIT YOU!!
KRIK
KRAK
GLORP
SEEA
KRAK
NOZEL !!
STAY CALM! YOU CAN'T FIGHT AT THIS POINT.
WORRY ABOUT YOUR-SELVES ...
!

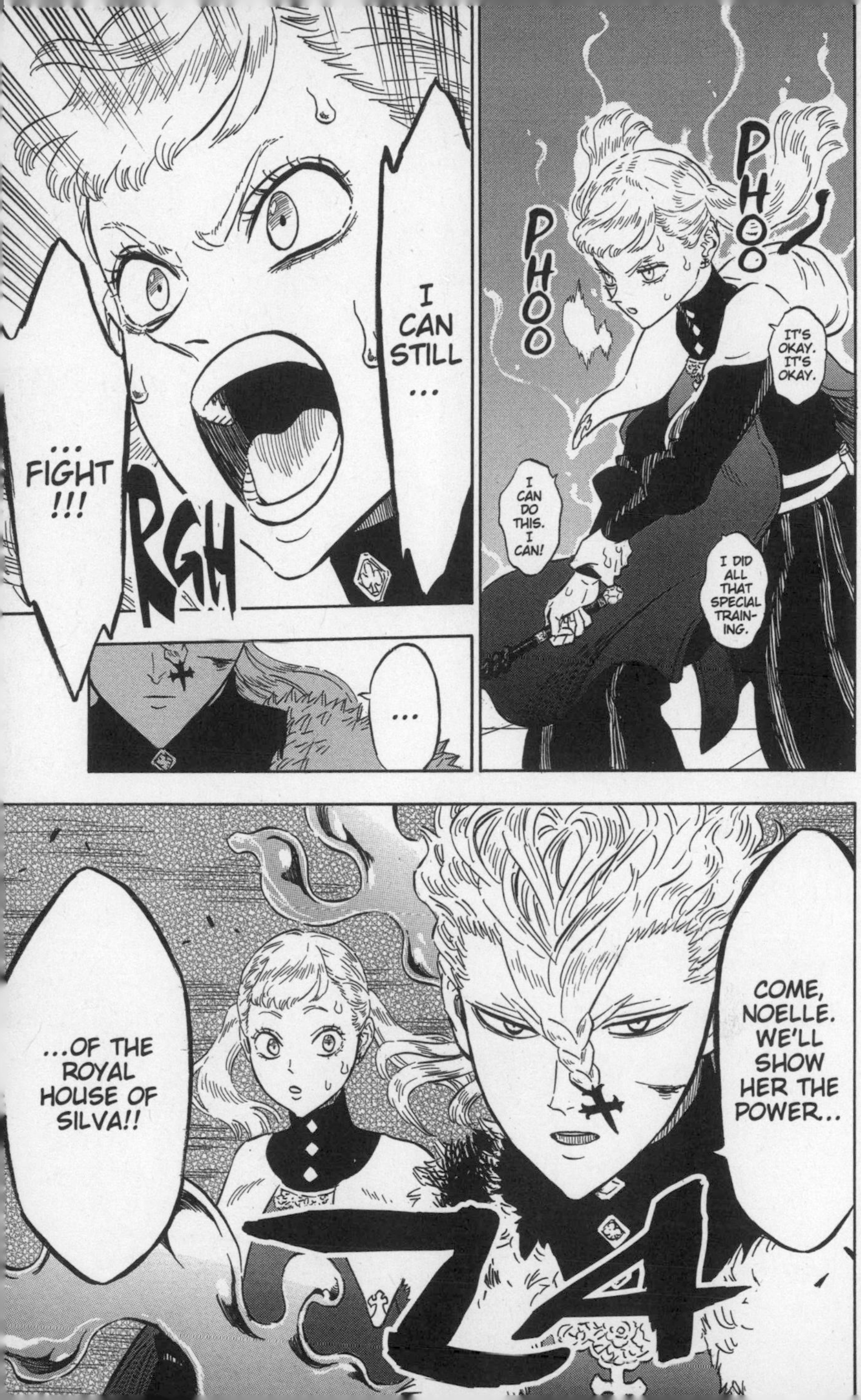
PHOO
PHOO
IT'S OKAY. IT'S OKAY.
I CAN DO THIS. I CAN!
I DID ALL THAT SPECIAL TRAIN-ING.
I CAN STILL ...
RGH
... FIGHT !!!
...
COME, NOELLE. WE'LL SHOW HER THE POWER...
...OF THE ROYAL HOUSE OF SILVA!!

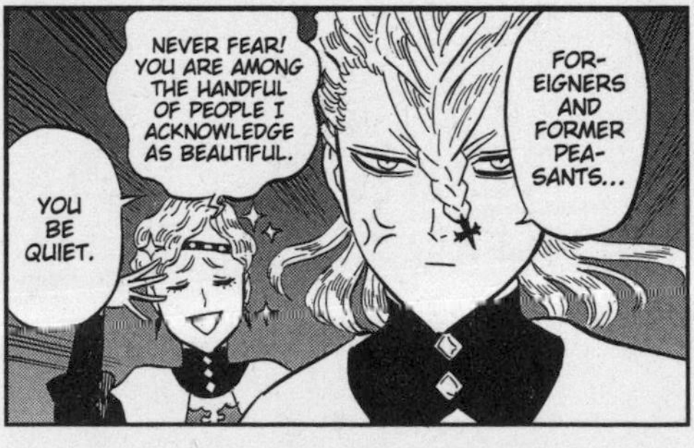
FOR-EIGNERS AND FORMER PEA-SANTS...
NEVER FEAR! YOU ARE AMONG THE HANDFUL OF PEOPLE I ACKNOWLEDGE AS BEAUTIFUL.
YOU BE QUIET.

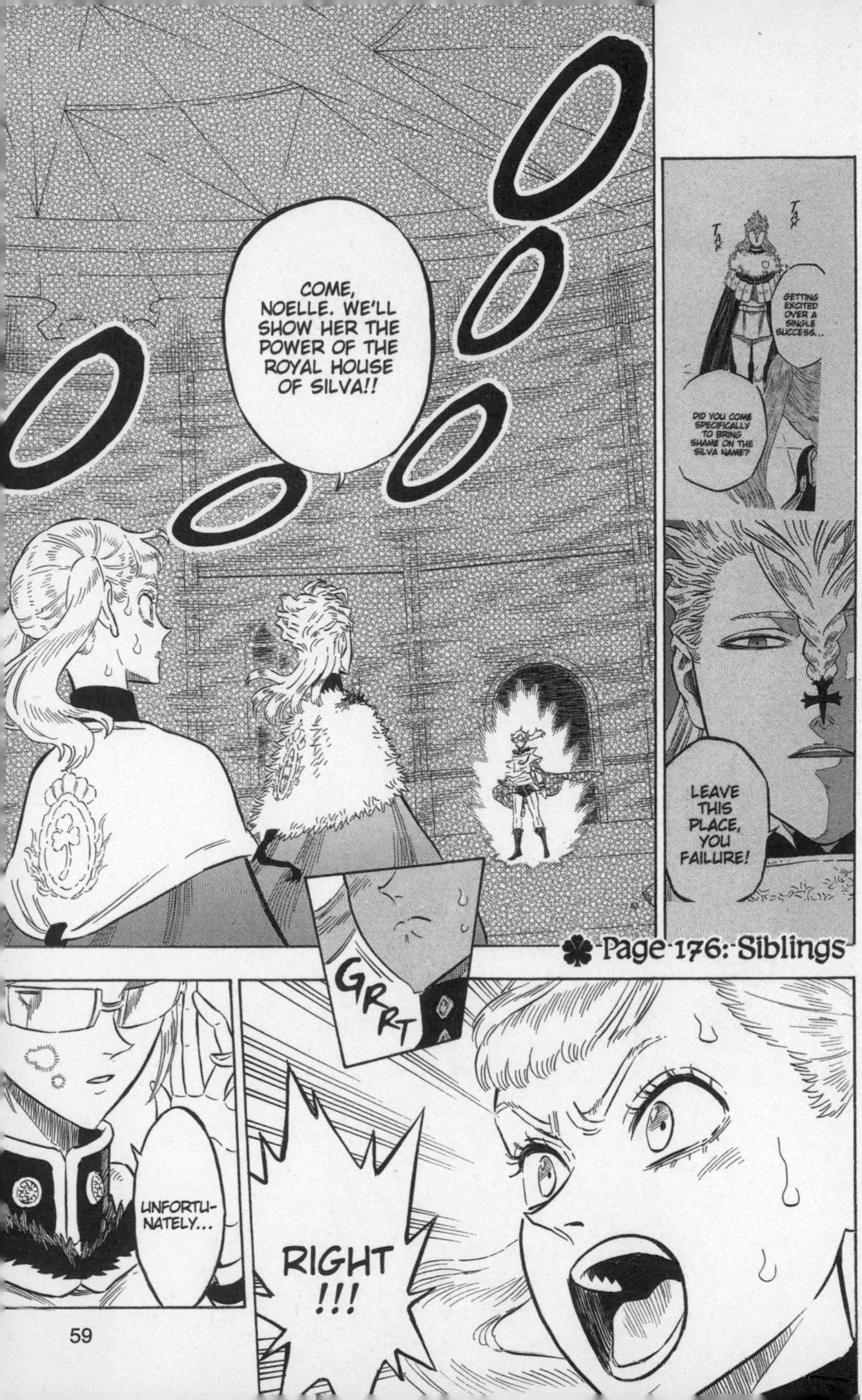
GETTING EXCITED OVER A SINGLE SUCCESS...
DID YOU COME SPECIFICALLY TO BRING SHAME ON THE SILVA NAME?
LEAVE THIS PLACE, YOU FAILURE!
COME, NOELLE. WE'LL SHOW HER THE POWER OF THE ROYAL HOUSE OF SILVA!!
GRRRT
Page 176: Siblings
RIGHT !!!
UNFORTU-NATELY...

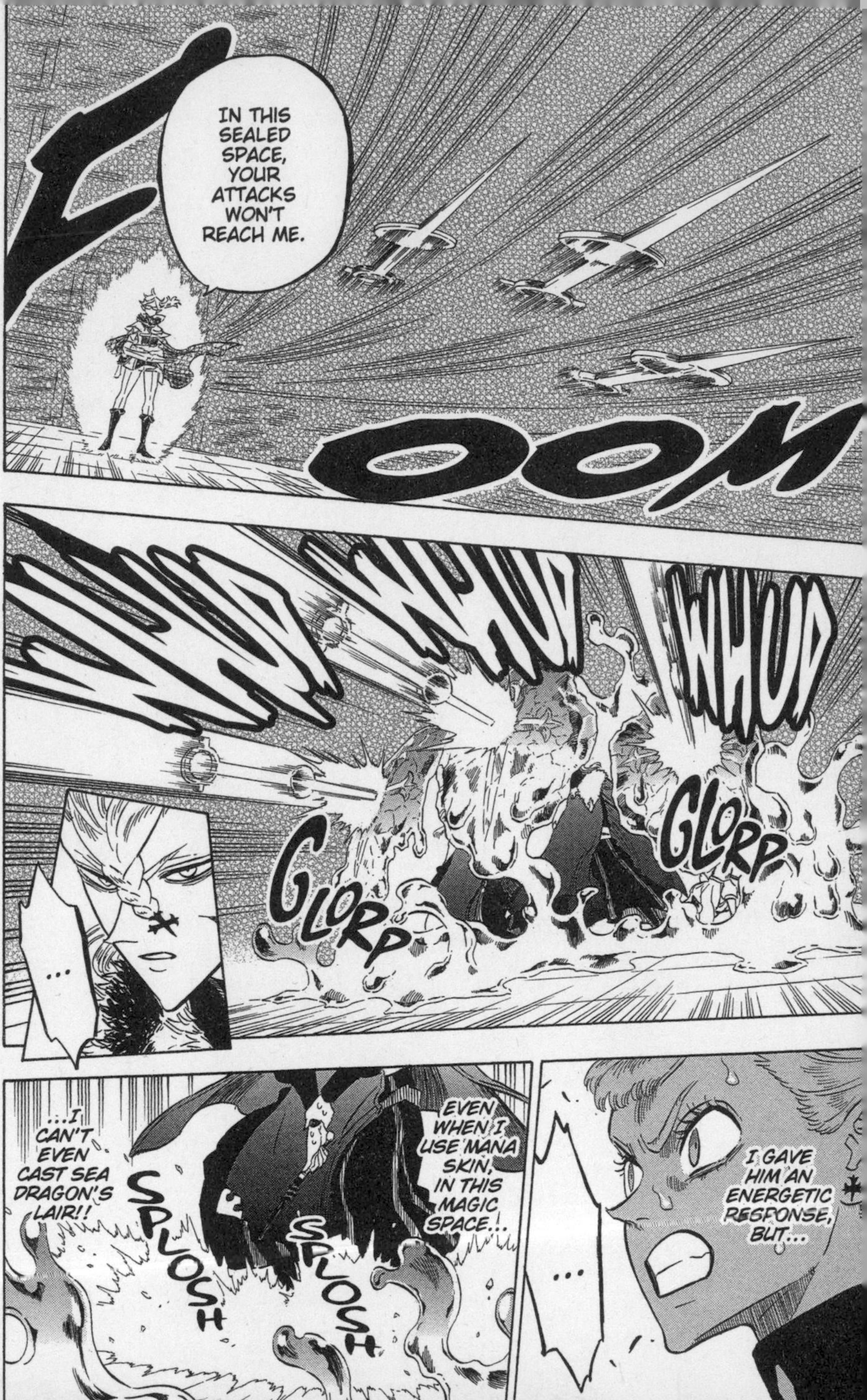
IN THIS SEALED SPACE, YOUR ATTACKS WON'T REACH ME.
OOM
WHUD
WHUD
WHUD
GLORP
GLORP
...
I GAVE HIM AN ENERGETIC RESPONSE, BUT...
...
EVEN WHEN I USE MANA SKIN, IN THIS MAGIC SPACE...
...I CAN'T EVEN CAST SEA DRAGON'S LAIR!!
SPLOSH
SPLOSH

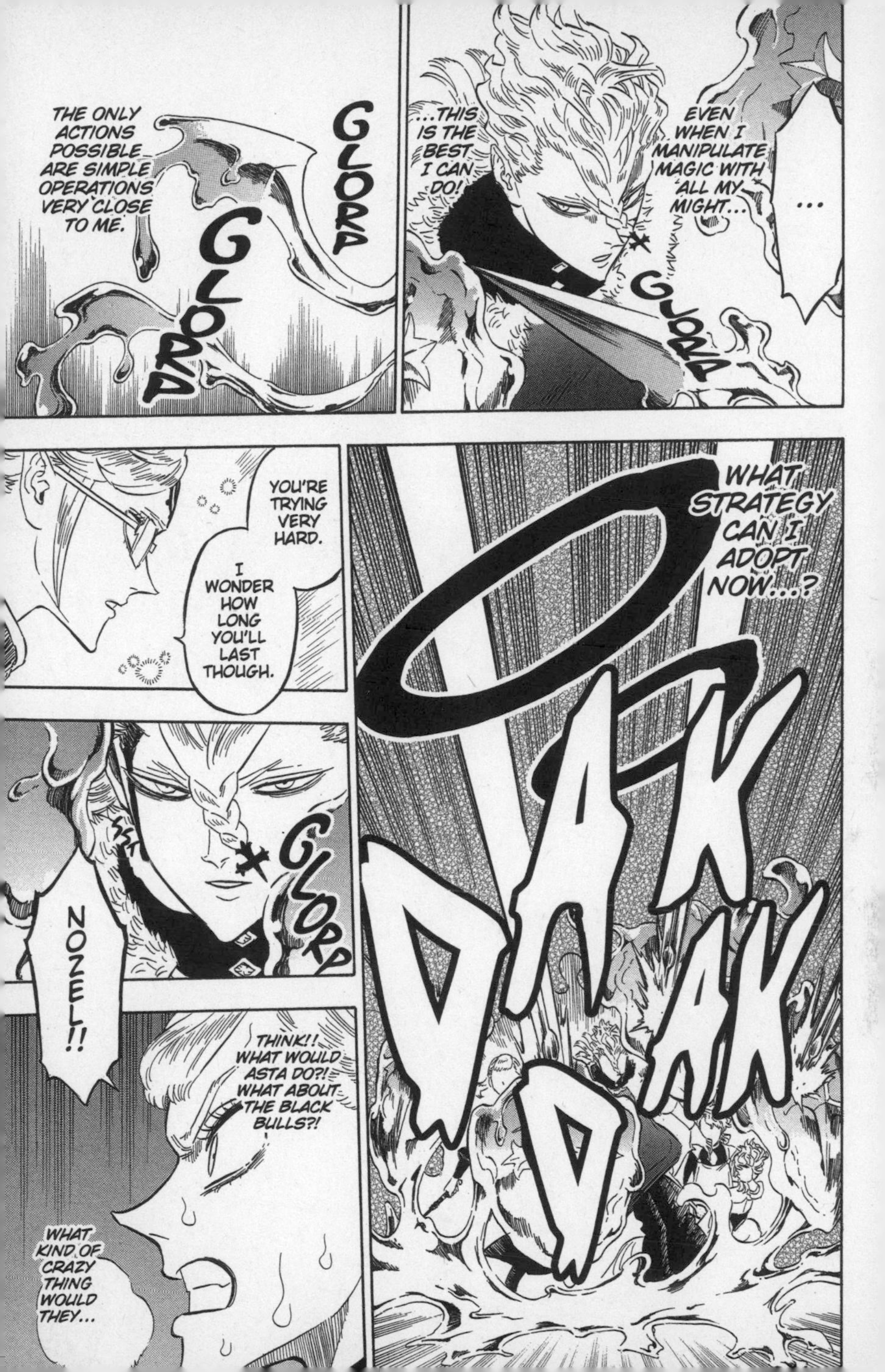
...
EVEN WHEN I MANIPULATE MAGIC WITH ALL MY MIGHT...
...THIS IS THE BEST I CAN DO!
GLORP
GLORP
GLORP
THE ONLY ACTIONS POSSIBLE ARE SIMPLE OPERATIONS VERY CLOSE TO ME.
WHAT STRATEGY CAN I ADOPT NOW...?
DAK
DAK
DAK
YOU'RE TRYING VERY HARD.
I WONDER HOW LONG YOU'LL LAST THOUGH.
GLORP
NOZEL!!
THINK!! WHAT WOULD ASTA DO?! WHAT ABOUT THE BLACK BULLS?!
WHAT KIND OF CRAZY THING WOULD THEY...

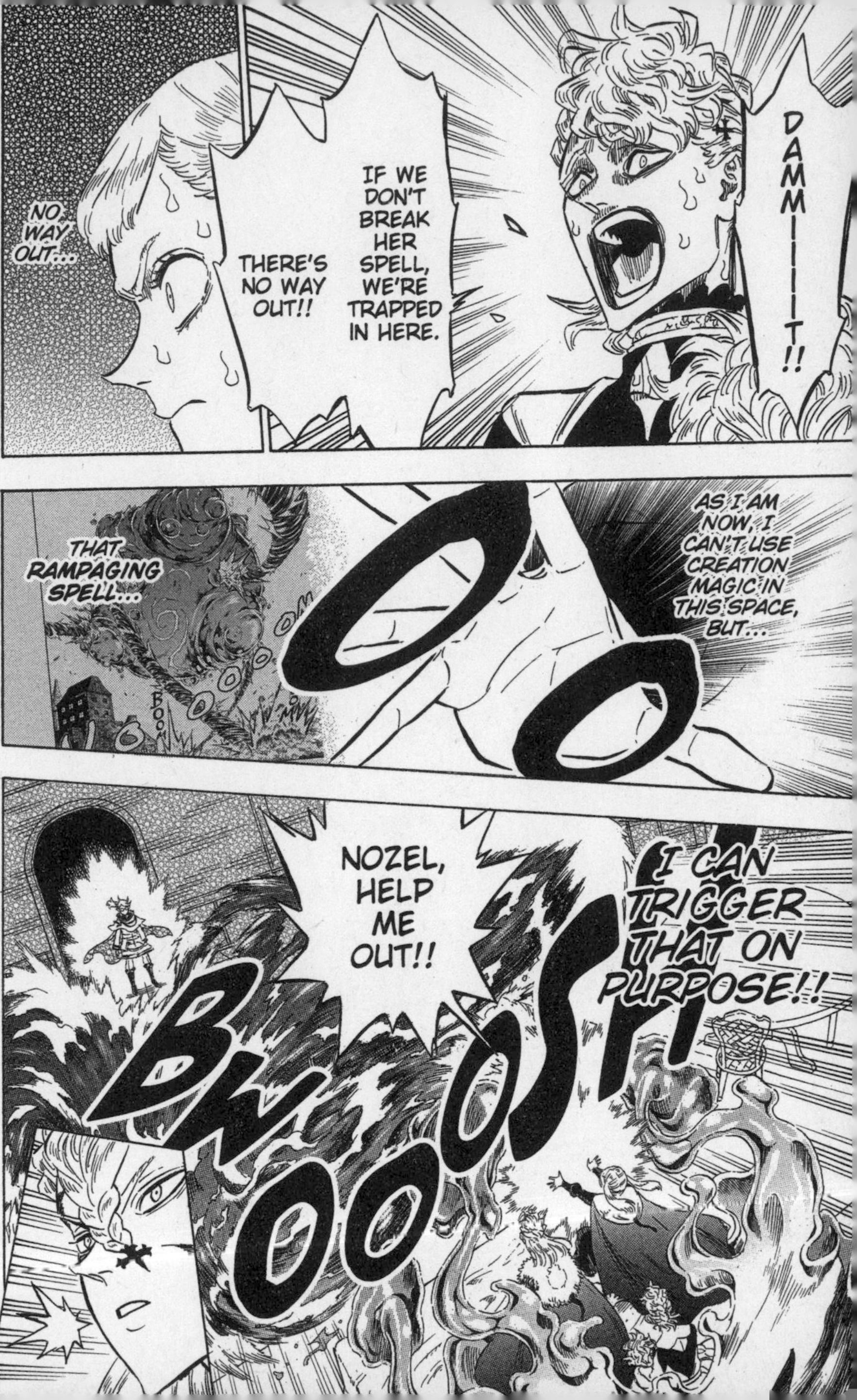
DAMMIIIIT!!
IF WE DON'T BREAK HER SPELL, WE'RE TRAPPED IN HERE.
THERE'S NO WAY OUT!!
NO WAY OUT...
AS I AM NOW, I CAN'T USE CREATION MAGIC IN THIS SPACE, BUT...
THAT RAMPAGING SPELL...
I CAN TRIGGER THAT ON PURPOSE!!
NOZEL, HELP ME OUT!!
BWOOOOSH

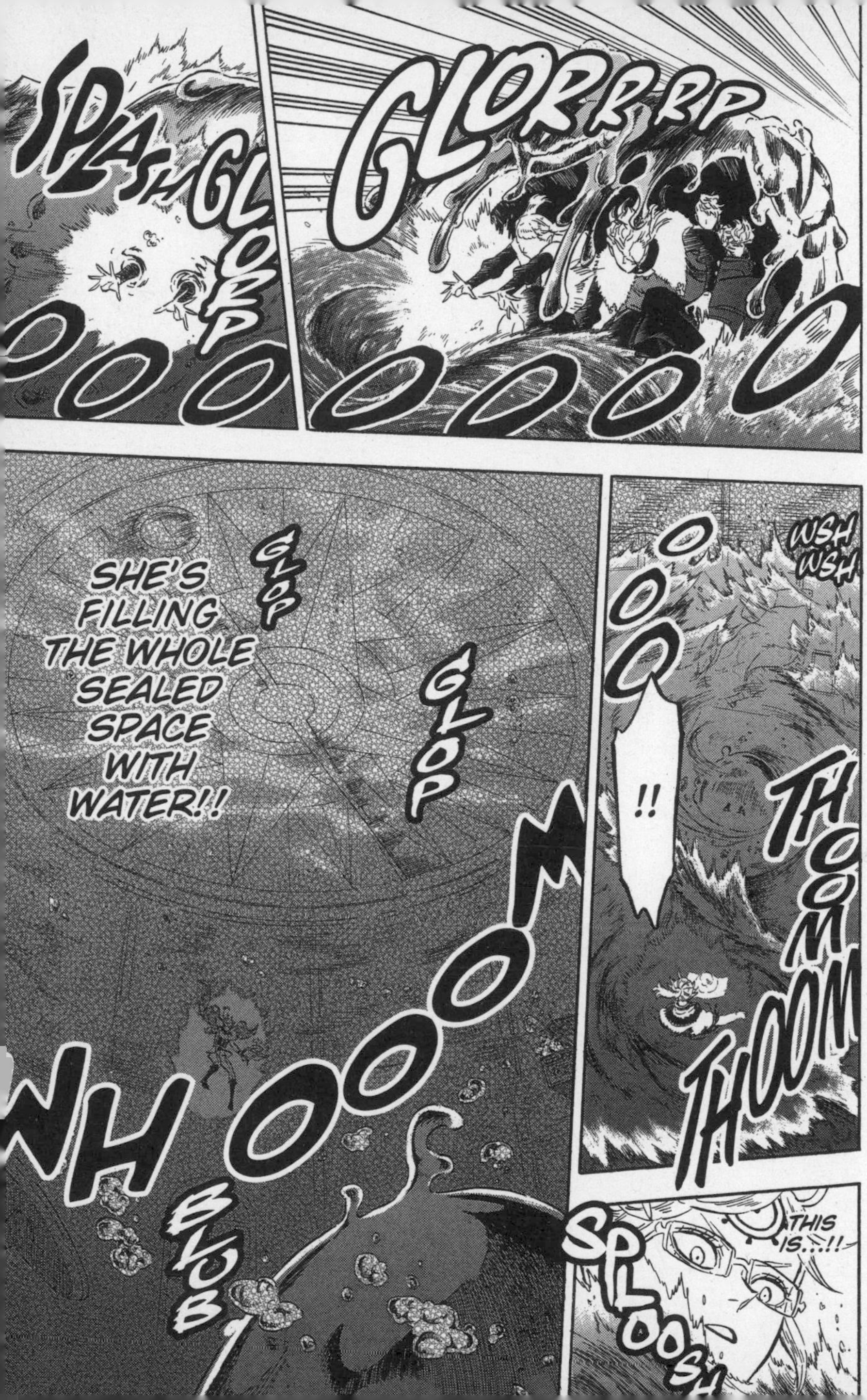
GLORRRRP
OOOOOO
SPLASH
GLOMP
OOOO
WSH WSH
OOO
!!
THOOM THOOM
SHE'S FILLING THE WHOLE SEALED SPACE WITH WATER!!
GLOP
GLOP
WHOOOOOM
BLOB
THIS IS...!!
SPLOOSH

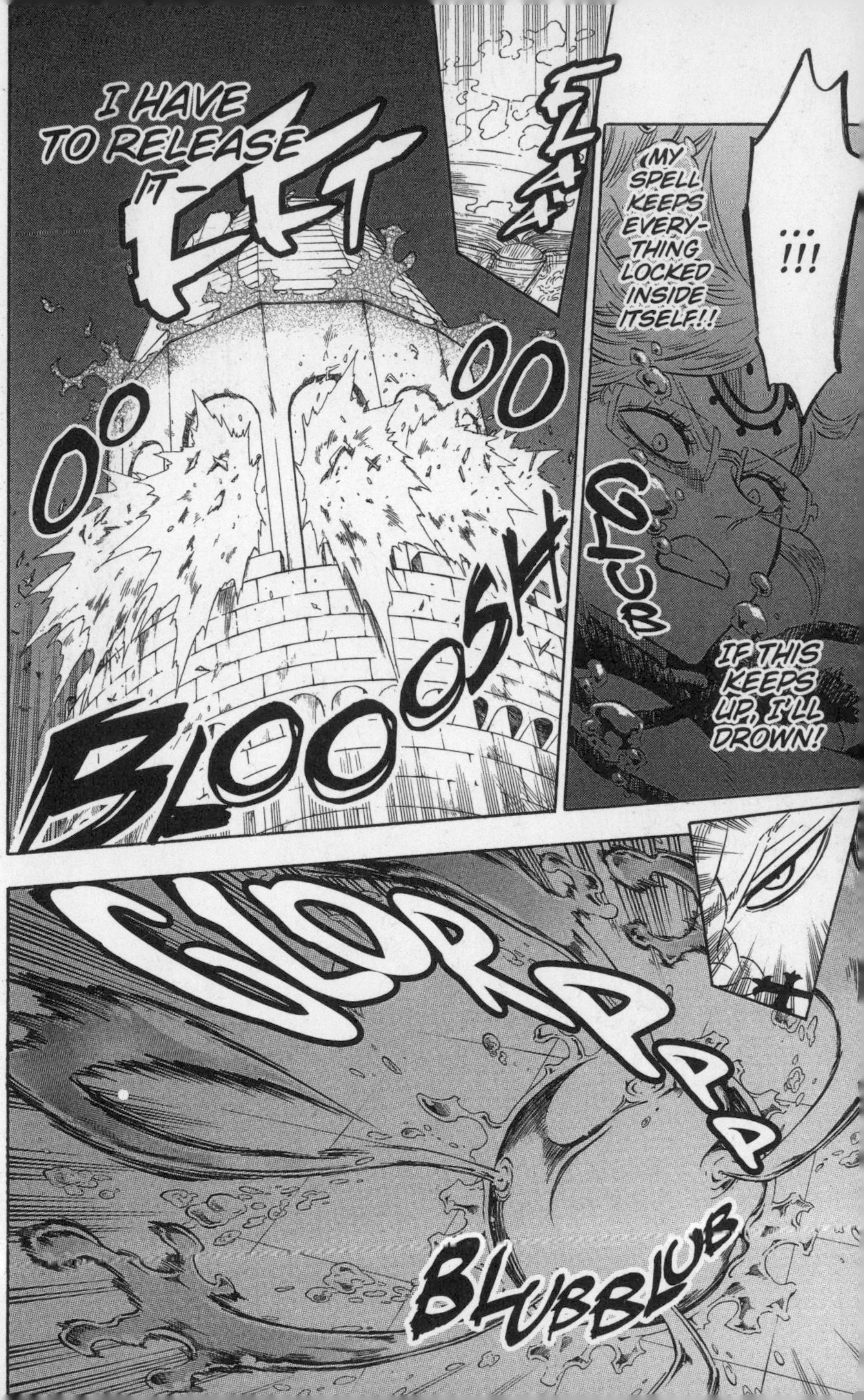
...
!!!
MY SPELL KEEPS EVERYTHING LOCKED INSIDE ITSELF!!
GLUB
IF THIS KEEPS UP, I'LL DROWN!
FLAAA
I HAVE TO RELEASE IT—
BLOOOOSH
BLUBBLUB

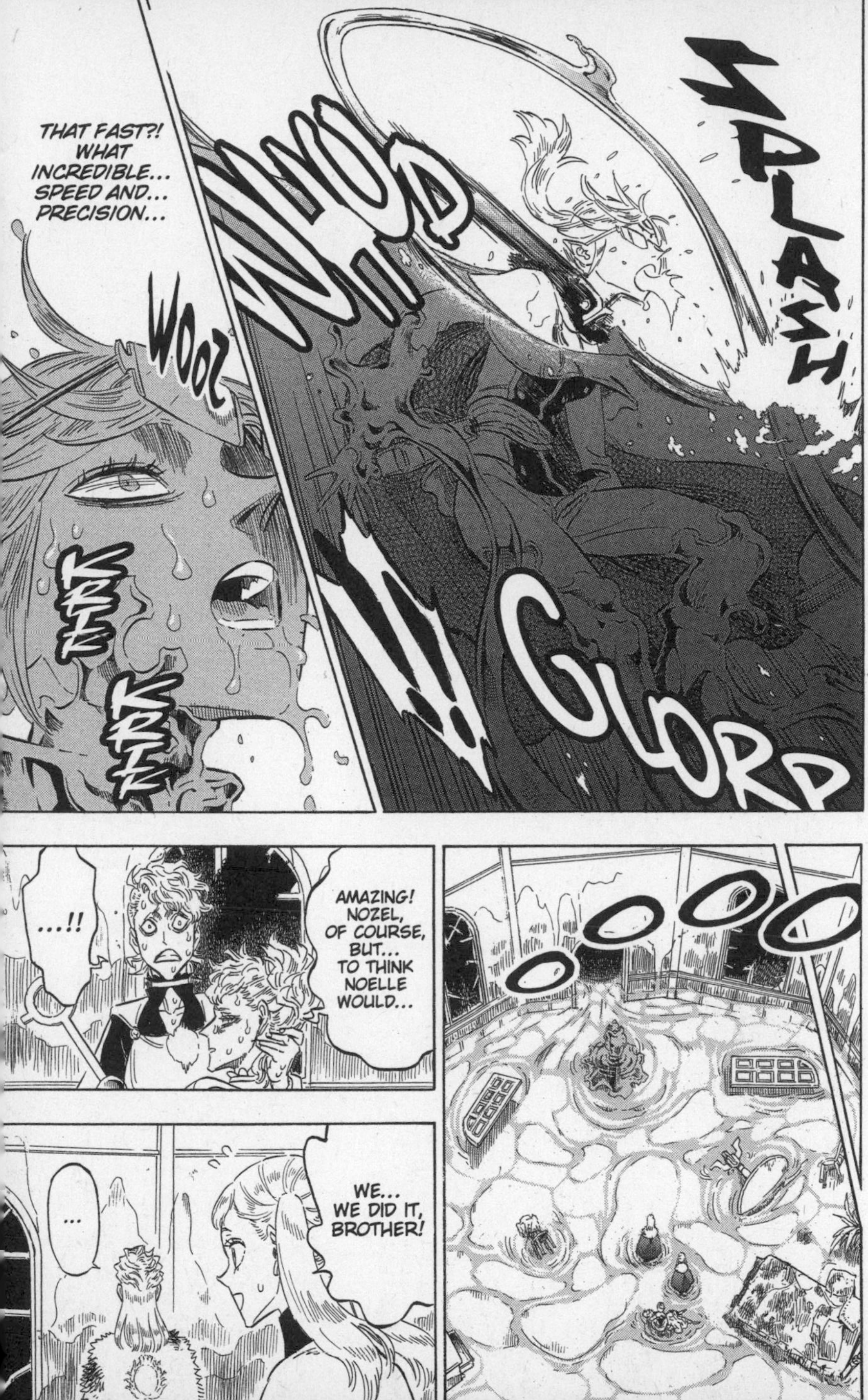
SPLASH
SWOOSH
THAT FAST?! WHAT INCREDIBLE... SPEED AND... PRECISION...
ZOOM
GLORP
KRIK
KRIK
OOOOO
AMAZING! NOZEL, OF COURSE, BUT... TO THINK NOELLE WOULD...
...!!
WE... WE DID IT, BROTHER!
...

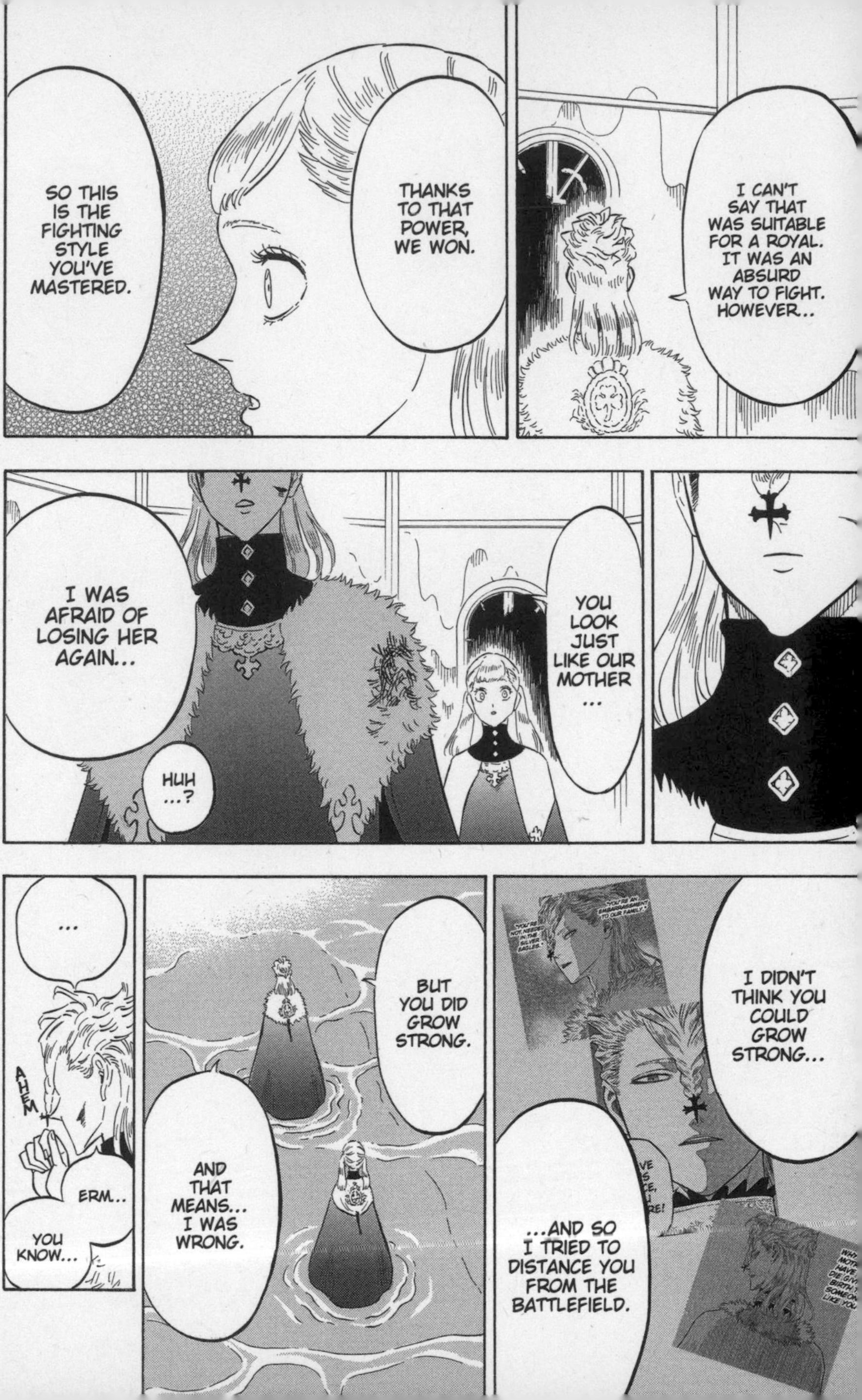
I CAN'T SAY THAT WAS SUITABLE FOR A ROYAL. IT WAS AN ABSURD WAY TO FIGHT. HOWEVER...
THANKS TO THAT POWER, WE WON.
SO THIS IS THE FIGHTING STYLE YOU'VE MASTERED.
YOU LOOK JUST LIKE OUR MOTHER...
I WAS AFRAID OF LOSING HER AGAIN...
HUH...?
I DIDN'T THINK YOU COULD GROW STRONG...
"YOU'RE AN EMBARRASSMENT TO OUR FAMILY."
"YOU'RE NOT NEEDED IN THE SILVER EAGLES."
...AND SO I TRIED TO DISTANCE YOU FROM THE BATTLEFIELD.
BUT YOU DID GROW STRONG.
AND THAT MEANS... I WAS WRONG.
...
AHEM
ERM...
YOU KNOW...

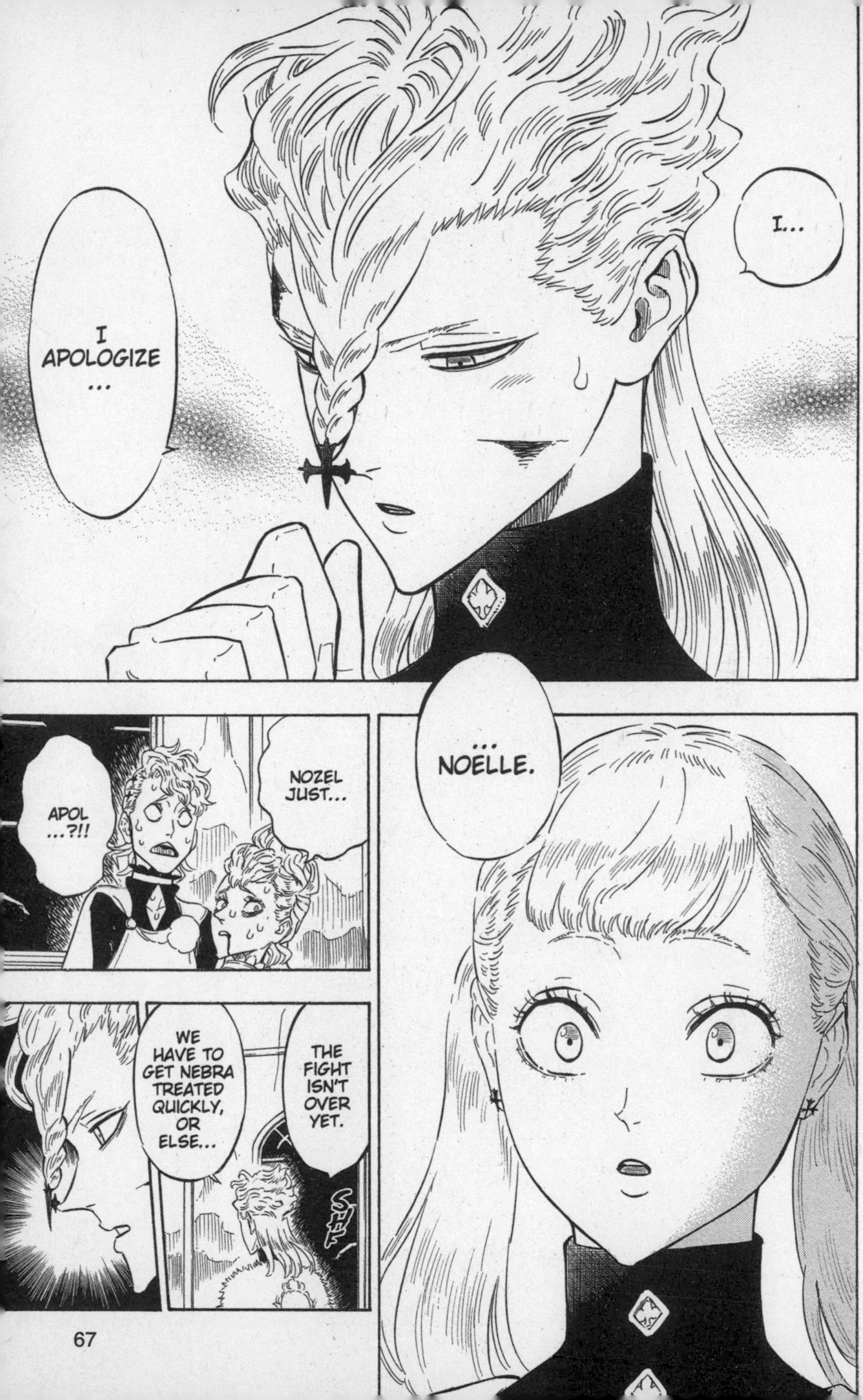
I...
I APOLOGIZE ...
... NOELLE.
NOZEL JUST...
APOL ...?!!
THE FIGHT ISN'T OVER YET.
WE HAVE TO GET NEBRA TREATED QUICKLY, OR ELSE...

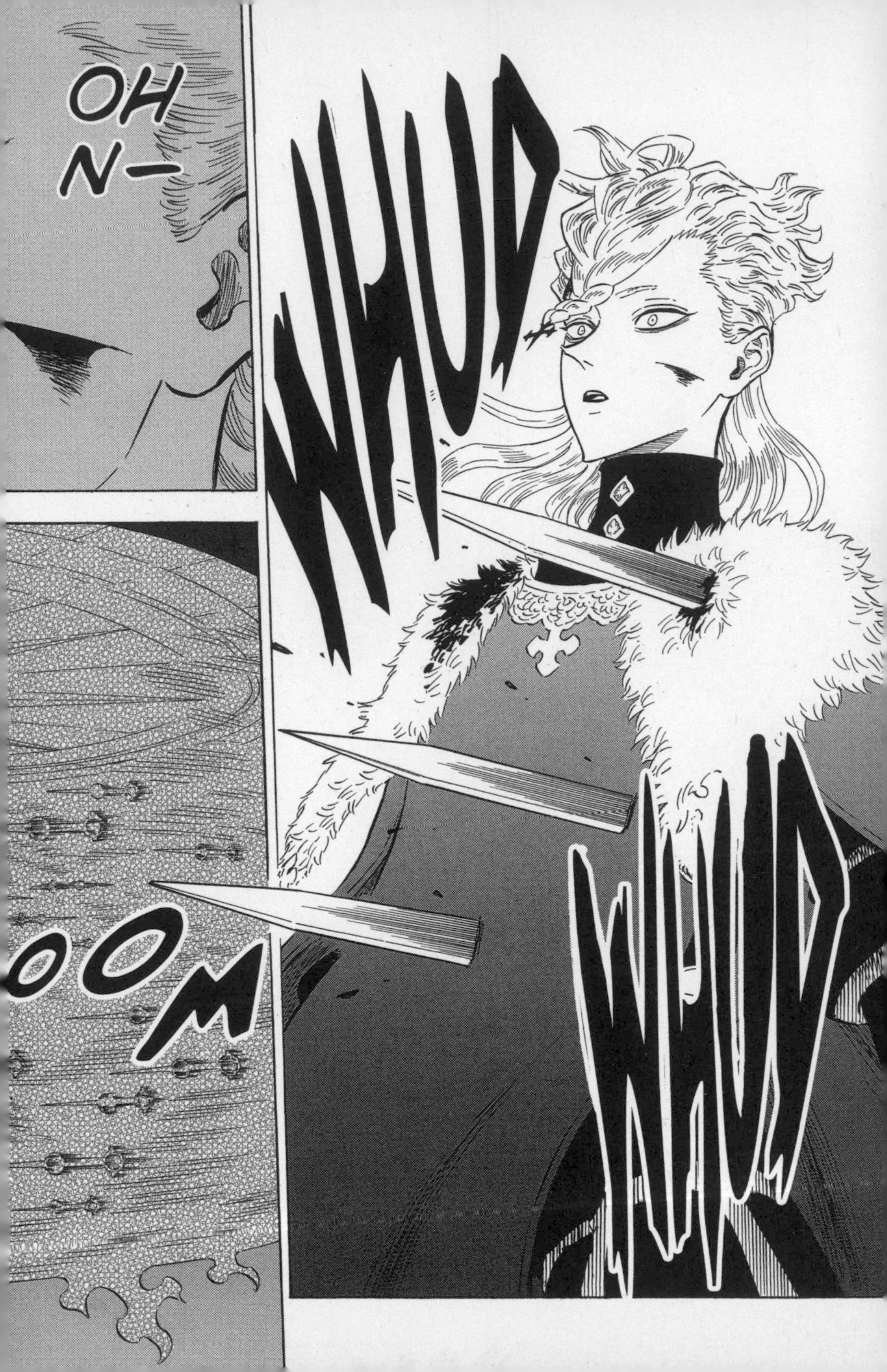
OH N—
WHUD
WHUD

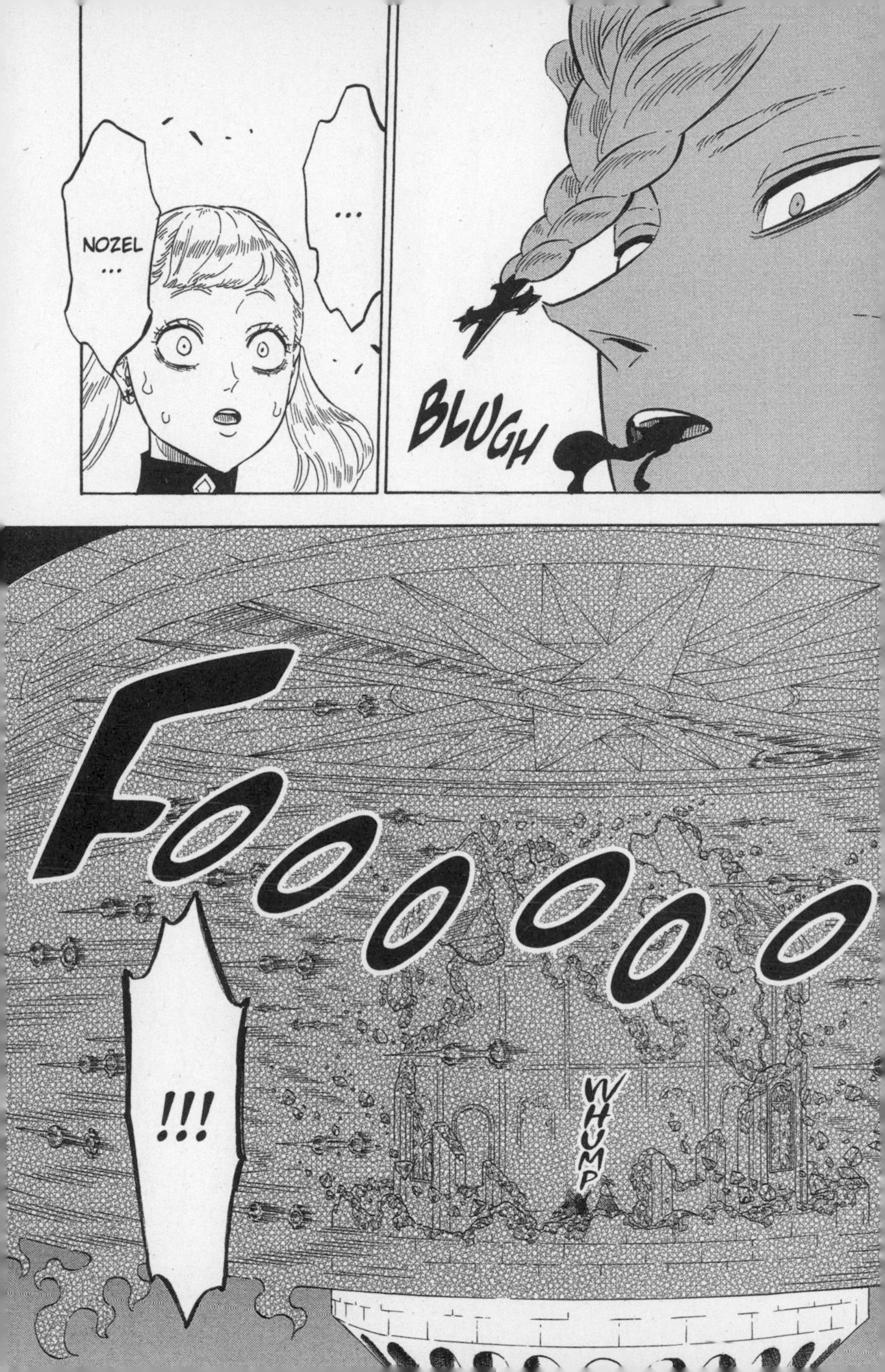
BLUGH
...
NOZEL ...
FOOOOOO
!!!
WHUMP

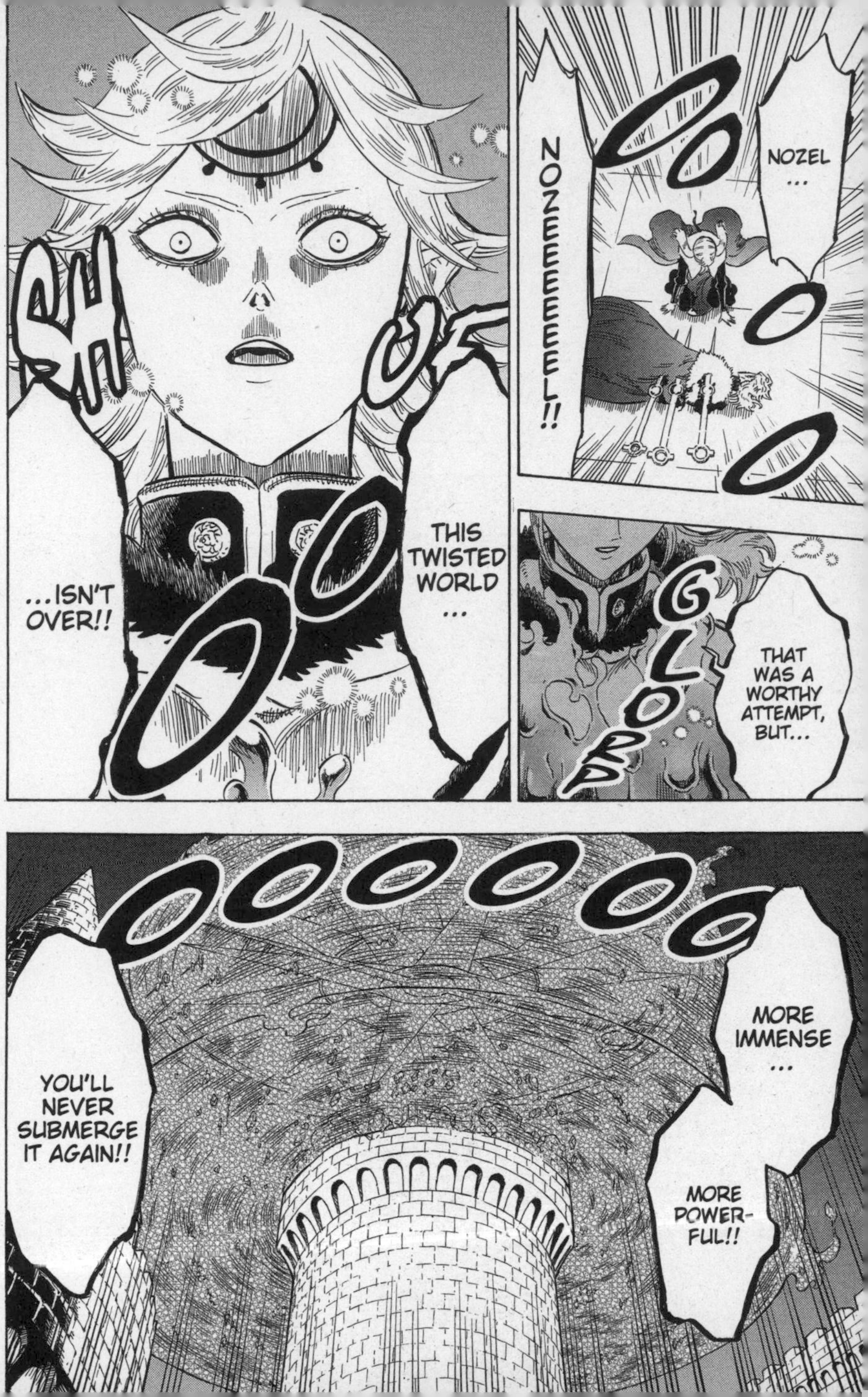
NOZEL ...
NOZEEEEEEEL!!
THAT WAS A WORTHY ATTEMPT, BUT...
THIS TWISTED WORLD ...
...ISN'T OVER!!
MORE IMMENSE ...
MORE POWER-FUL!!
YOU'LL NEVER SUBMERGE IT AGAIN!!

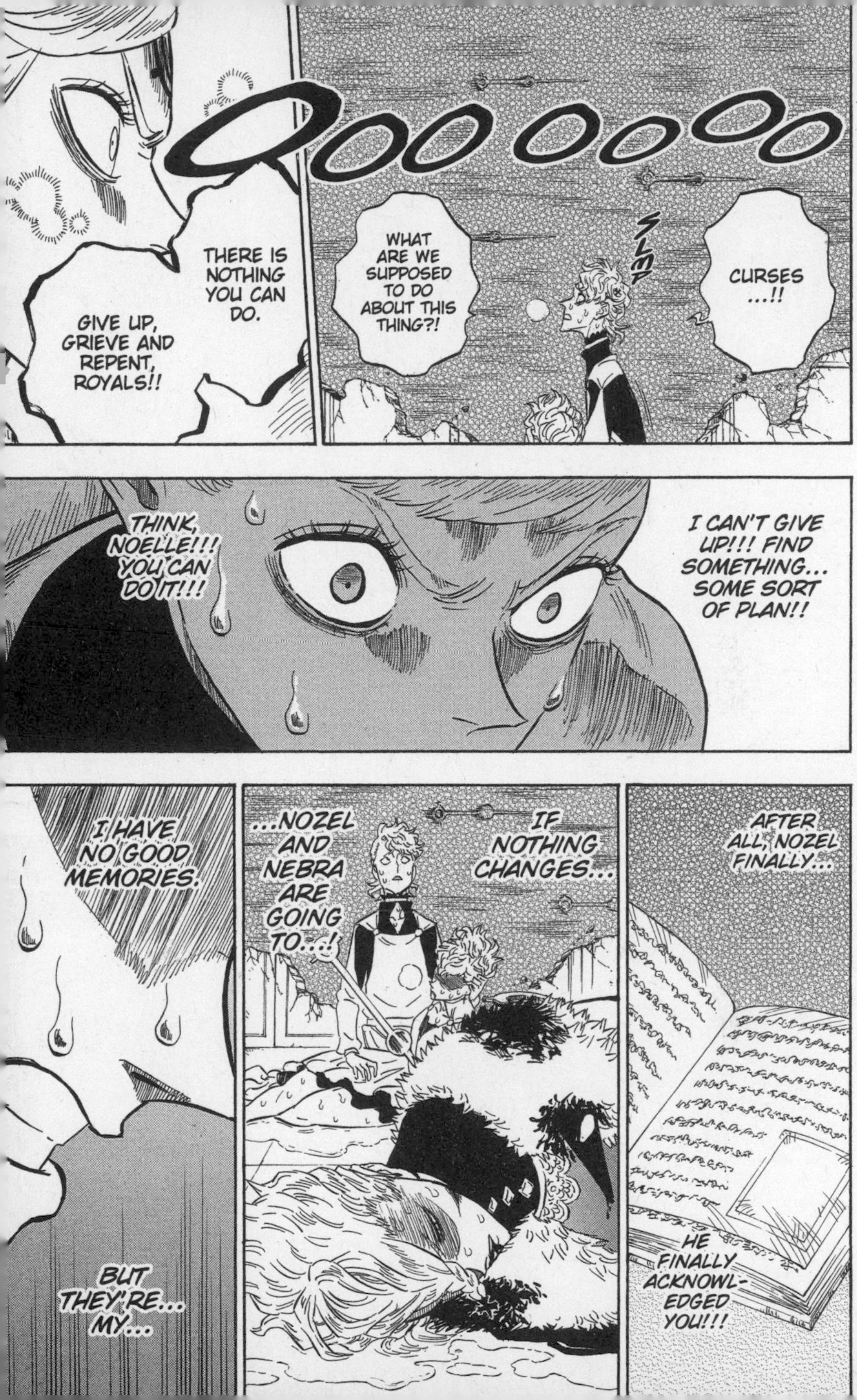
QOOOOOOO
CURSES ...!!
SLMA
WHAT ARE WE SUPPOSED TO DO ABOUT THIS THING?!
THERE IS NOTHING YOU CAN DO.
GIVE UP, GRIEVE AND REPENT, ROYALS!!
I CAN'T GIVE UP!!! FIND SOMETHING... SOME SORT OF PLAN!!
THINK, NOELLE!!! YOU CAN DO IT!!!
AFTER ALL, NOZEL FINALLY...
HE FINALLY ACKNOWL-EDGED YOU!!!
IF NOTHING CHANGES...
...NOZEL AND NEBRA ARE GOING TO...!
I HAVE NO GOOD MEMORIES.
BUT THEY'RE... MY...

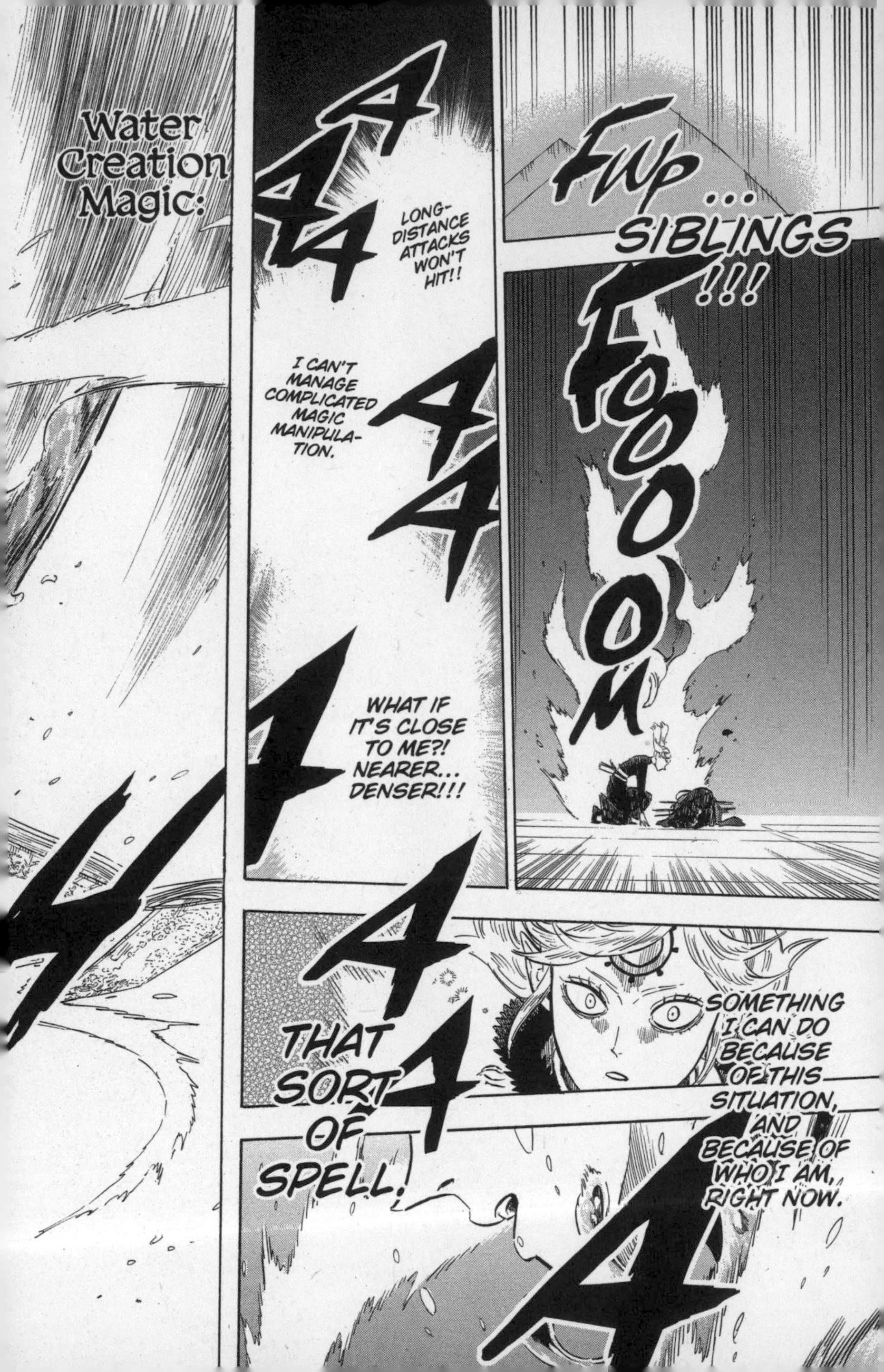
FWP... SIBLINGS!!!
FOOOOOM
LONG-DISTANCE ATTACKS WON'T HIT!!
I CAN'T MANAGE COMPLICATED MAGIC MANIPULA-TION.
WHAT IF IT'S CLOSE TO ME?! NEARER... DENSER!!!
SOMETHING I CAN DO BECAUSE OF THIS SITUATION, AND BECAUSE OF WHO I AM, RIGHT NOW.
THAT SORT OF SPELL.
Water Creation Magic:

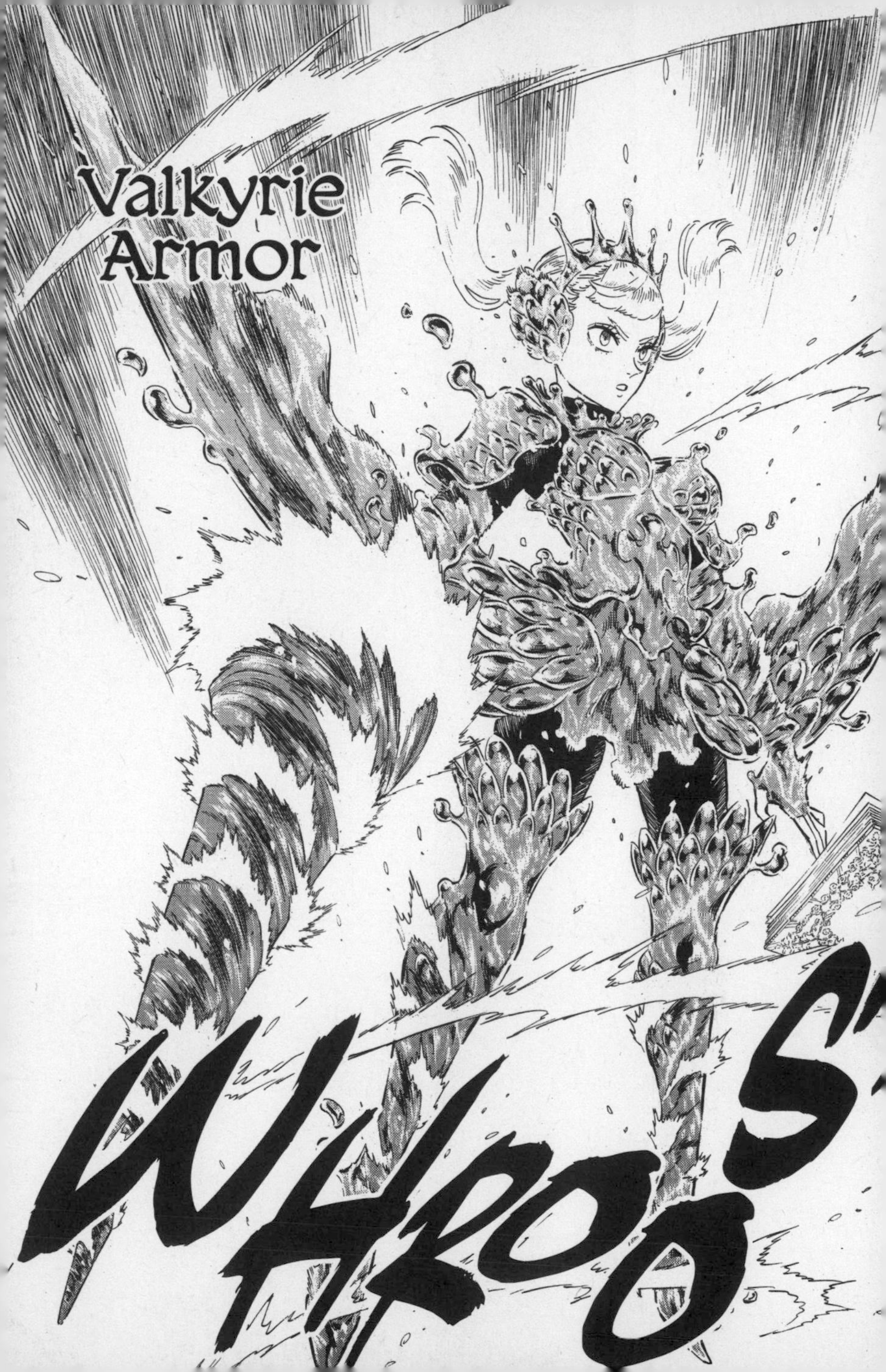
Valkyrie
Armor

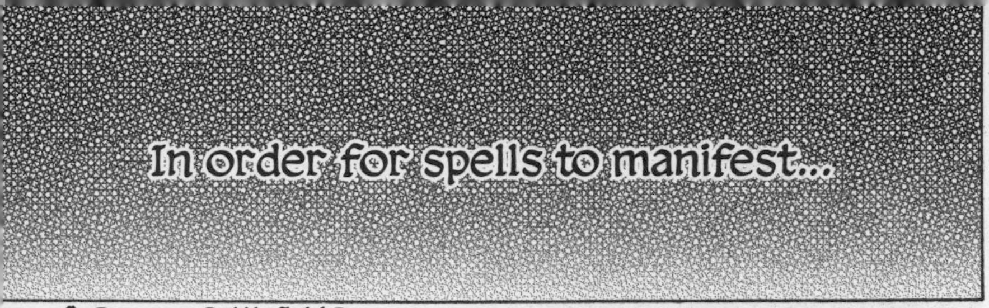
In order for spells to manifest...

Page 177: Battlefield Dancer

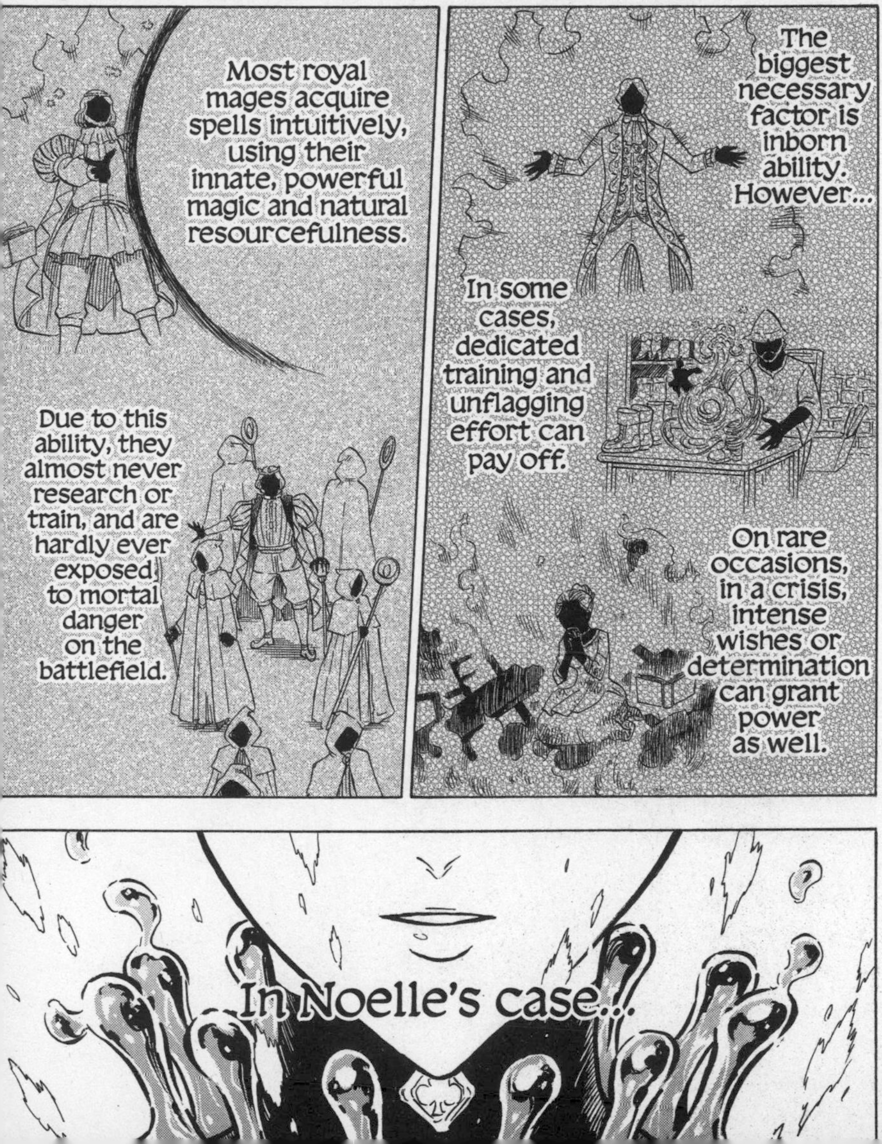
The biggest necessary factor is inborn ability. However...
In some cases, dedicated training and unflagging effort can pay off.
On rare occasions, in a crisis, intense wishes or determination can grant power as well.
Most royal mages acquire spells intuitively, using their innate, powerful magic and natural resourcefulness.
Due to this ability, they almost never research or train, and are hardly ever exposed to mortal danger on the battlefield.
In Noelle's case...

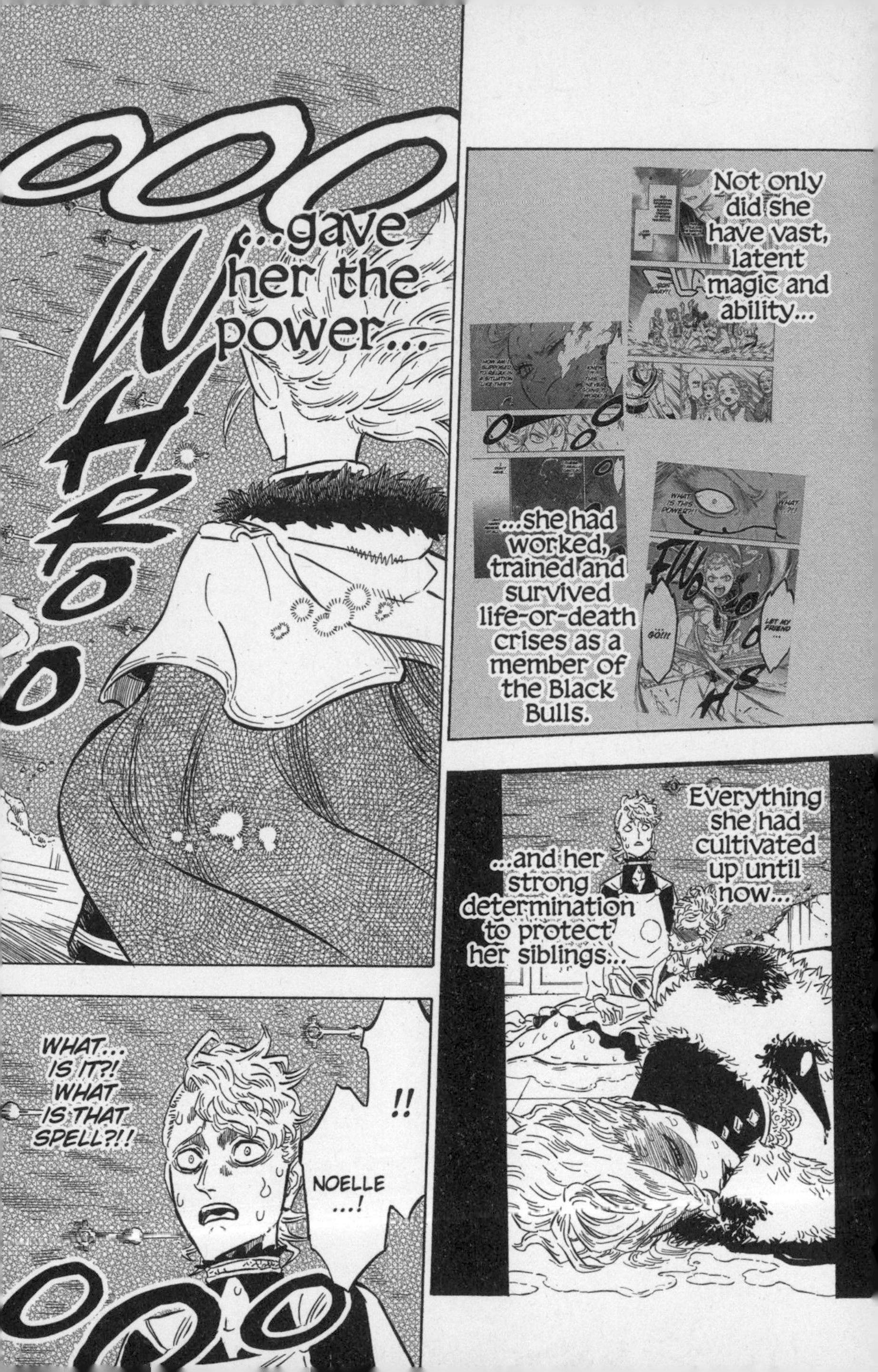
Not only did she have vast, latent magic and ability...
...she had worked, trained and survived life-or-death crises as a member of the Black Bulls.
WHROOOOO
...gave her the power...
Everything she had cultivated up until now...
...and her strong determination to protect her siblings...
!!
NOELLE ...!
WHAT... IS IT?! WHAT IS THAT SPELL?!!
OOOO

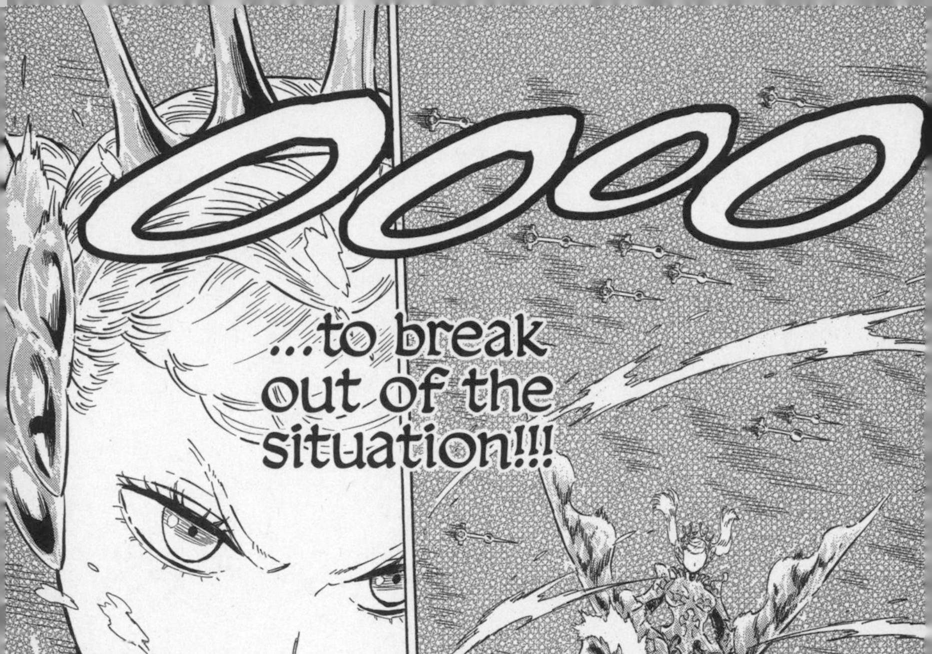
...to break out of the situation!!!

Page 177: Battlefield Dancer

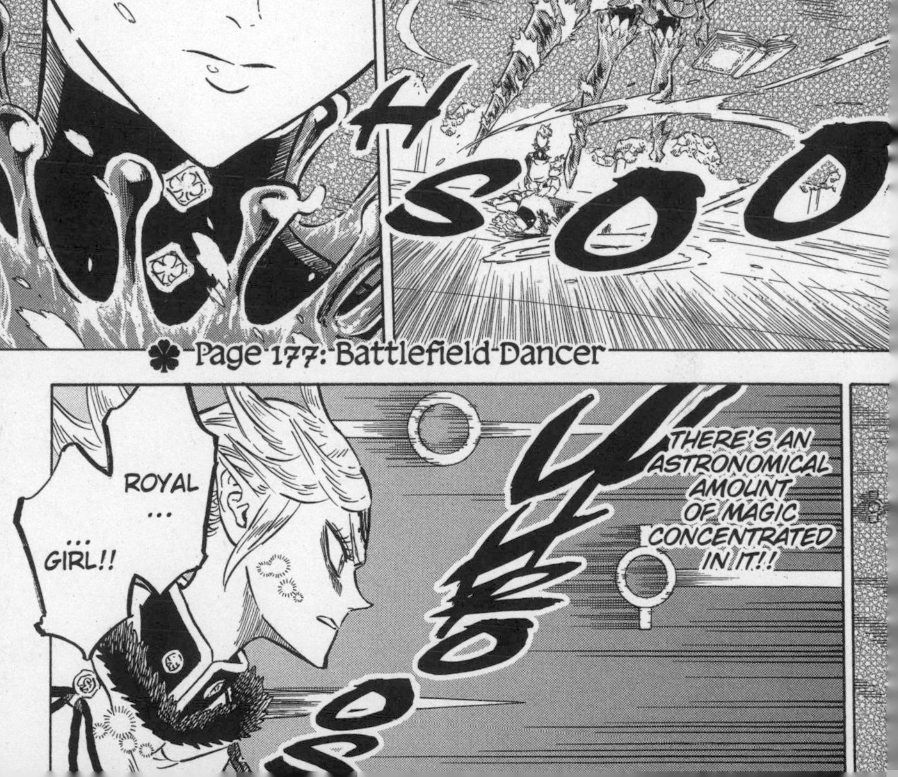
THERE'S AN ASTRONOMICAL AMOUNT OF MAGIC CONCENTRATED IN IT!!
ROYAL ... ... GIRL!!

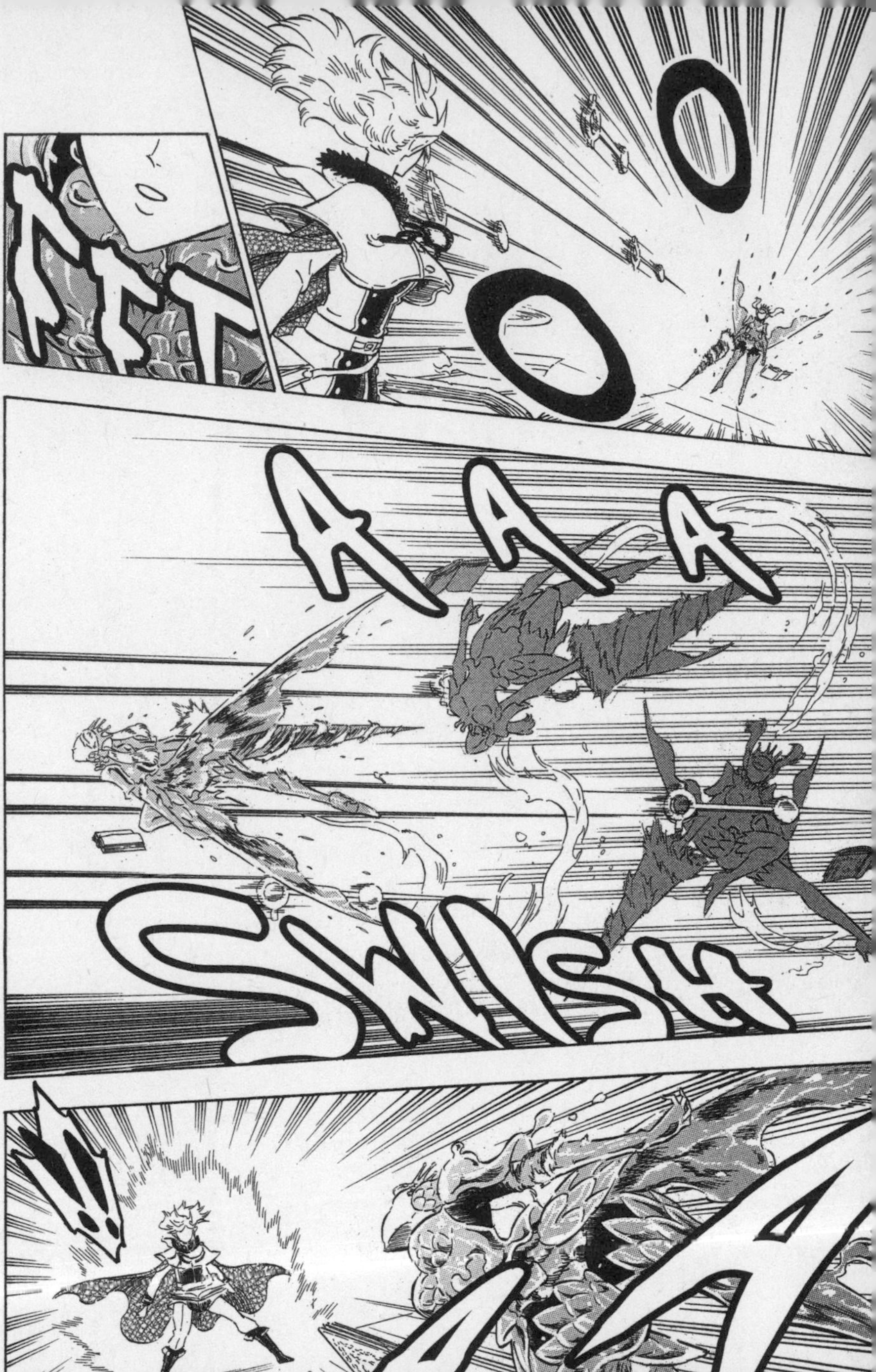
OO
AAA
SWISH
AA
!!

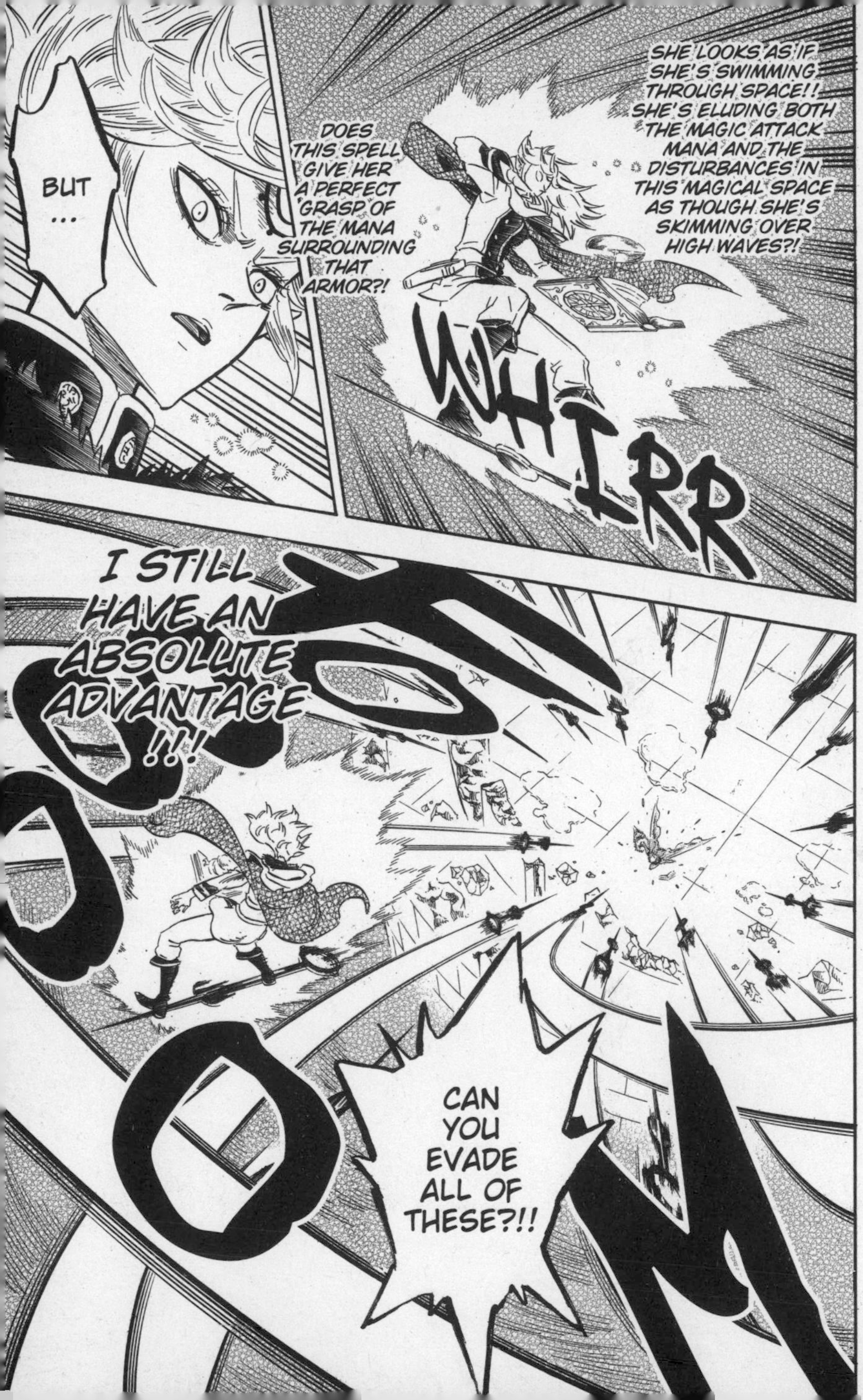
SHE LOOKS AS IF SHE'S SWIMMING THROUGH SPACE!! SHE'S ELUDING BOTH THE MAGIC ATTACK MANA AND THE DISTURBANCES IN THIS MAGICAL SPACE AS THOUGH SHE'S SKIMMING OVER HIGH WAVES?!
DOES THIS SPELL GIVE HER A PERFECT GRASP OF THE MANA SURROUNDING THAT ARMOR?!
WHIRR
BUT ...
I STILL HAVE AN ABSOLUTE ADVANTAGE!!!
CAN YOU EVADE ALL OF THESE?!!

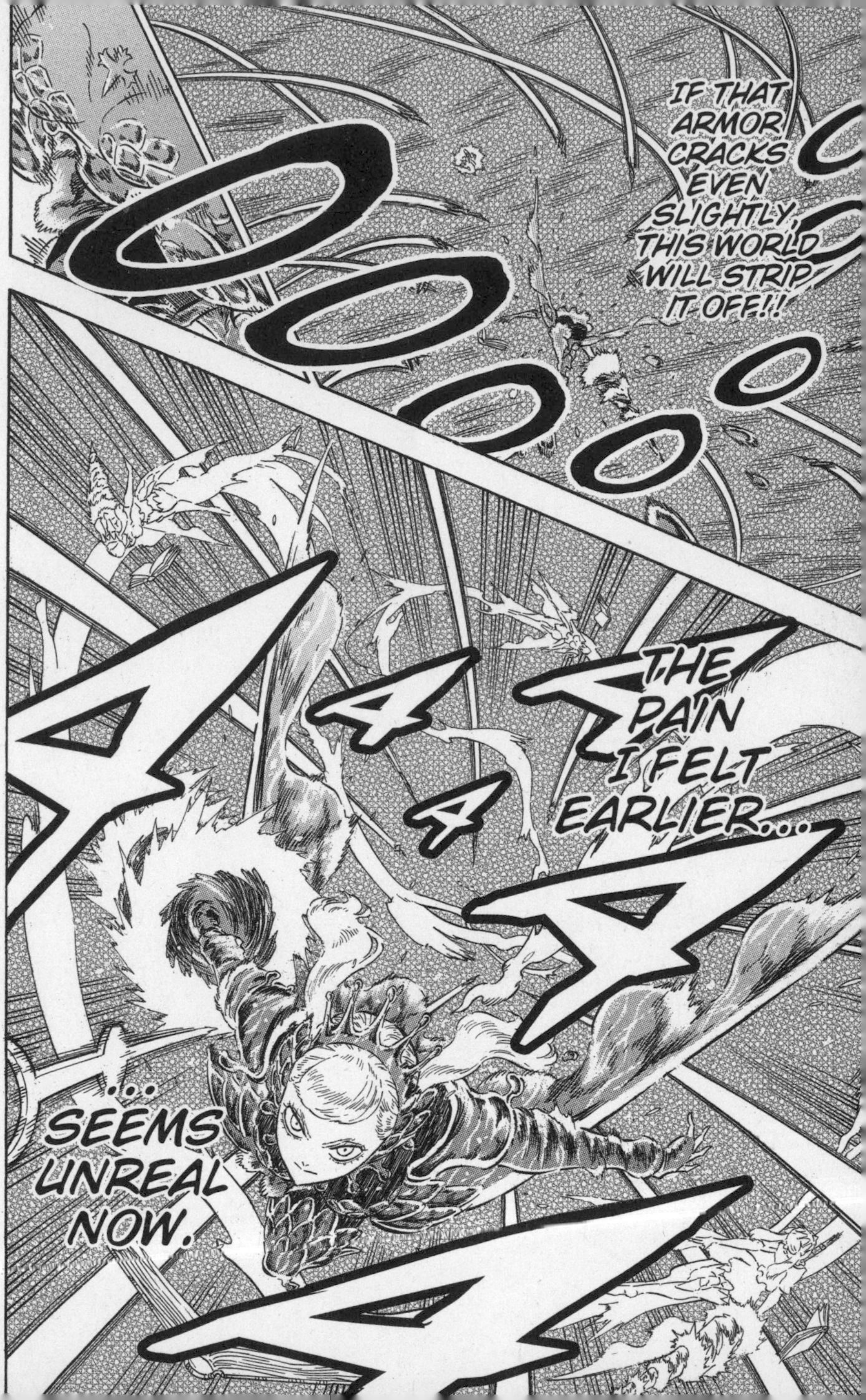
IF THAT ARMOR CRACKS EVEN SLIGHTLY, THIS WORLD WILL STRIP IT OFF!!
THE PAIN I FELT EARLIER...
...SEEMS UNREAL NOW.

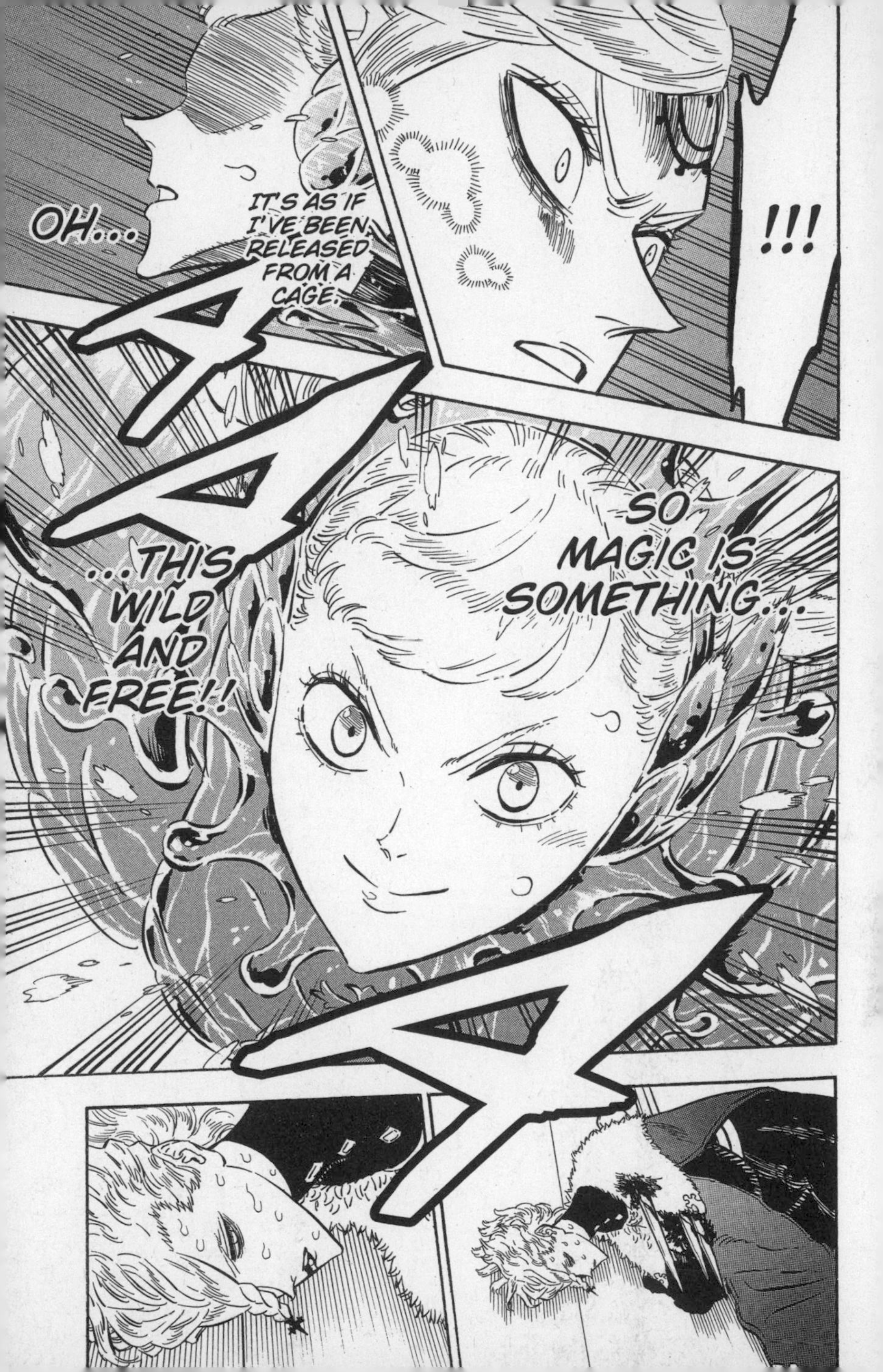
!!!
IT'S AS IF I'VE BEEN RELEASED FROM A CAGE.
OH...
SO MAGIC IS SOMETHING...
...THIS WILD AND FREE!!

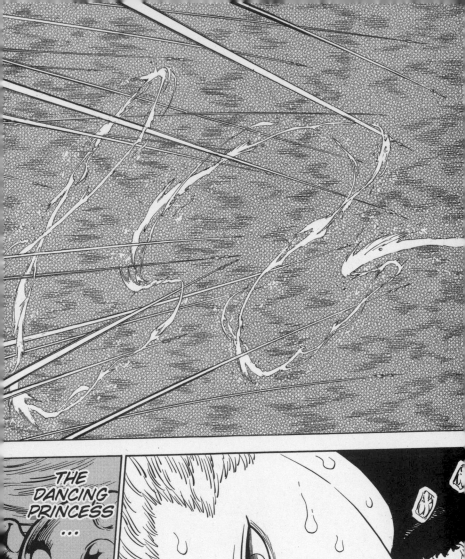

THE
DANCING
PRINCESS
...

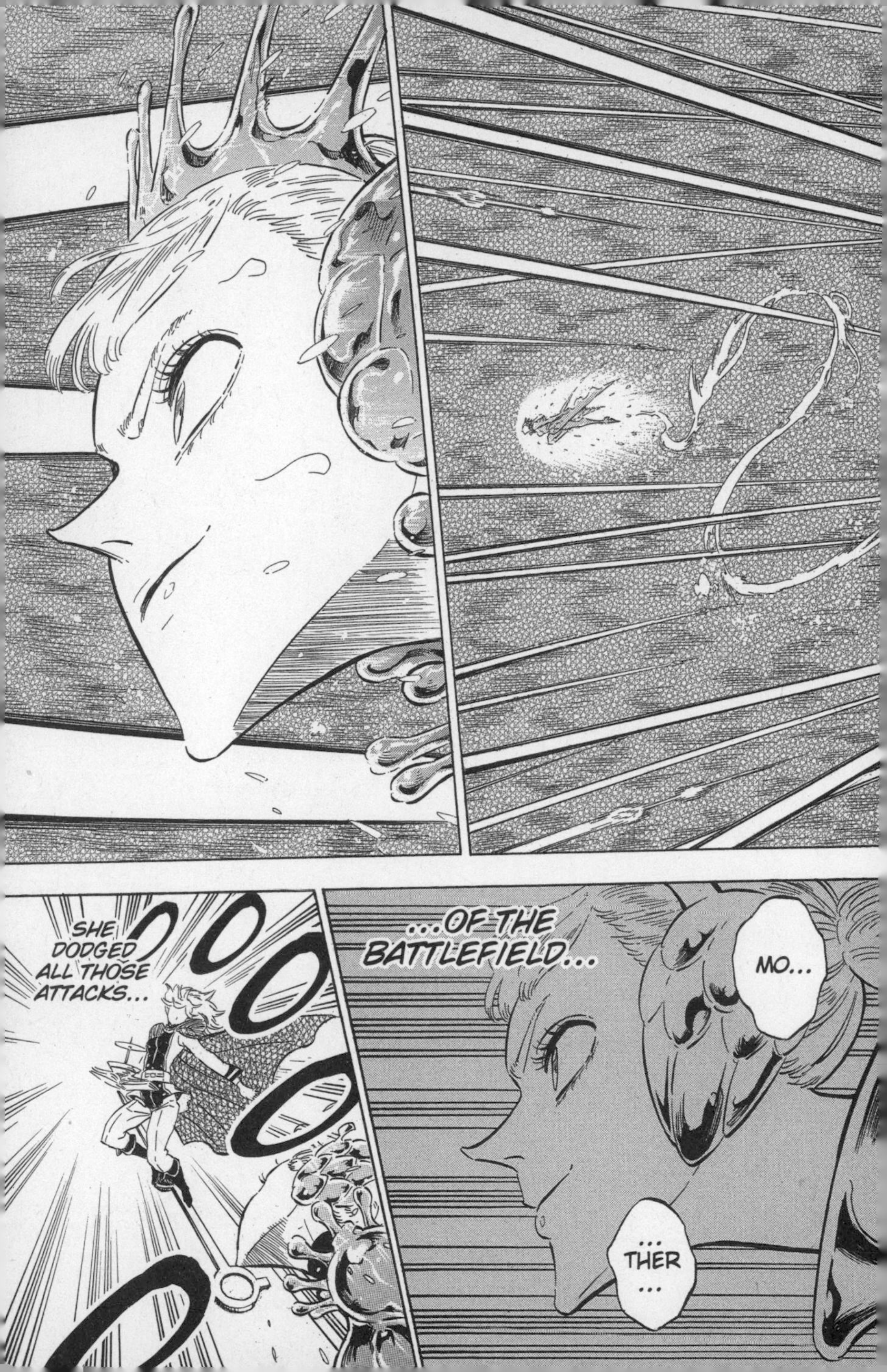
MO...
...OF THE BATTLEFIELD...
...THER...
SHE DODGED ALL THOSE ATTACKS...

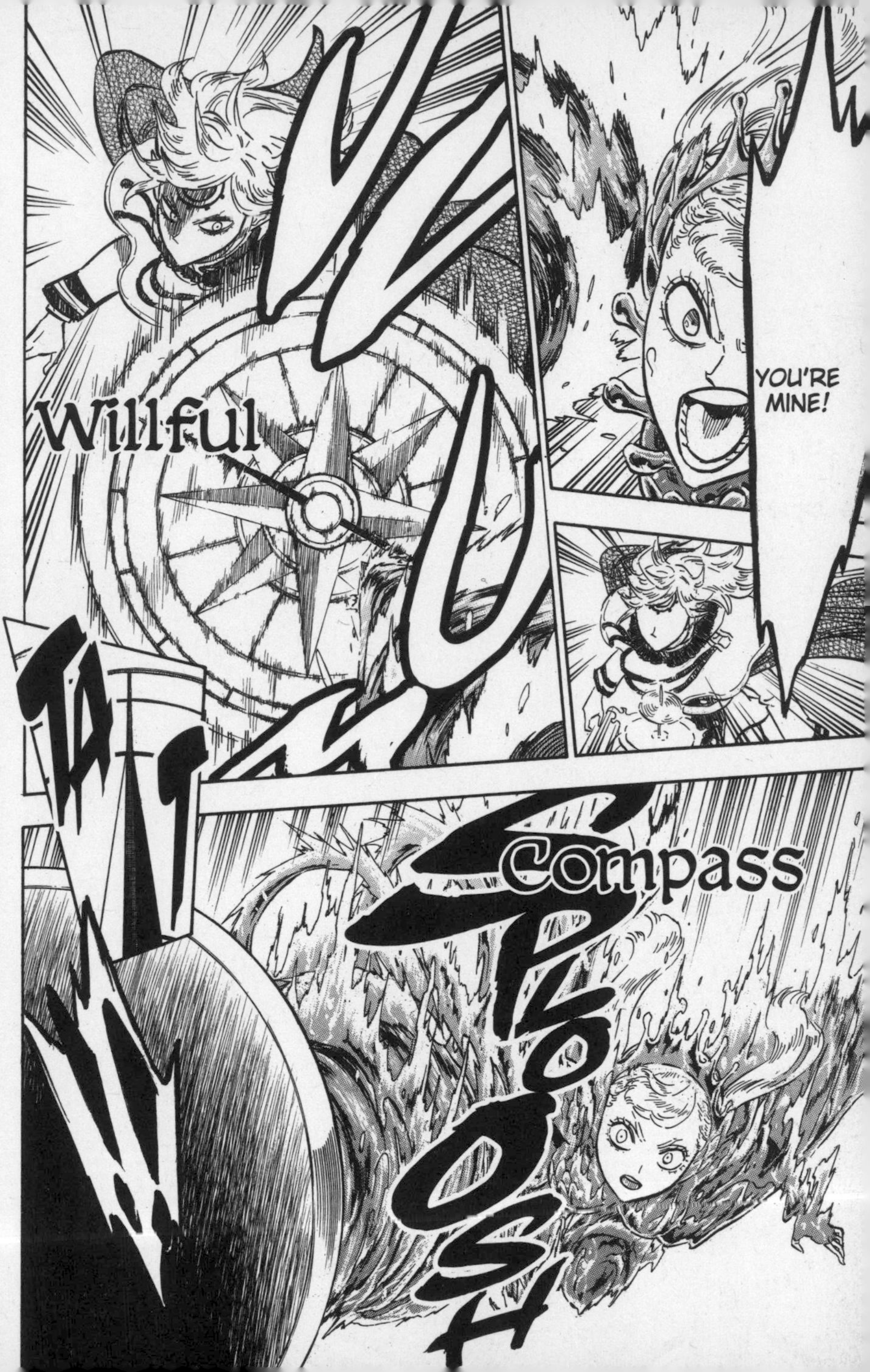
YOU'RE MINE!
Willful
Compass

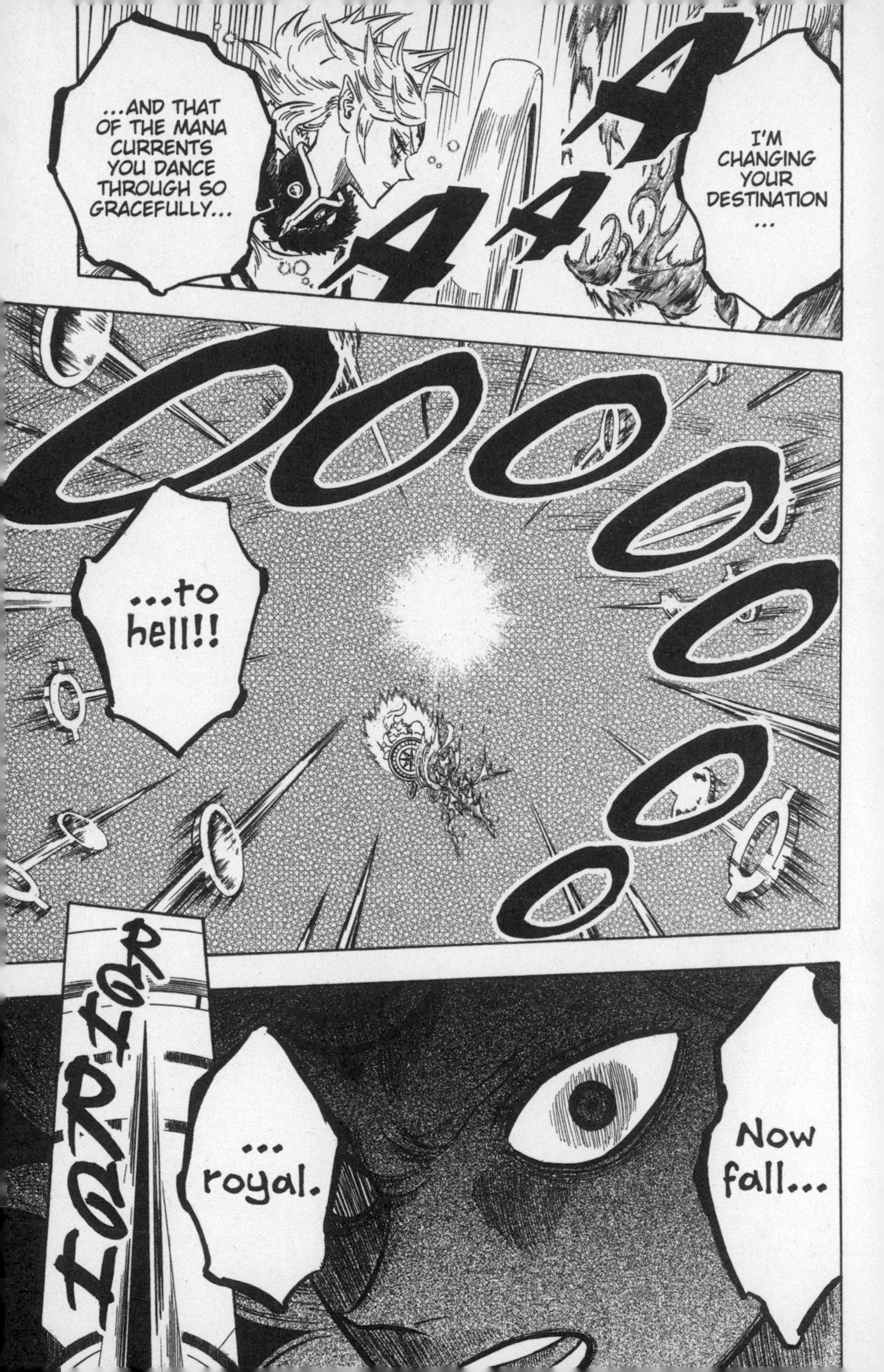
I'M CHANGING YOUR DESTINATION...
...AND THAT OF THE MANA CURRENTS YOU DANCE THROUGH SO GRACEFULLY...
AAA
...to hell!!
Now fall...
...royal.

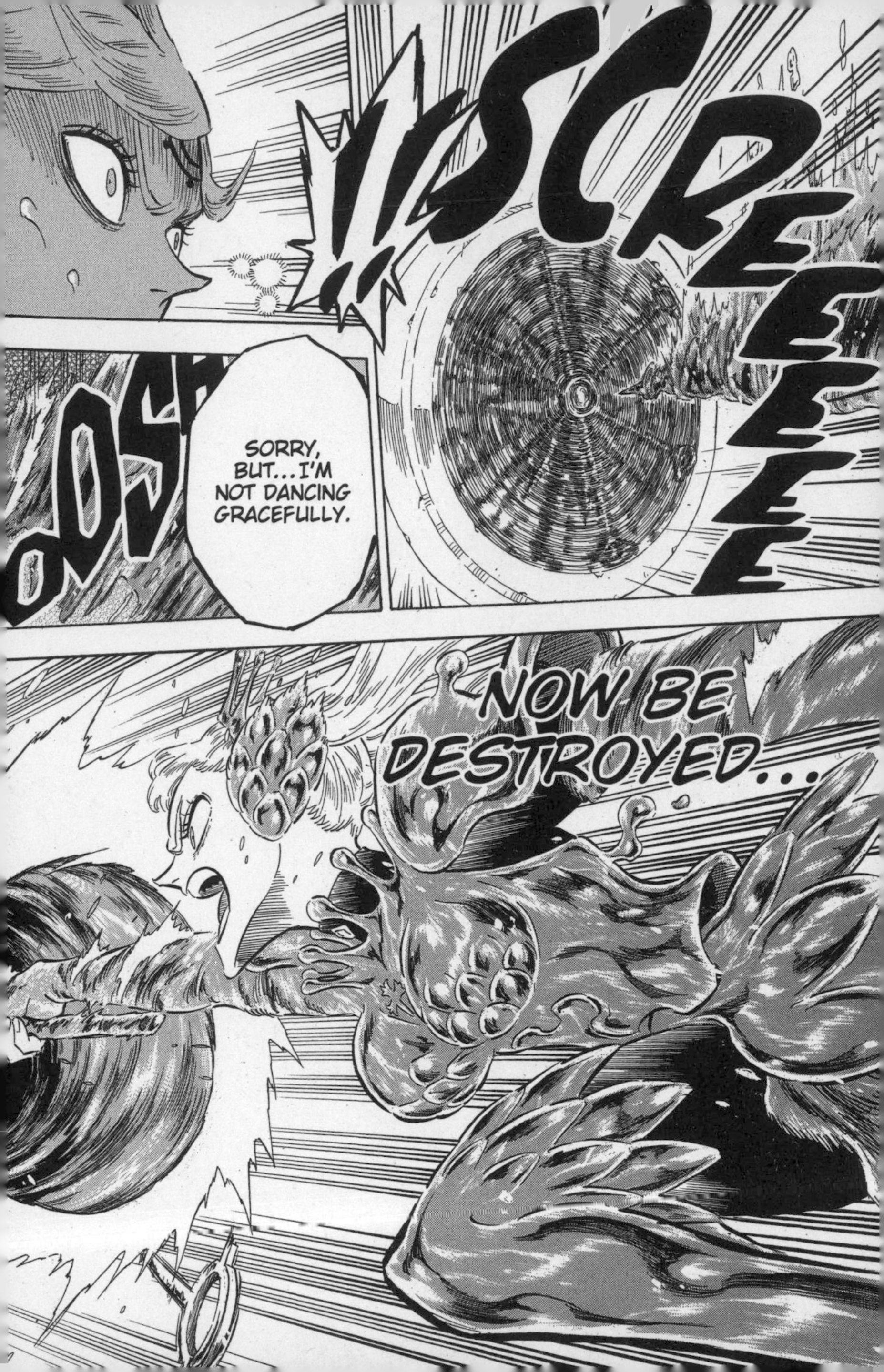

!!SCREEEEE
SORRY, BUT...I'M NOT DANCING GRACEFULLY.
NOW BE DESTROYED...

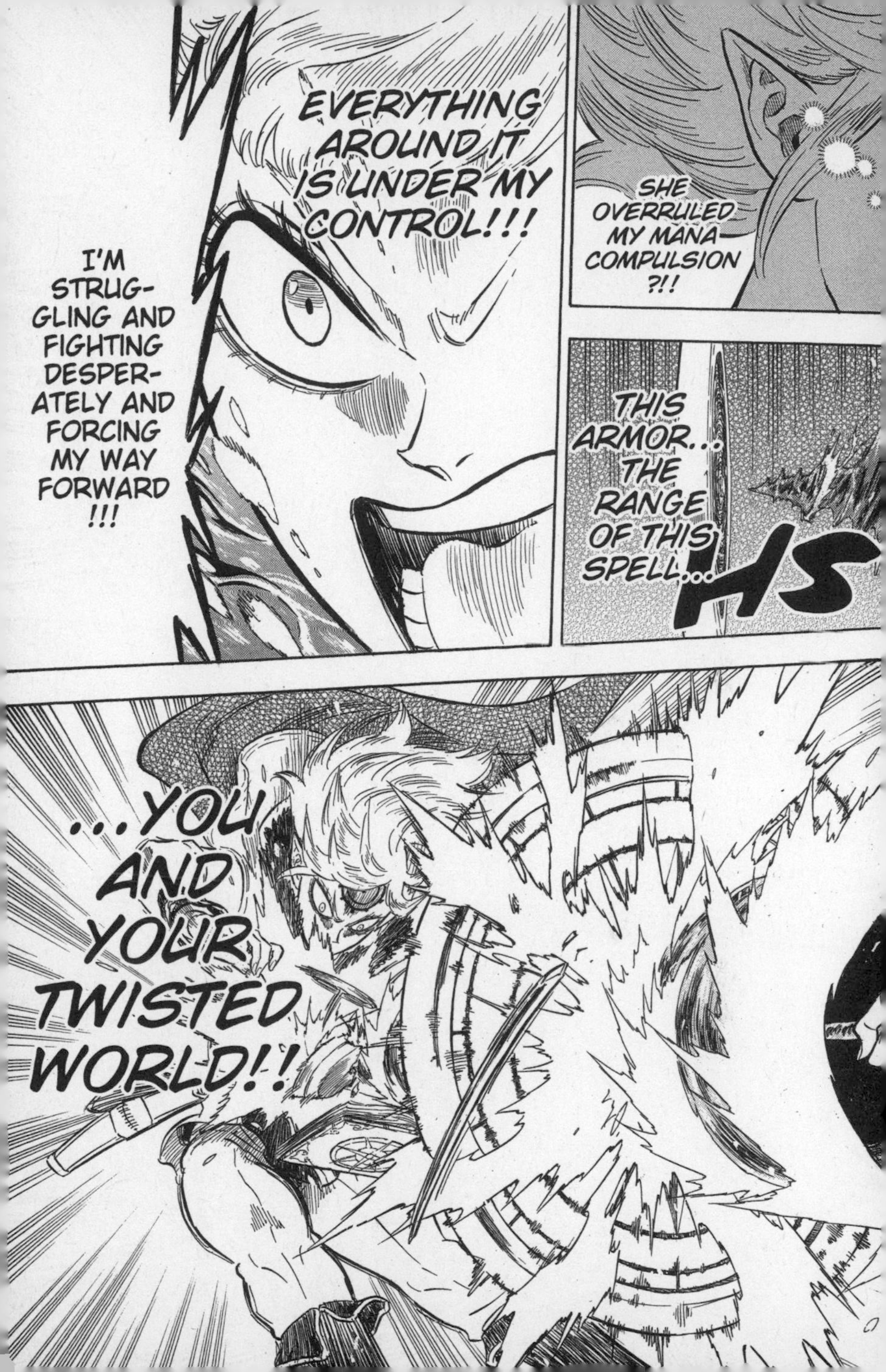
SHE OVERRULED MY MANA COMPULSION ?!!
THIS ARMOR... THE RANGE OF THIS SPELL...
HS
EVERYTHING AROUND IT IS UNDER MY CONTROL!!!
I'M STRUG-GLING AND FIGHTING DESPER-ATELY AND FORCING MY WAY FORWARD !!!
...YOU AND YOUR TWISTED WORLD!!

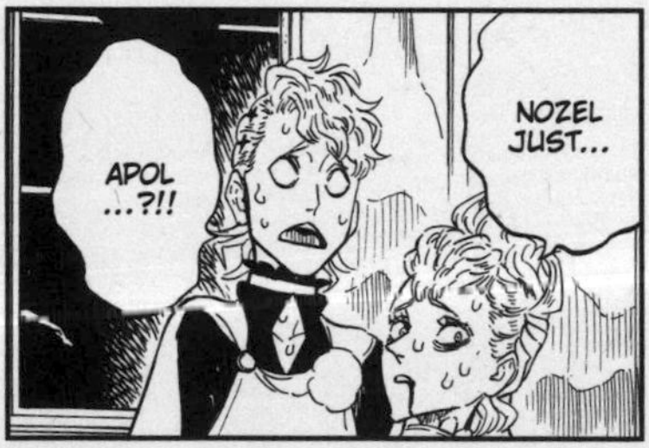
NOZEL JUST...
APOL ...?!!

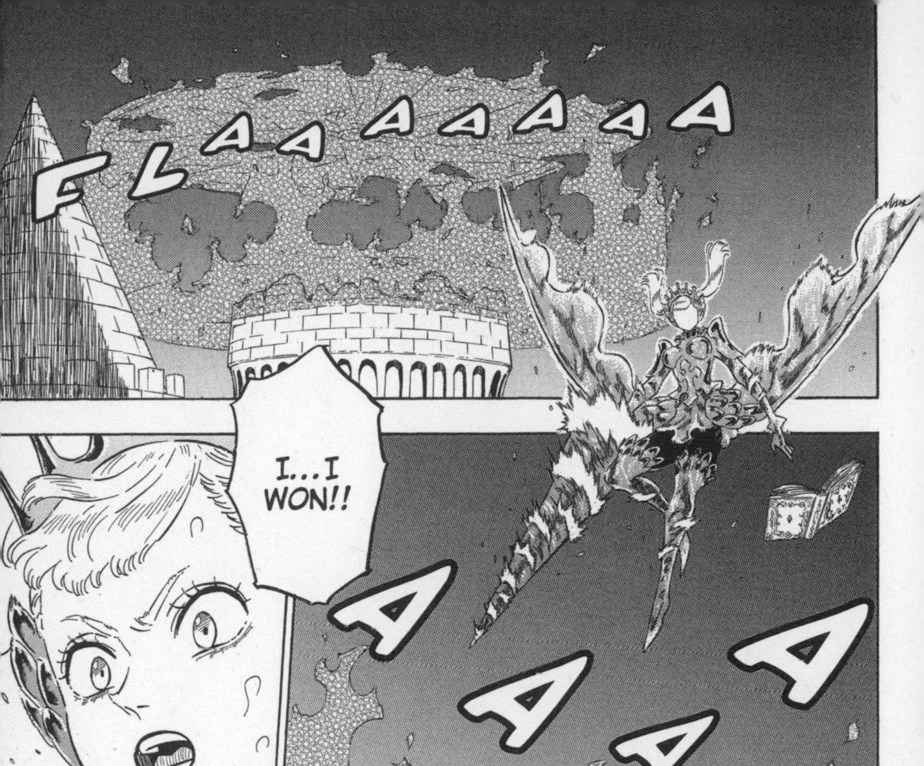
FLAAAAAAAA
AAAAA
I...I WON!!

Page 178: Human Magic

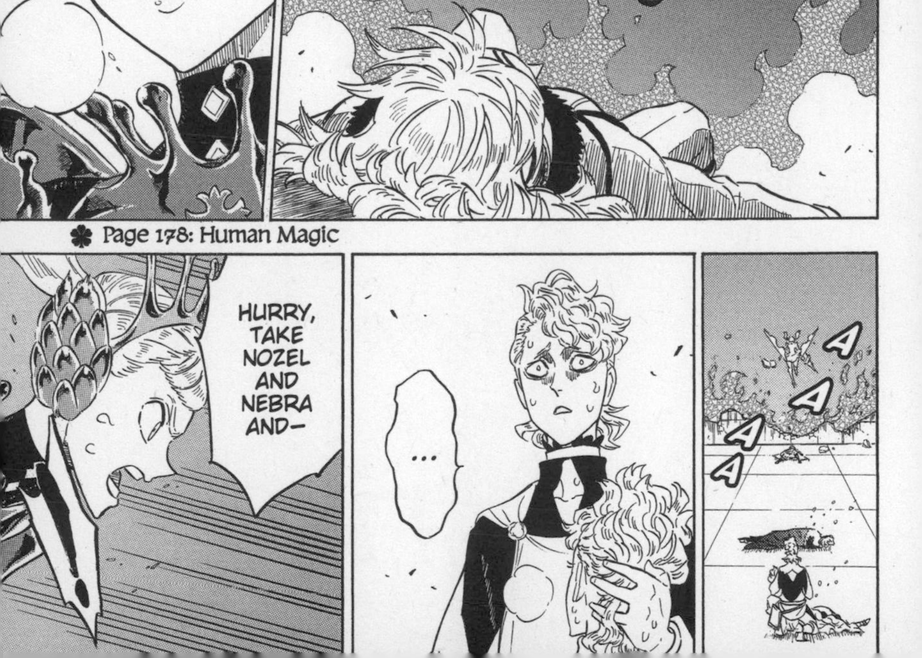
AAAA
...
HURRY, TAKE NOZEL AND NEBRA AND–

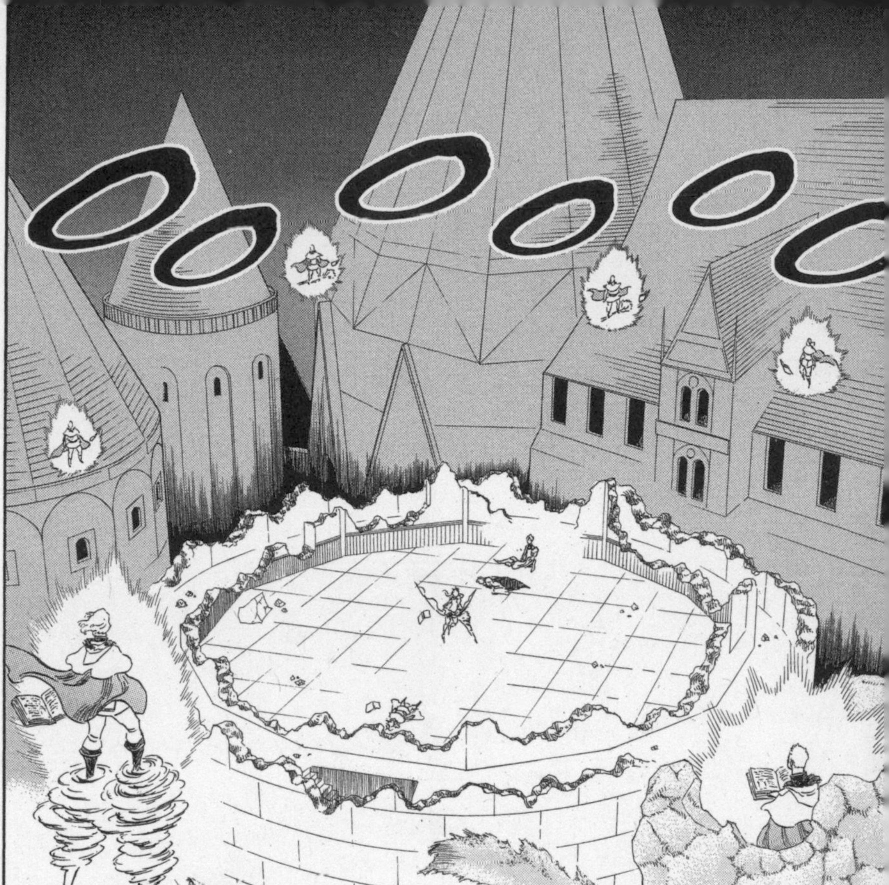
Page 178: Human Magic
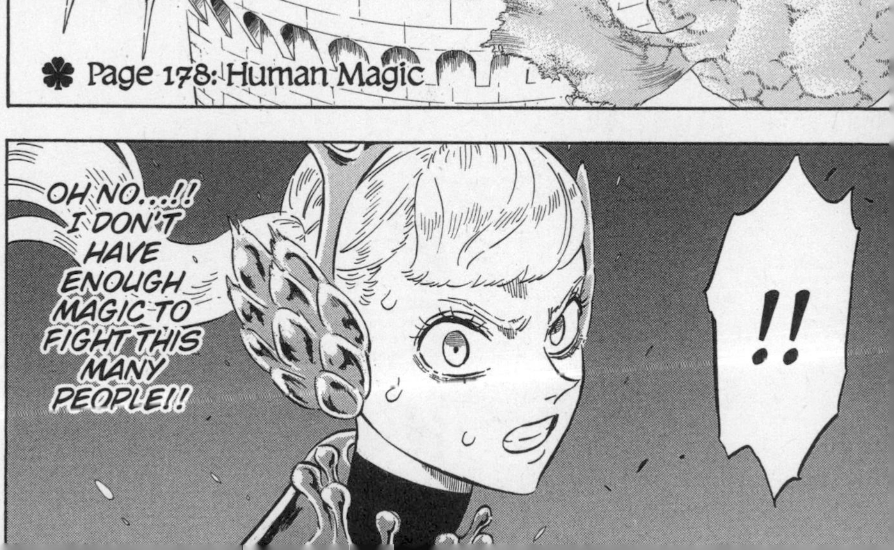
!!
OH NO...!! I DON'T HAVE ENOUGH MAGIC TO FIGHT THIS MANY PEOPLE!!

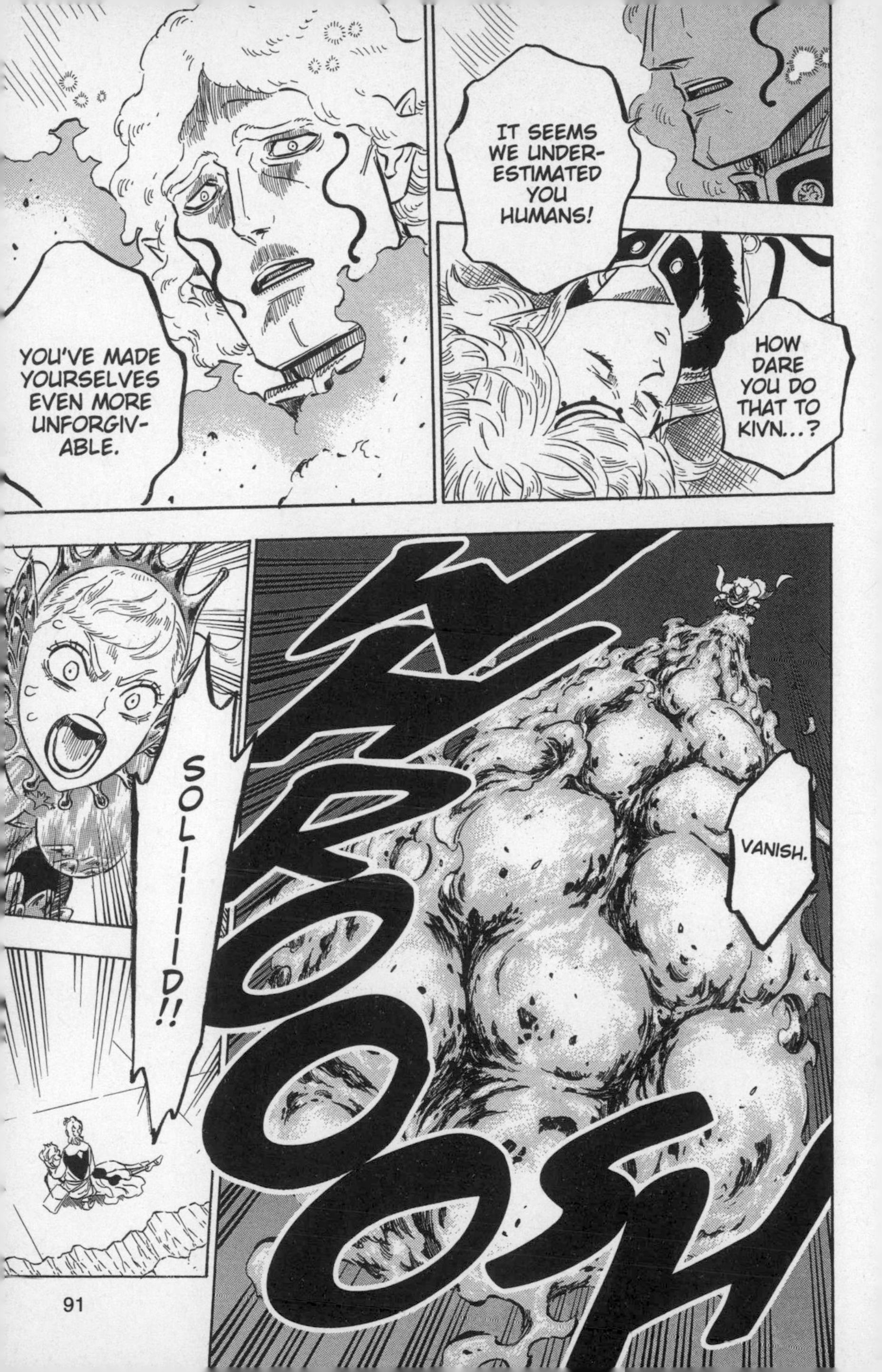
IT SEEMS WE UNDER-ESTIMATED YOU HUMANS!
HOW DARE YOU DO THAT TO KIVN...?
YOU'VE MADE YOURSELVES EVEN MORE UNFORGIV-ABLE.
VANISH.
SOLIIIID!!

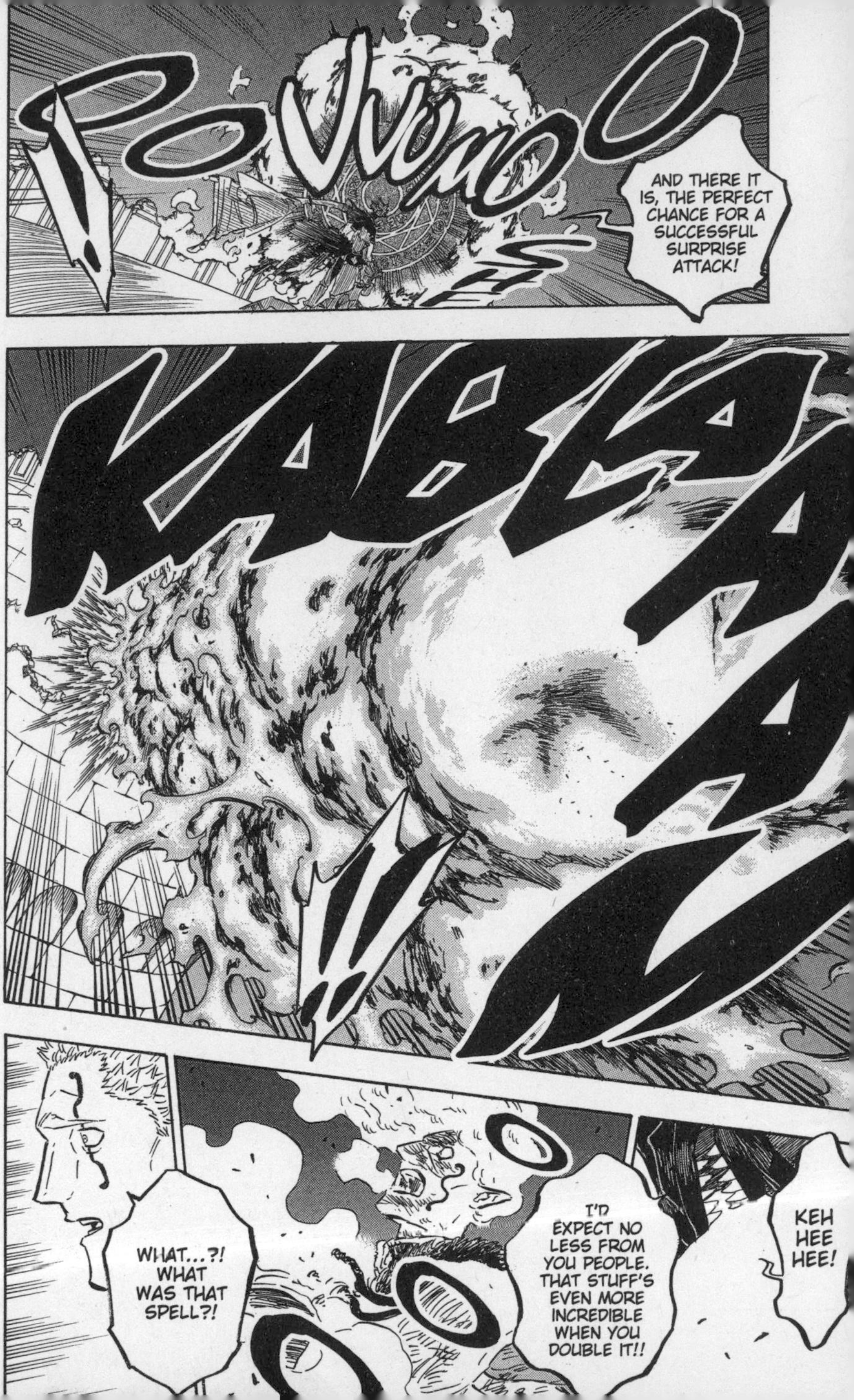
AND THERE IT IS, THE PERFECT CHANCE FOR A SUCCESSFUL SURPRISE ATTACK!
KEH HEE HEE!
I'D EXPECT NO LESS FROM YOU PEOPLE. THAT STUFF'S EVEN MORE INCREDIBLE WHEN YOU DOUBLE IT!!
WHAT...?! WHAT WAS THAT SPELL?!

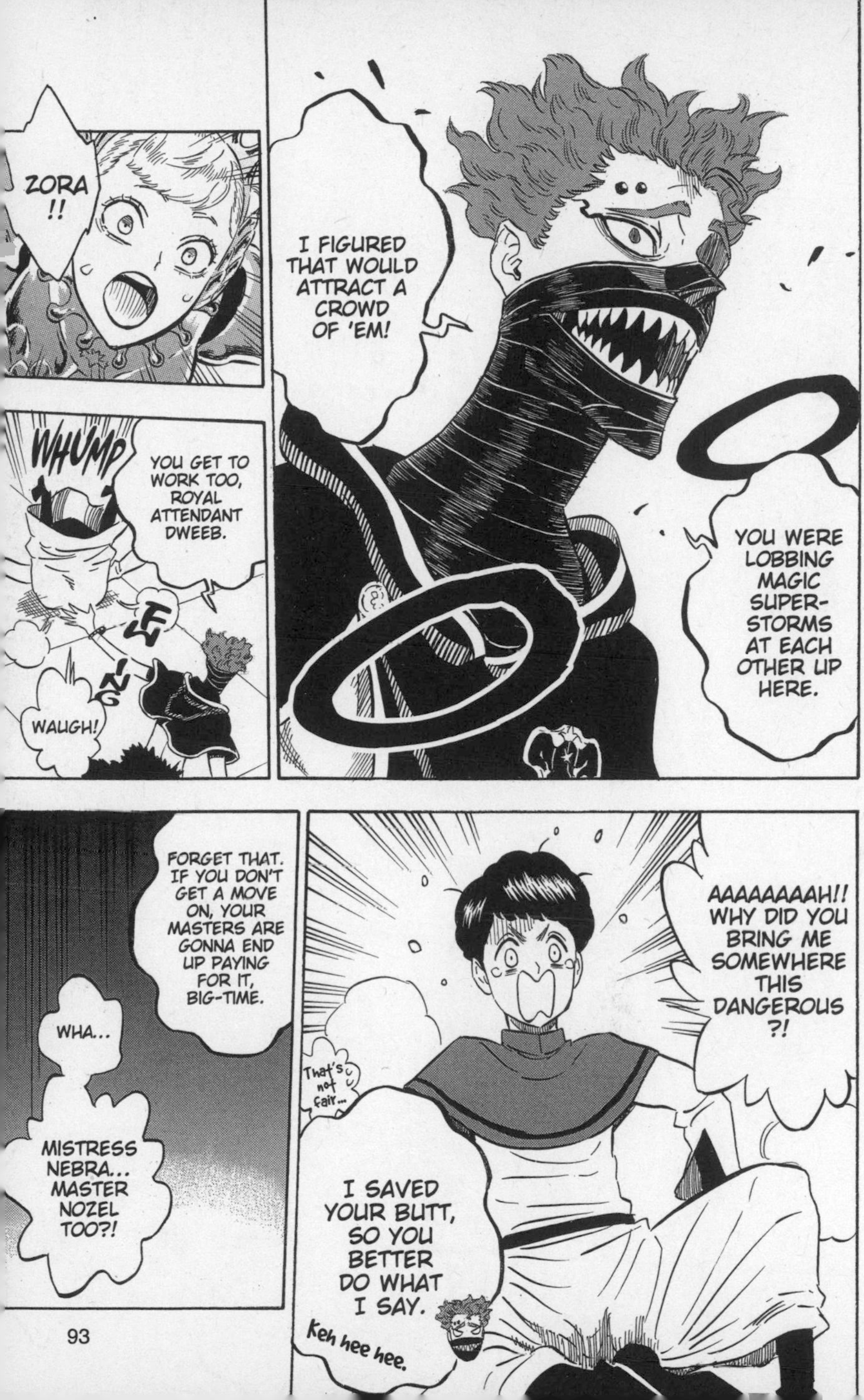
YOU WERE LOBBING MAGIC SUPER-STORMS AT EACH OTHER UP HERE.
I FIGURED THAT WOULD ATTRACT A CROWD OF 'EM!
ZORA!!
WHUMP
YOU GET TO WORK TOO, ROYAL ATTENDANT DWEEB.
FWING
WAUGH!
AAAAAAAAH!! WHY DID YOU BRING ME SOMEWHERE THIS DANGEROUS?!
That's not fair...
I SAVED YOUR BUTT, SO YOU BETTER DO WHAT I SAY.
Keh hee hee.
FORGET THAT. IF YOU DON'T GET A MOVE ON, YOUR MASTERS ARE GONNA END UP PAYING FOR IT, BIG-TIME.
WHA...
MISTRESS NEBRA... MASTER NOZEL TOO?!

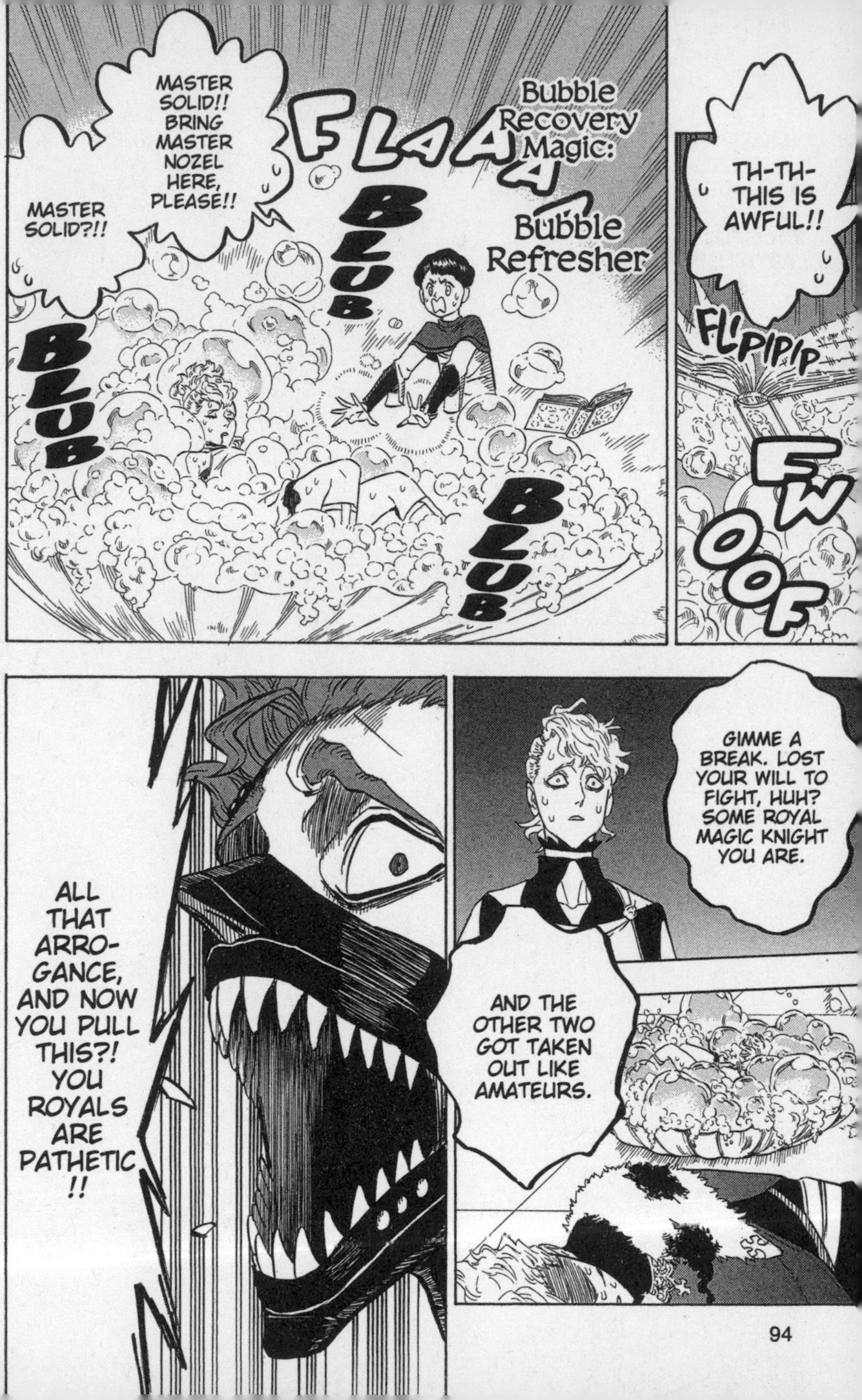
TH-TH-THIS IS AWFUL!!
FLIPIPIP
FWOOOF
Bubble Recovery Magic:
Bubble Refresher
FLAAA
MASTER SOLID!! BRING MASTER NOZEL HERE, PLEASE!!
BLUB BLUB
MASTER SOLID?!!
BLUB
BLUB
GIMME A BREAK. LOST YOUR WILL TO FIGHT, HUH? SOME ROYAL MAGIC KNIGHT YOU ARE.
AND THE OTHER TWO GOT TAKEN OUT LIKE AMATEURS.
ALL THAT ARRO-GANCE, AND NOW YOU PULL THIS?! YOU ROYALS ARE PATHETIC!!

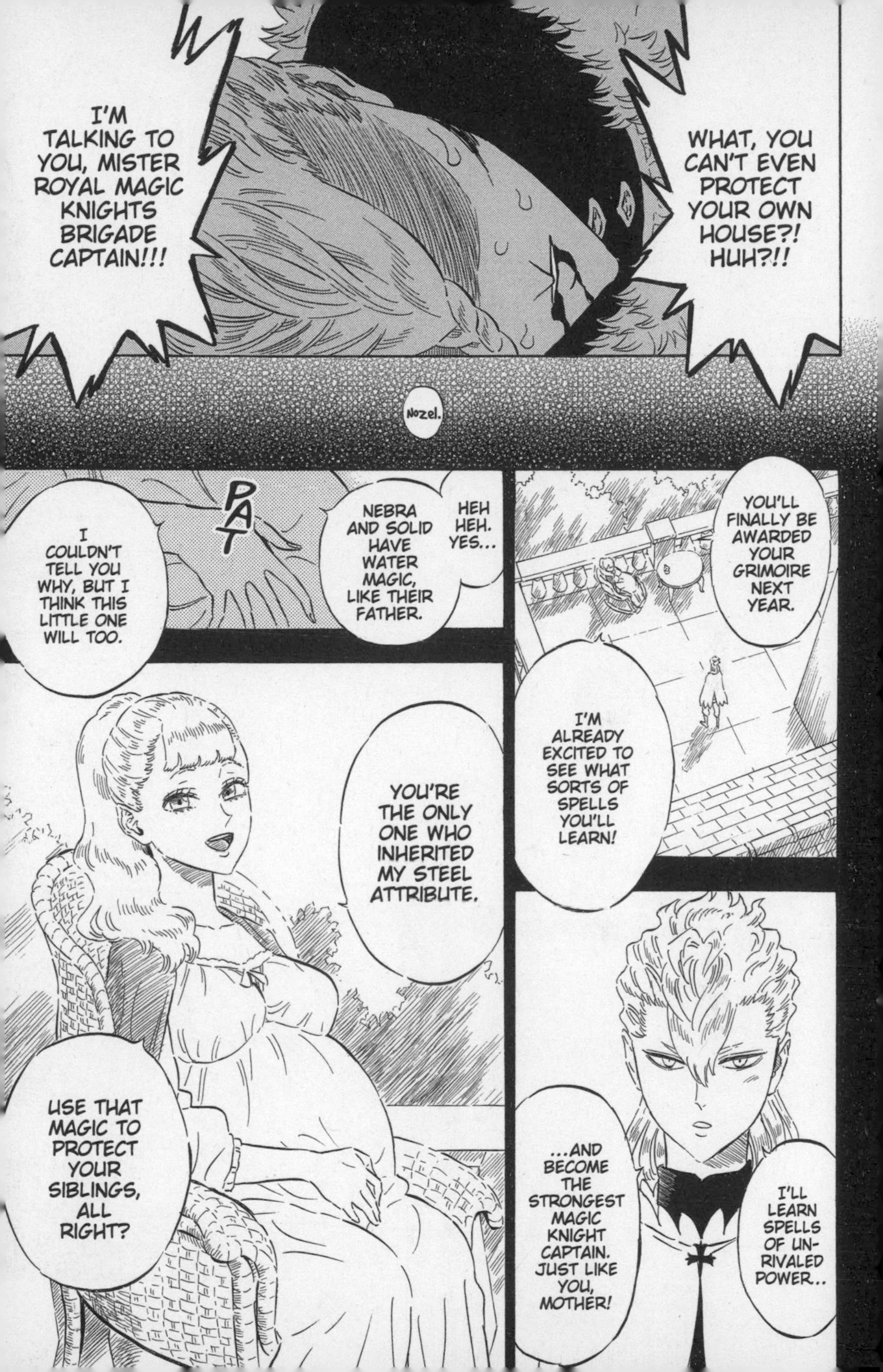
WHAT, YOU CAN'T EVEN PROTECT YOUR OWN HOUSE?! HUH?!!
I'M TALKING TO YOU, MISTER ROYAL MAGIC KNIGHTS BRIGADE CAPTAIN!!!
Nozel.
YOU'LL FINALLY BE AWARDED YOUR GRIMOIRE NEXT YEAR.
I'M ALREADY EXCITED TO SEE WHAT SORTS OF SPELLS YOU'LL LEARN!
I'LL LEARN SPELLS OF UNRIVALED POWER..
...AND BECOME THE STRONGEST MAGIC KNIGHT CAPTAIN. JUST LIKE YOU, MOTHER!
PAT
HEH HEH. YES...
NEBRA AND SOLID HAVE WATER MAGIC, LIKE THEIR FATHER.
I COULDN'T TELL YOU WHY, BUT I THINK THIS LITTLE ONE WILL TOO.
YOU'RE THE ONLY ONE WHO INHERITED MY STEEL ATTRIBUTE.
USE THAT MAGIC TO PROTECT YOUR SIBLINGS, ALL RIGHT?

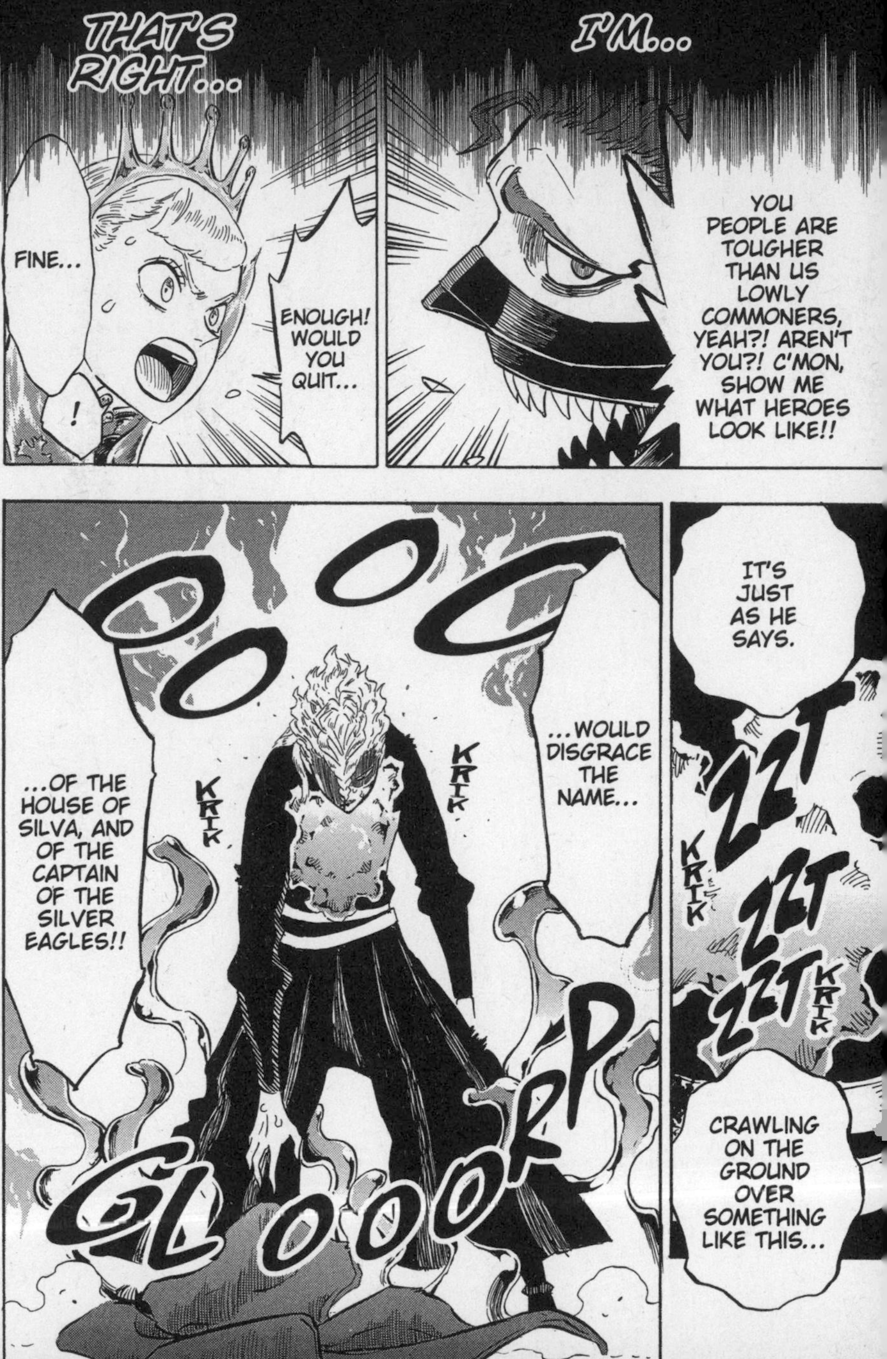
I'M...
YOU PEOPLE ARE TOUGHER THAN US LOWLY COMMONERS, YEAH?! AREN'T YOU?! C'MON, SHOW ME WHAT HEROES LOOK LIKE!!
THAT'S RIGHT...
ENOUGH! WOULD YOU QUIT...
FINE...
!
IT'S JUST AS HE SAYS.
ZZT
ZZT
ZZT
KRIK
KRIK
CRAWLING ON THE GROUND OVER SOMETHING LIKE THIS...
OOO
...WOULD DISGRACE THE NAME...
KRIK
KRIK
...OF THE HOUSE OF SILVA, AND OF THE CAPTAIN OF THE SILVER EAGLES!!
GLOOOORP

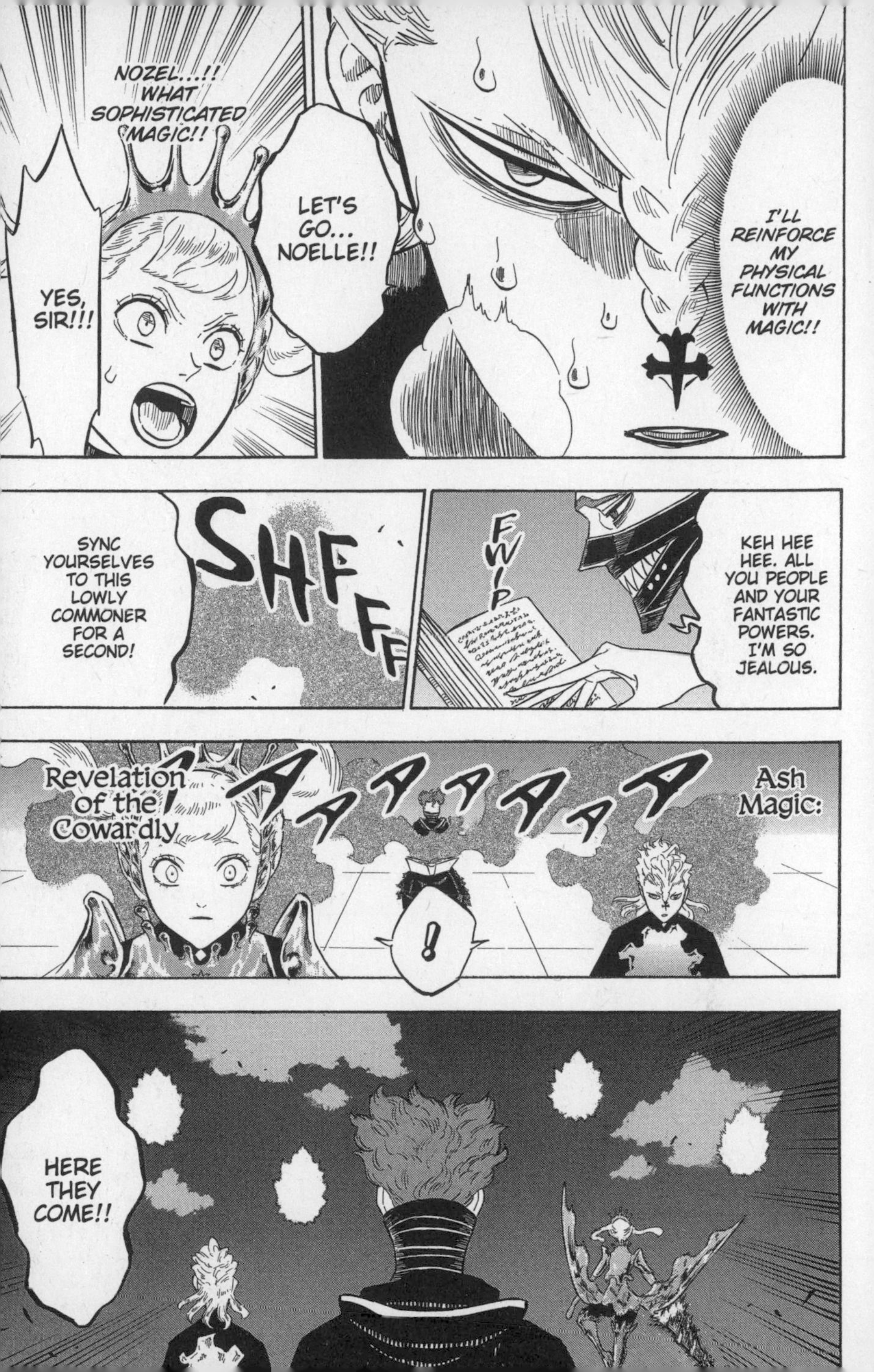
I'LL REINFORCE MY PHYSICAL FUNCTIONS WITH MAGIC!!
LET'S GO... NOELLE!!
NOZEL...!! WHAT SOPHISTICATED MAGIC!!
YES, SIR!!!
KEH HEE HEE. ALL YOU PEOPLE AND YOUR FANTASTIC POWERS. I'M SO JEALOUS.
FWIP
SHFFF
SYNC YOURSELVES TO THIS LOWLY COMMONER FOR A SECOND!
Ash Magic:
Revelation of the Cowardly
AAAAAAAA
!
HERE THEY COME!!

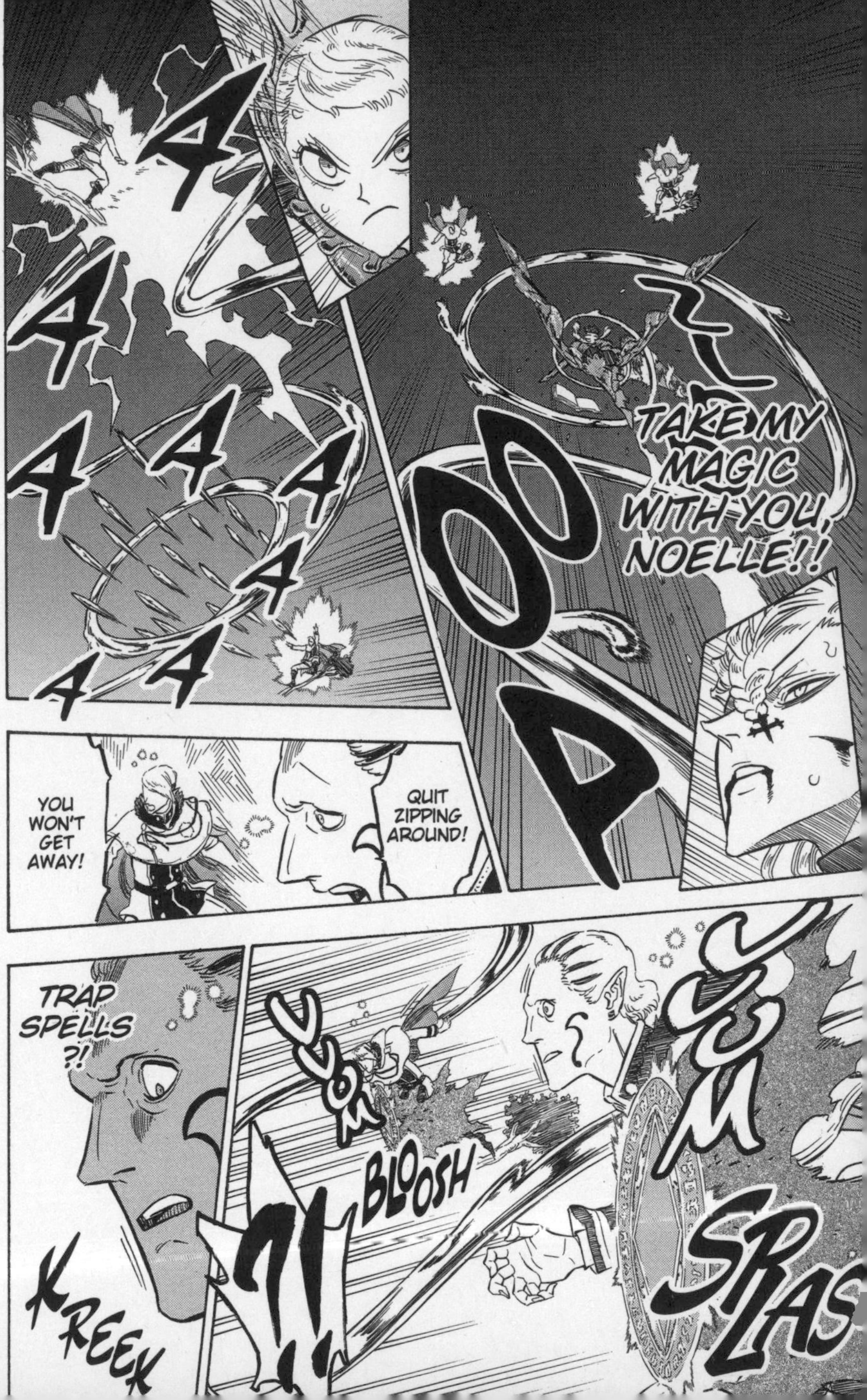
TAKE MY MAGIC WITH YOU, NOELLE!!
QUIT ZIPPING AROUND!
YOU WON'T GET AWAY!
SPLAS
BLOOSH
TRAP SPELLS ?!
KREEK

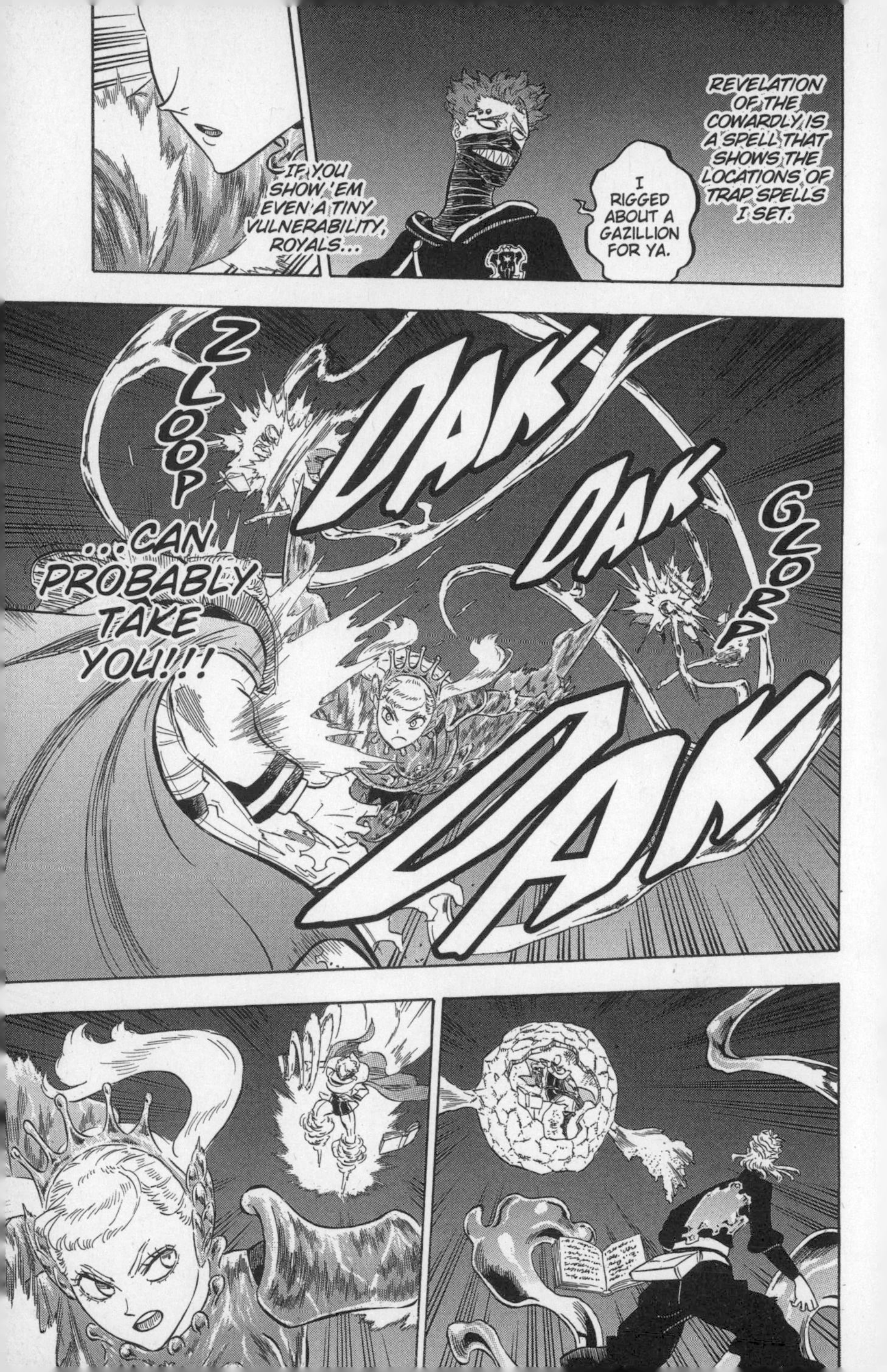

REVELATION OF THE COWARDLY IS A SPELL THAT SHOWS THE LOCATIONS OF TRAP SPELLS I SET.
I RIGGED ABOUT A GAZILLION FOR YA.
IF YOU SHOW 'EM EVEN A TINY VULNERABILITY, ROYALS...
DAK
GLORP
DAK
ZLOOP
...CAN PROBABLY TAKE YOU!!!
DAK

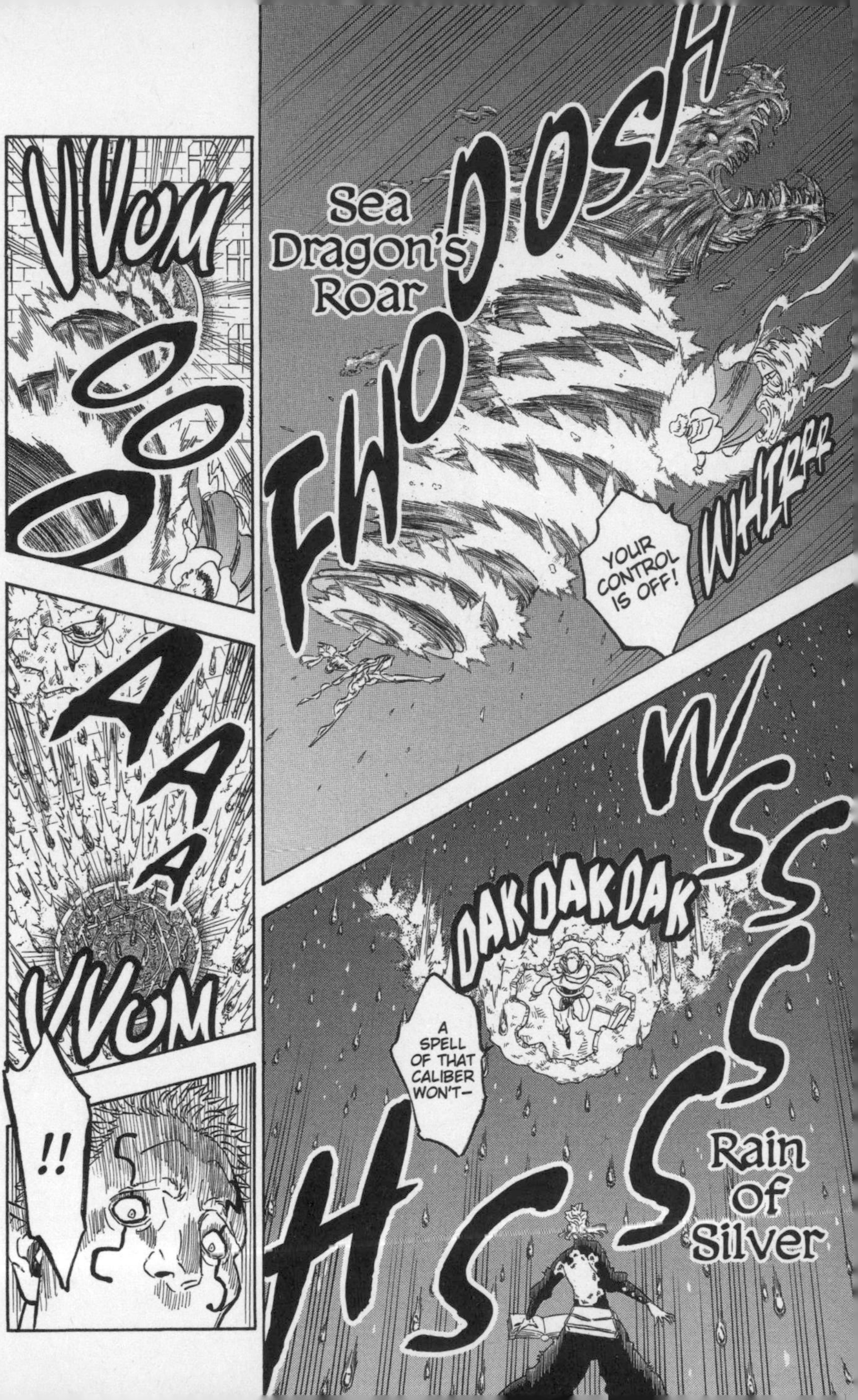
Sea Dragon's Roar
FWOOOSH
YOUR CONTROL IS OFF!
WHIRRR
DAK DAK DAK
A SPELL OF THAT CALIBER WON'T—
WHSSSS
Rain of Silver
VWOM
OOOO
AAAA
VWOM
!!

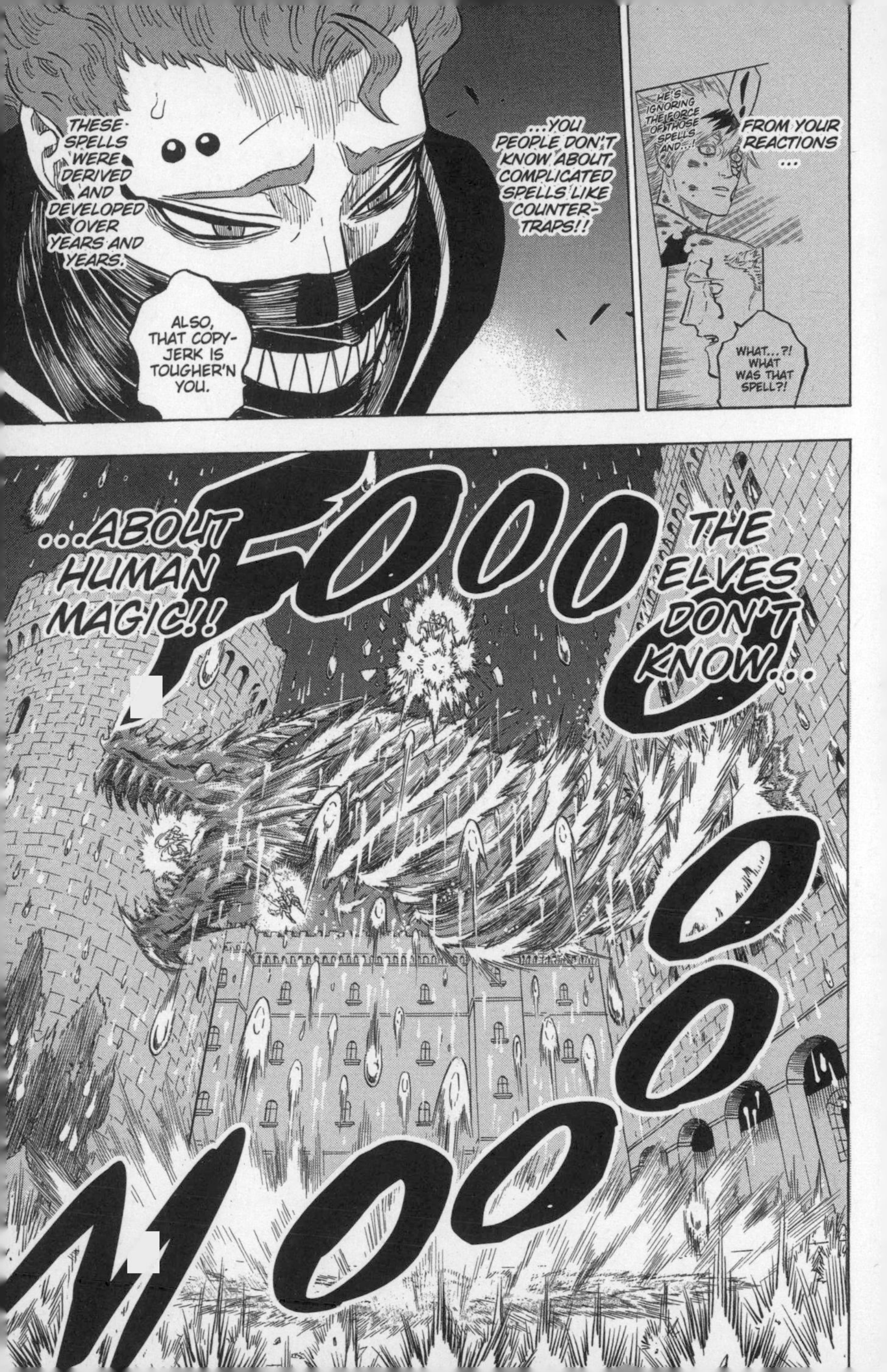
FROM YOUR REACTIONS ...
HE'S IGNORING THE FORCE OF THOSE SPELLS AND...!
WHAT...?! WHAT WAS THAT SPELL?!
...YOU PEOPLE DON'T KNOW ABOUT COMPLICATED SPELLS LIKE COUNTER-TRAPS!!
THESE SPELLS WERE DERIVED AND DEVELOPED OVER YEARS AND YEARS.
ALSO, THAT COPY-JERK IS TOUGHER'N YOU.
THE ELVES DON'T KNOW...
...ABOUT HUMAN MAGIC!!

The first *Black Clover* spin-off!

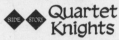

Black Clover

SIDE STORY Quartet Knights

Yumiya Tashiro Sensei dropped by for a visit!

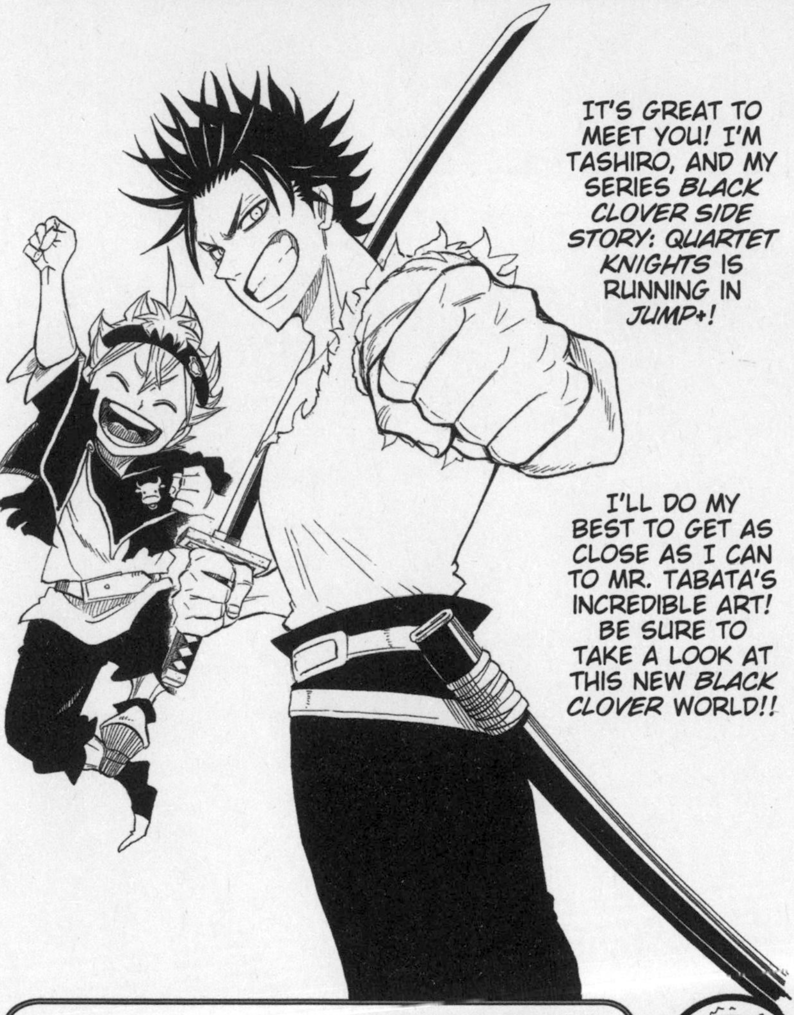
IT'S GREAT TO MEET YOU! I'M TASHIRO, AND MY SERIES *BLACK CLOVER SIDE STORY: QUARTET KNIGHTS* IS RUNNING IN *JUMP+*!
I'LL DO MY BEST TO GET AS CLOSE AS I CAN TO MR. TABATA'S INCREDIBLE ART! BE SURE TO TAKE A LOOK AT THIS NEW *BLACK CLOVER* WORLD!!

Thanks for drawing this picture just for this volume!! I feel lucky to have you contributing such enthusiastic, energetic art skills to the side story!! I'll be giving the spin-off my full support!!

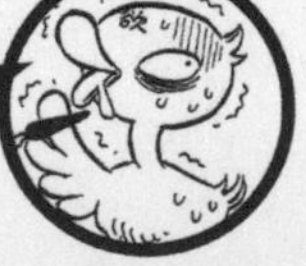

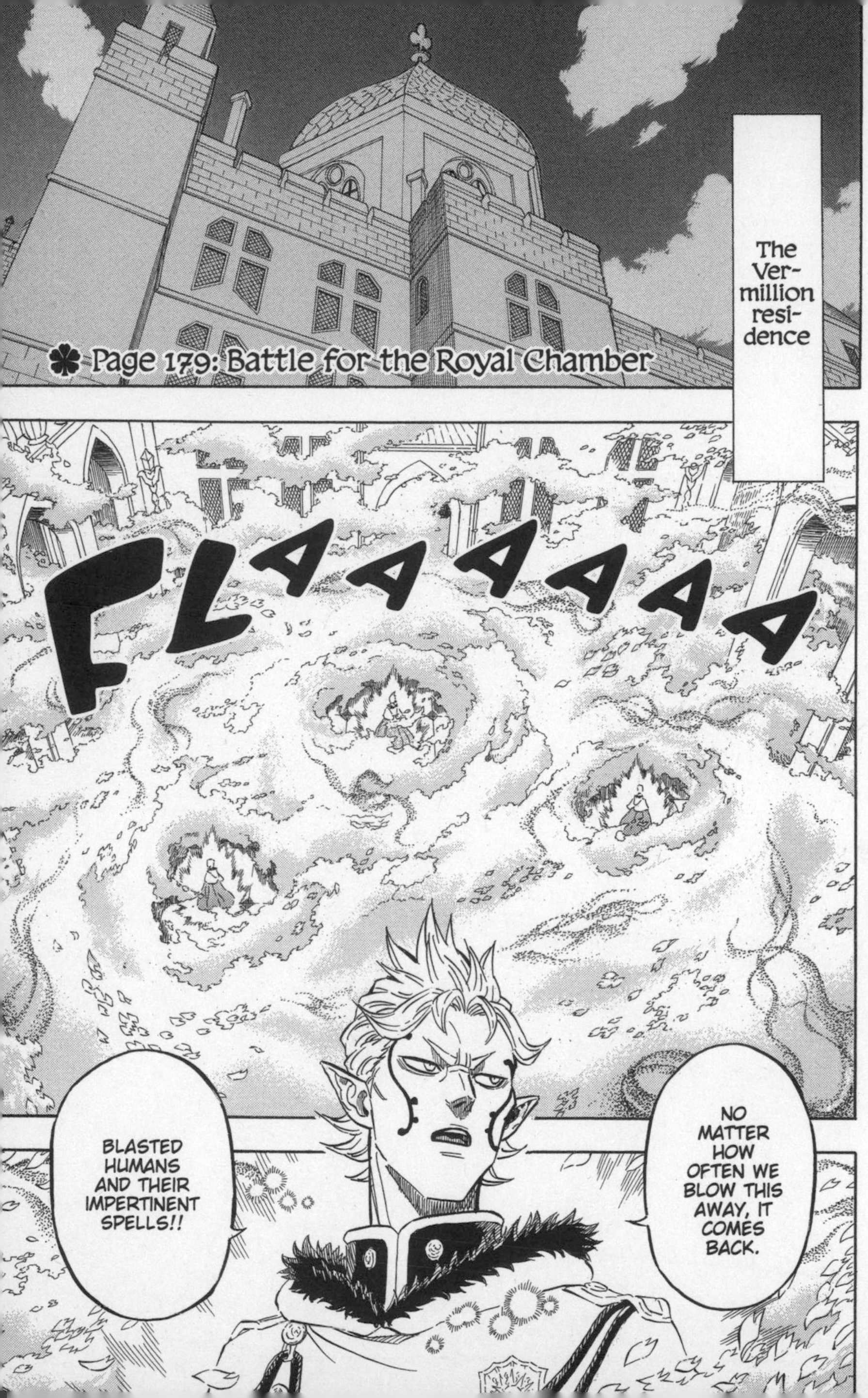
Page 179: Battle for the Royal Chamber
The Vermillion residence
FLAAAAAA
NO MATTER HOW OFTEN WE BLOW THIS AWAY, IT COMES BACK.
BLASTED HUMANS AND THEIR IMPERTINENT SPELLS!!

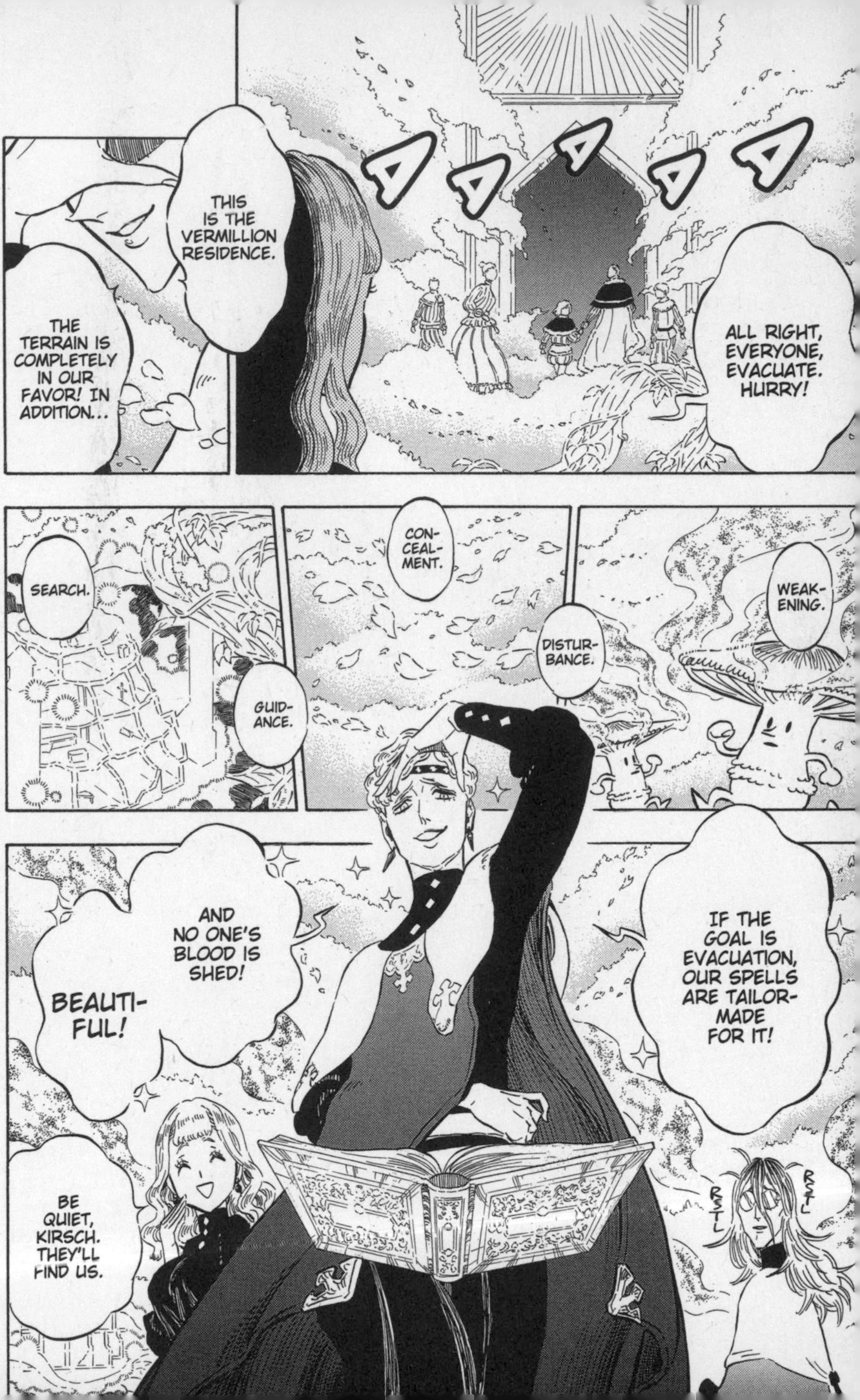
AAAAA
ALL RIGHT, EVERYONE, EVACUATE. HURRY!
THIS IS THE VERMILLION RESIDENCE.
THE TERRAIN IS COMPLETELY IN OUR FAVOR! IN ADDITION...
WEAK-ENING.
DISTUR-BANCE.
CON-CEAL-MENT.
SEARCH.
GUID-ANCE.
IF THE GOAL IS EVACUATION, OUR SPELLS ARE TAILOR-MADE FOR IT!
RSTL
RSTL
AND NO ONE'S BLOOD IS SHED!
BEAUTI-FUL!
BE QUIET, KIRSCH. THEY'LL FIND US.

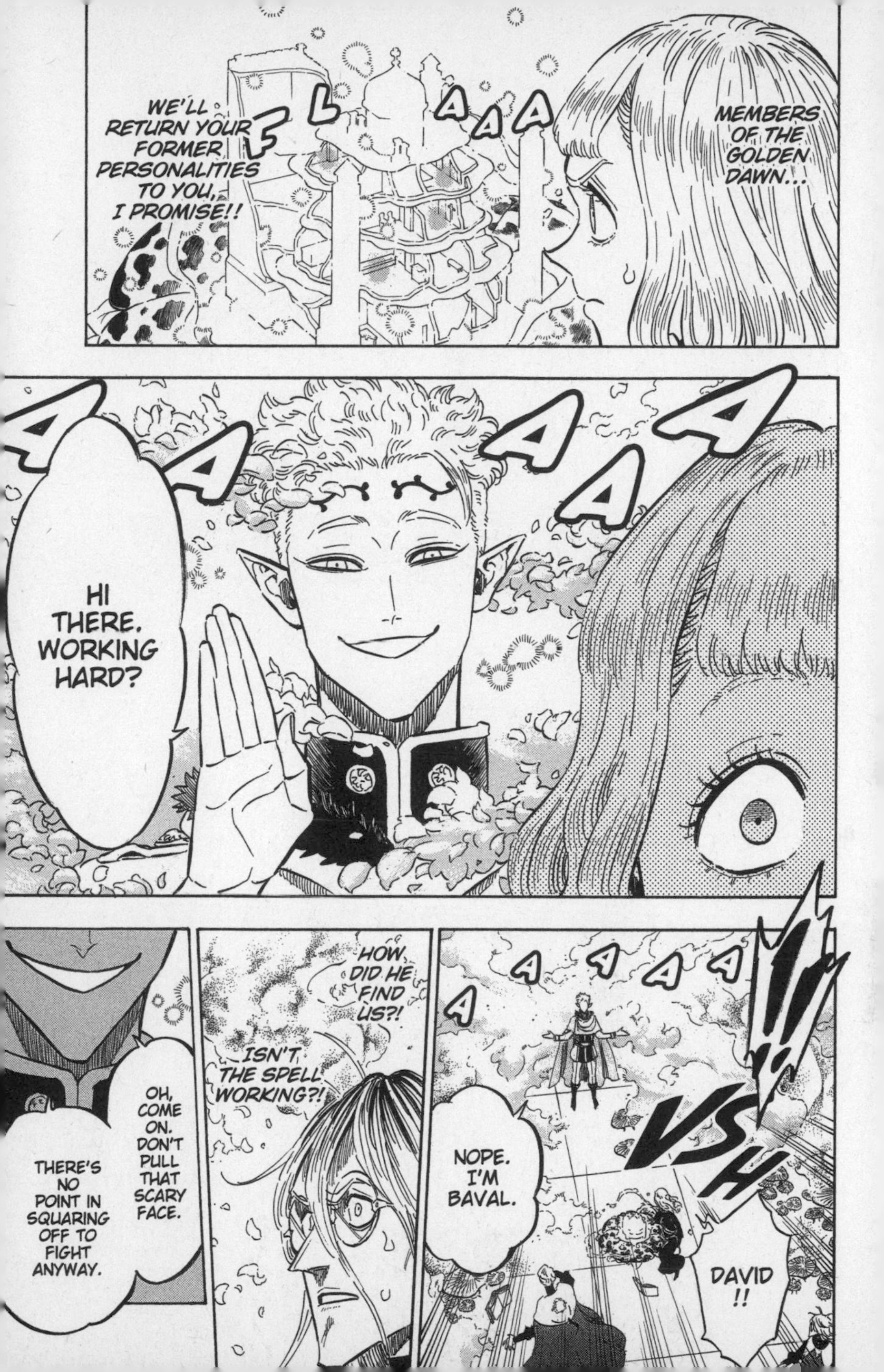
MEMBERS OF THE GOLDEN DAWN...
FLAAAA
WE'LL RETURN YOUR FORMER PERSONALITIES TO YOU, I PROMISE!!
AAAAA
HI THERE. WORKING HARD?
AAAAAA
!!
VSH
NOPE. I'M BAVAL.
DAVID !!
HOW DID HE FIND US?!
ISN'T THE SPELL WORKING?!
OH, COME ON. DON'T PULL THAT SCARY FACE.
THERE'S NO POINT IN SQUARING OFF TO FIGHT ANYWAY.

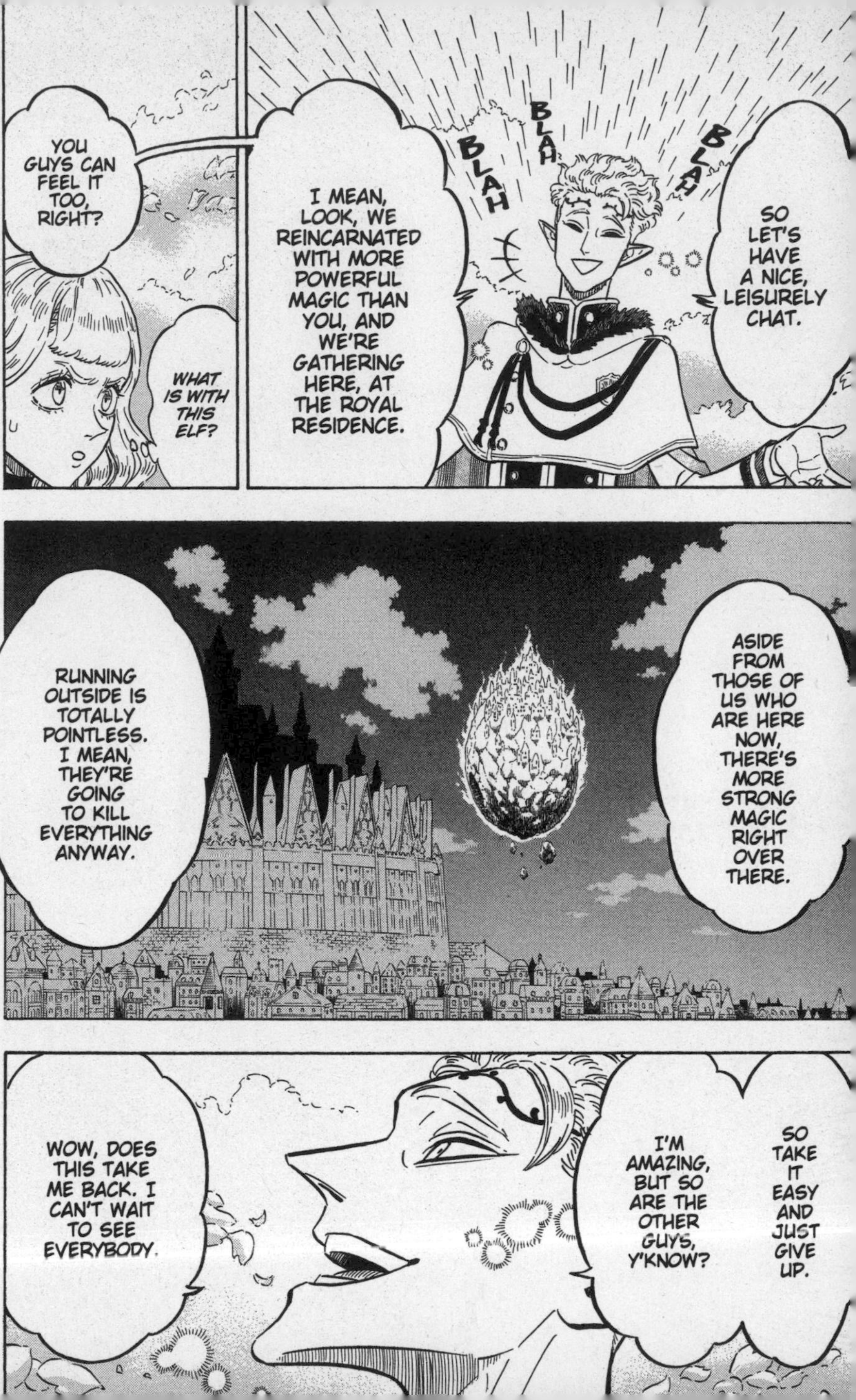
SO LET'S HAVE A NICE, LEISURELY CHAT.
BLAH
BLAH
BLAH
I MEAN, LOOK, WE REINCARNATED WITH MORE POWERFUL MAGIC THAN YOU, AND WE'RE GATHERING HERE, AT THE ROYAL RESIDENCE.
YOU GUYS CAN FEEL IT TOO, RIGHT?
WHAT IS WITH THIS ELF?
ASIDE FROM THOSE OF US WHO ARE HERE NOW, THERE'S MORE STRONG MAGIC RIGHT OVER THERE.
RUNNING OUTSIDE IS TOTALLY POINTLESS. I MEAN, THEY'RE GOING TO KILL EVERYTHING ANYWAY.
I'M AMAZING, BUT SO ARE THE OTHER GUYS, Y'KNOW? SO TAKE IT EASY AND JUST GIVE UP.
WOW, DOES THIS TAKE ME BACK. I CAN'T WAIT TO SEE EVERYBODY.

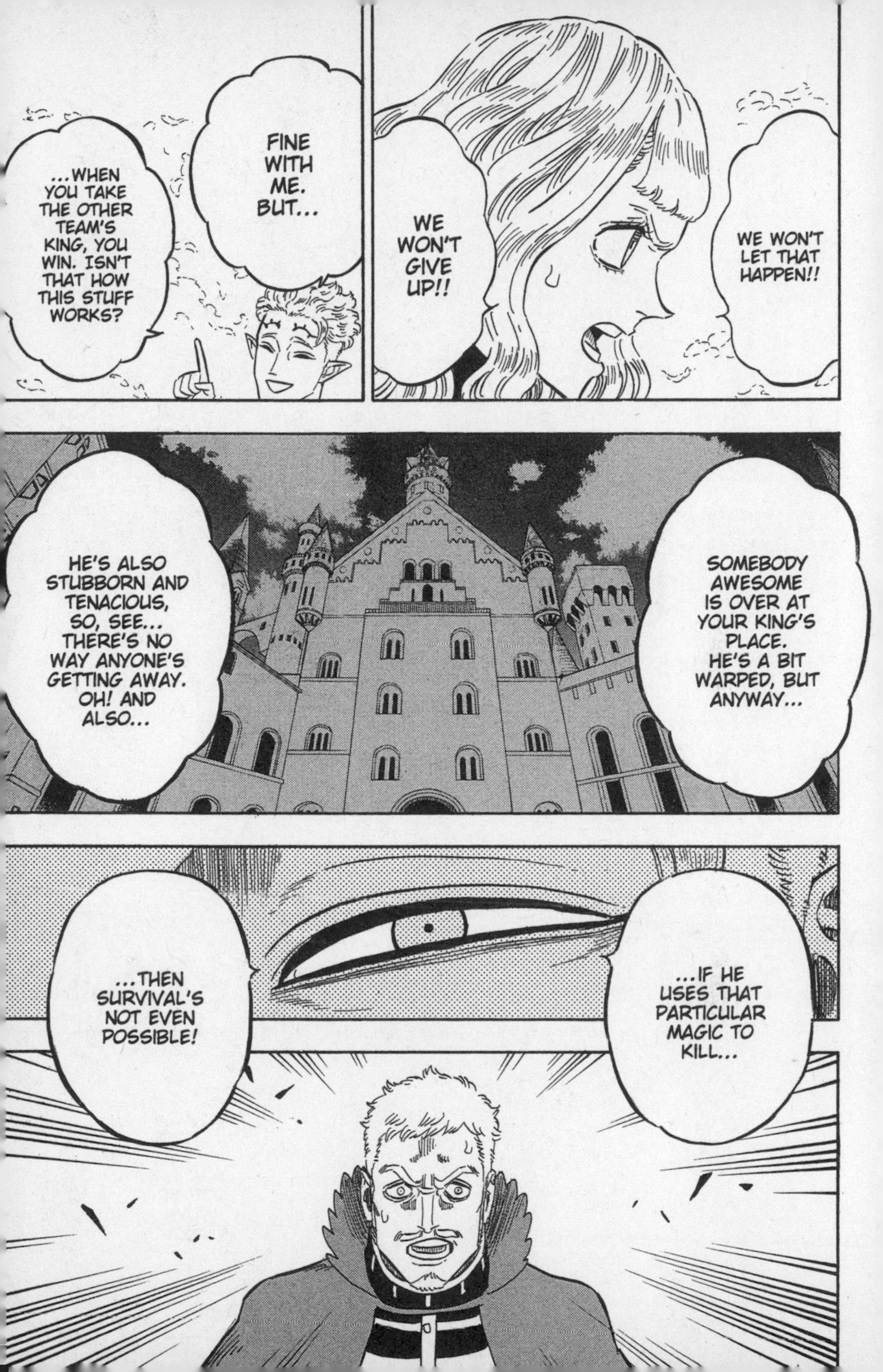
WE WON'T LET THAT HAPPEN!!
WE WON'T GIVE UP!!
FINE WITH ME. BUT...
...WHEN YOU TAKE THE OTHER TEAM'S KING, YOU WIN. ISN'T THAT HOW THIS STUFF WORKS?
SOMEBODY AWESOME IS OVER AT YOUR KING'S PLACE. HE'S A BIT WARPED, BUT ANYWAY...
HE'S ALSO STUBBORN AND TENACIOUS, SO, SEE... THERE'S NO WAY ANYONE'S GETTING AWAY. OH! AND ALSO...
...IF HE USES THAT PARTICULAR MAGIC TO KILL...
...THEN SURVIVAL'S NOT EVEN POSSIBLE!

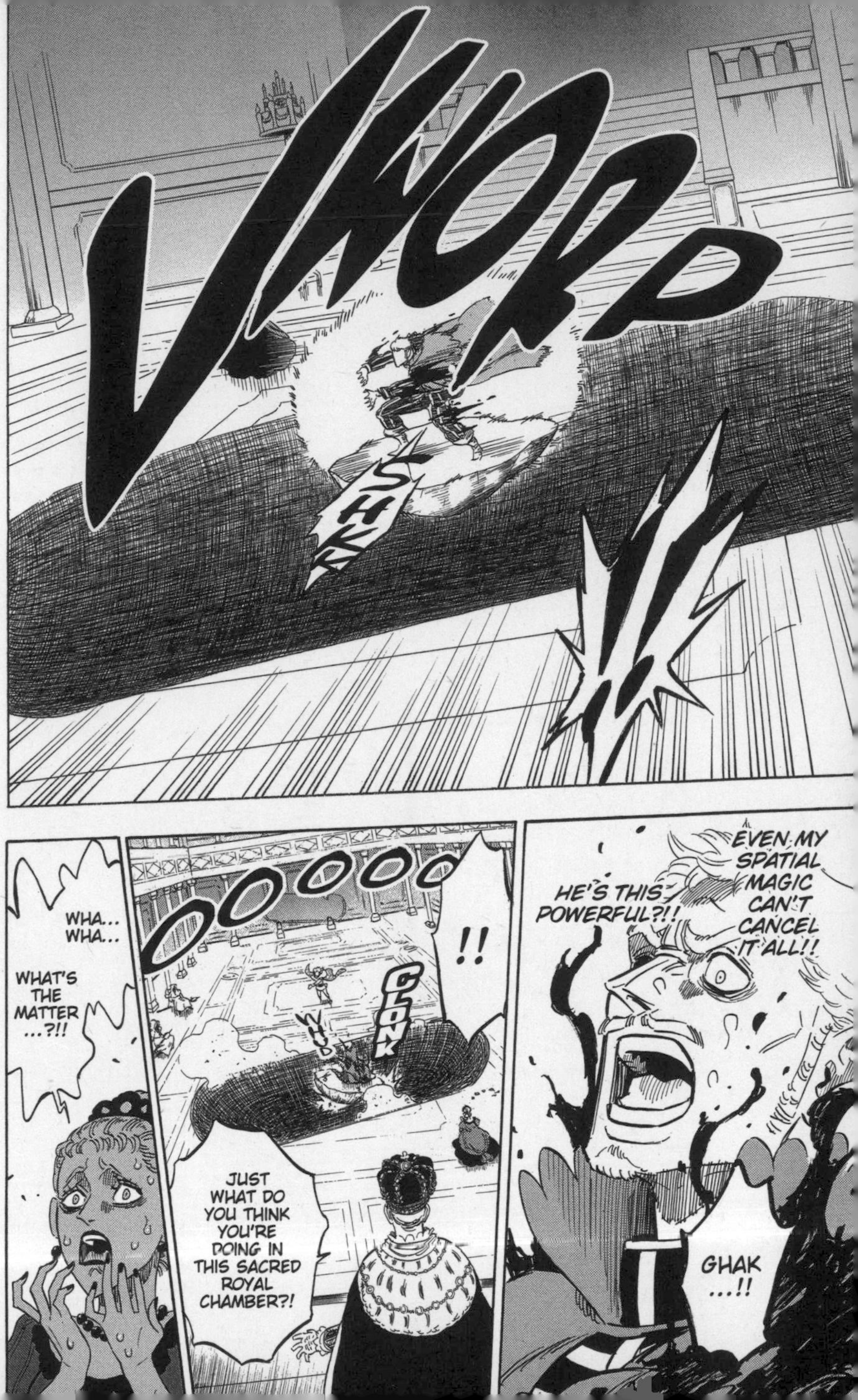
VWORP
SHKK
!!
EVEN MY SPATIAL MAGIC CAN'T CANCEL IT ALL!!
HE'S THIS POWERFUL?!!
GHAK ...!!
OOOOO
!!
CLONK
WHUD
JUST WHAT DO YOU THINK YOU'RE DOING IN THIS SACRED ROYAL CHAMBER?!
WHA... WHA...
WHAT'S THE MATTER ...?!!

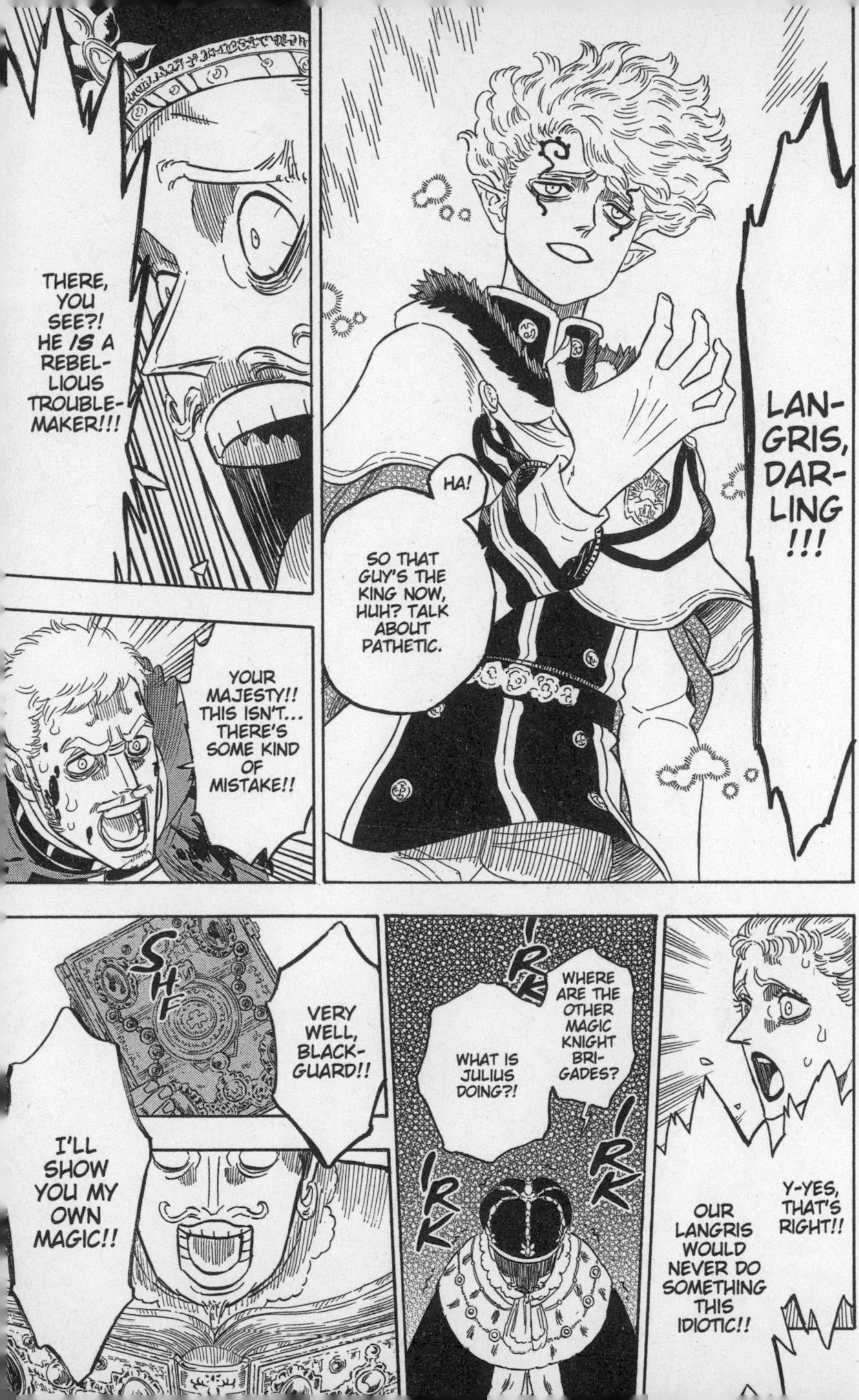
LANGRIS, DARLING!!!
HA!
SO THAT GUY'S THE KING NOW, HUH? TALK ABOUT PATHETIC.
THERE, YOU SEE?! HE *IS* A REBELLIOUS TROUBLEMAKER!!!
YOUR MAJESTY!! THIS ISN'T... THERE'S SOME KIND OF MISTAKE!!
Y-YES, THAT'S RIGHT!!
OUR LANGRIS WOULD NEVER DO SOMETHING THIS IDIOTIC!!
IRK
WHERE ARE THE OTHER MAGIC KNIGHT BRIGADES?
WHAT IS JULIUS DOING?!
IRK
IRK
SHF
VERY WELL, BLACKGUARD!!
I'LL SHOW YOU MY OWN MAGIC!!

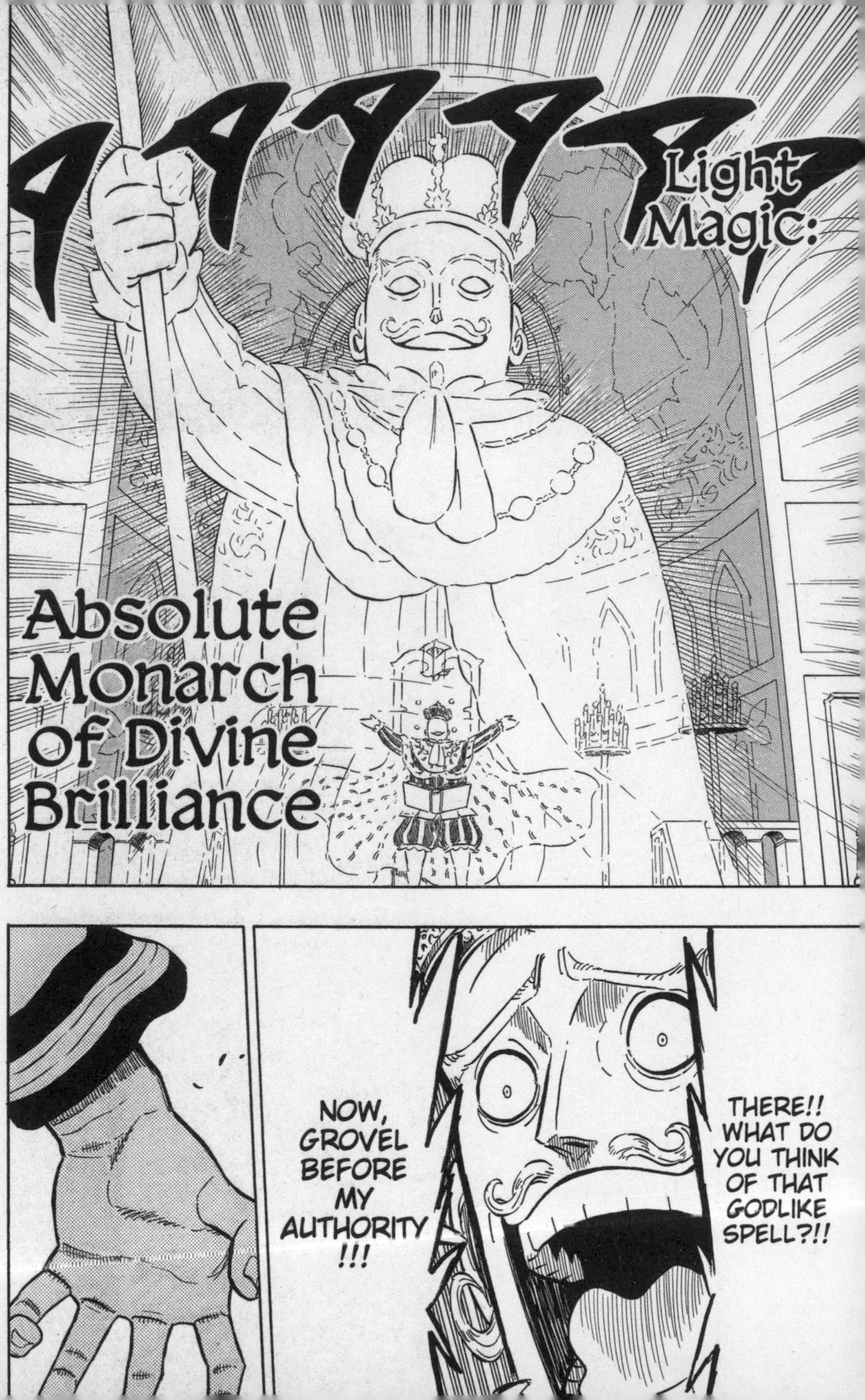
Light Magic:
Absolute Monarch of Divine Brilliance
THERE!! WHAT DO YOU THINK OF THAT GODLIKE SPELL?!!
NOW, GROVEL BEFORE MY AUTHORITY!!!

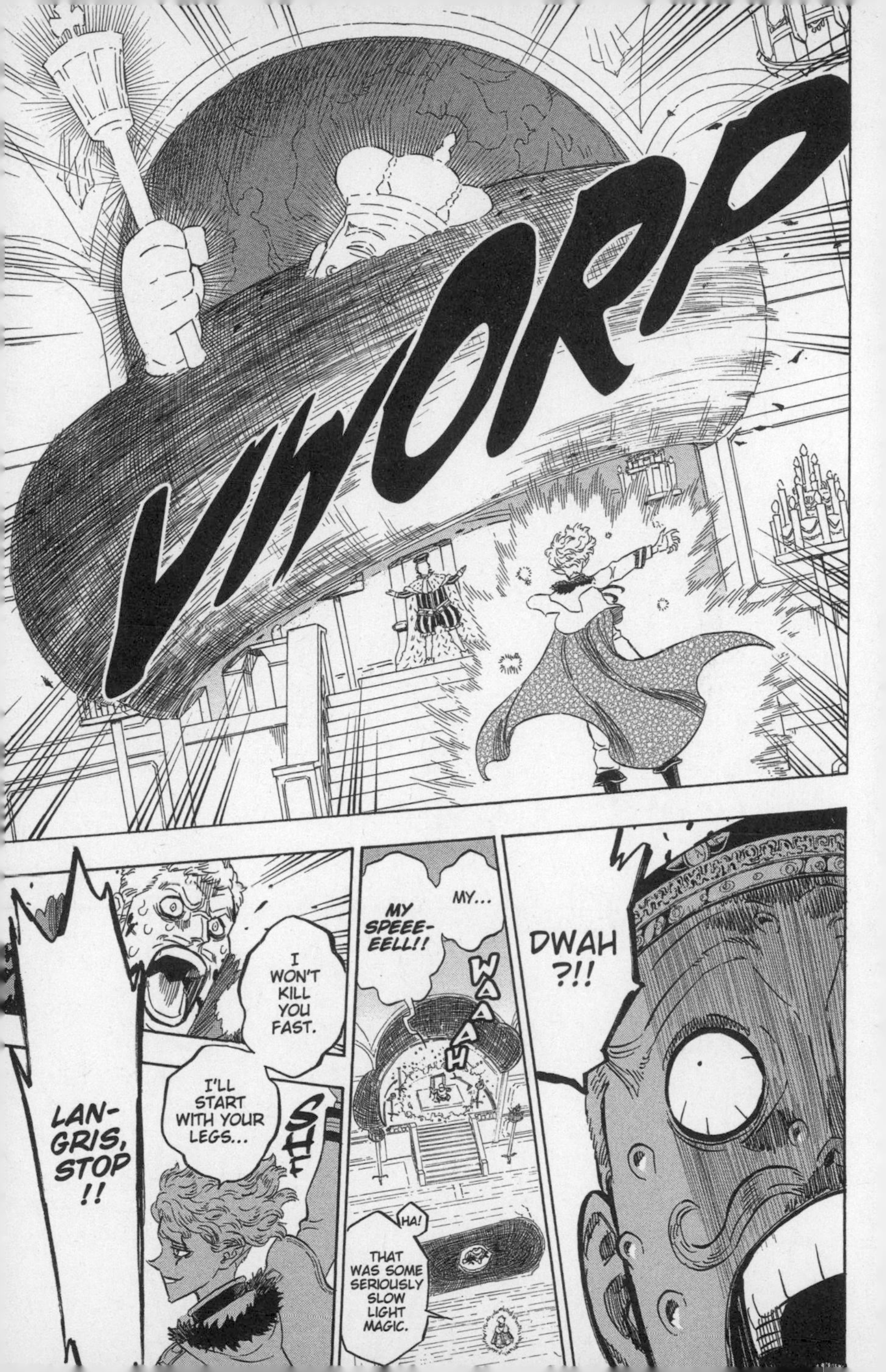
VWORP
DWAH ?!!
MY...
MY SPEEE-EELL!!
WAAAAH
HA!
THAT WAS SOME SERIOUSLY SLOW LIGHT MAGIC.
I WON'T KILL YOU FAST.
I'LL START WITH YOUR LEGS...
SHF
LAN-GRIS, STOP!!

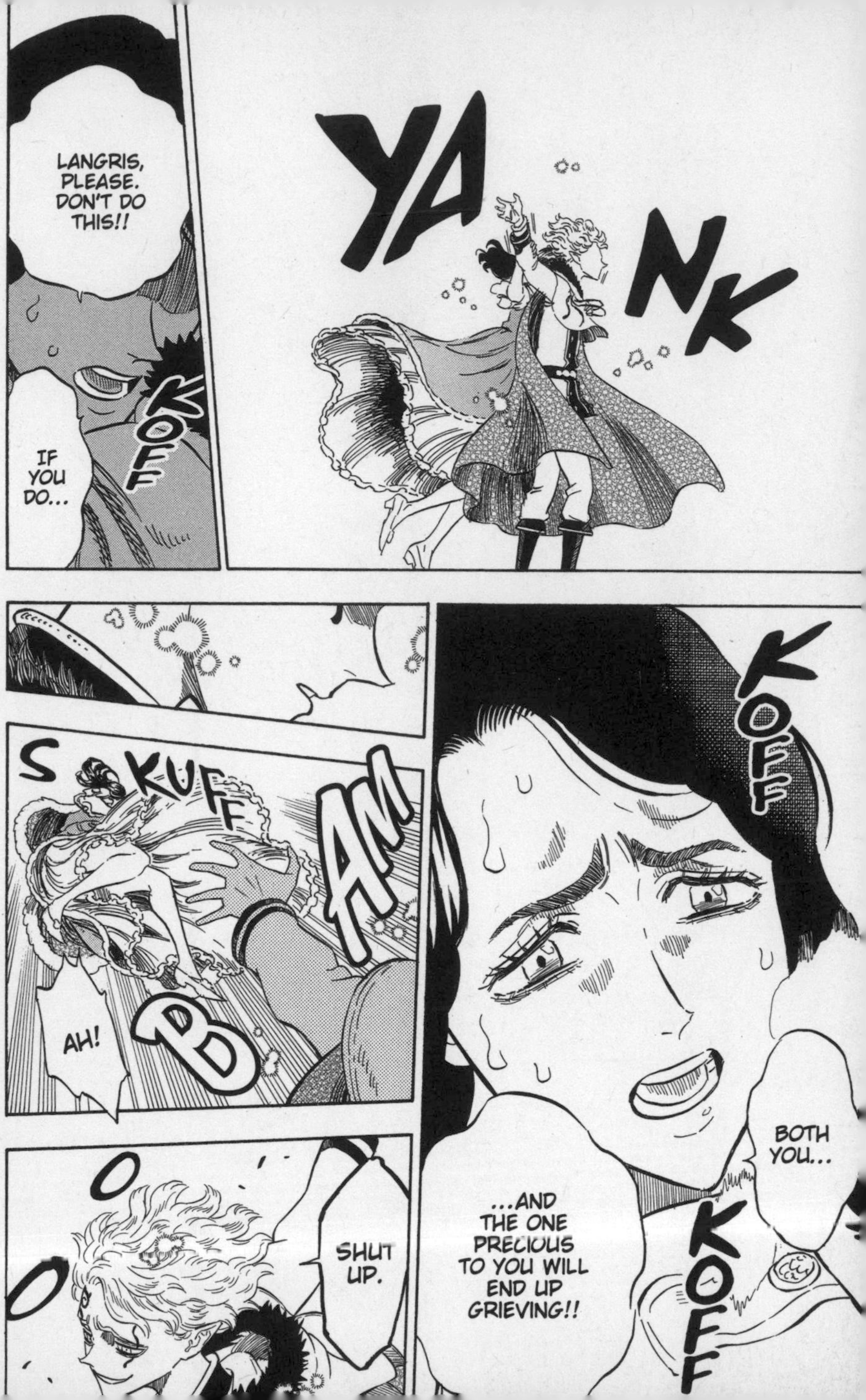
YANK
LANGRIS, PLEASE. DON'T DO THIS!!
KOFF
IF YOU DO...
KOFF
BOTH YOU...
...AND THE ONE PRECIOUS TO YOU WILL END UP GRIEVING!!
KOFF
SKUFF
BAM
AH!
OO
SHUT UP.

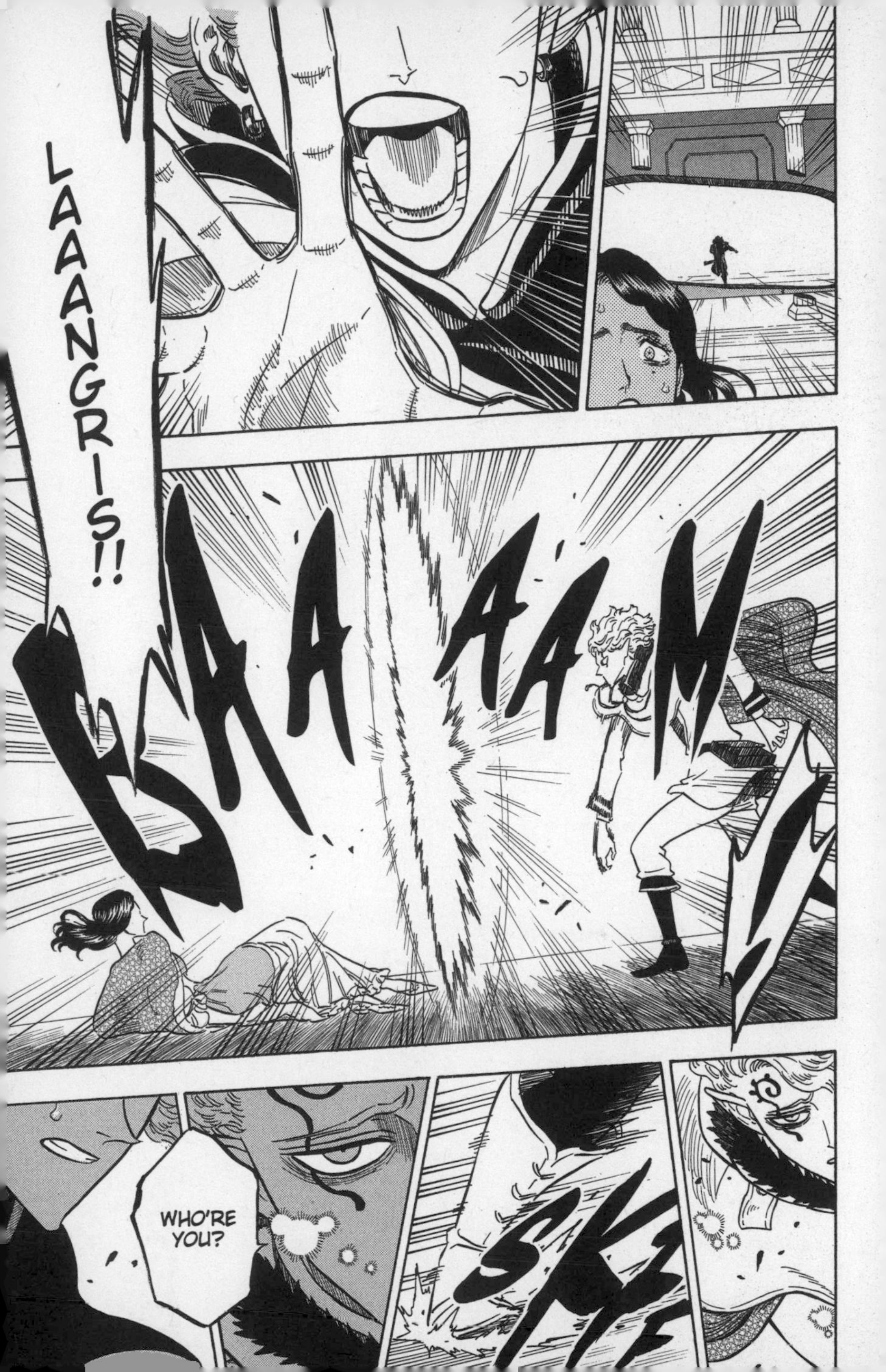
LAAANGRIS!!
BAAAAM
WHO'RE YOU?

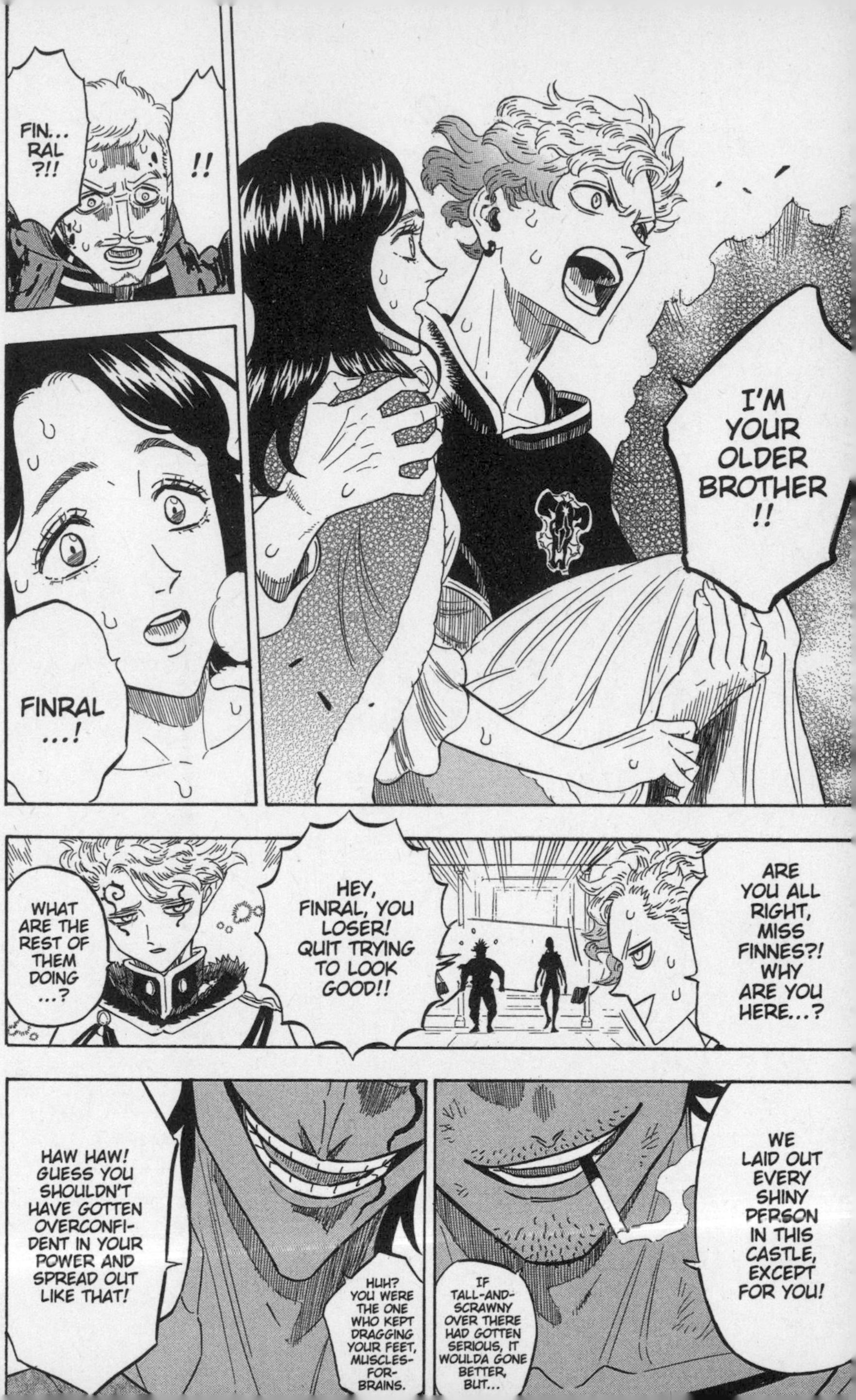
I'M YOUR OLDER BROTHER!!
FIN... RAL?!!
!!
FINRAL...!
ARE YOU ALL RIGHT, MISS FINNES?! WHY ARE YOU HERE...?
HEY, FINRAL, YOU LOSER! QUIT TRYING TO LOOK GOOD!!
WHAT ARE THE REST OF THEM DOING...?
WE LAID OUT EVERY SHINY PERSON IN THIS CASTLE, EXCEPT FOR YOU!
IF TALL-AND-SCRAWNY OVER THERE HAD GOTTEN SERIOUS, IT WOULDA GONE BETTER, BUT...
HAW HAW! GUESS YOU SHOULDN'T HAVE GOTTEN OVERCONFIDENT IN YOUR POWER AND SPREAD OUT LIKE THAT!
HUH? YOU WERE THE ONE WHO KEPT DRAGGING YOUR FEET, MUSCLES-FOR-BRAINS.

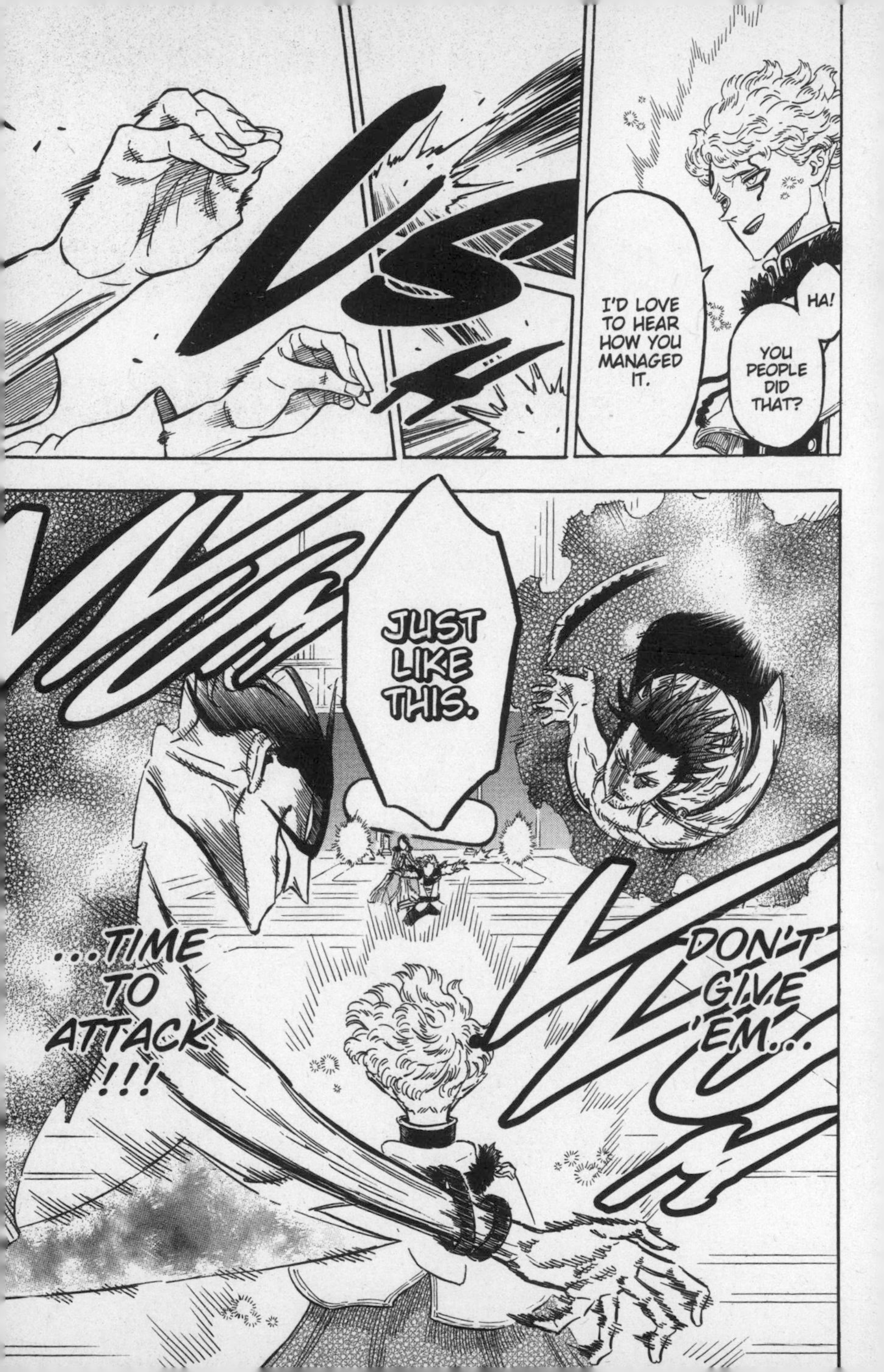
HA!
YOU PEOPLE DID THAT?
I'D LOVE TO HEAR HOW YOU MANAGED IT.
JUST LIKE THIS.
DON'T GIVE 'EM...
...TIME TO ATTACK!!!

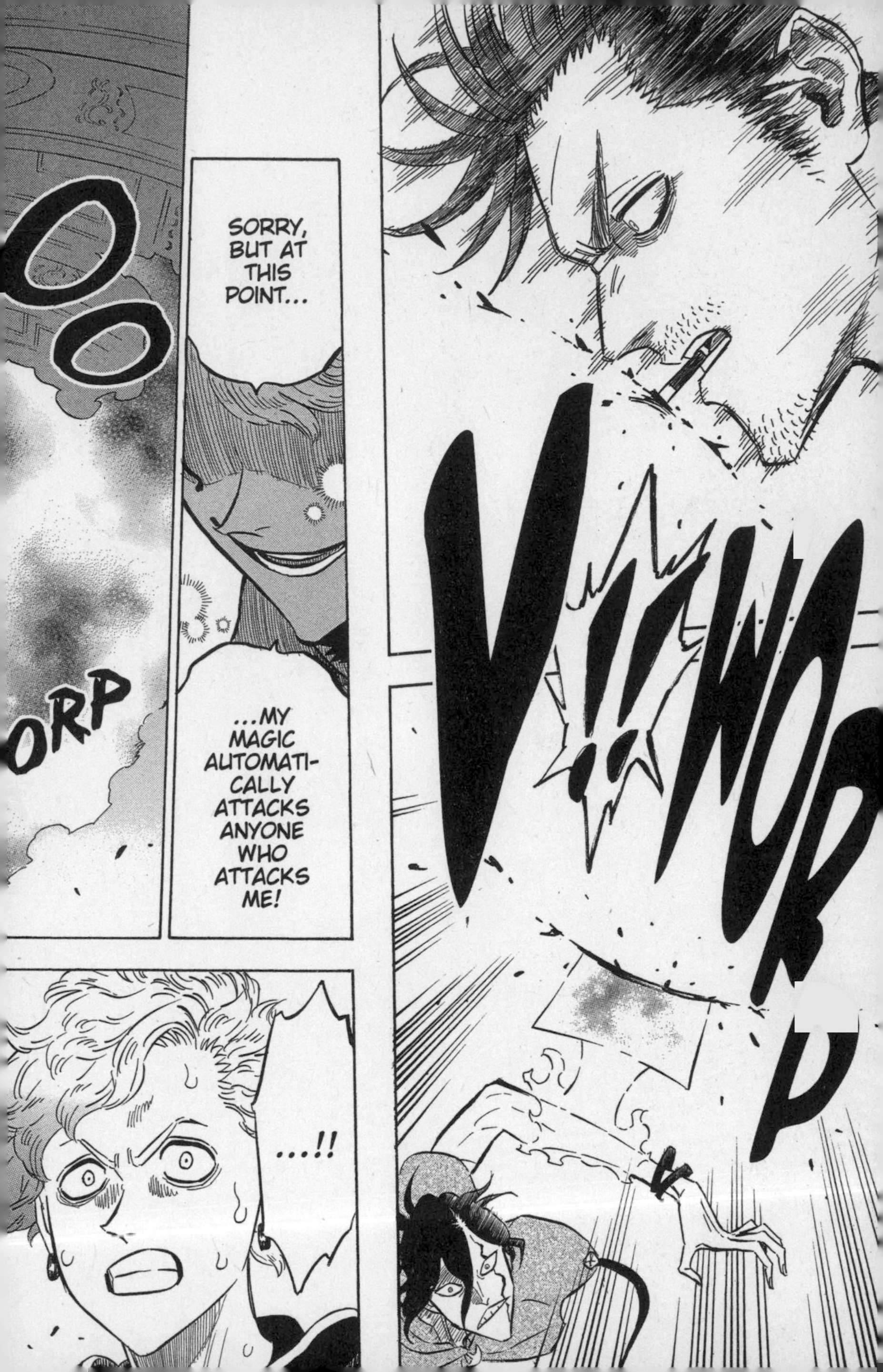
SORRY, BUT AT THIS POINT...
...MY MAGIC AUTOMATICALLY ATTACKS ANYONE WHO ATTACKS ME!
OO
ORP
...!!

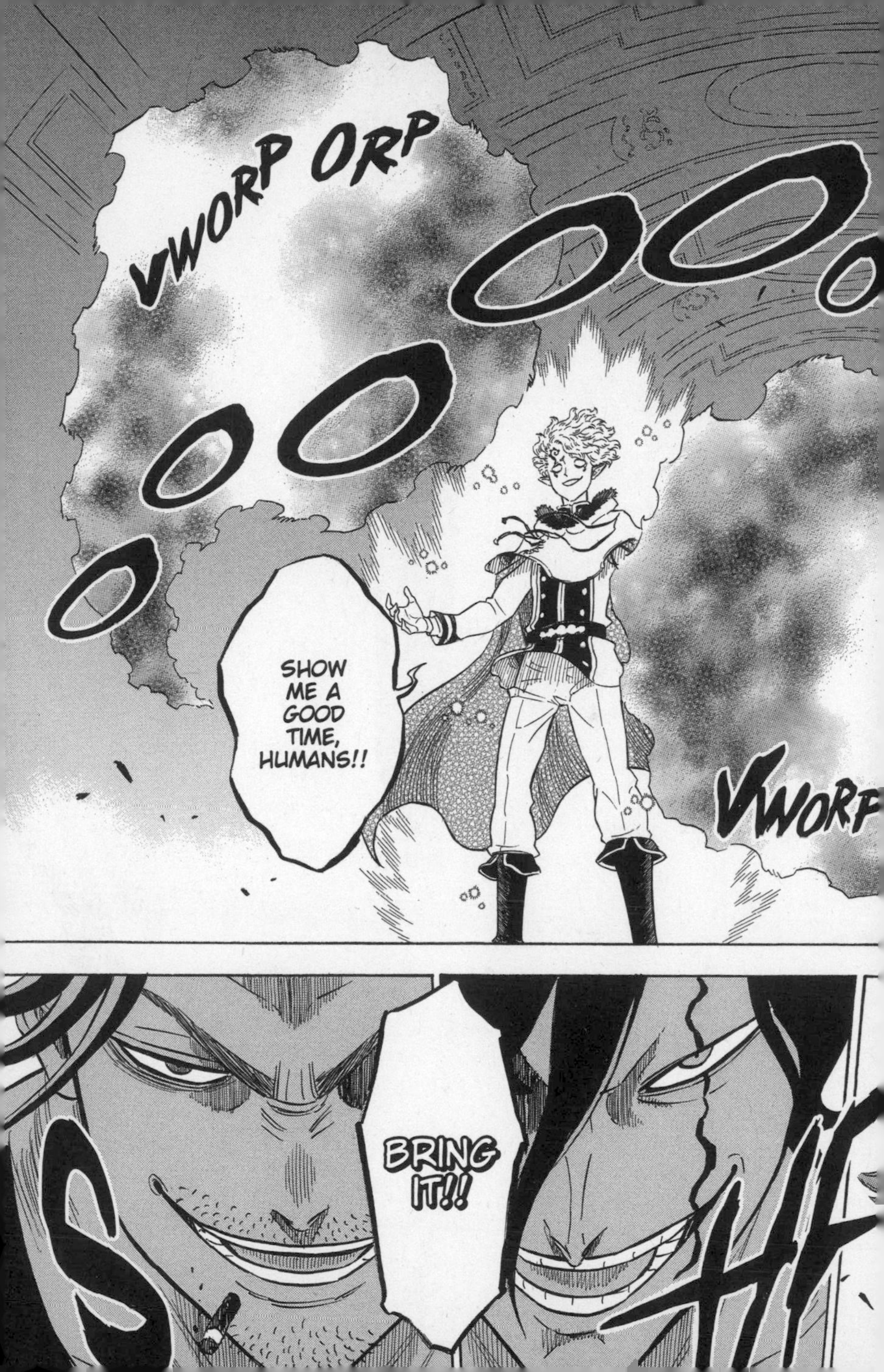

VWORP ORP
SHOW ME A GOOD TIME, HUMANS!!
VWORP
BRING IT!!

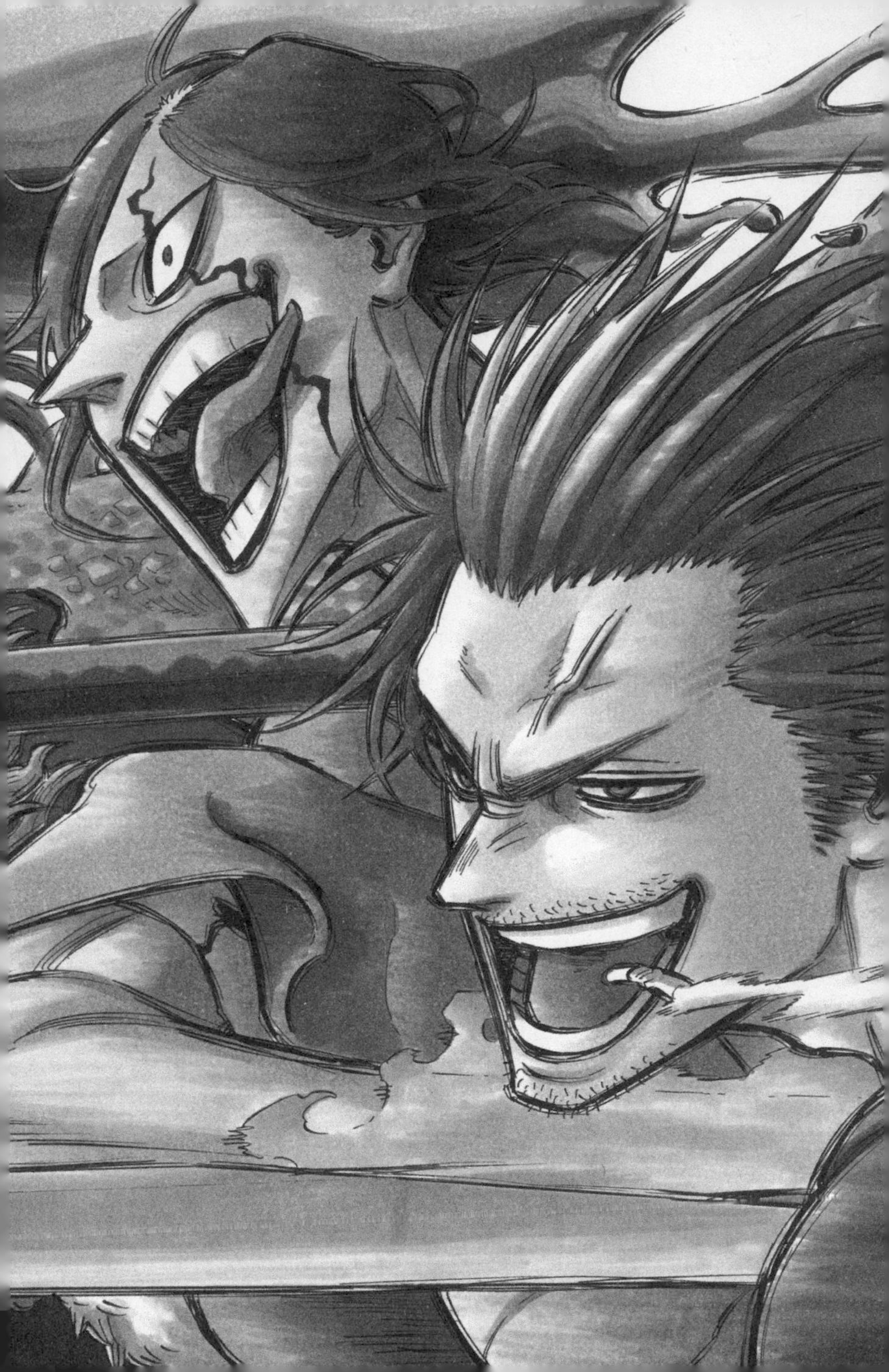

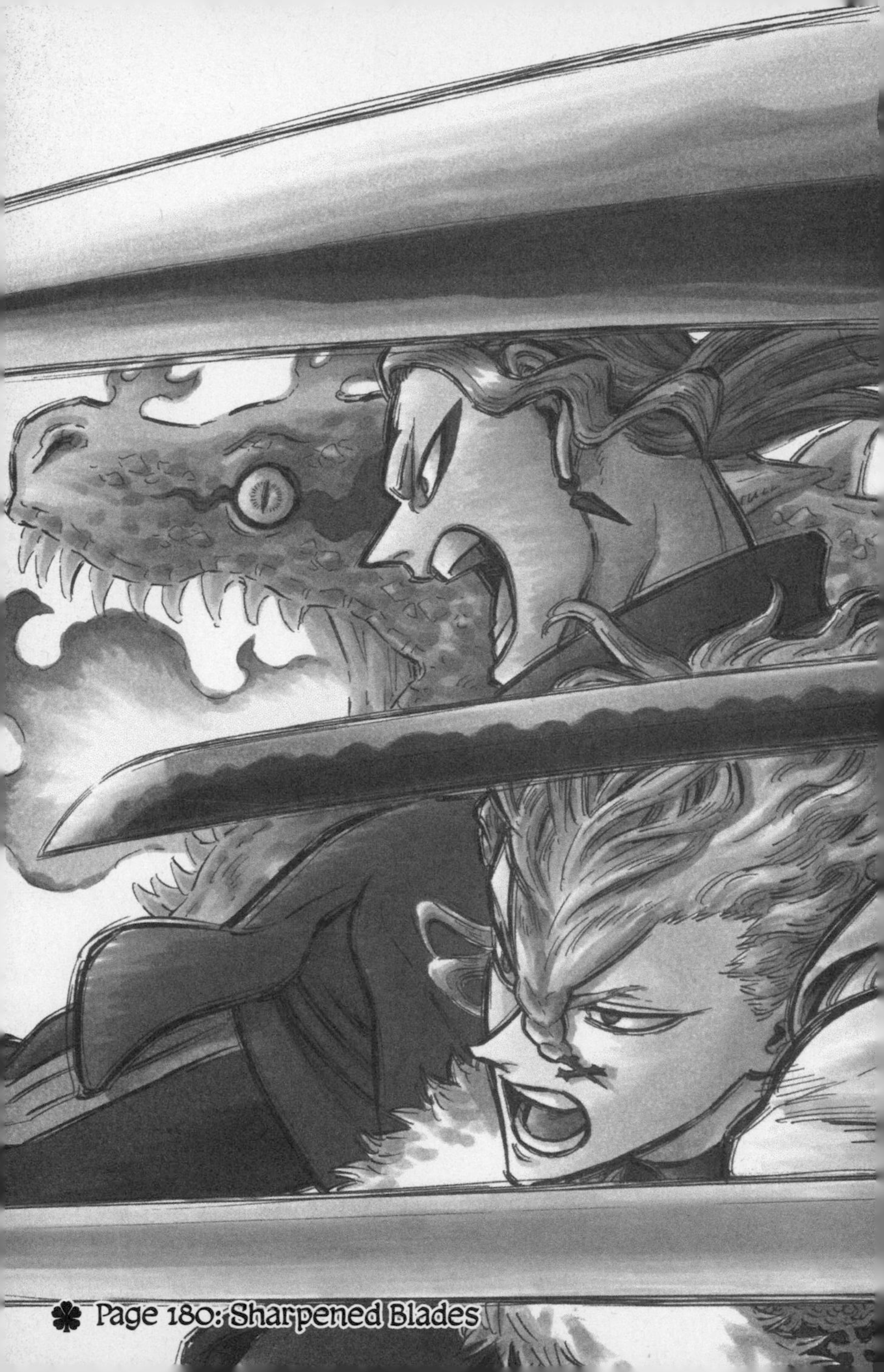
Page 180: Sharpened Blades

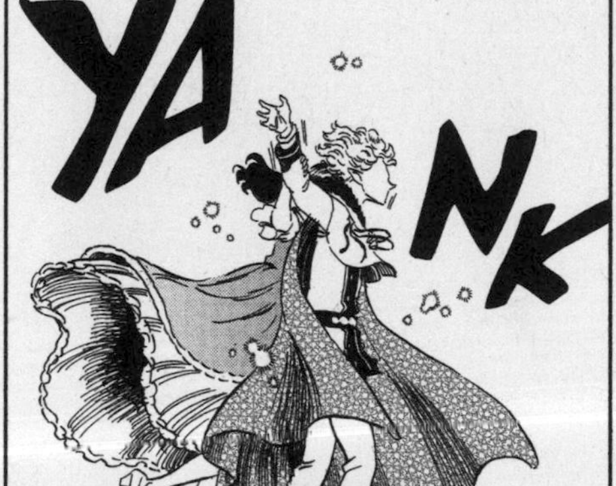
YANK

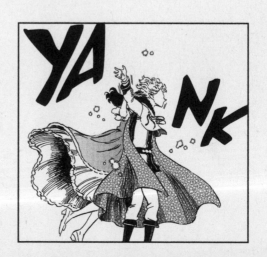

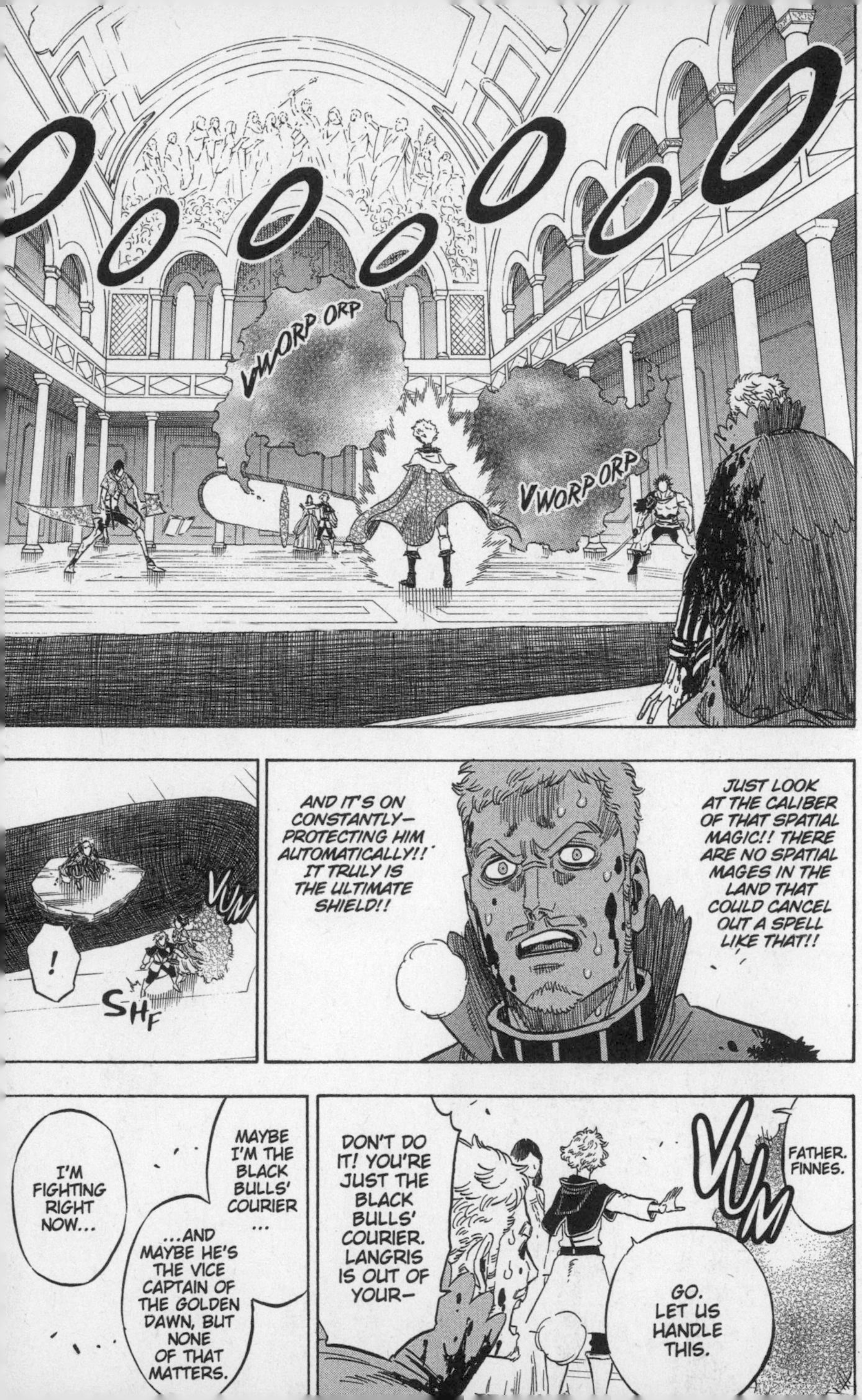
VWORP ORP
VWORP ORP
JUST LOOK AT THE CALIBER OF THAT SPATIAL MAGIC!! THERE ARE NO SPATIAL MAGES IN THE LAND THAT COULD CANCEL OUT A SPELL LIKE THAT!!
AND IT'S ON CONSTANTLY— PROTECTING HIM AUTOMATICALLY!! IT TRULY IS THE ULTIMATE SHIELD!!
VUM
!
SHF
FATHER. FINNES.
GO. LET US HANDLE THIS.
VUM
DON'T DO IT! YOU'RE JUST THE BLACK BULLS' COURIER. LANGRIS IS OUT OF YOUR—
MAYBE I'M THE BLACK BULLS' COURIER...
...AND MAYBE HE'S THE VICE CAPTAIN OF THE GOLDEN DAWN, BUT NONE OF THAT MATTERS.
I'M FIGHTING RIGHT NOW...

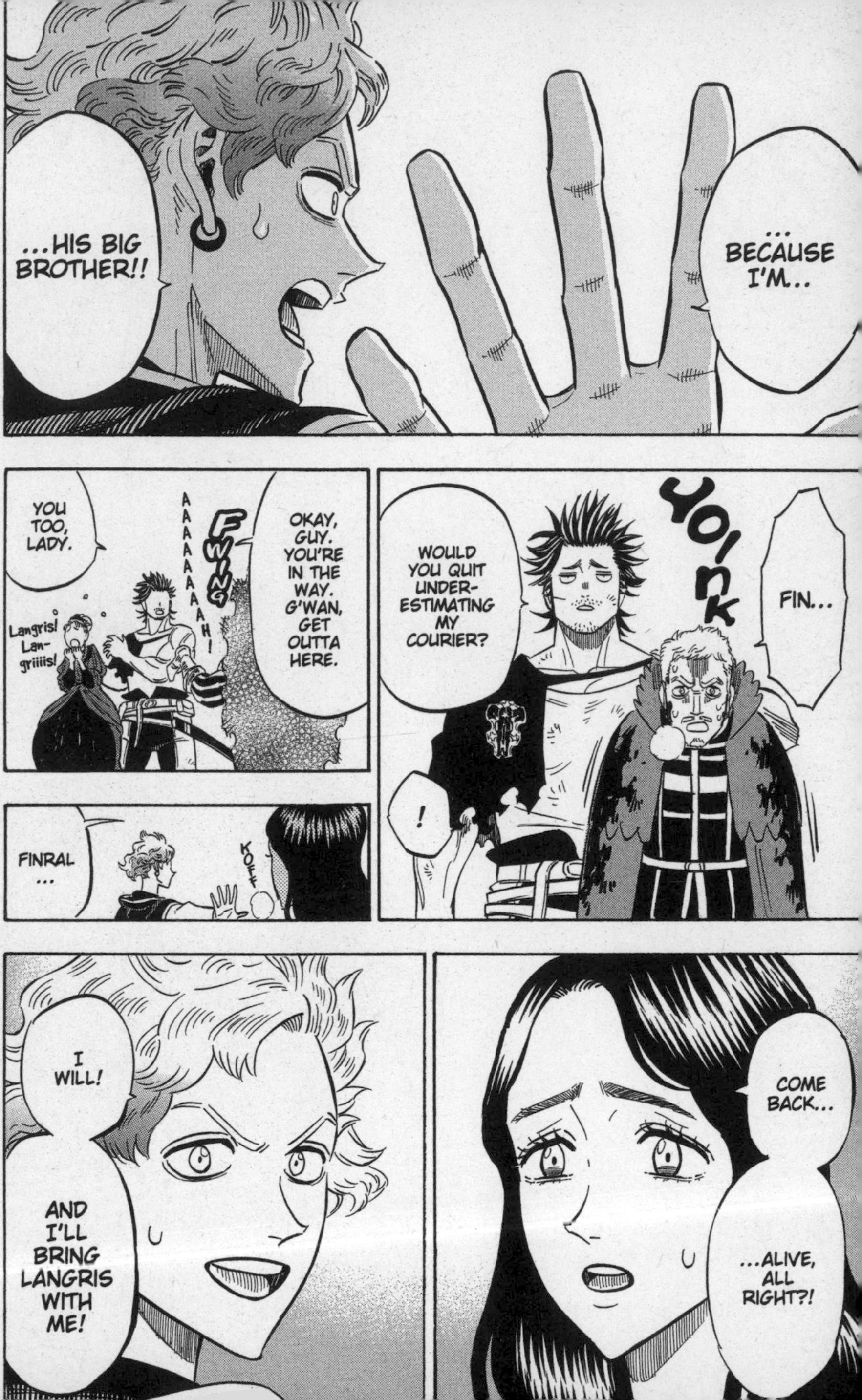
...BECAUSE I'M...
...HIS BIG BROTHER!!
FIN...
YOINK
WOULD YOU QUIT UNDER-ESTIMATING MY COURIER?
!
OKAY, GUY. YOU'RE IN THE WAY. G'WAN, GET OUTTA HERE.
FWING
AAAAAAAAAH!
YOU TOO, LADY.
Langris! Langriiiis!
KOFF
FINRAL...
COME BACK...
...ALIVE, ALL RIGHT?!
I WILL!
AND I'LL BRING LANGRIS WITH ME!

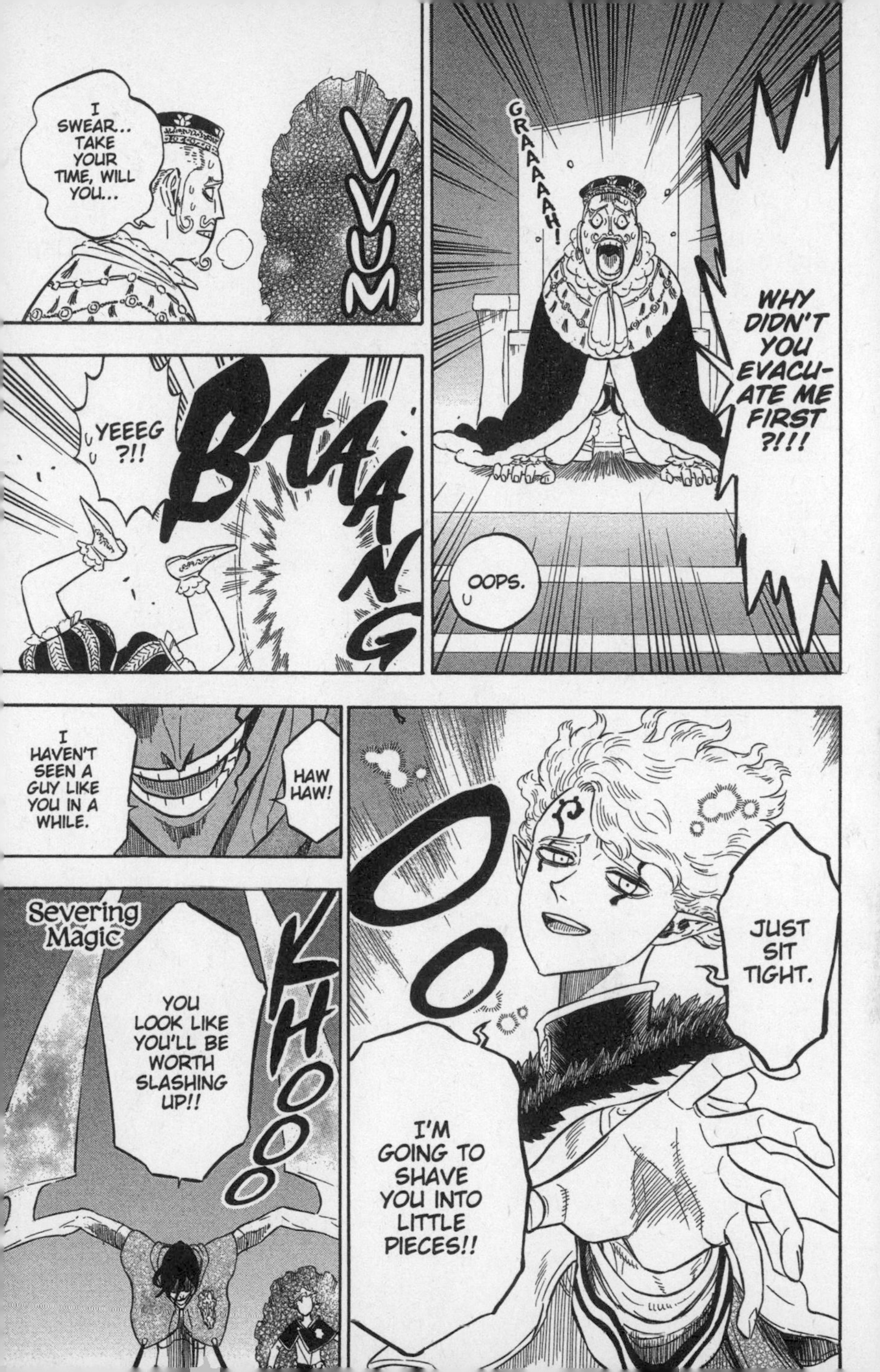
GRAAAAAH!
WHY DIDN'T YOU EVACUATE ME FIRST ?!!!
OOPS.
I SWEAR... TAKE YOUR TIME, WILL YOU...
VVVUM
YEEEG ?!!
BAAAANG
JUST SIT TIGHT.
I'M GOING TO SHAVE YOU INTO LITTLE PIECES!!
I HAVEN'T SEEN A GUY LIKE YOU IN A WHILE.
HAW HAW!
Severing Magic
YOU LOOK LIKE YOU'LL BE WORTH SLASHING UP!!
KHOOOO

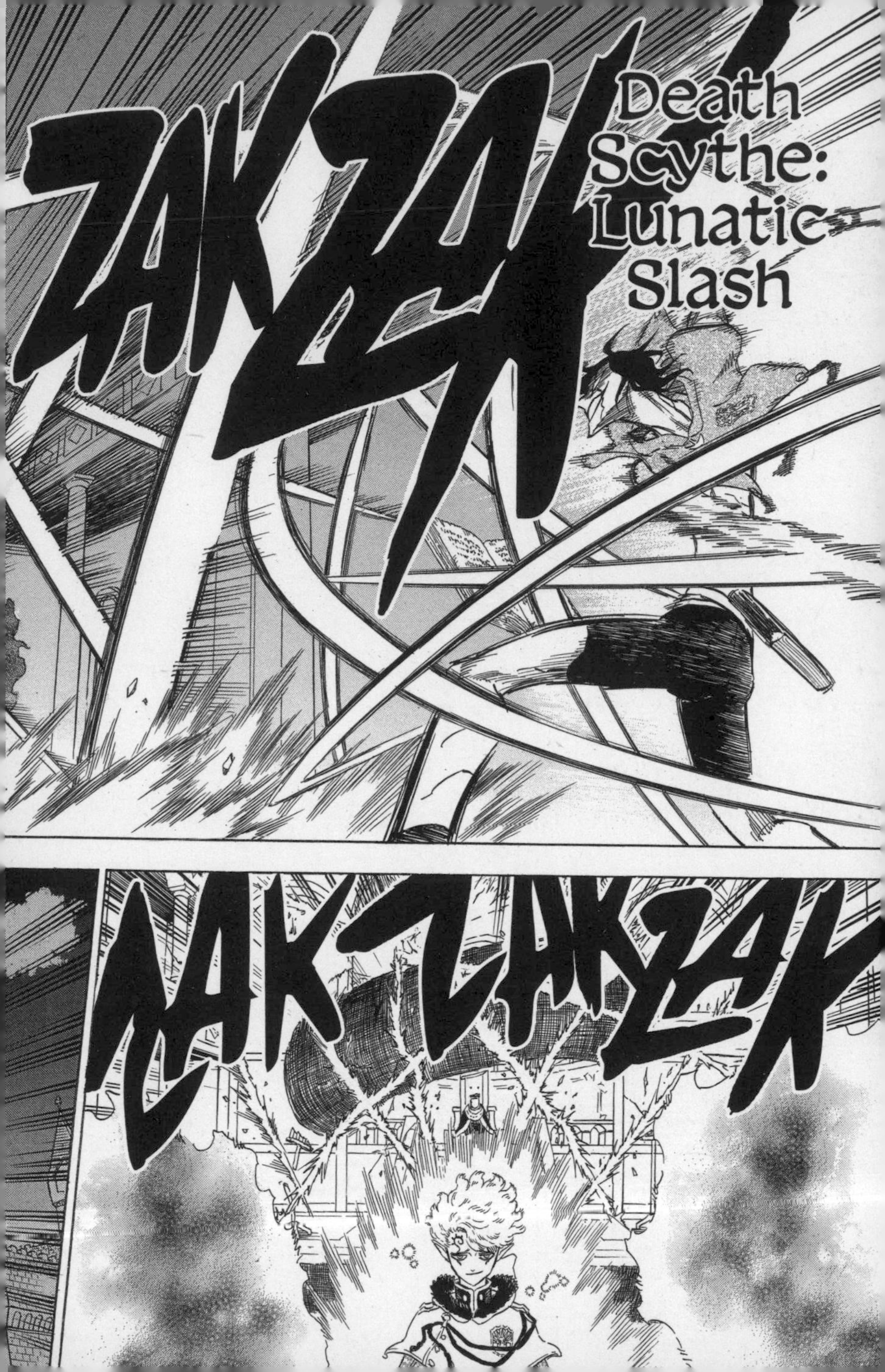
Death Scythe: Lunatic Slash
ZAKZAK
ZAKZAKZAK

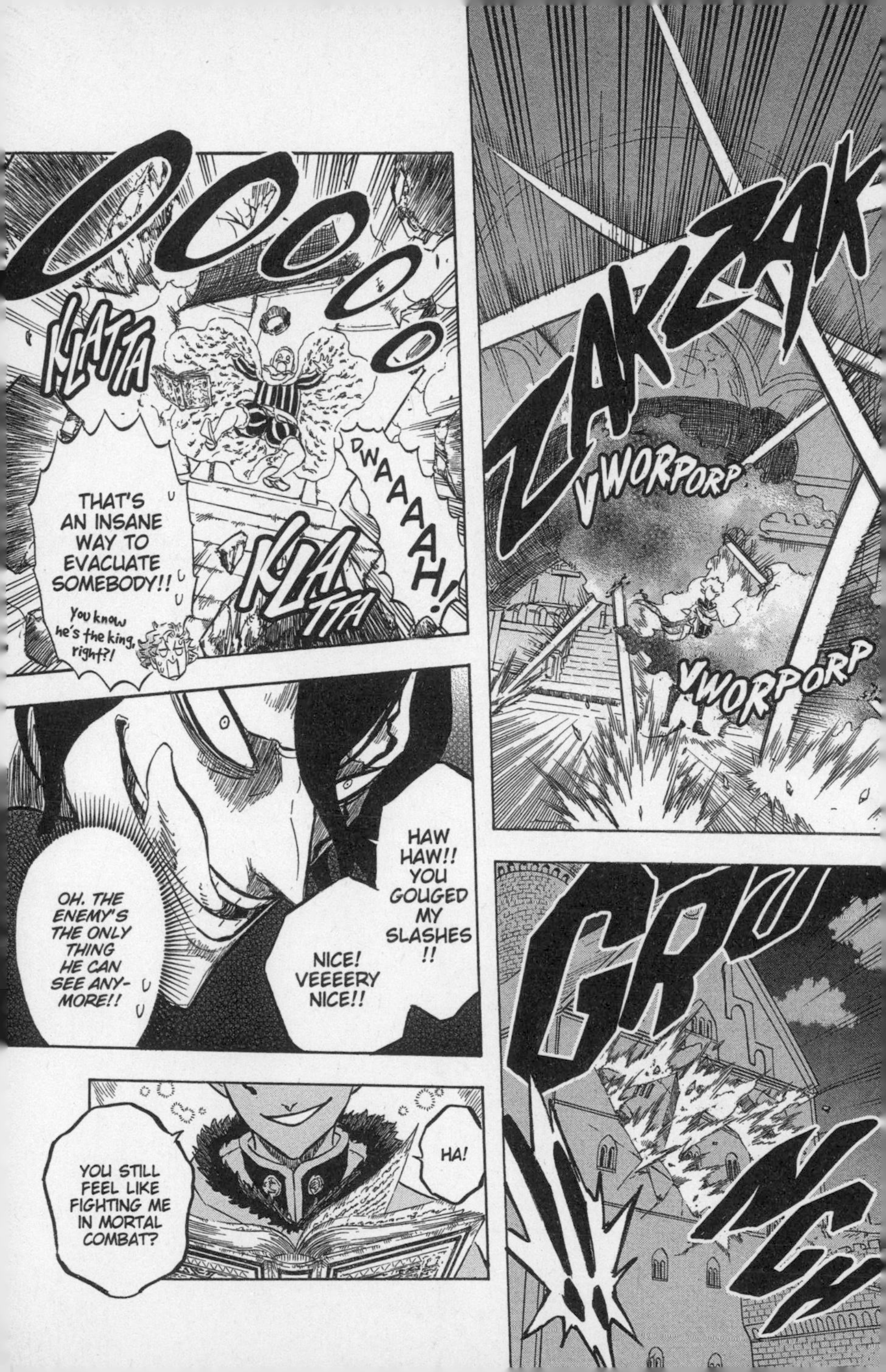
ZAKZAK
VWORPORP
VWORPORP
OOOOOO
KLATTA
DWAAAAAH!!
THAT'S AN INSANE WAY TO EVACUATE SOMEBODY!!
KLATTA
You know he's the king, right?!
HAW HAW!! YOU GOUGED MY SLASHES!!
NICE! VEEEERY NICE!!
OH. THE ENEMY'S THE ONLY THING HE CAN SEE ANYMORE!!
HA!
YOU STILL FEEL LIKE FIGHTING ME IN MORTAL COMBAT?

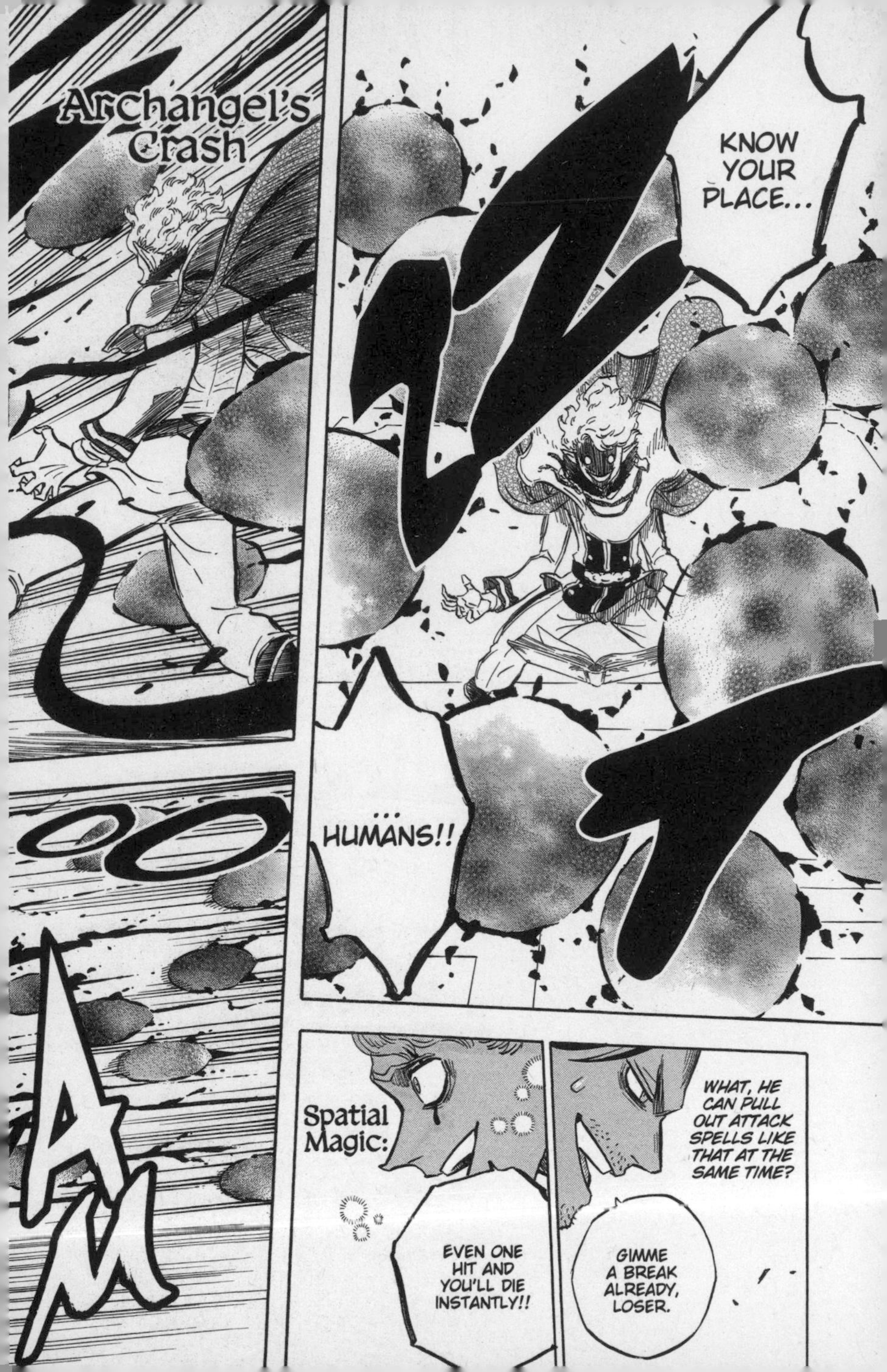
KNOW YOUR PLACE...
...HUMANS!!
WHAT, HE CAN PULL OUT ATTACK SPELLS LIKE THAT AT THE SAME TIME?
GIMME A BREAK ALREADY, LOSER.
Spatial Magic:
EVEN ONE HIT AND YOU'LL DIE INSTANTLY!!
Archangel's Crash

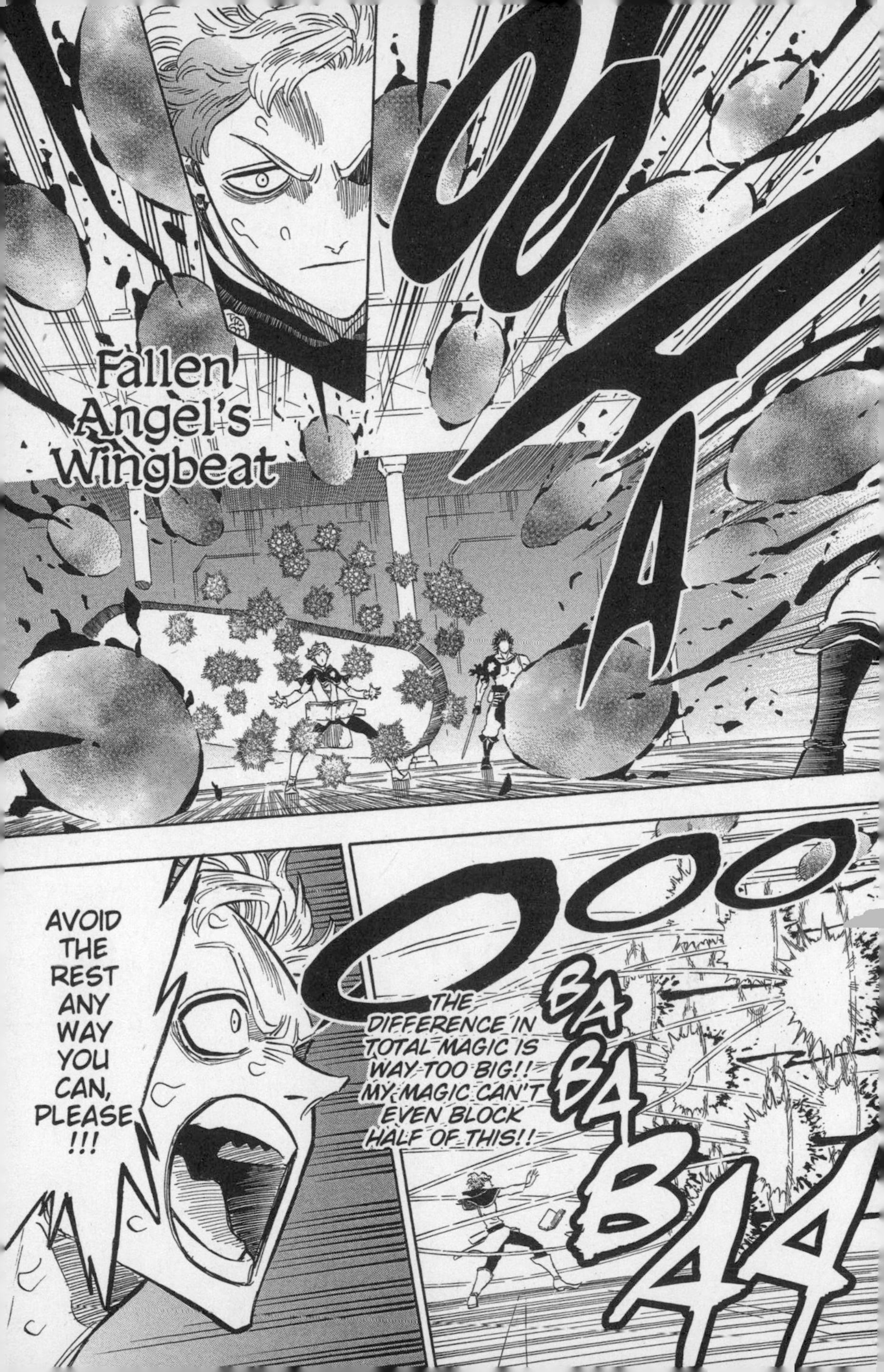
Fallen Angel's Wingbeat
BA BA BAA
THE DIFFERENCE IN TOTAL MAGIC IS WAY TOO BIG!! MY MAGIC CAN'T EVEN BLOCK HALF OF THIS!!
AVOID THE REST ANY WAY YOU CAN, PLEASE!!!

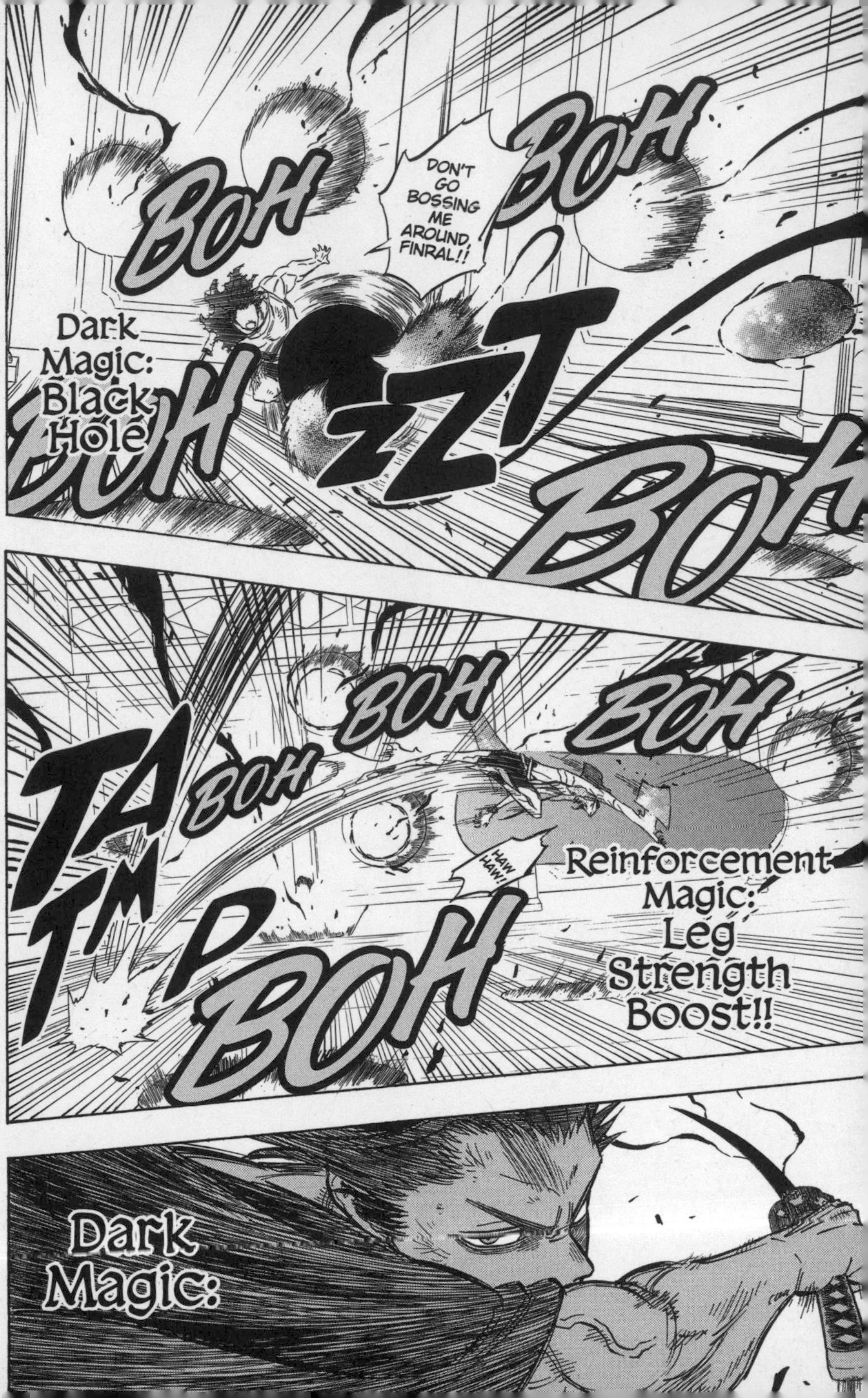
BOH
BOH
DON'T GO BOSSING ME AROUND, FINRAL!!
BOH
BOH
ZZT
Dark Magic: Black Hole
BOH
BOH
BOH
Reinforcement Magic: Leg Strength Boost!!
HAW HAW!
BOH
BOH
TAP
Dark Magic:

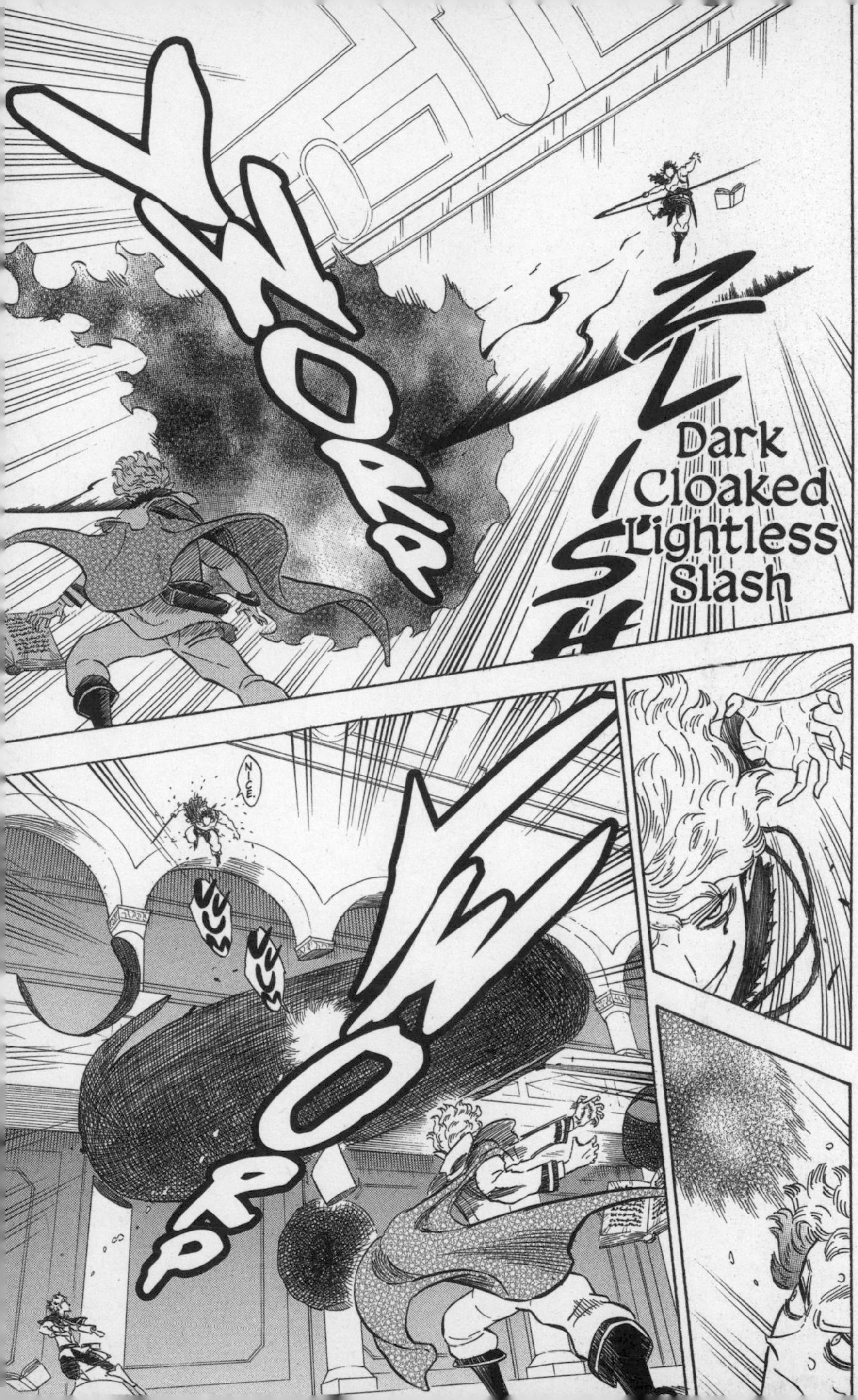
VWORR
Dark Cloaked Lightless Slash
NICE.
VUUM
VUUM

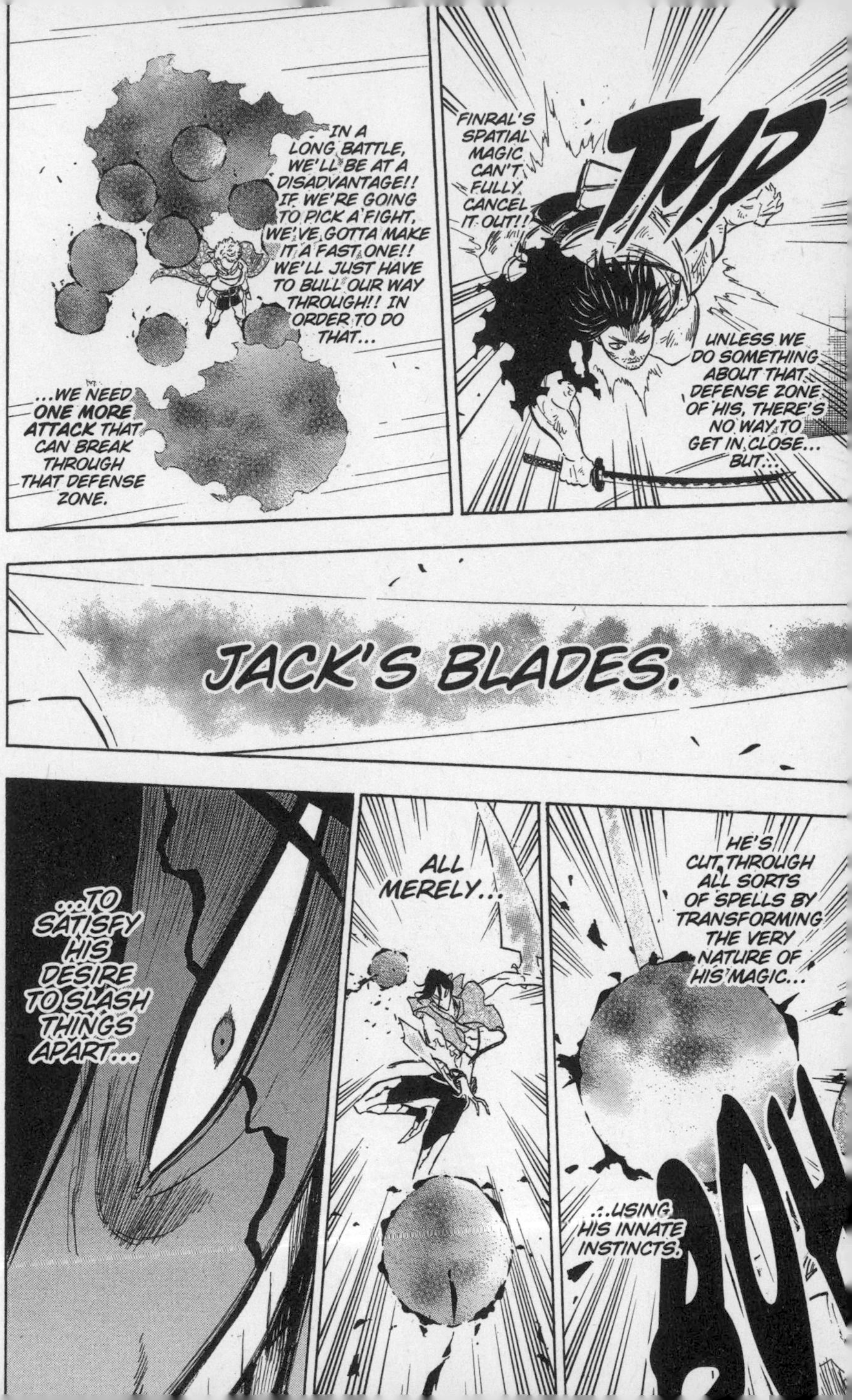
FINRAL'S SPATIAL MAGIC CAN'T FULLY CANCEL IT OUT!!
TMP
UNLESS WE DO SOMETHING ABOUT THAT DEFENSE ZONE OF HIS, THERE'S NO WAY TO GET IN CLOSE... BUT...
IN A LONG BATTLE, WE'LL BE AT A DISADVANTAGE!! IF WE'RE GOING TO PICK A FIGHT, WE'VE GOTTA MAKE IT A FAST ONE!! WE'LL JUST HAVE TO BULL OUR WAY THROUGH!! IN ORDER TO DO THAT...
...WE NEED ONE MORE ATTACK THAT CAN BREAK THROUGH THAT DEFENSE ZONE.
JACK'S BLADES.
HE'S CUT THROUGH ALL SORTS OF SPELLS BY TRANSFORMING THE VERY NATURE OF HIS MAGIC...
...USING HIS INNATE INSTINCTS.
ALL MERELY...
...TO SATISFY HIS DESIRE TO SLASH THINGS APART...

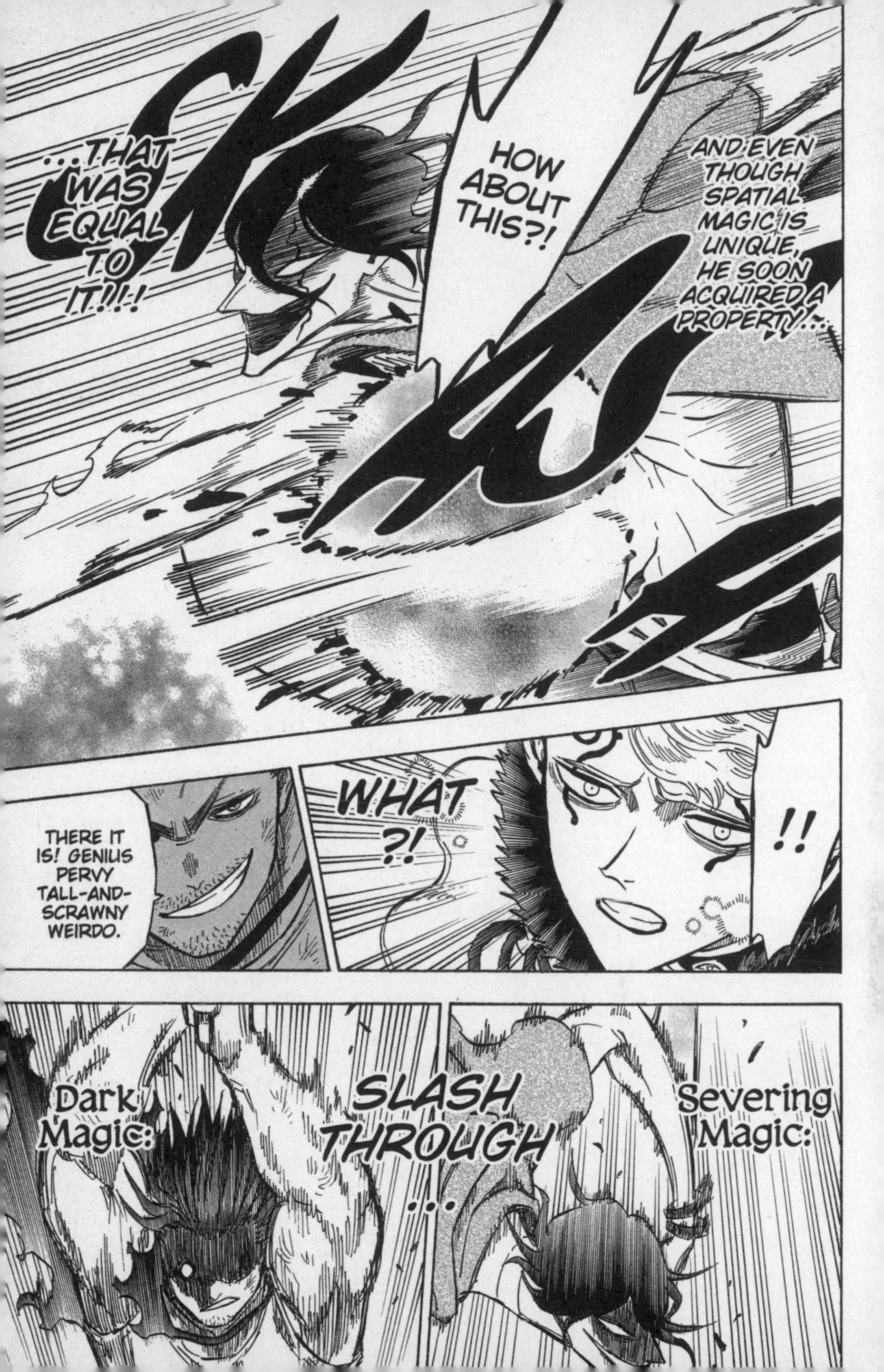
AND EVEN THOUGH SPATIAL MAGIC IS UNIQUE, HE SOON ACQUIRED A PROPERTY...
HOW ABOUT THIS?!
...THAT WAS EQUAL TO IT!!!!
!!
WHAT ?!
THERE IT IS! GENIUS PERVY TALL-AND-SCRAWNY WEIRDO.
Severing Magic:
SLASH THROUGH...
Dark Magic:

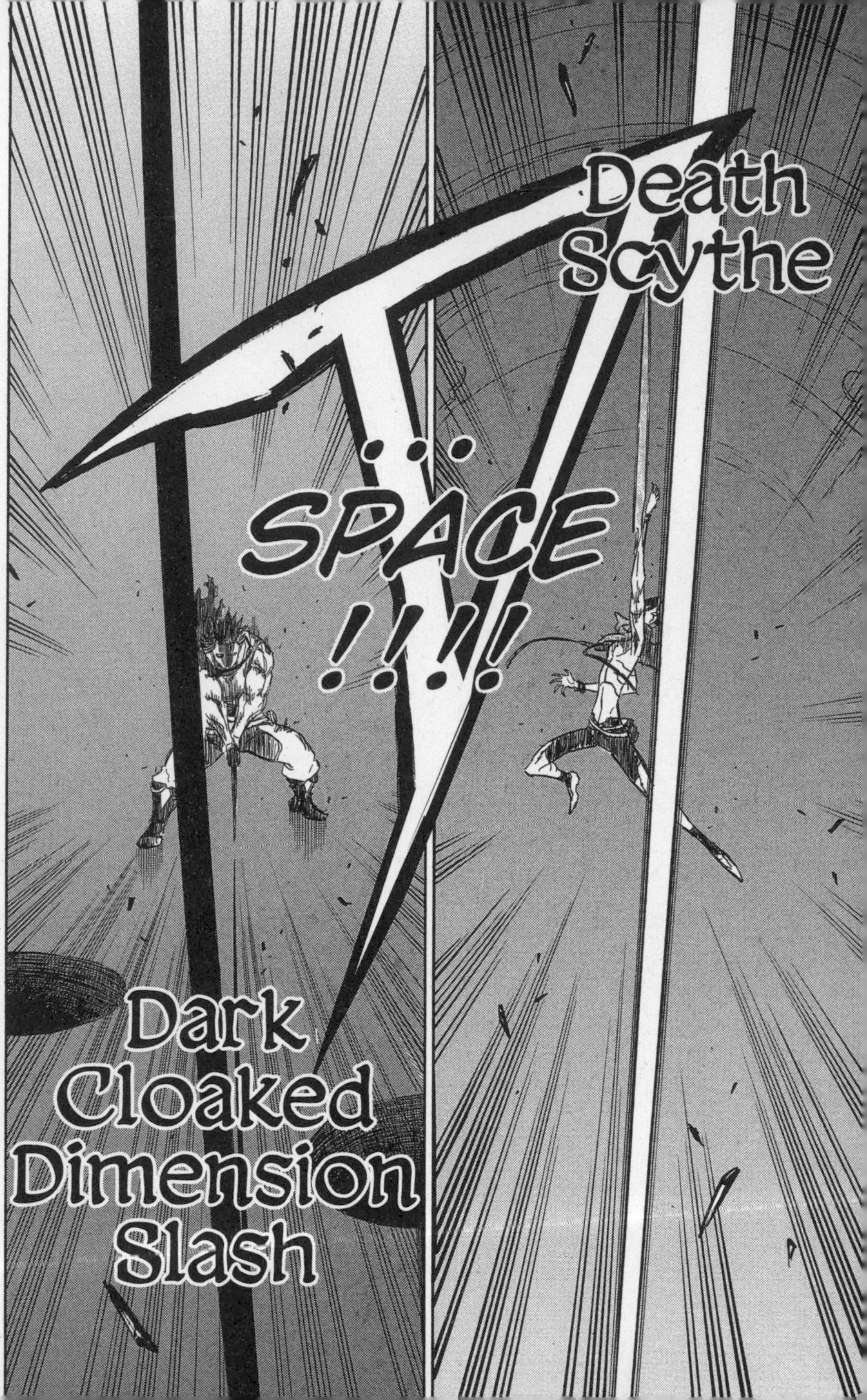
Death Scythe
...SPACE!!!!
Dark Cloaked Dimension Slash

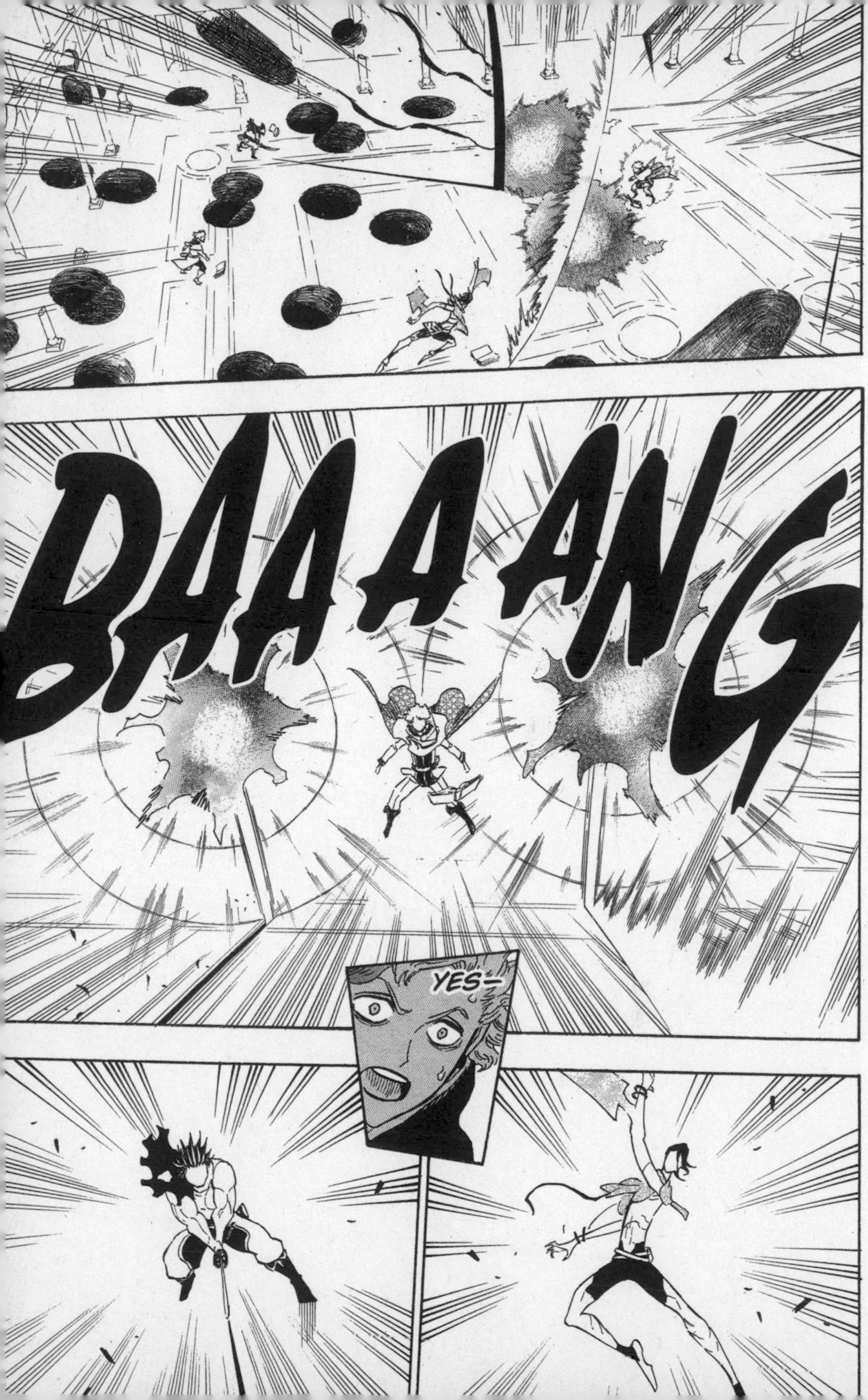
DAAAANG
YES—

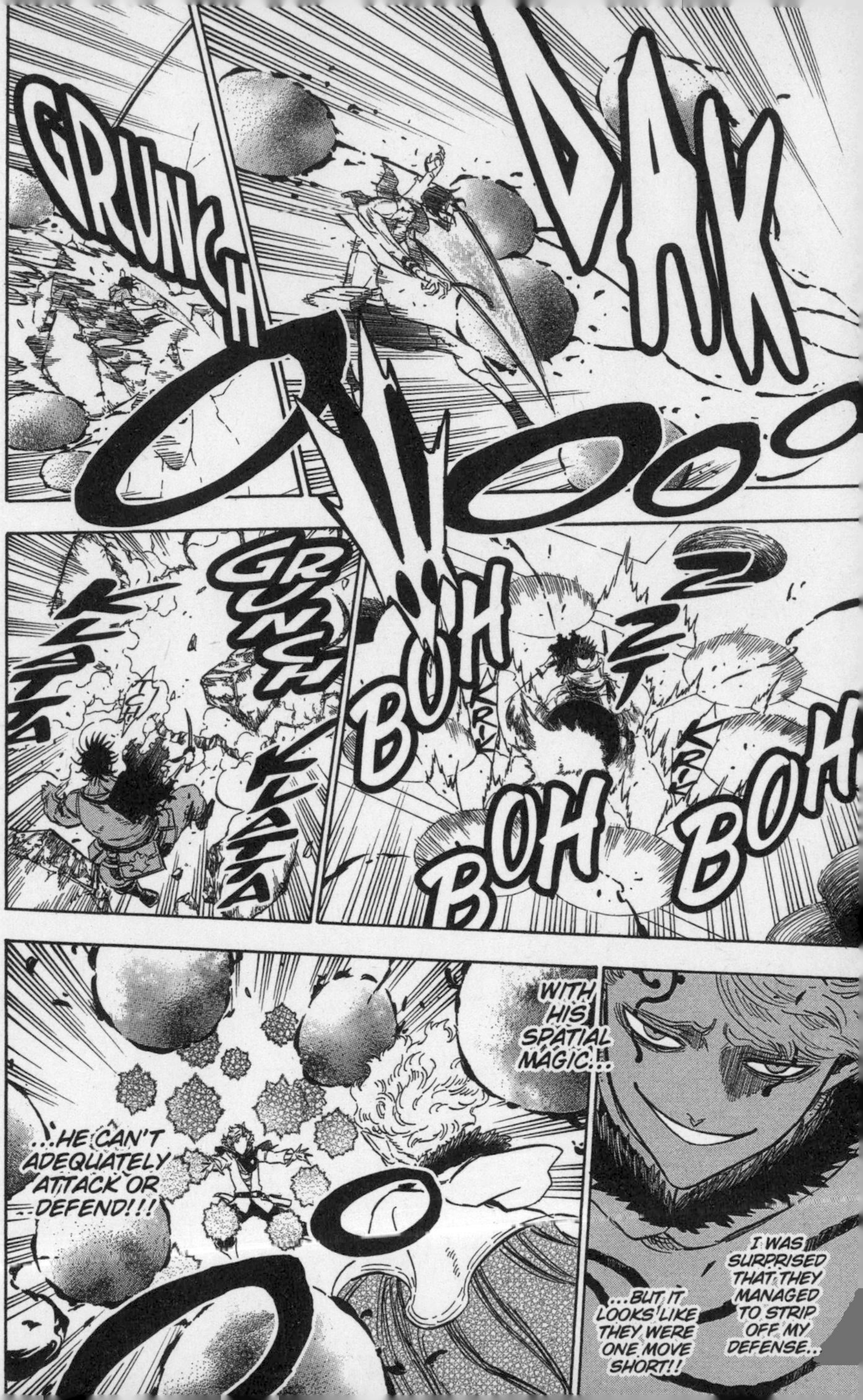
DAK
GRUNCH
BOH
BOH
BOH
KRIK
KRIK
GRUNCH
I WAS SURPRISED THAT THEY MANAGED TO STRIP OFF MY DEFENSE...
...BUT IT LOOKS LIKE THEY WERE ONE MOVE SHORT!!
WITH HIS SPATIAL MAGIC...
...HE CAN'T ADEQUATELY ATTACK OR DEFEND!!!

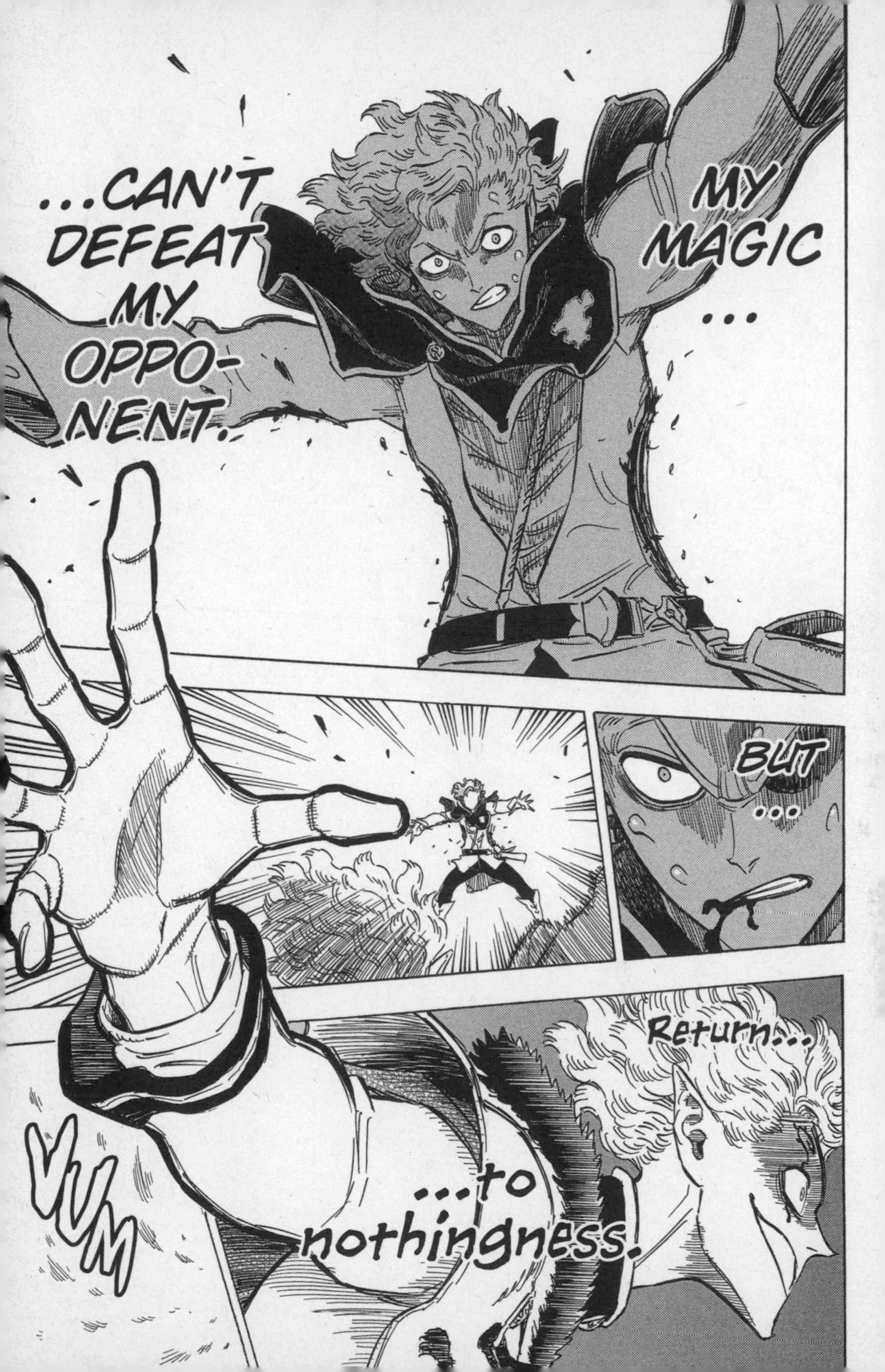
MY MAGIC...
...CAN'T DEFEAT MY OPPONENT.
BUT...
Return...
...to nothingness.
VUM

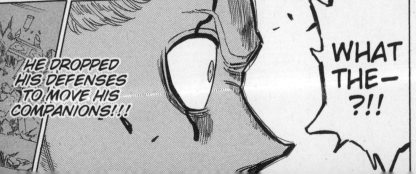
HE DROPPED HIS DEFENSES TO MOVE HIS COMPANIONS!!!

WHAT THE—?!!

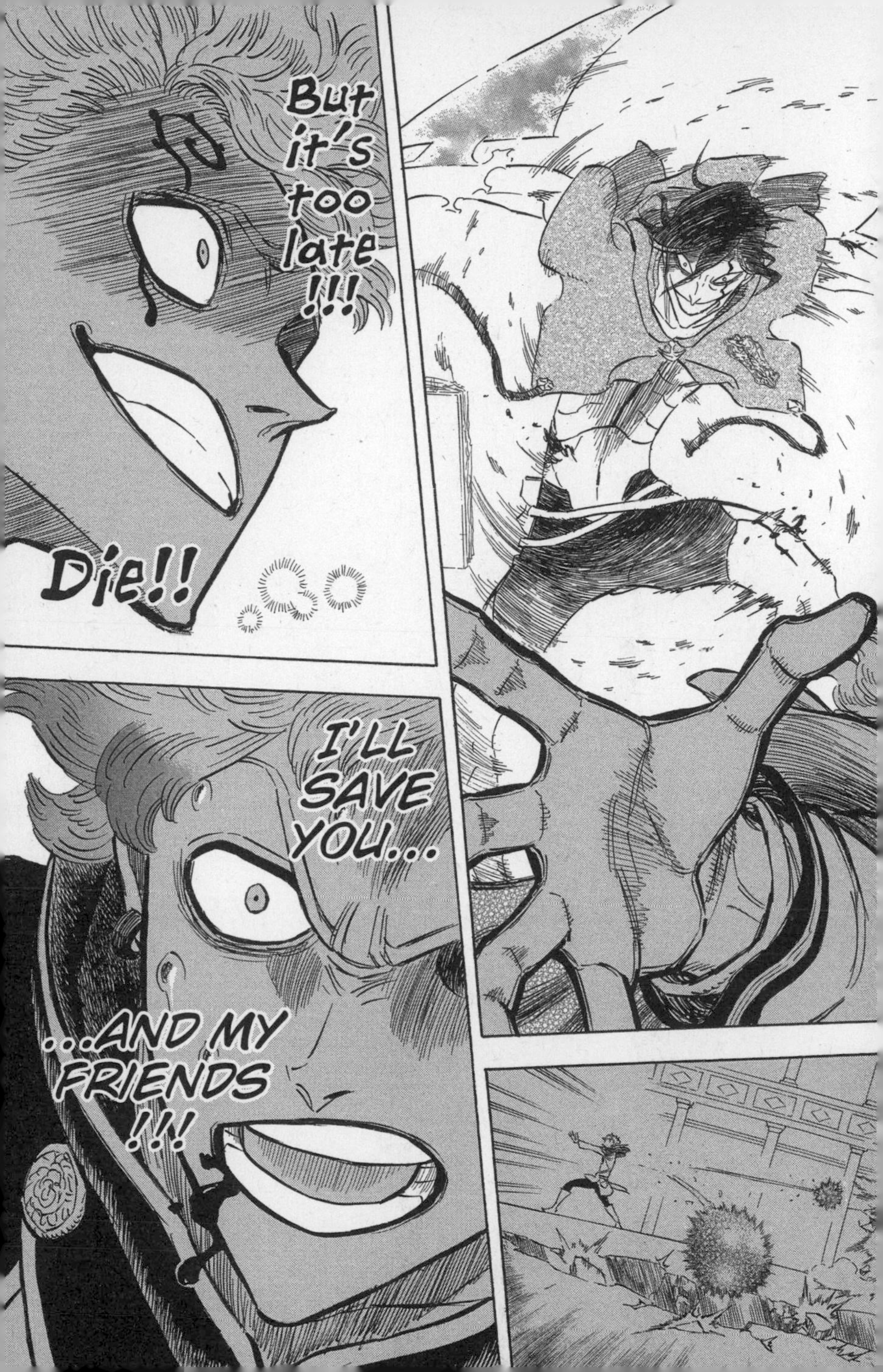
But it's too late!!!
Die!!
I'LL SAVE YOU...
...AND MY FRIENDS!!!

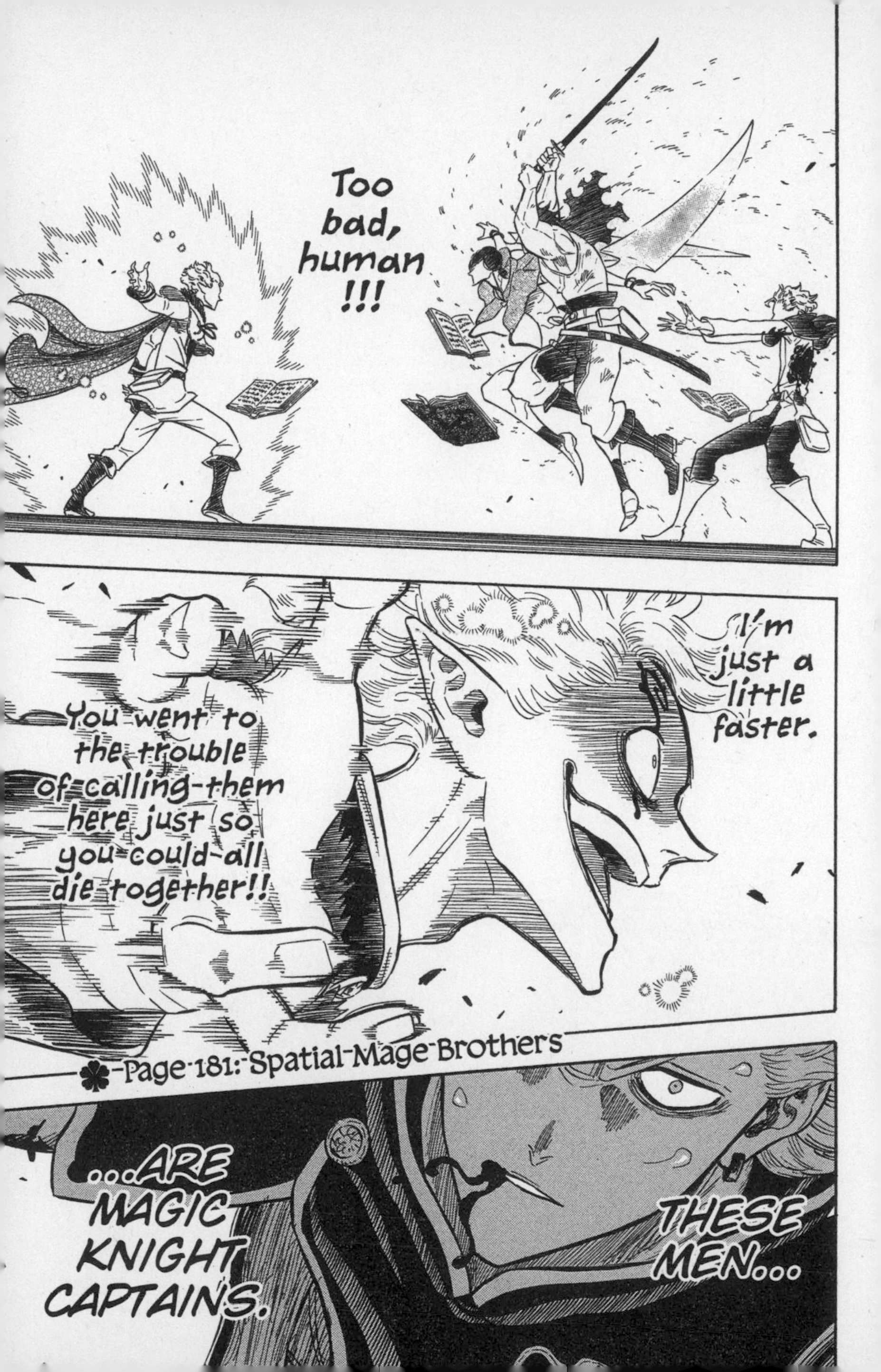
Too bad, human!!!
I'm just a little faster.
You went to the trouble of calling them here just so you could all die together!!
Page 181: Spatial Mage Brothers
THESE MEN...
...ARE MAGIC KNIGHT CAPTAINS.

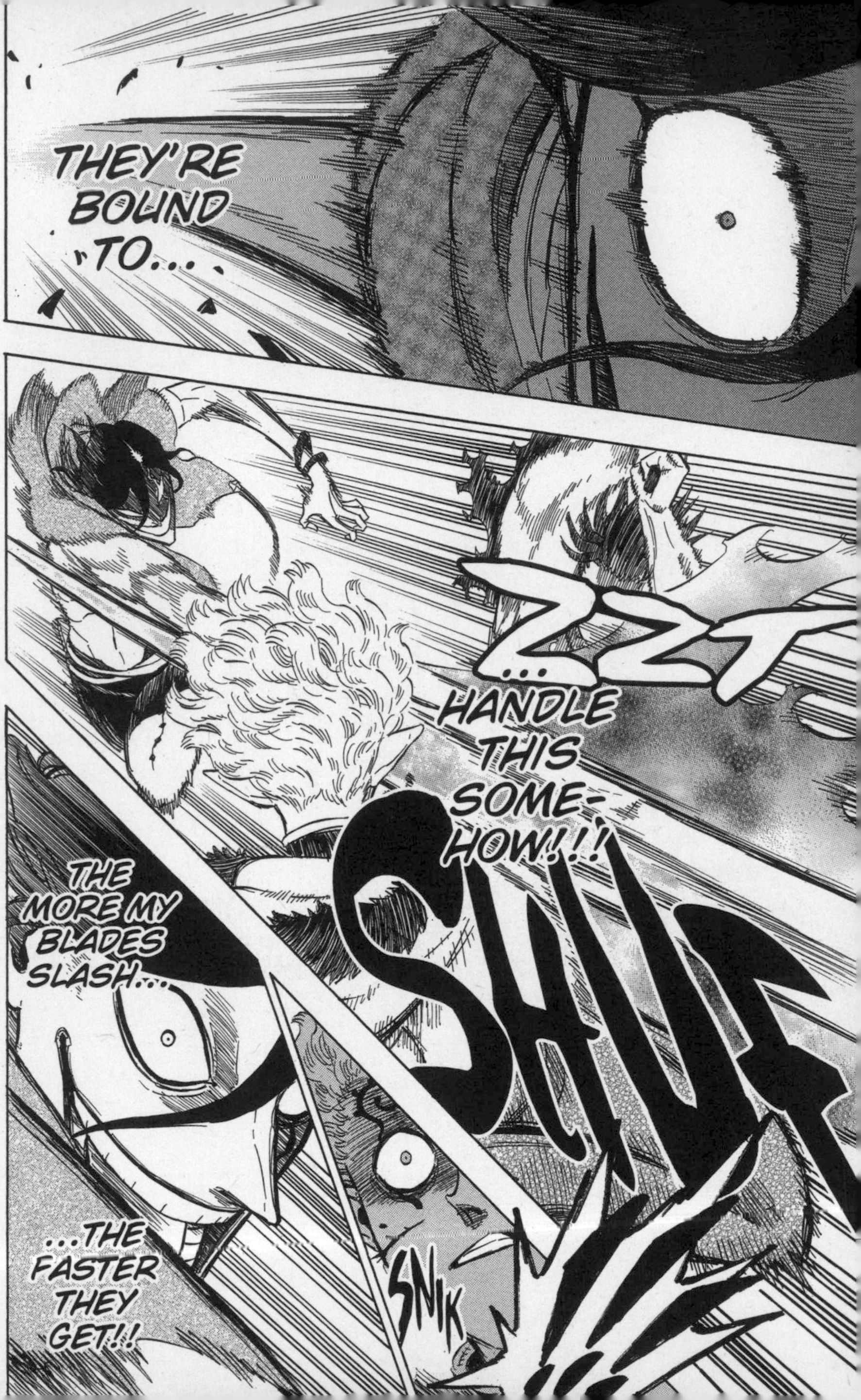
THEY'RE BOUND TO...
ZZZT
...HANDLE THIS SOME-HOW!!!
THE MORE MY BLADES SLASH...
SHUF
SNIK
...THE FASTER THEY GET!!

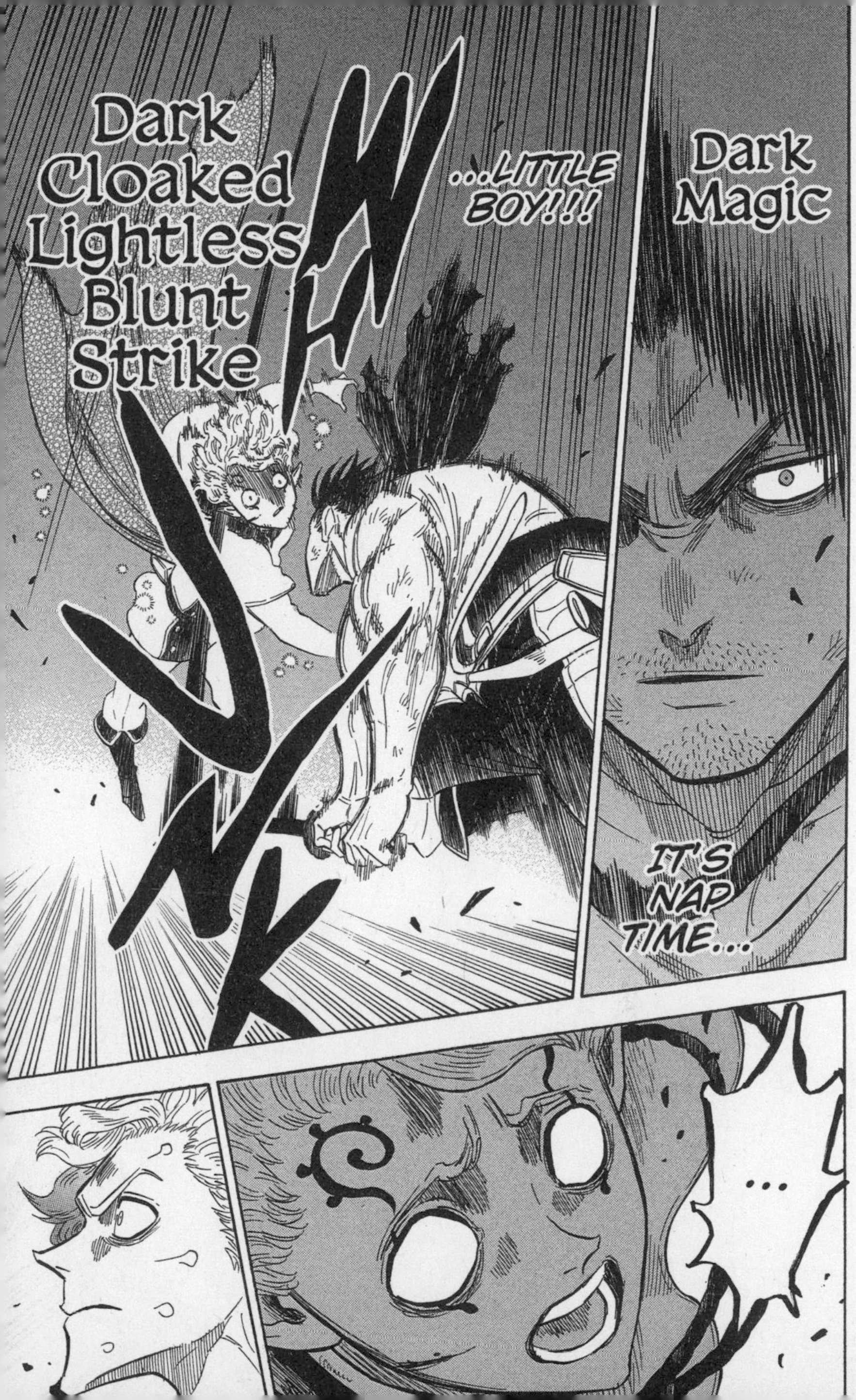
Dark Magic
IT'S NAP TIME...
...LITTLE BOY!!!
Dark Cloaked Lightless Blunt Strike
...

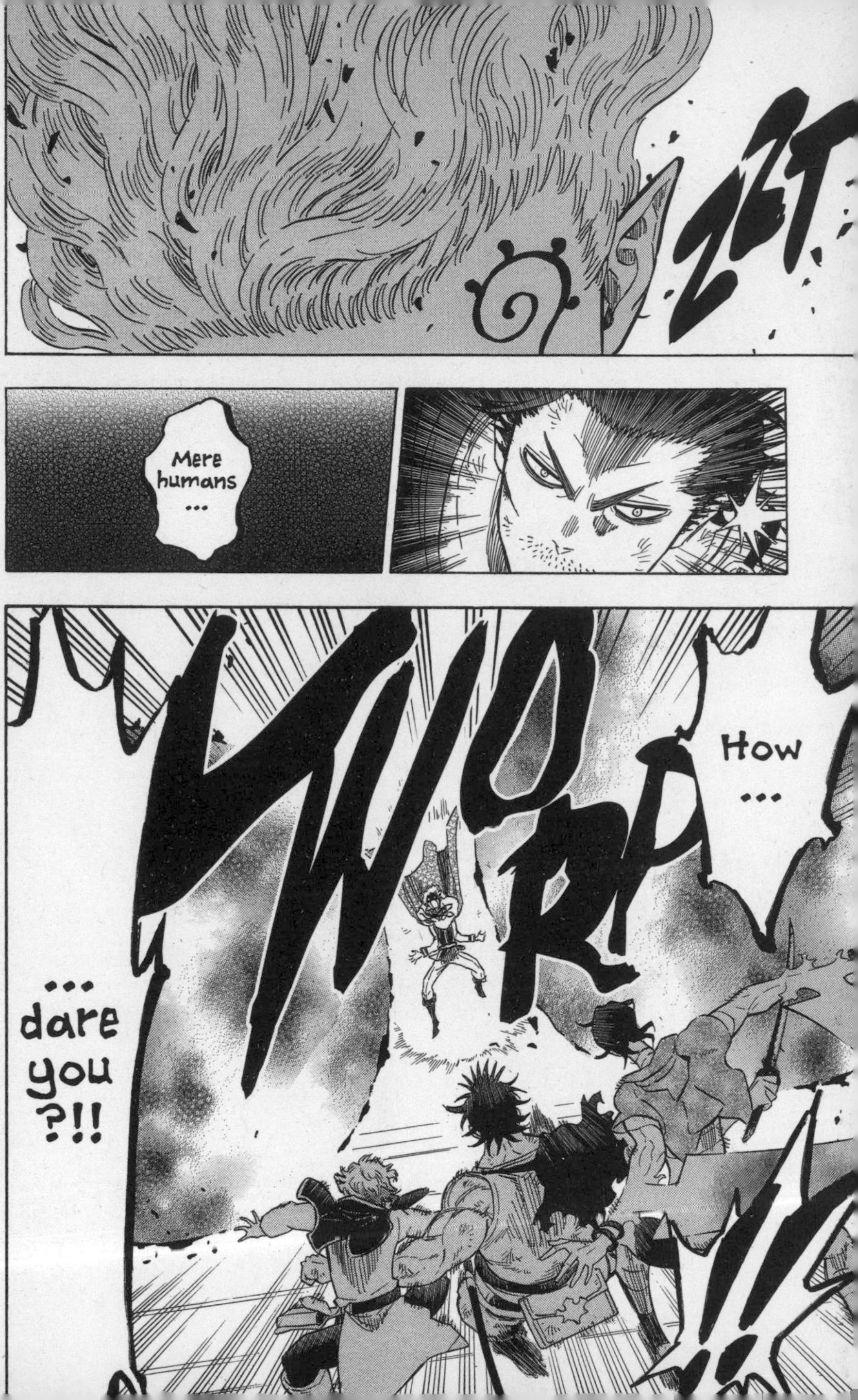
Mere humans ...
How ...
... dare you ?!!

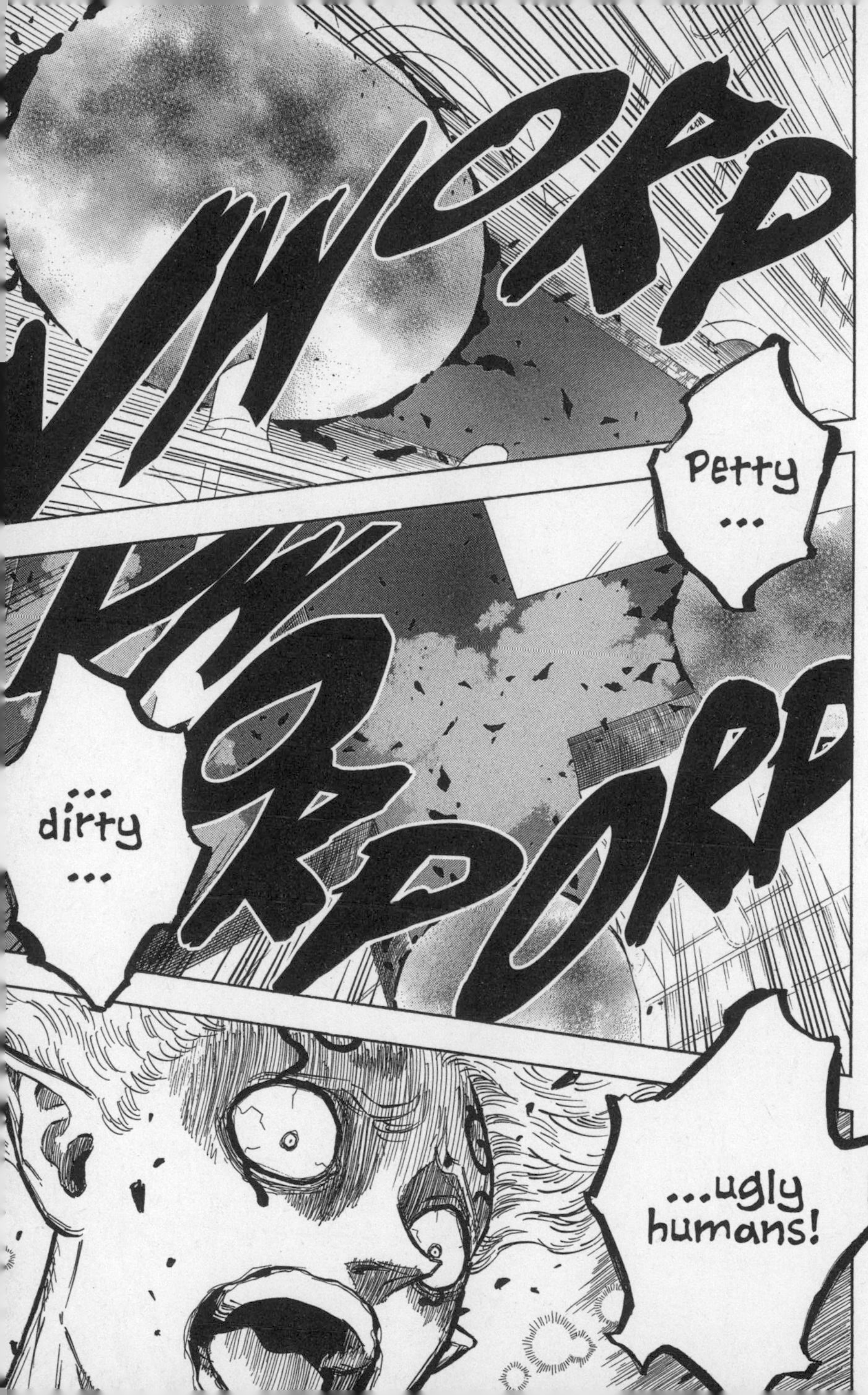
Petty ...
... dirty ...
...ugly humans!

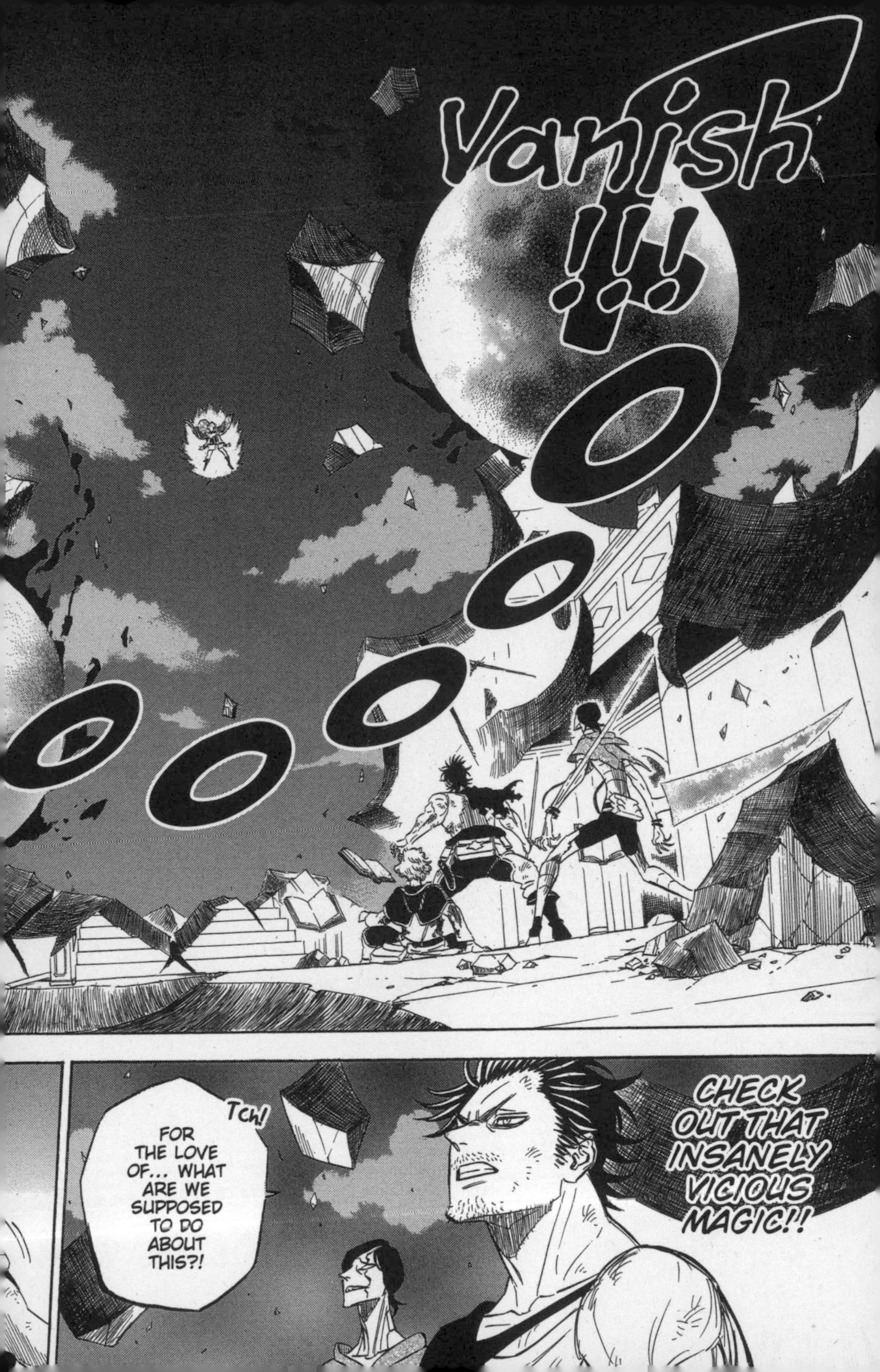
Vanish!!!
CHECK OUT THAT INSANELY VICIOUS MAGIC!!
Tch!
FOR THE LOVE OF... WHAT ARE WE SUPPOSED TO DO ABOUT THIS?!

...IT TOOK ME A WHILE. I'M SORRY.

I'M WEAK, SO...

LANGRIS!

SHF

LAN... GRIS...

WOBB

SHF

WOBB

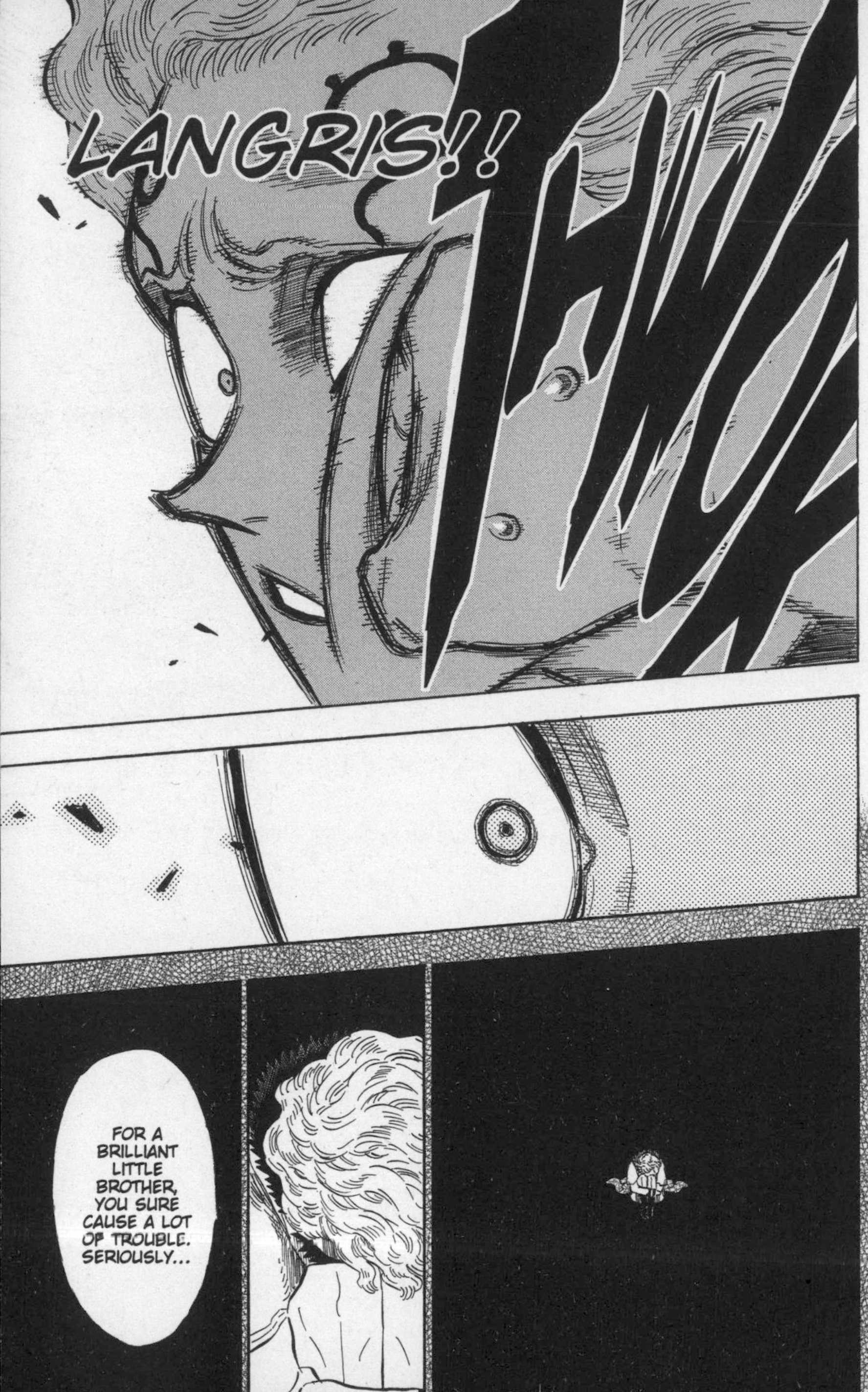
LANGRIS!!
FOR A BRILLIANT LITTLE BROTHER, YOU SURE CAUSE A LOT OF TROUBLE. SERIOUSLY...

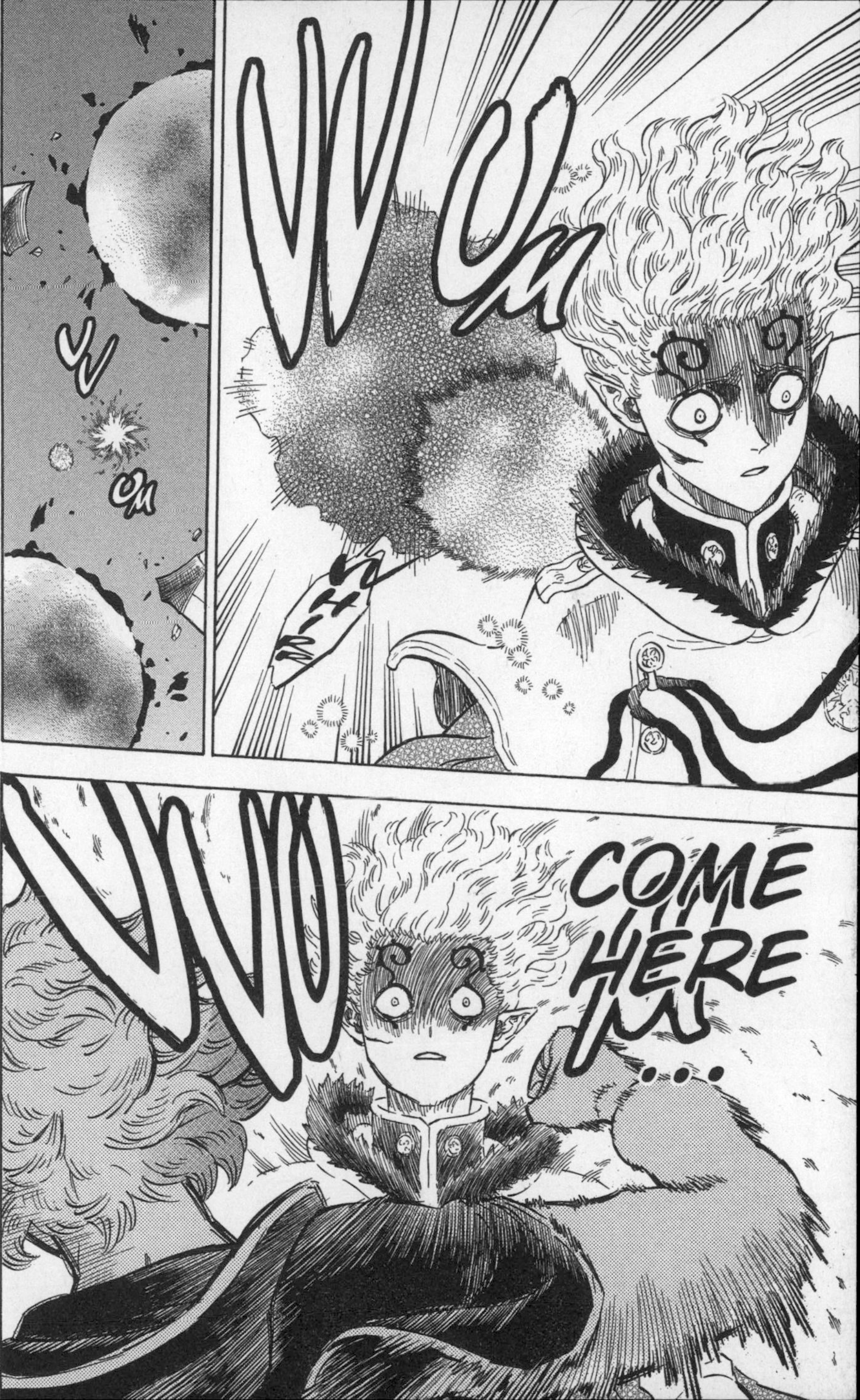
VVOM
WHIR
VVOM
VVOOM
COME HERE...

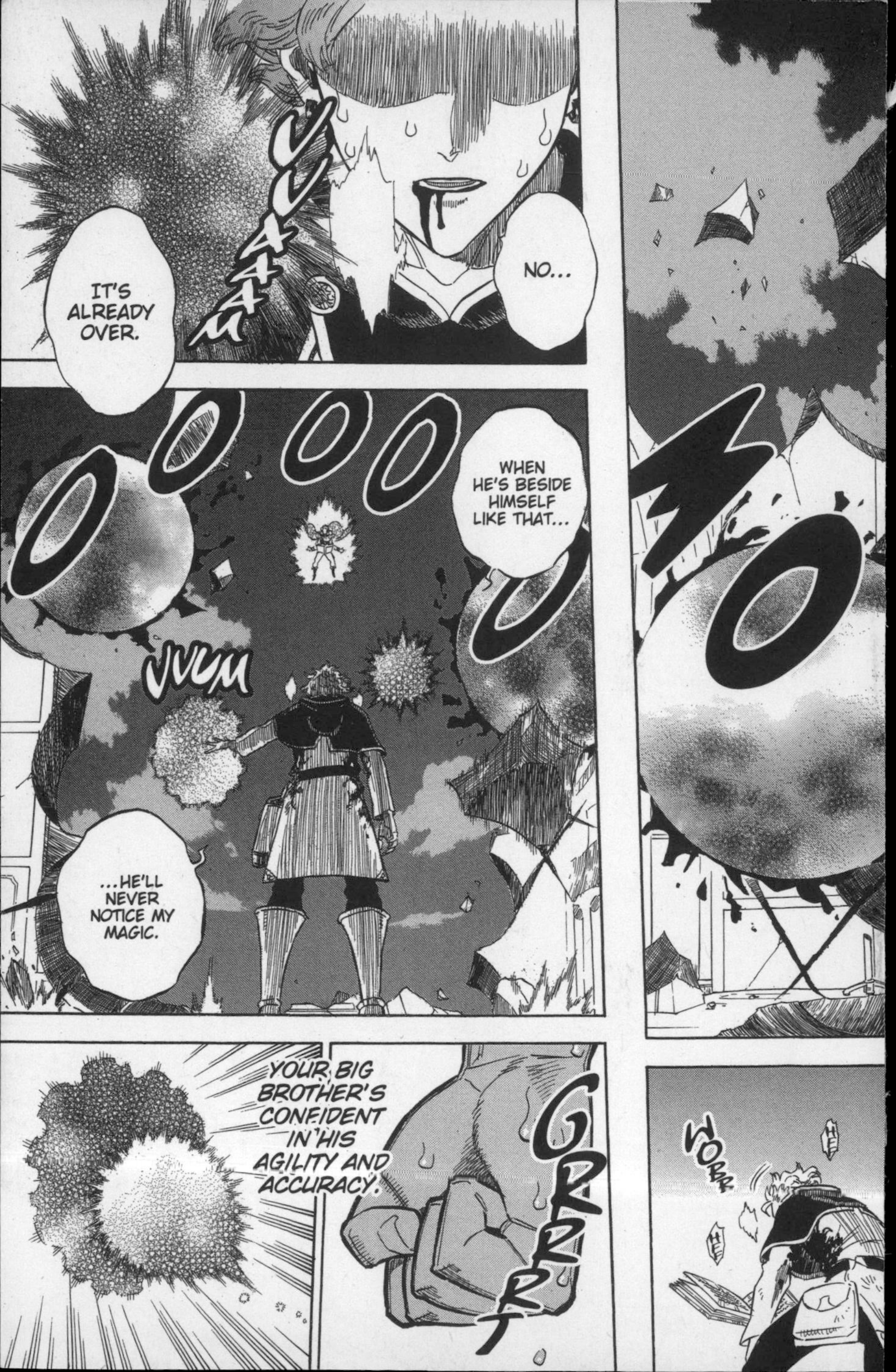
NO...
IT'S ALREADY OVER.
WHEN HE'S BESIDE HIMSELF LIKE THAT...
JVUM
...HE'LL NEVER NOTICE MY MAGIC.
HE
WOBB
HE
YOUR BIG BROTHER'S CONFIDENT IN HIS AGILITY AND ACCURACY.
GRRRT

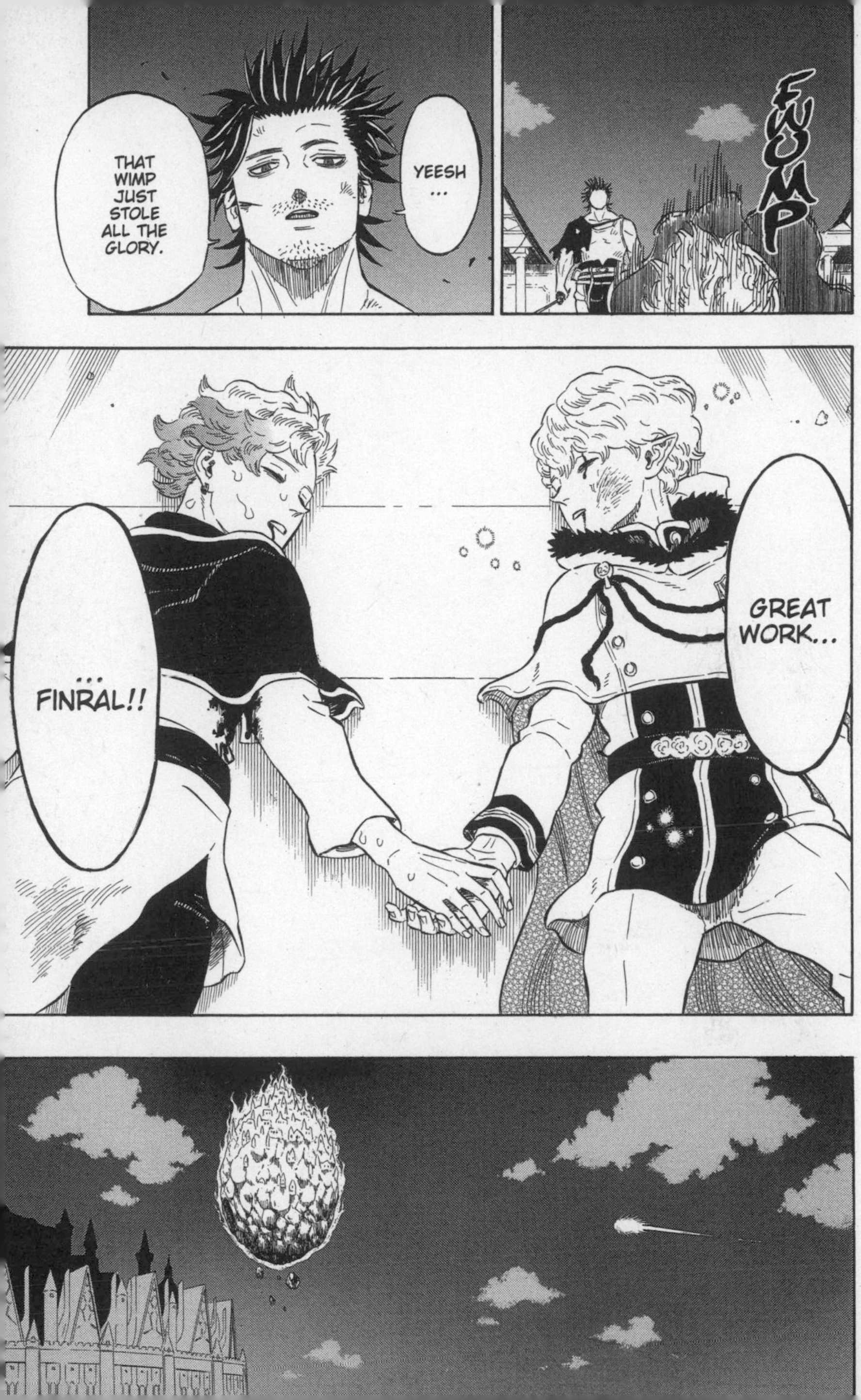
FWUMP
YEESH...
THAT WIMP JUST STOLE ALL THE GLORY.
GREAT WORK...
...FINRAL!!

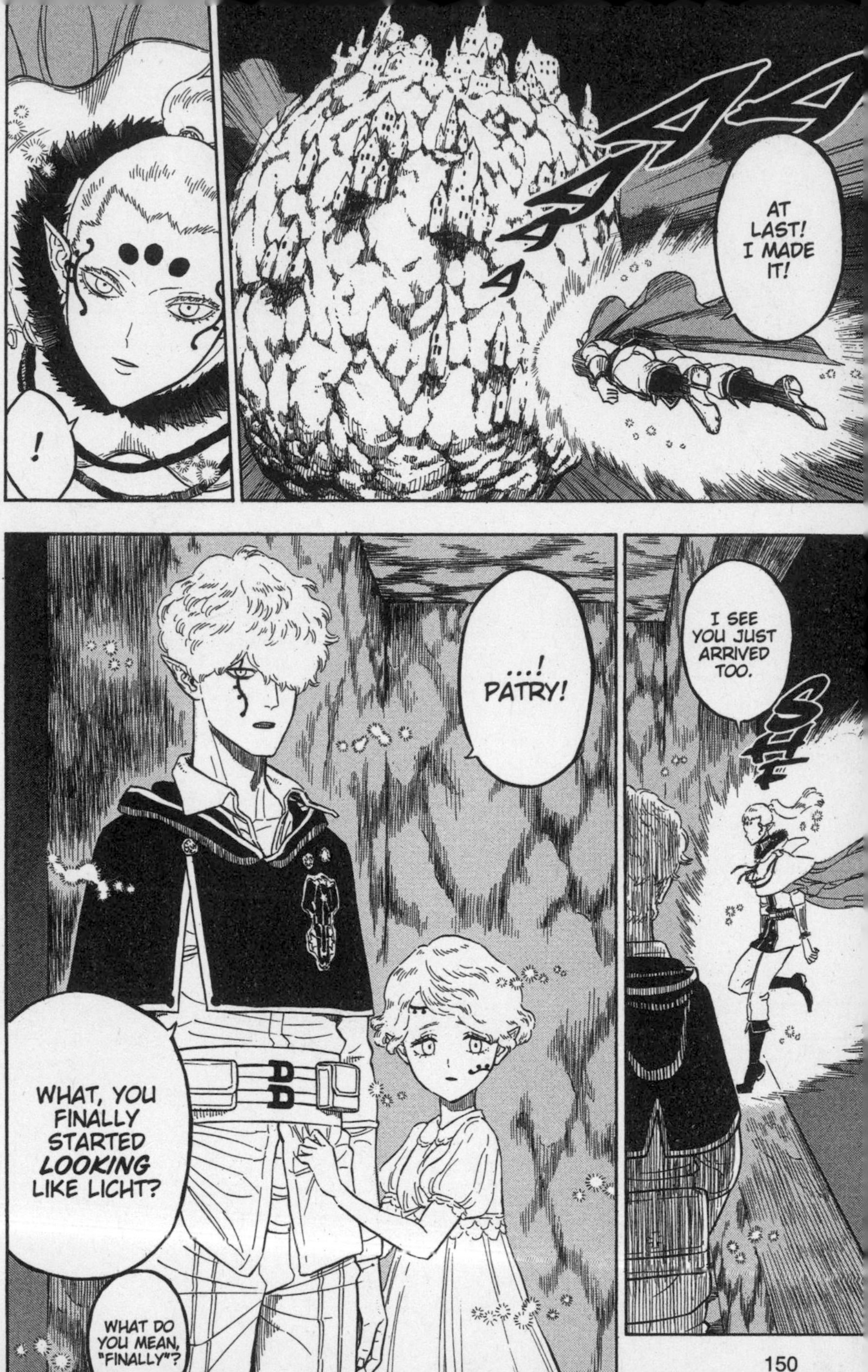

AT LAST! I MADE IT!
!
I SEE YOU JUST ARRIVED TOO.
...! PATRY!
WHAT, YOU FINALLY STARTED *LOOKING* LIKE LICHT?
WHAT DO YOU MEAN, "FINALLY"?

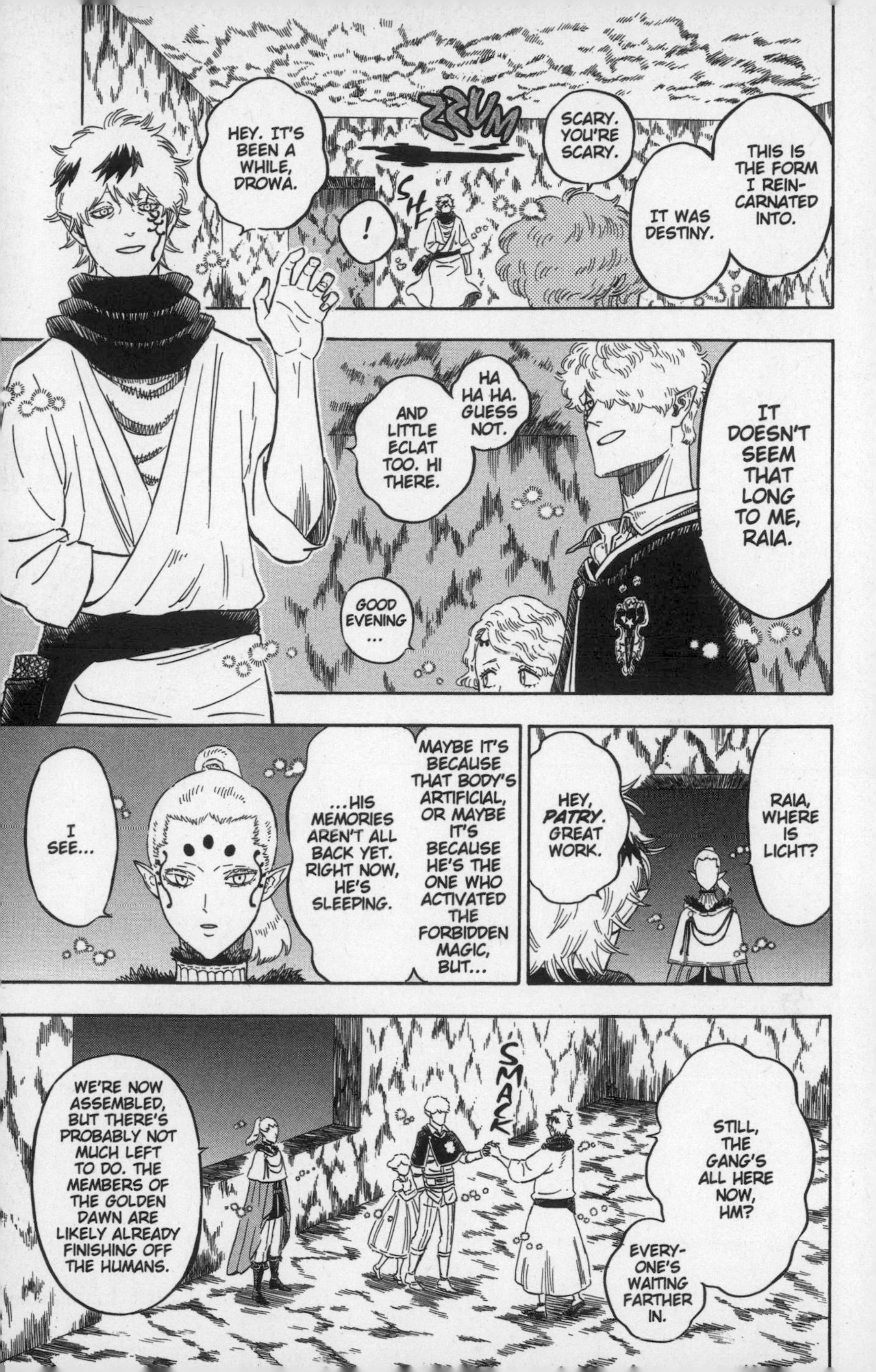
THIS IS THE FORM I REINCARNATED INTO.
IT WAS DESTINY.
SCARY. YOU'RE SCARY.
ZZUM
SHF
!
HEY. IT'S BEEN A WHILE, DROWA.
IT DOESN'T SEEM THAT LONG TO ME, RAIA.
HA HA HA. GUESS NOT.
AND LITTLE ECLAT TOO. HI THERE.
GOOD EVENING ...
RAIA, WHERE IS LICHT?
HEY, **PATRY**. GREAT WORK.
MAYBE IT'S BECAUSE THAT BODY'S ARTIFICIAL, OR MAYBE IT'S BECAUSE HE'S THE ONE WHO ACTIVATED THE FORBIDDEN MAGIC, BUT...
...HIS MEMORIES AREN'T ALL BACK YET. RIGHT NOW, HE'S SLEEPING.
I SEE...
STILL, THE GANG'S ALL HERE NOW, HM?
EVERYONE'S WAITING FARTHER IN.
SMACK
WE'RE NOW ASSEMBLED, BUT THERE'S PROBABLY NOT MUCH LEFT TO DO. THE MEMBERS OF THE GOLDEN DAWN ARE LIKELY ALREADY FINISHING OFF THE HUMANS.

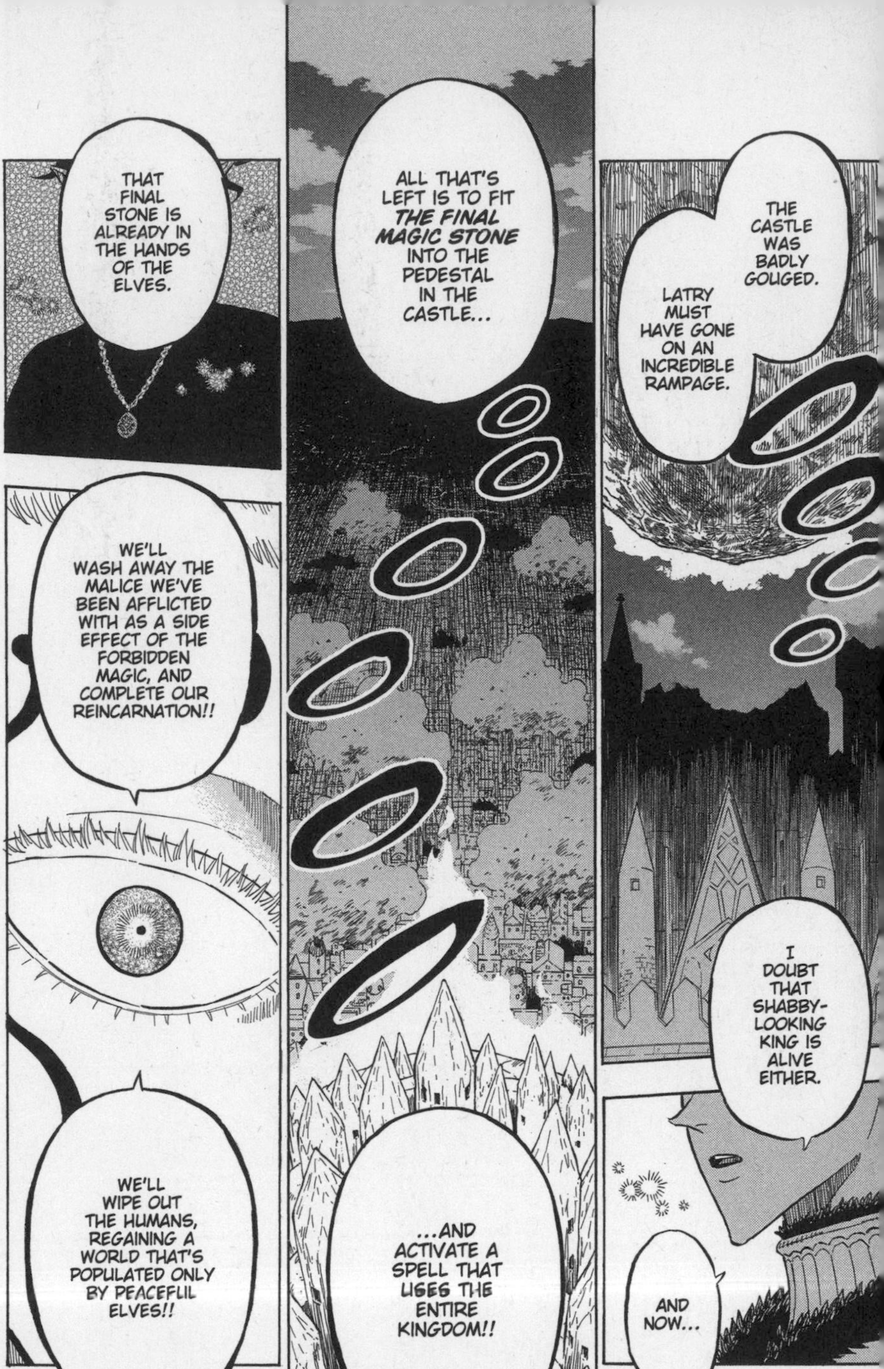
THE CASTLE WAS BADLY GOUGED.
LATRY MUST HAVE GONE ON AN INCREDIBLE RAMPAGE.
I DOUBT THAT SHABBY-LOOKING KING IS ALIVE EITHER.
AND NOW...
ALL THAT'S LEFT IS TO FIT *THE FINAL MAGIC STONE* INTO THE PEDESTAL IN THE CASTLE...
...AND ACTIVATE A SPELL THAT USES THE ENTIRE KINGDOM!!
THAT FINAL STONE IS ALREADY IN THE HANDS OF THE ELVES.
WE'LL WASH AWAY THE MALICE WE'VE BEEN AFFLICTED WITH AS A SIDE EFFECT OF THE FORBIDDEN MAGIC, AND COMPLETE OUR REINCARNATION!!
WE'LL WIPE OUT THE HUMANS, REGAINING A WORLD THAT'S POPULATED ONLY BY PEACEFUL ELVES!!

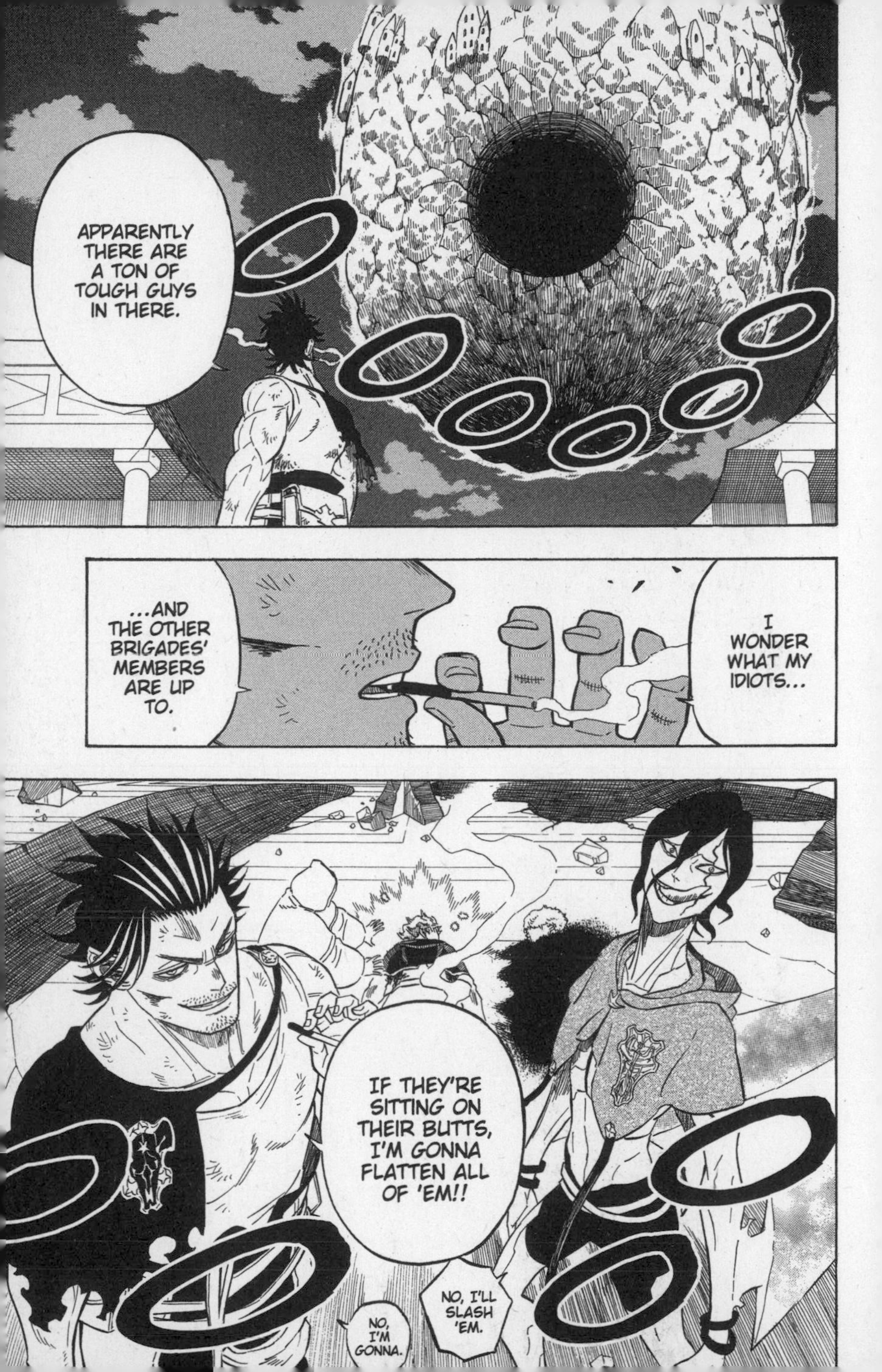
APPARENTLY THERE ARE A TON OF TOUGH GUYS IN THERE.
I WONDER WHAT MY IDIOTS...
...AND THE OTHER BRIGADES' MEMBERS ARE UP TO.
IF THEY'RE SITTING ON THEIR BUTTS, I'M GONNA FLATTEN ALL OF 'EM!!
NO, I'LL SLASH 'EM.
NO, I'M GONNA.

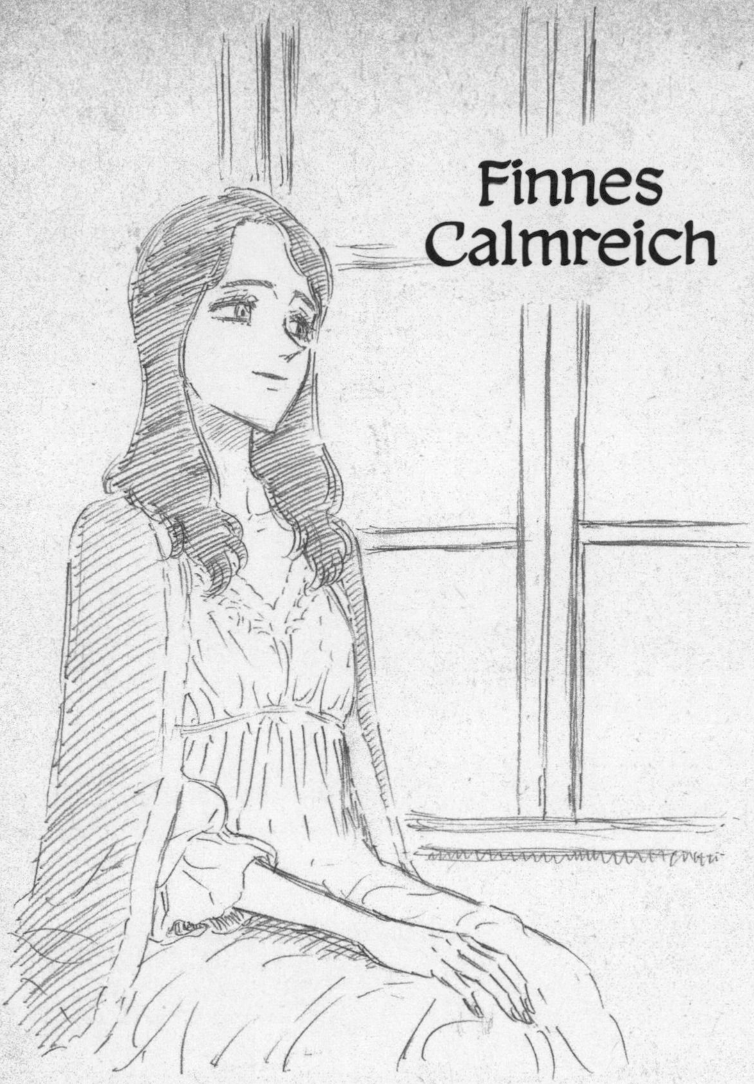

Finnes Calmreich

Age: 25 Height: 163 cm
Birthday: June 2 Sign: Gemini Blood Type: O
Likes: Hot vegetable soup, kindhearted people

Character Profile

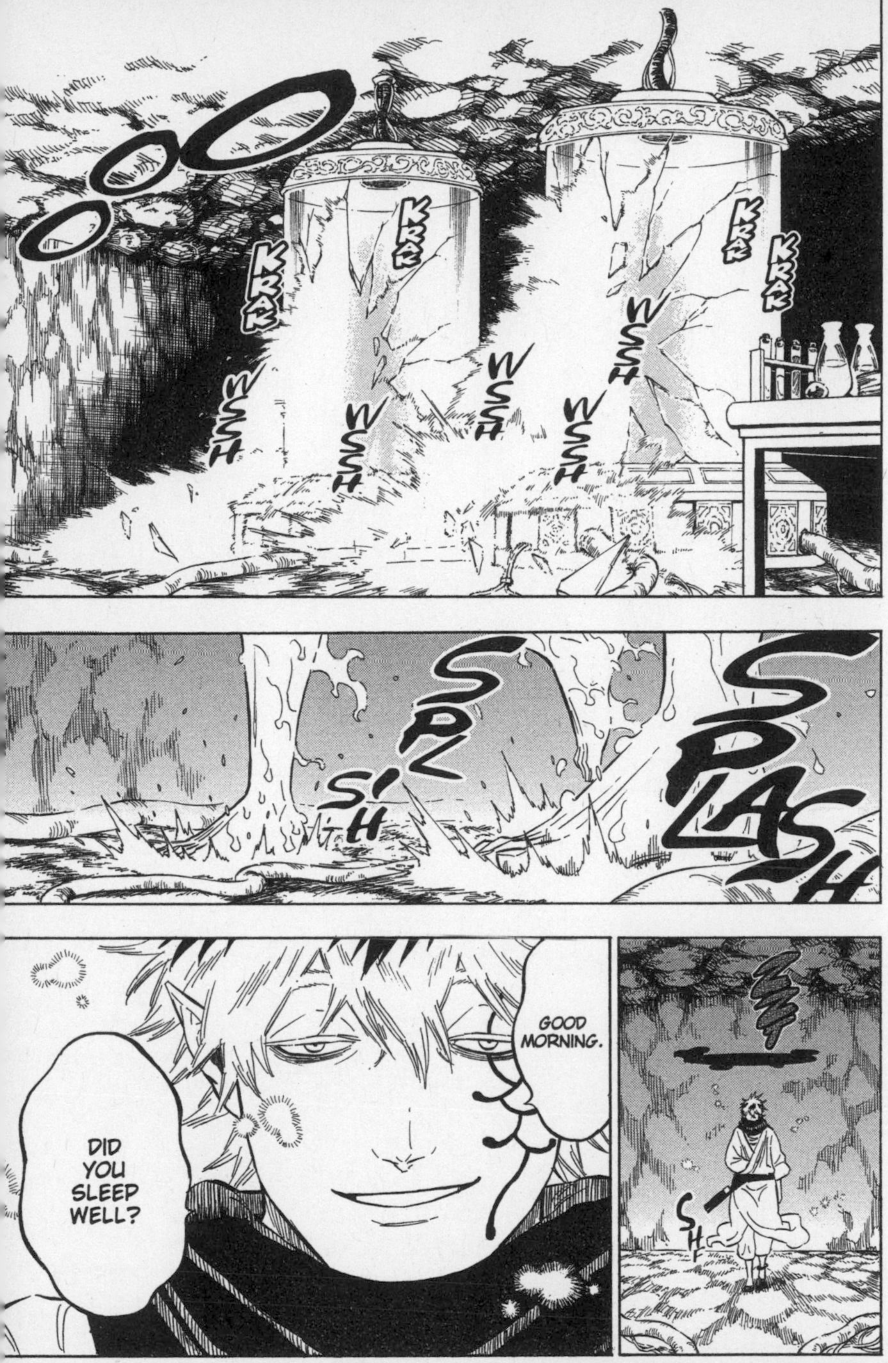
KRAK
KRAK
KRAK
WSSH
KRAK
WSSH
WSSH
WSSH
WSSH
SPLASH
SPLISH
SH
GOOD MORNING.
DID YOU SLEEP WELL?

Page 182: The Apostles of Sephira

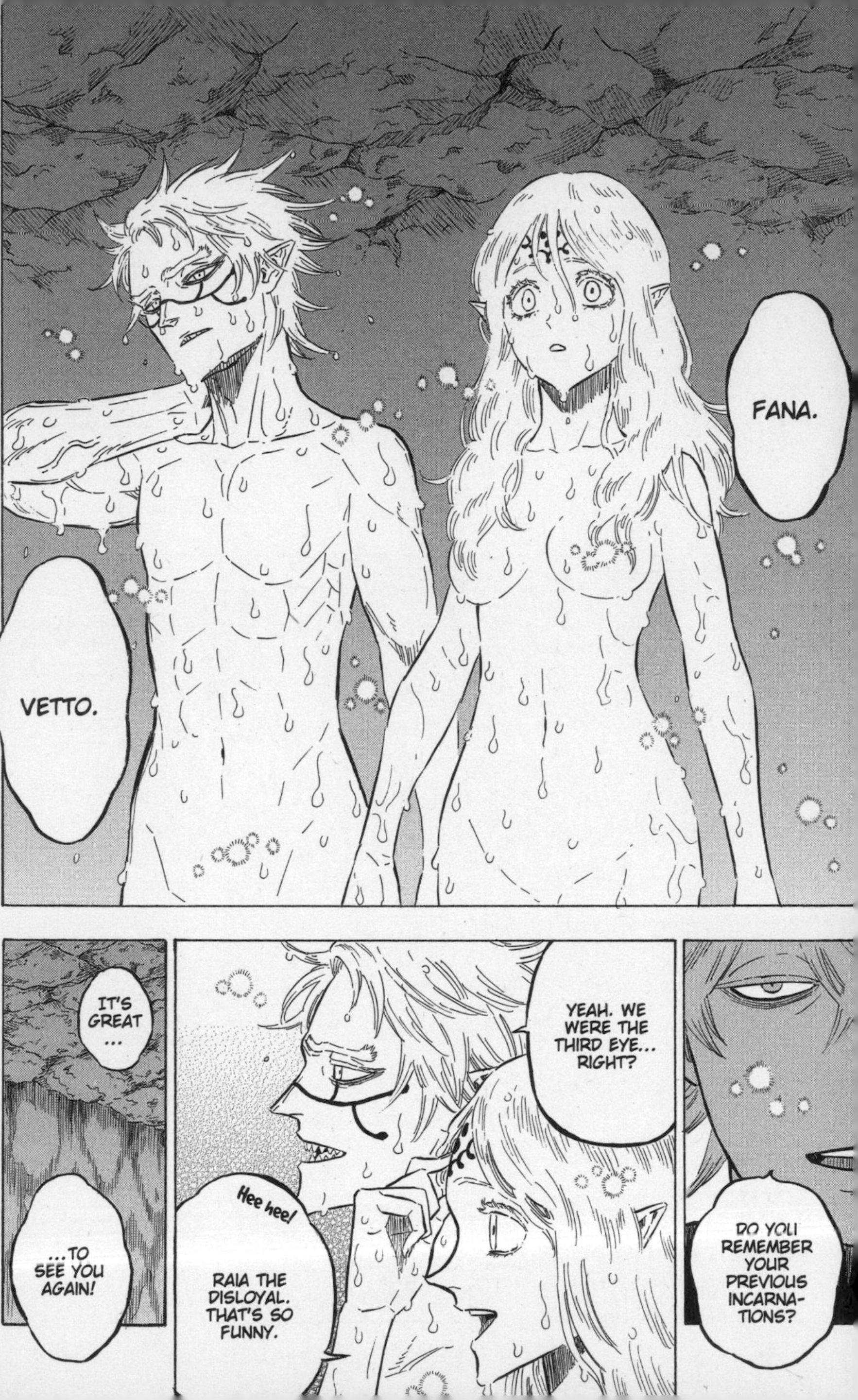
FANA.
VETTO.
DO YOU REMEMBER YOUR PREVIOUS INCARNATIONS?
YEAH. WE WERE THE THIRD EYE... RIGHT?
Hee hee!
RAIA THE DISLOYAL. THAT'S SO FUNNY.
IT'S GREAT...
...TO SEE YOU AGAIN!

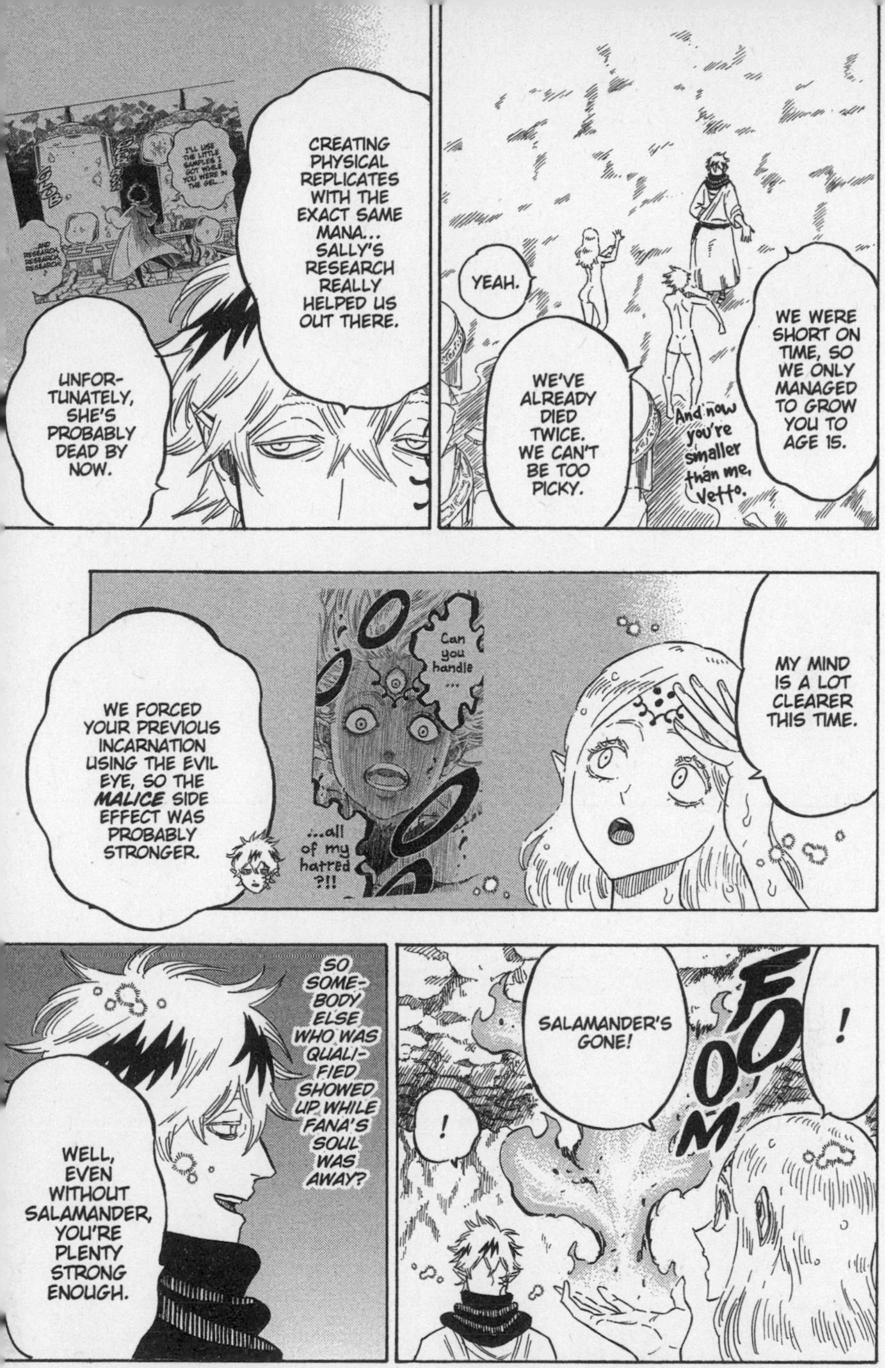
WE WERE SHORT ON TIME, SO WE ONLY MANAGED TO GROW YOU TO AGE 15.
And now you're smaller than me, Vetto.
WE'VE ALREADY DIED TWICE. WE CAN'T BE TOO PICKY.
YEAH.
CREATING PHYSICAL REPLICATES WITH THE EXACT SAME MANA... SALLY'S RESEARCH REALLY HELPED US OUT THERE.
I'LL USE THE LITTLE SAMPLES I GOT WHILE YOU WERE IN THE GEL...
...AND RESEARCH RESEARCH RESEARCH?
UNFORTUNATELY, SHE'S PROBABLY DEAD BY NOW.
MY MIND IS A LOT CLEARER THIS TIME.
Can you handle...
...all of my hatred?!!
WE FORCED YOUR PREVIOUS INCARNATION USING THE EVIL EYE, SO THE ***MALICE*** SIDE EFFECT WAS PROBABLY STRONGER.
!
FOOOM
SALAMANDER'S GONE!
!
SO SOMEBODY ELSE WHO WAS QUALIFIED SHOWED UP WHILE FANA'S SOUL WAS AWAY?
WELL, EVEN WITHOUT SALAMANDER, YOU'RE PLENTY STRONG ENOUGH.

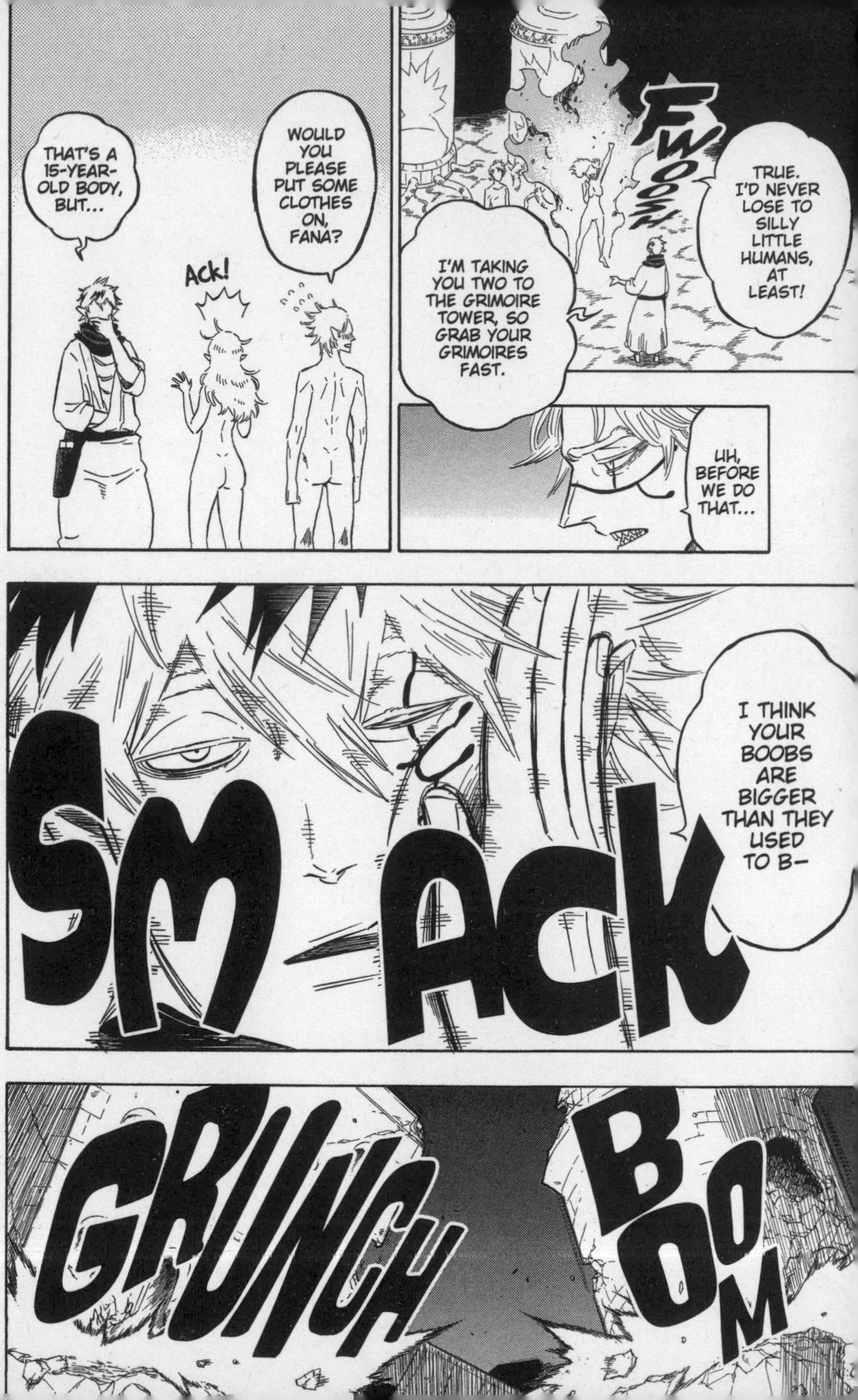

TRUE. I'D NEVER LOSE TO SILLY LITTLE HUMANS, AT LEAST!
FWOOMH
I'M TAKING YOU TWO TO THE GRIMOIRE TOWER, SO GRAB YOUR GRIMOIRES FAST.
UH, BEFORE WE DO THAT...
WOULD YOU PLEASE PUT SOME CLOTHES ON, FANA?
THAT'S A 15-YEAR-OLD BODY, BUT...
ACK!
I THINK YOUR BOOBS ARE BIGGER THAN THEY USED TO B—
SMACK
BOOM
CRUNCH

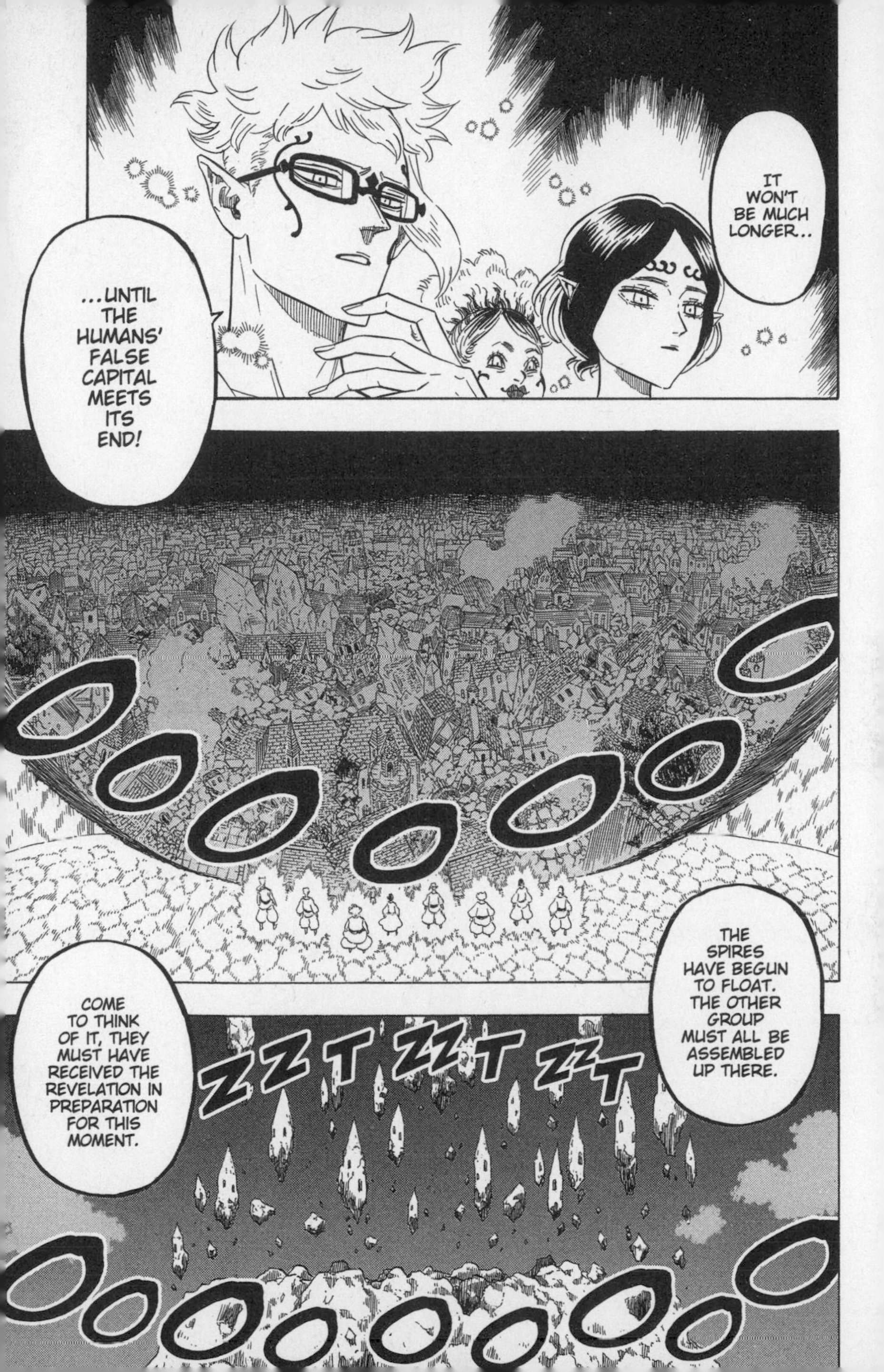
IT WON'T BE MUCH LONGER...
...UNTIL THE HUMANS' FALSE CAPITAL MEETS ITS END!
THE SPIRES HAVE BEGUN TO FLOAT. THE OTHER GROUP MUST ALL BE ASSEMBLED UP THERE.
ZZT ZZT ZZT
COME TO THINK OF IT, THEY MUST HAVE RECEIVED THE REVELATION IN PREPARATION FOR THIS MOMENT.

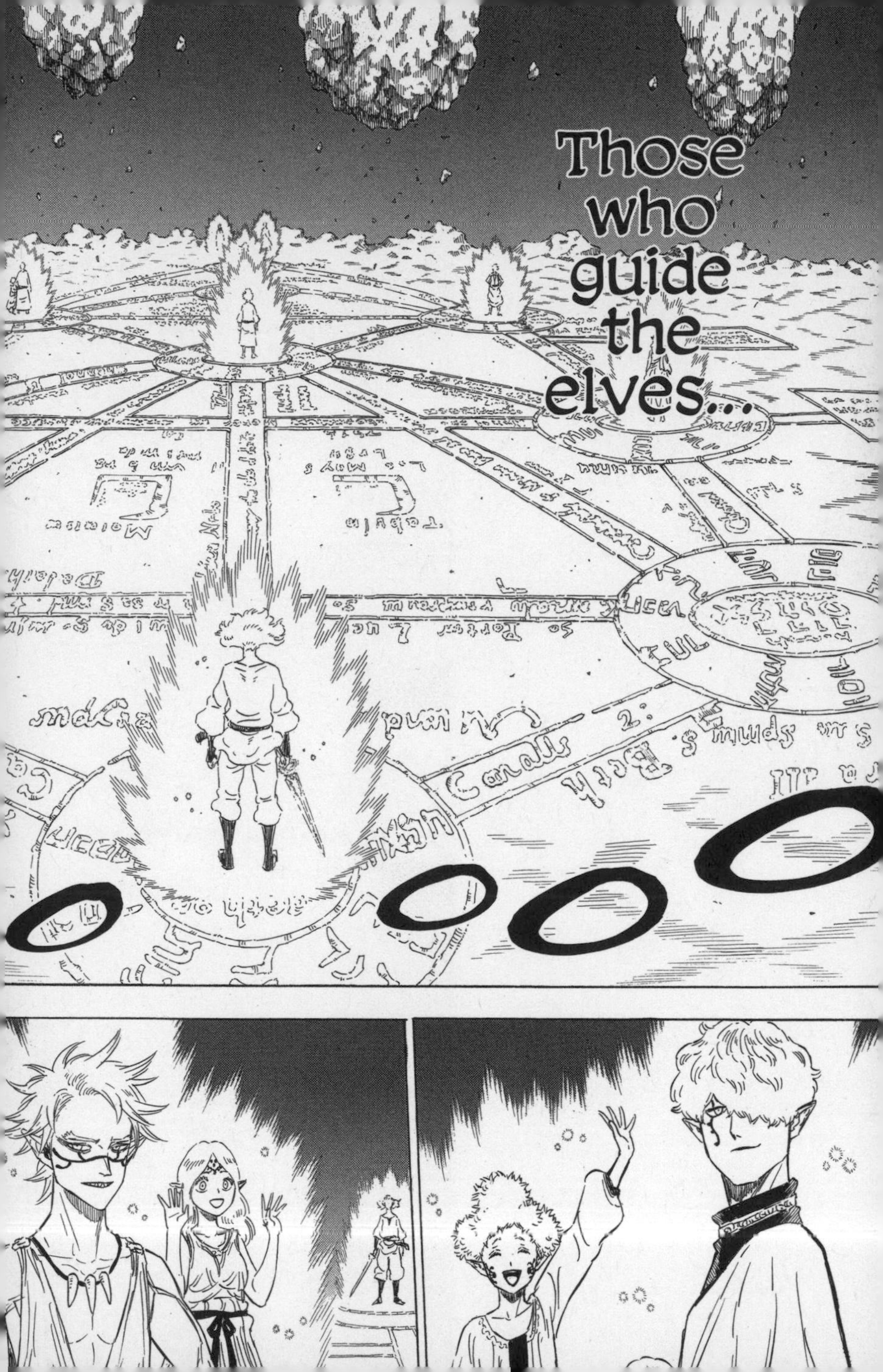

Those who guide the elves...
OOOO

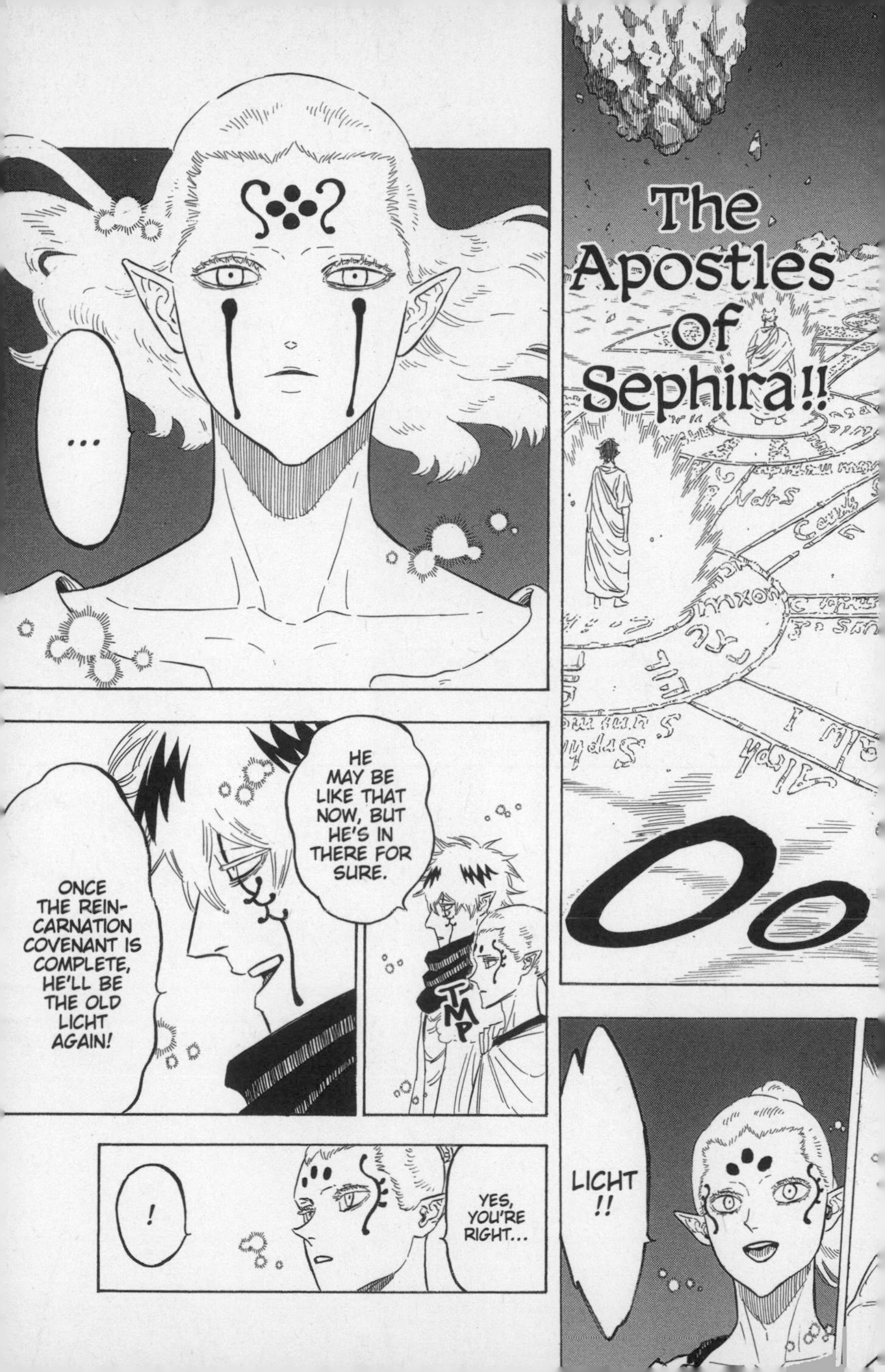
The Apostles of Sephira!!
LICHT!!
...
HE MAY BE LIKE THAT NOW, BUT HE'S IN THERE FOR SURE.
TMP
ONCE THE REIN-CARNATION COVENANT IS COMPLETE, HE'LL BE THE OLD LICHT AGAIN!
YES, YOU'RE RIGHT...
!

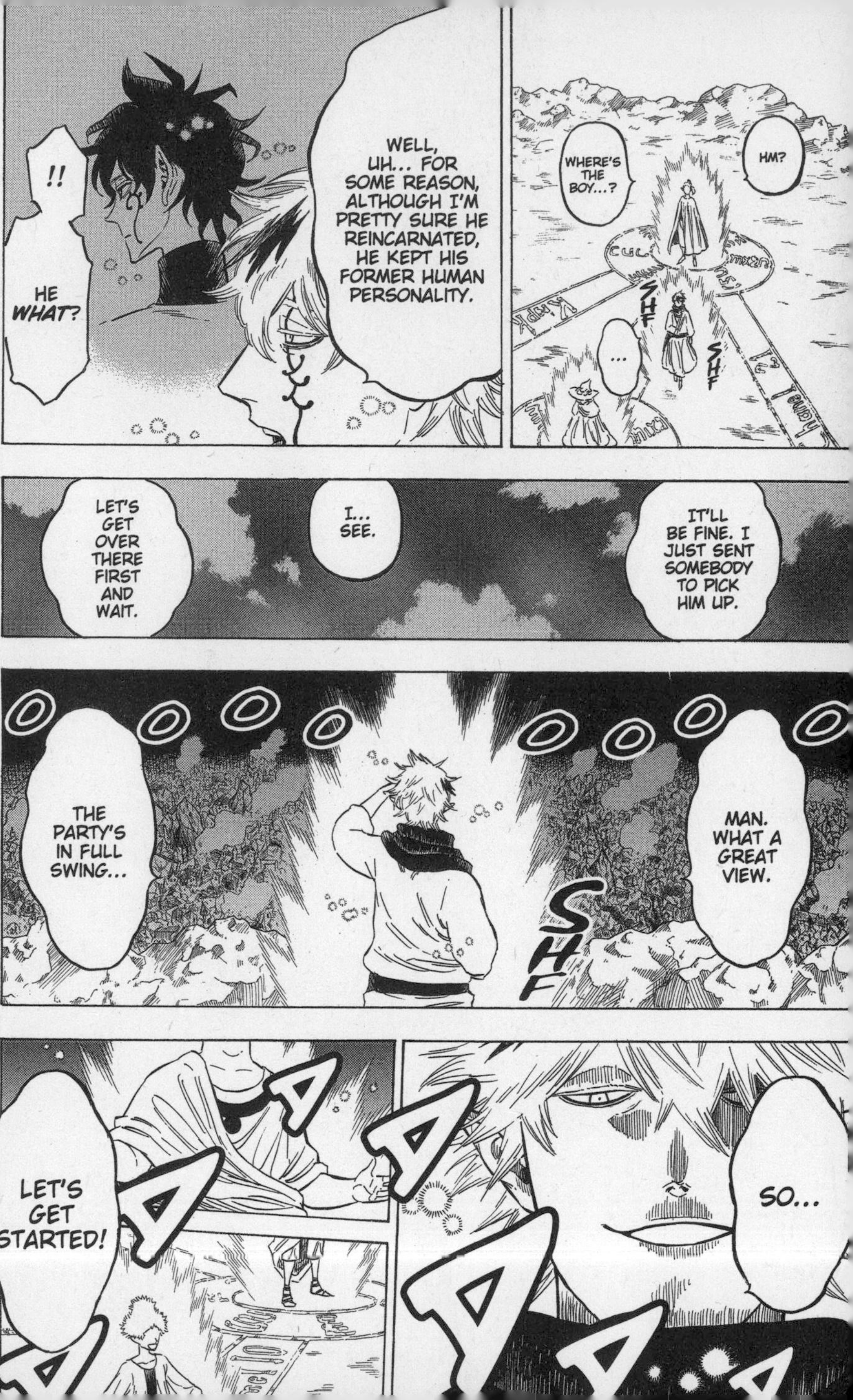
HM?
WHERE'S THE BOY...?
SHF
SHF
...
WELL, UH... FOR SOME REASON, ALTHOUGH I'M PRETTY SURE HE REINCARNATED, HE KEPT HIS FORMER HUMAN PERSONALITY.
!!
HE *WHAT?*
IT'LL BE FINE. I JUST SENT SOMEBODY TO PICK HIM UP.
I... SEE.
LET'S GET OVER THERE FIRST AND WAIT.
OOOOOOOOOO
MAN. WHAT A GREAT VIEW.
SHF
THE PARTY'S IN FULL SWING...
SO...
LET'S GET STARTED!
AAAAAAAAAA

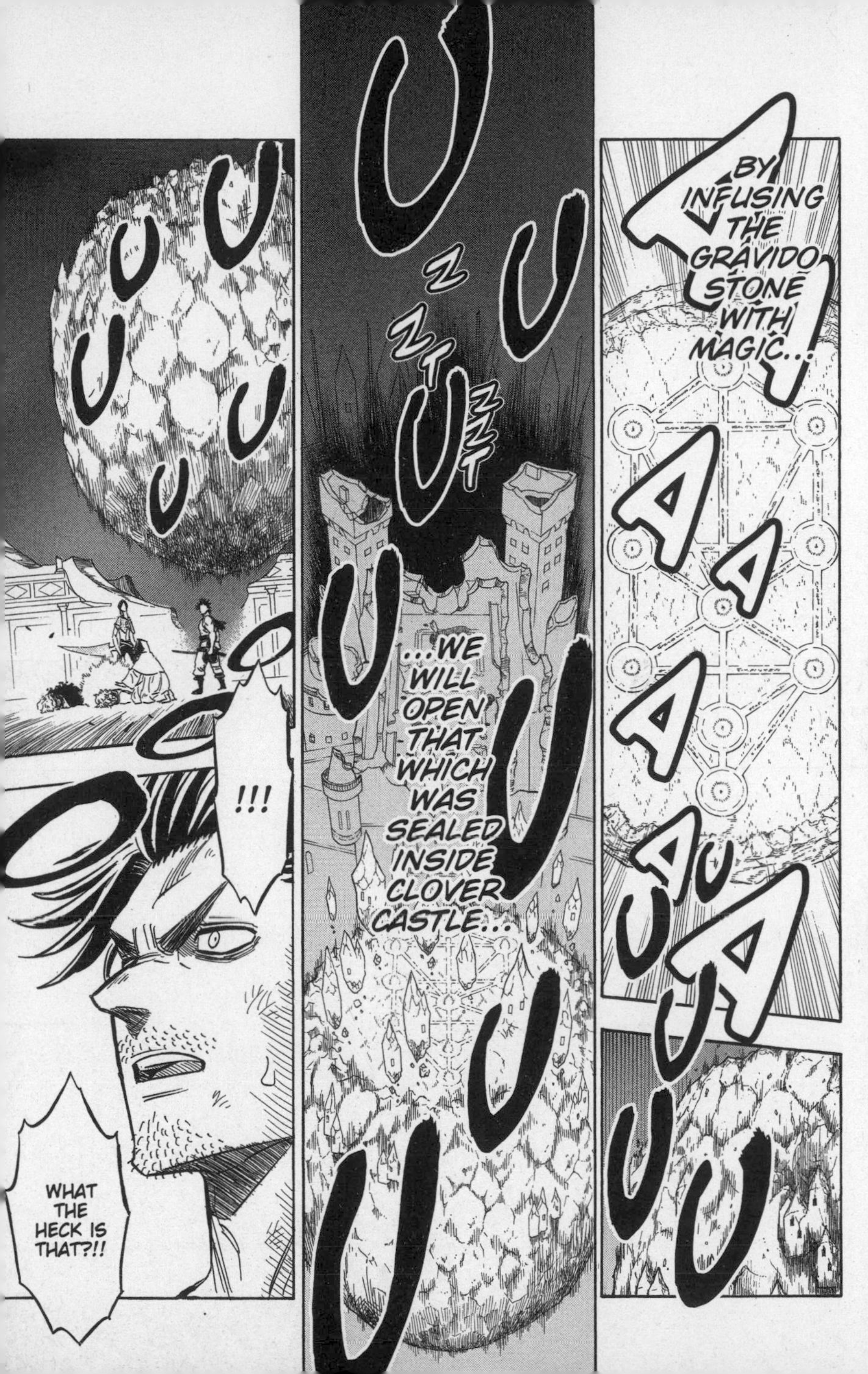
BY INFUSING THE GRAVIDO STONE WITH MAGIC...
...WE WILL OPEN THAT WHICH WAS SEALED INSIDE CLOVER CASTLE...
!!!
WHAT THE HECK IS THAT?!!

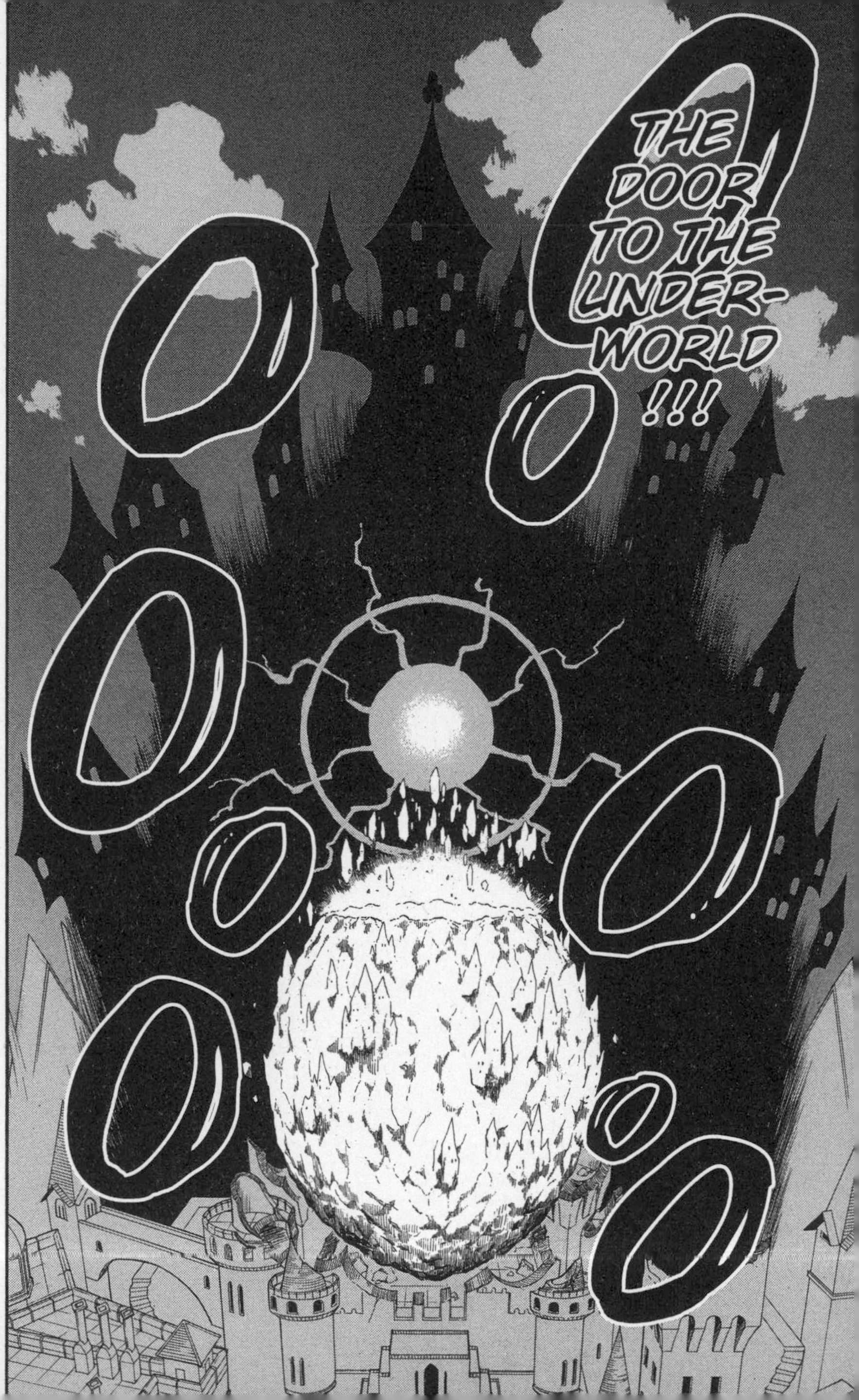
THE DOOR TO THE UNDER-WORLD !!!

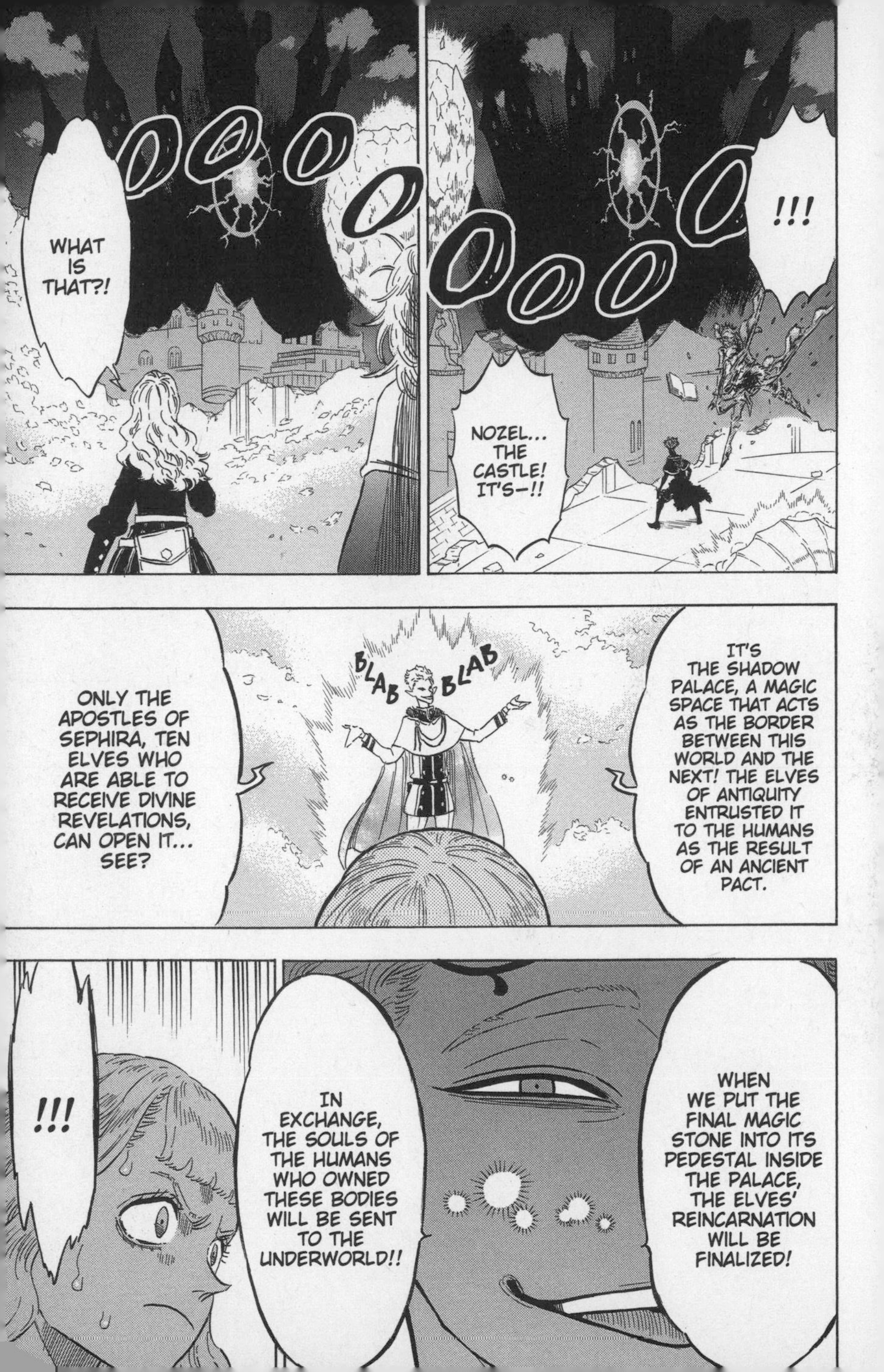
!!!
NOZEL... THE CASTLE! IT'S—!!
WHAT IS THAT?!
IT'S THE SHADOW PALACE, A MAGIC SPACE THAT ACTS AS THE BORDER BETWEEN THIS WORLD AND THE NEXT! THE ELVES OF ANTIQUITY ENTRUSTED IT TO THE HUMANS AS THE RESULT OF AN ANCIENT PACT.
BLAB BLAB
ONLY THE APOSTLES OF SEPHIRA, TEN ELVES WHO ARE ABLE TO RECEIVE DIVINE REVELATIONS, CAN OPEN IT... SEE?
WHEN WE PUT THE FINAL MAGIC STONE INTO ITS PEDESTAL INSIDE THE PALACE, THE ELVES' REINCARNATION WILL BE FINALIZED!
IN EXCHANGE, THE SOULS OF THE HUMANS WHO OWNED THESE BODIES WILL BE SENT TO THE UNDERWORLD!!
!!!

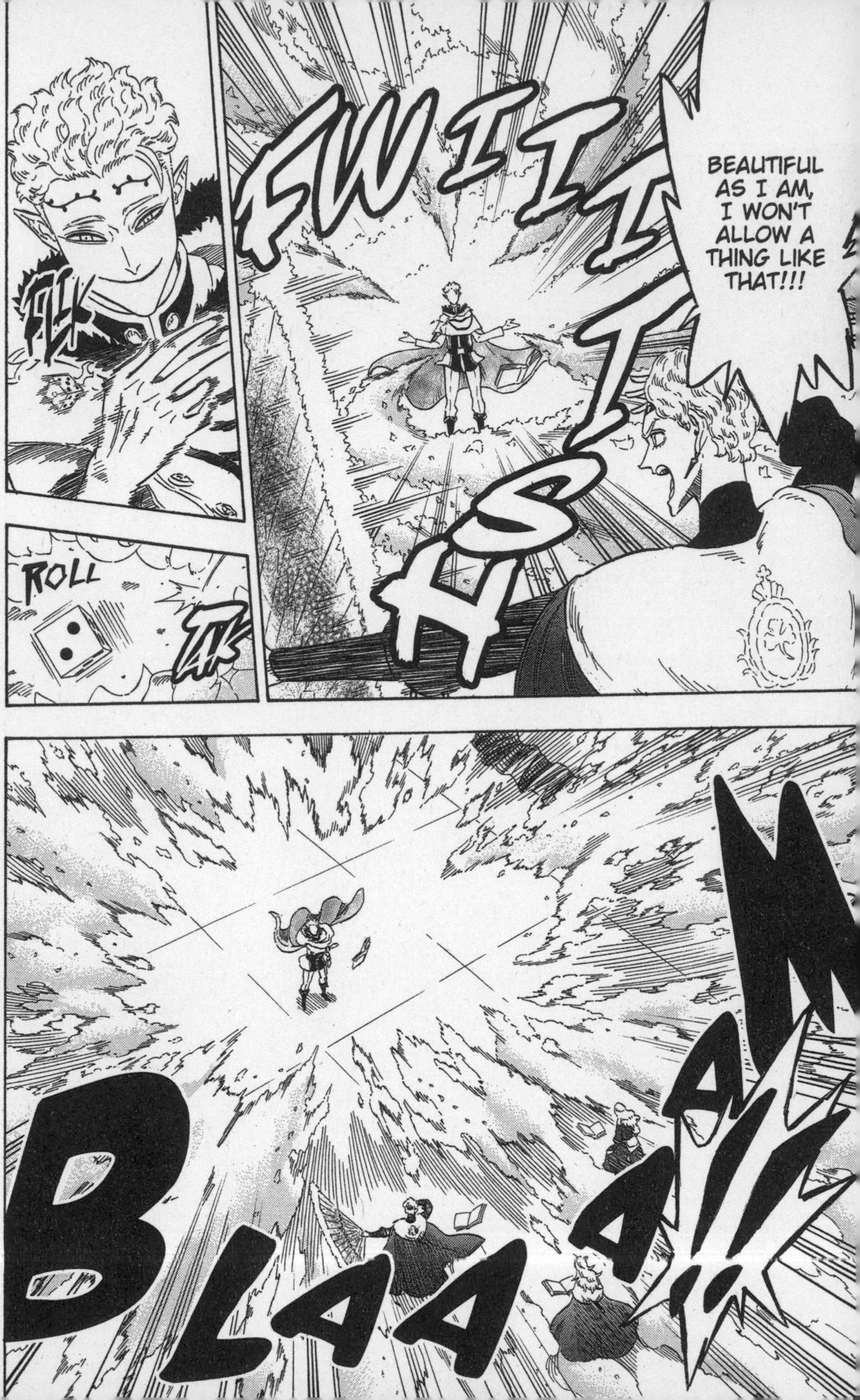
FWIIIISH
BEAUTIFUL AS I AM, I WON'T ALLOW A THING LIKE THAT!!!
ROLL
TAK
BLAAAM!!

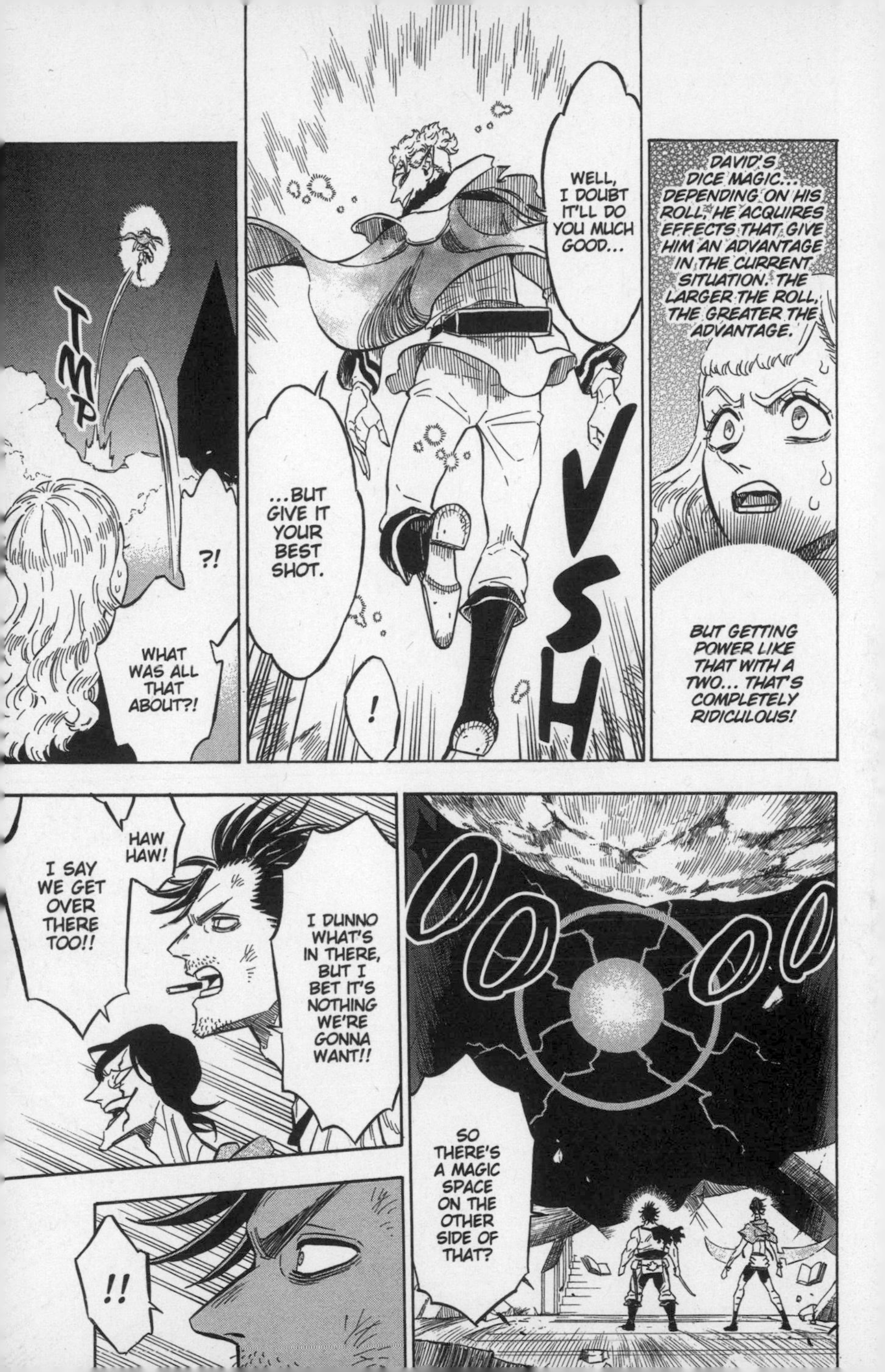
DAVID'S DICE MAGIC... DEPENDING ON HIS ROLL, HE ACQUIRES EFFECTS THAT GIVE HIM AN ADVANTAGE IN THE CURRENT SITUATION. THE LARGER THE ROLL, THE GREATER THE ADVANTAGE.
BUT GETTING POWER LIKE THAT WITH A TWO... THAT'S COMPLETELY RIDICULOUS!
WELL, I DOUBT IT'LL DO YOU MUCH GOOD...
...BUT GIVE IT YOUR BEST SHOT.
VSH
!
TMP
?!
WHAT WAS ALL THAT ABOUT?!
SO THERE'S A MAGIC SPACE ON THE OTHER SIDE OF THAT?
I DUNNO WHAT'S IN THERE, BUT I BET IT'S NOTHING WE'RE GONNA WANT!!
HAW HAW!
I SAY WE GET OVER THERE TOO!!
!!

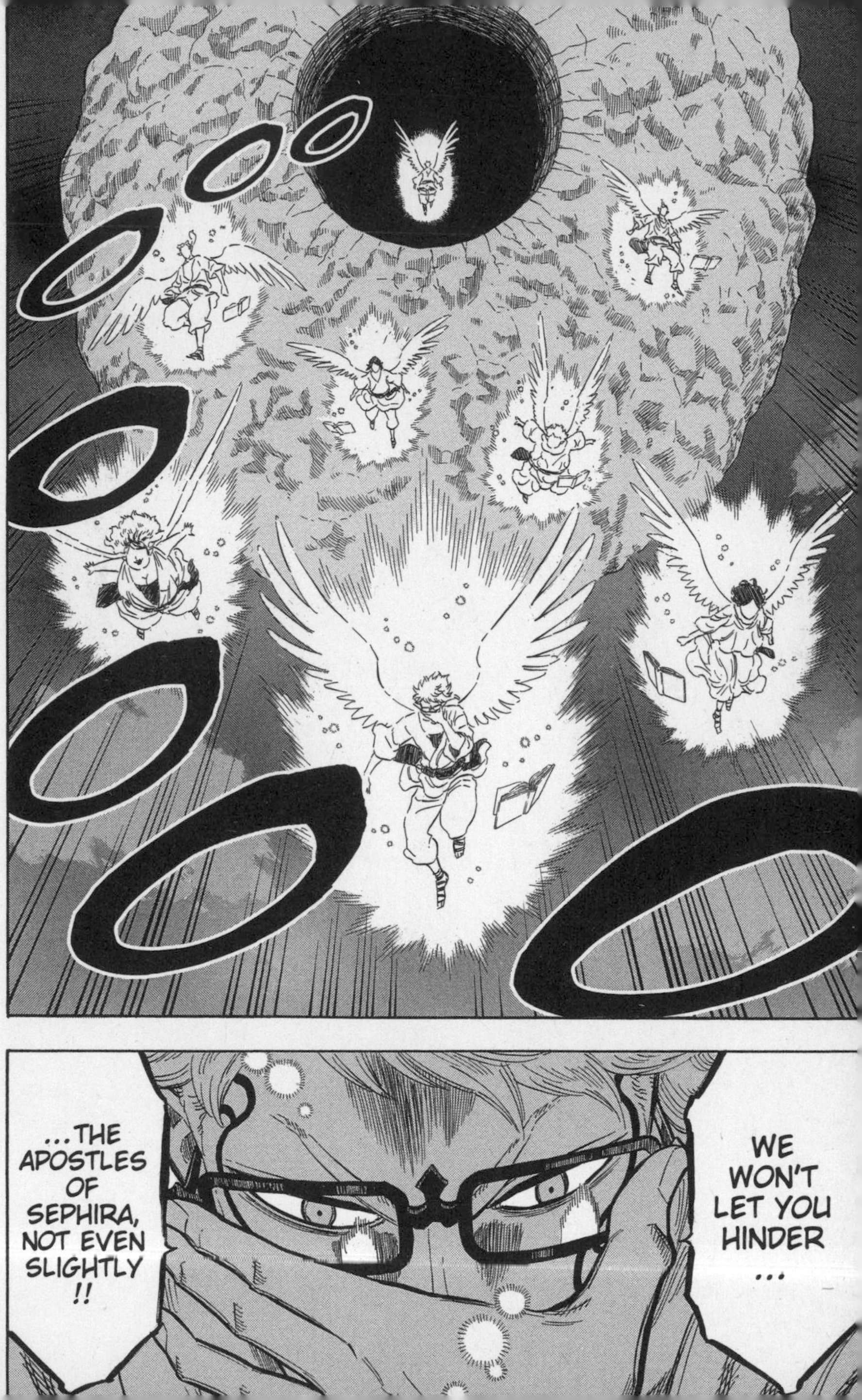
WE WON'T LET YOU HINDER ...
...THE APOSTLES OF SEPHIRA, NOT EVEN SLIGHTLY!!

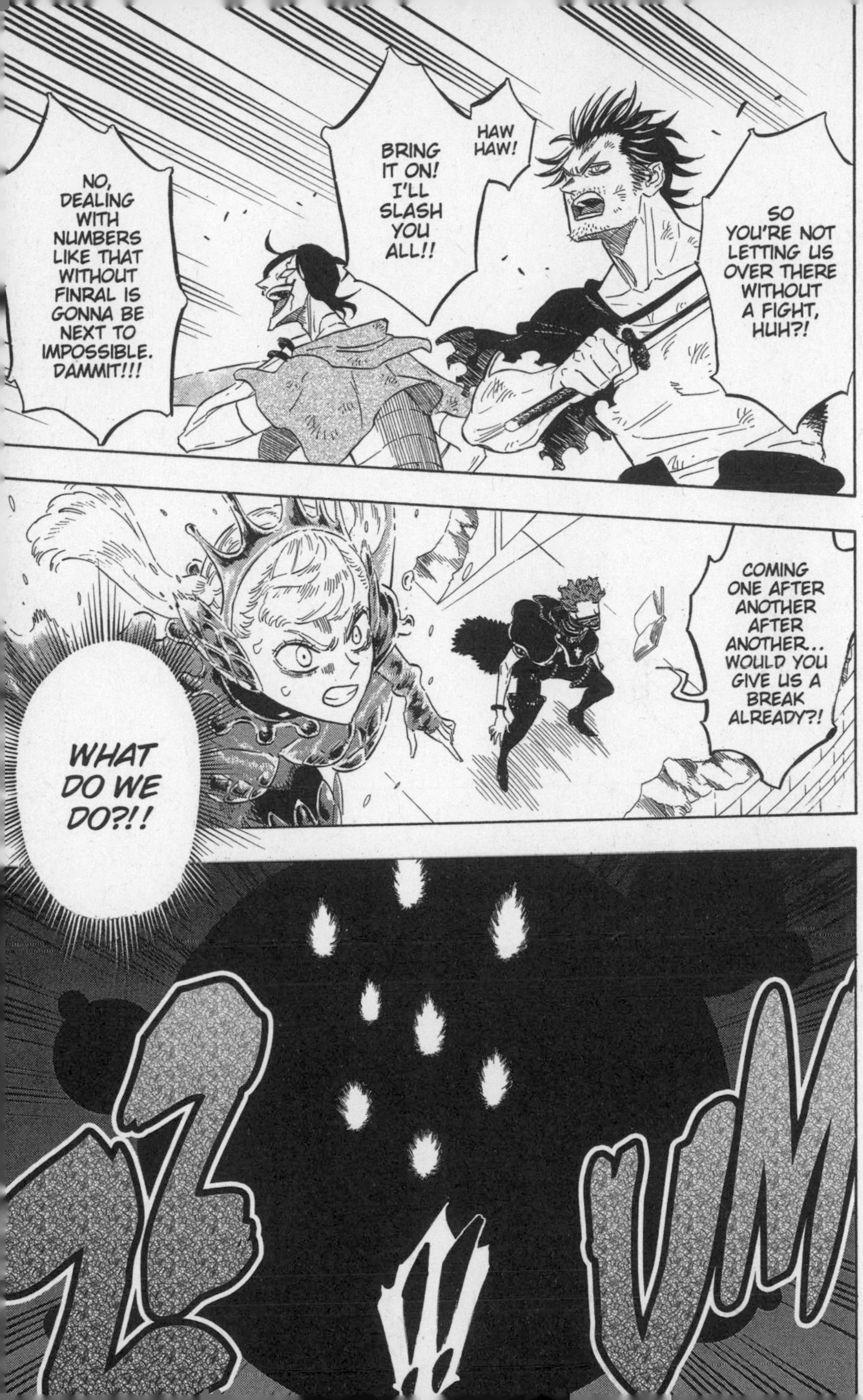
SO YOU'RE NOT LETTING US OVER THERE WITHOUT A FIGHT, HUH?!
HAW HAW!
BRING IT ON! I'LL SLASH YOU ALL!!
NO, DEALING WITH NUMBERS LIKE THAT WITHOUT FINRAL IS GONNA BE NEXT TO IMPOSSIBLE. DAMMIT!!!
COMING ONE AFTER ANOTHER AFTER ANOTHER... WOULD YOU GIVE US A BREAK ALREADY?!
WHAT DO WE DO?!!

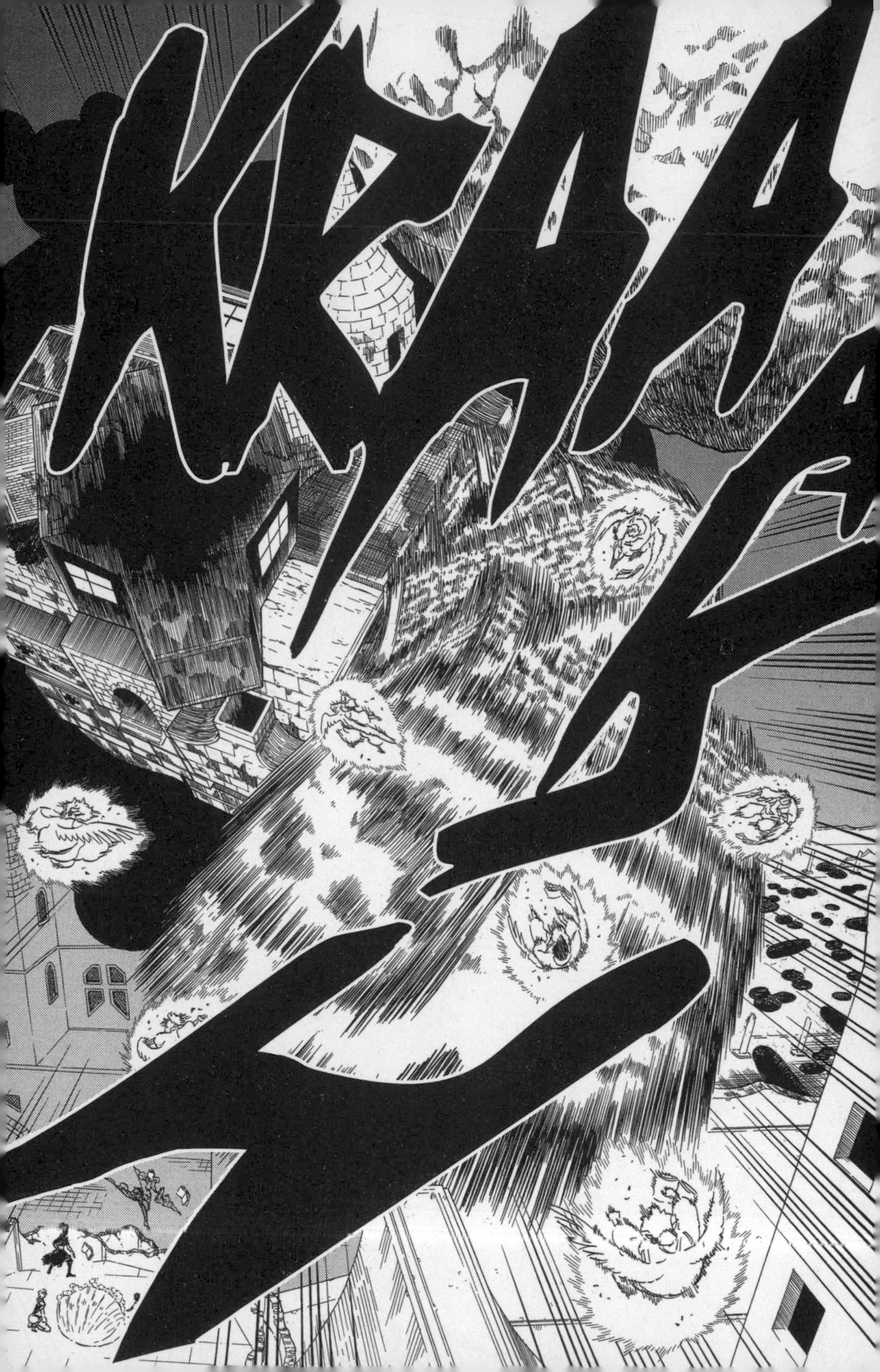

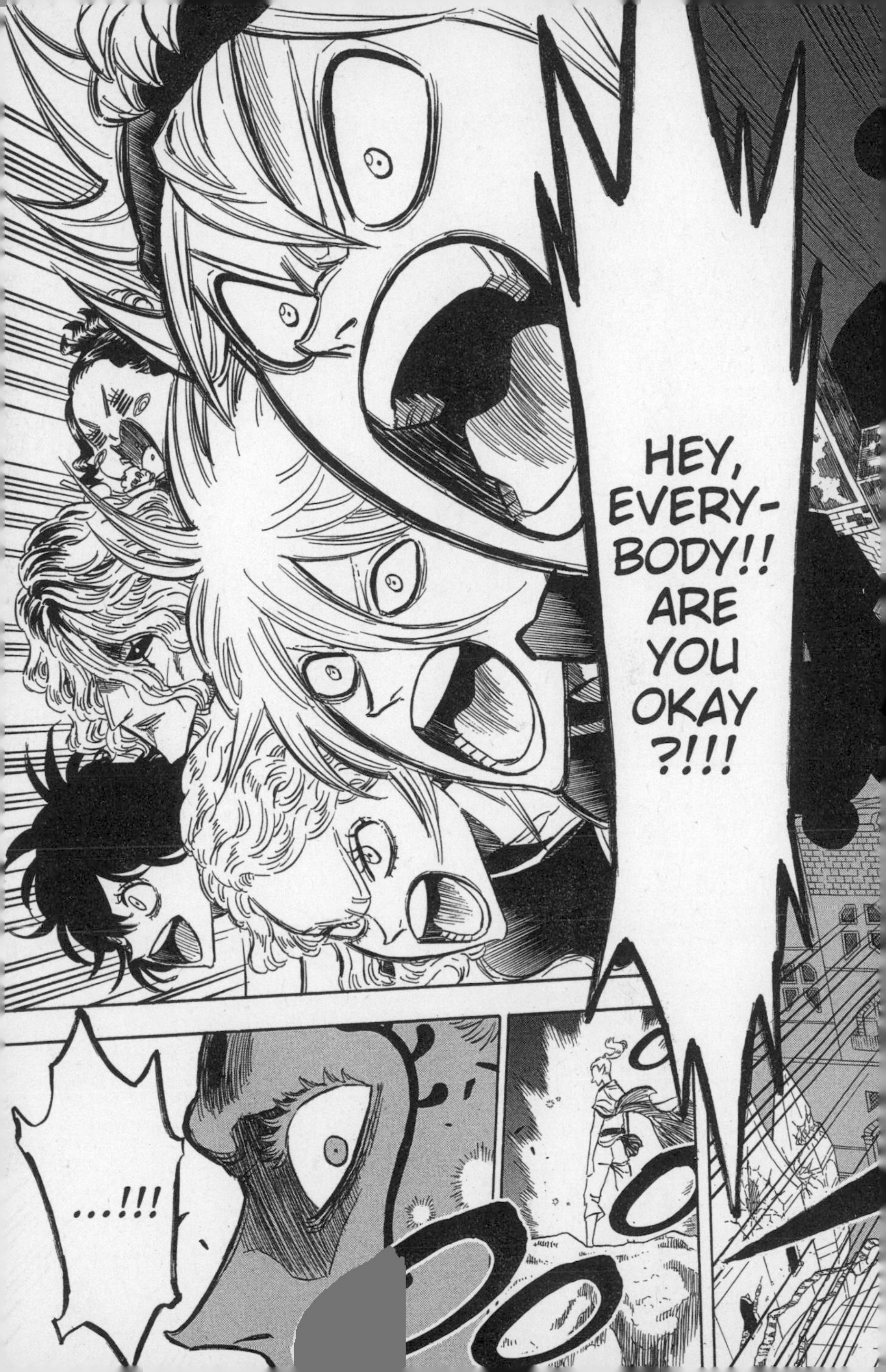

HEY, EVERY-BODY!! ARE YOU OKAY ?!!!
...!!!

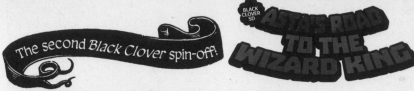

The second *Black Clover* spin-off!

BLACK CLOVER SD
ASTA'S ROAD TO THE WIZARD KING

Setta Kobayashi Sensei dropped by for a visit!

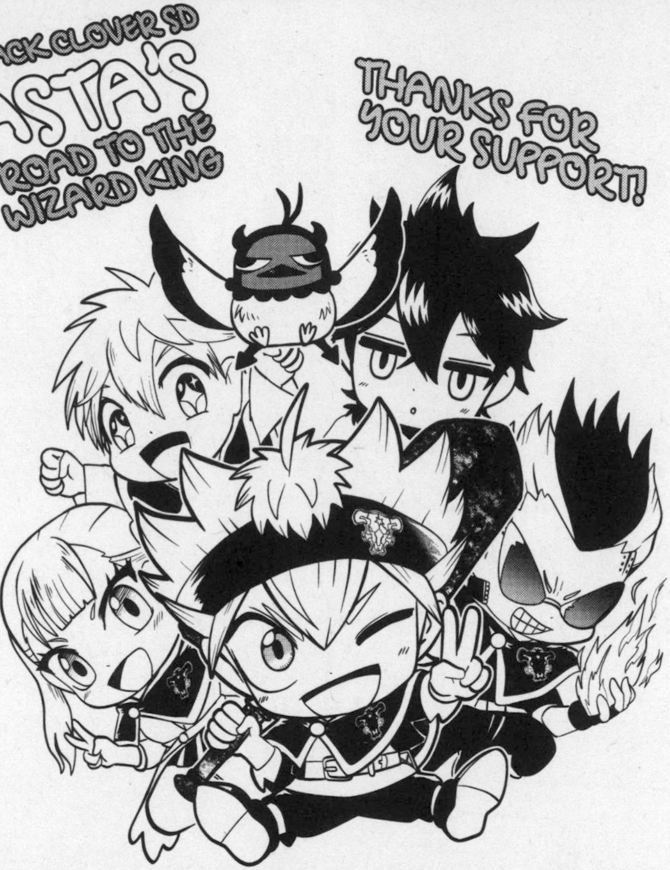
BLACK CLOVER SD
ASTA'S
ROAD TO THE
WIZARD KING
THANKS FOR
YOUR SUPPORT!

IT'S NICE TO MEET YOU! I'M SETTA KOBAYASHI!
I LOVE *BLACK CLOVER*, AND I'M THRILLED THAT I GET
TO DRAW A SPIN-OFF! DON'T MISS ASTA AND COMPANY'S
DYNAMIC CHIBI ADVENTURES!

Thanks for drawing this picture just for this volume!!
Your versions of Asta and the other characters are
way too cute and funny. (LOL) I'll be supporting the
heck out of this super-deformed spin-off!!

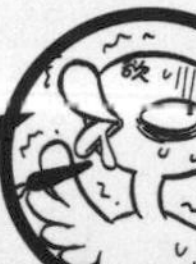

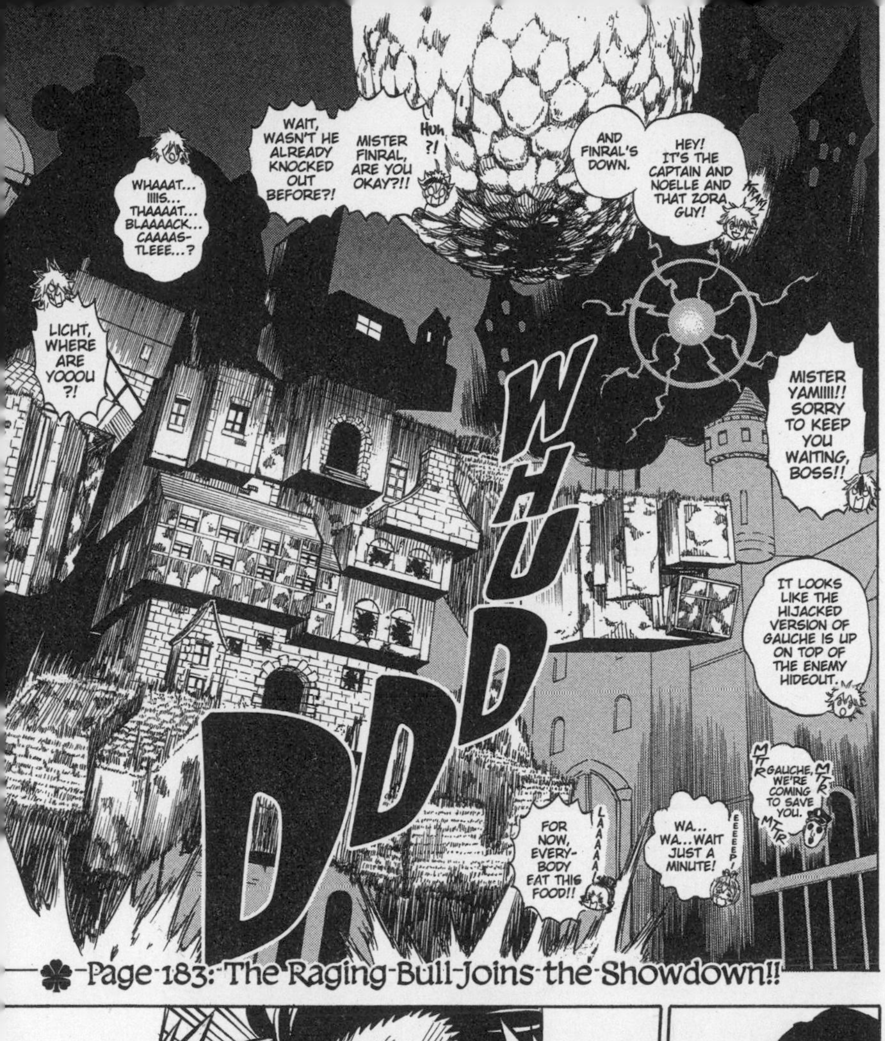
HEY! IT'S THE CAPTAIN AND NOELLE AND THAT ZORA GUY!
AND FINRAL'S DOWN.
HUH ?!
MISTER FINRAL, ARE YOU OKAY?!!
WAIT, WASN'T HE ALREADY KNOCKED OUT BEFORE?!
WHAAAT... IIIIS... THAAAAT... BLAAAACK... CAAAAS-TLEEE...?
MISTER YAMIIII!! SORRY TO KEEP YOU WAITING, BOSS!!
LICHT, WHERE ARE YOOOU ?!
WHUDDDD
IT LOOKS LIKE THE HIJACKED VERSION OF GAUCHE IS UP ON TOP OF THE ENEMY HIDEOUT.
MTTR
GAUCHE, WE'RE COMING TO SAVE YOU.
MTTR
MTTR
WA... WA...WAIT JUST A MINUTE!
EEEEEP!
LAAAAA
FOR NOW, EVERY-BODY EAT THIS FOOD!!

Page 183: The Raging Bull Joins the Showdown!!

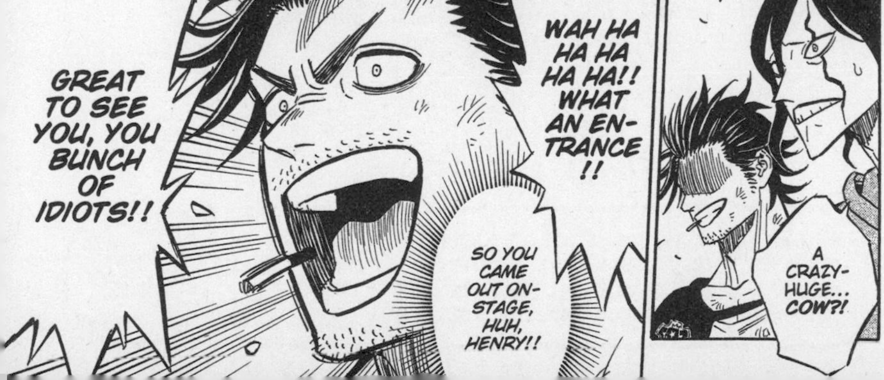
A CRAZY-HUGE... COW?!
WAH HA HA HA HA HA!! WHAT AN EN-TRANCE !!
SO YOU CAME OUT ON-STAGE, HUH, HENRY!!
GREAT TO SEE YOU, YOU BUNCH OF IDIOTS!!

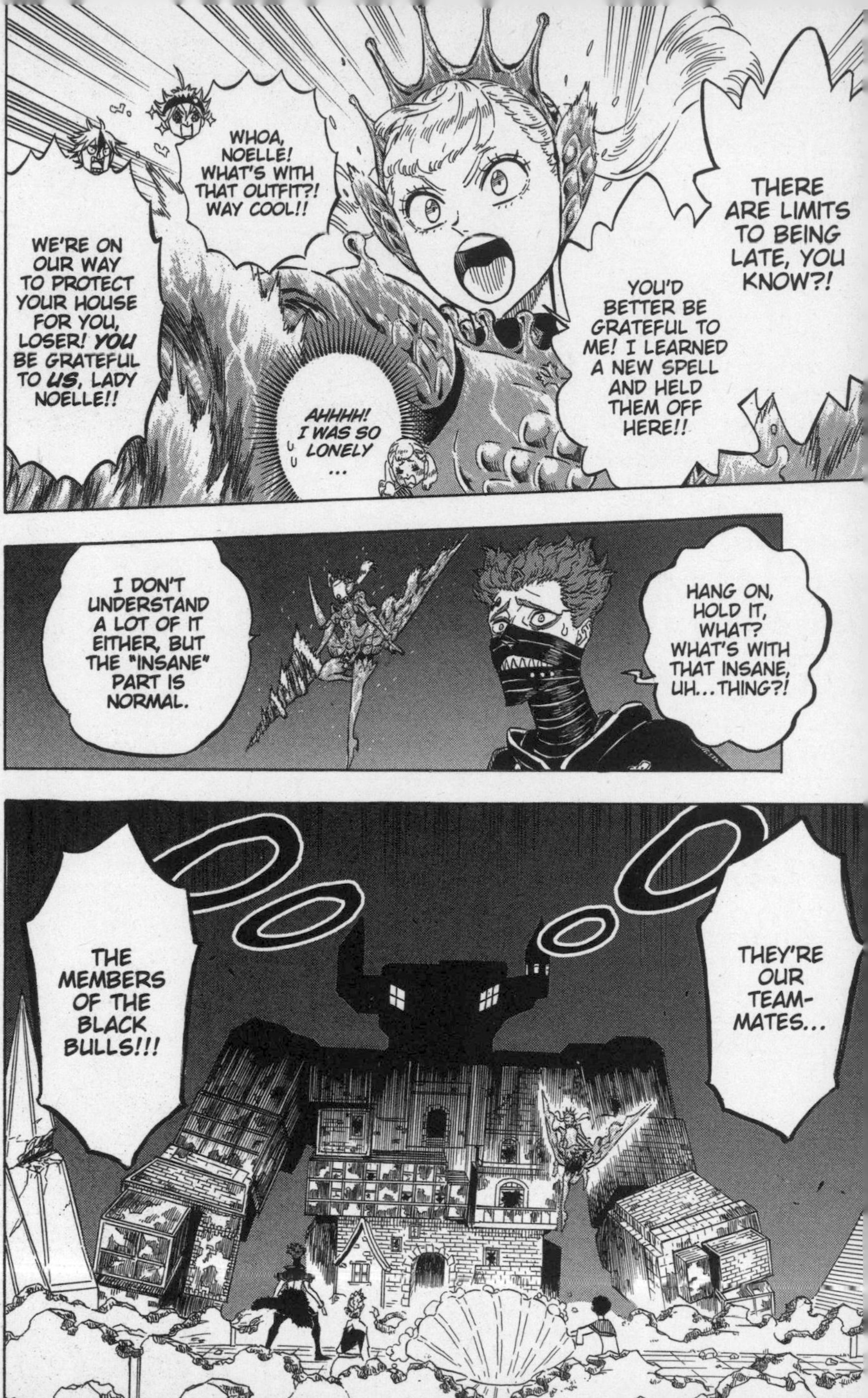
THERE ARE LIMITS TO BEING LATE, YOU KNOW?!
YOU'D BETTER BE GRATEFUL TO ME! I LEARNED A NEW SPELL AND HELD THEM OFF HERE!!
AHHHH! I WAS SO LONELY...
WHOA, NOELLE! WHAT'S WITH THAT OUTFIT?! WAY COOL!!
WE'RE ON OUR WAY TO PROTECT YOUR HOUSE FOR YOU, LOSER! *YOU* BE GRATEFUL TO *US*, LADY NOELLE!!
HANG ON, HOLD IT, WHAT? WHAT'S WITH THAT INSANE, UH...THING?!
I DON'T UNDERSTAND A LOT OF IT EITHER, BUT THE "INSANE" PART IS NORMAL.
THEY'RE OUR TEAMMATES...
THE MEMBERS OF THE BLACK BULLS!!!

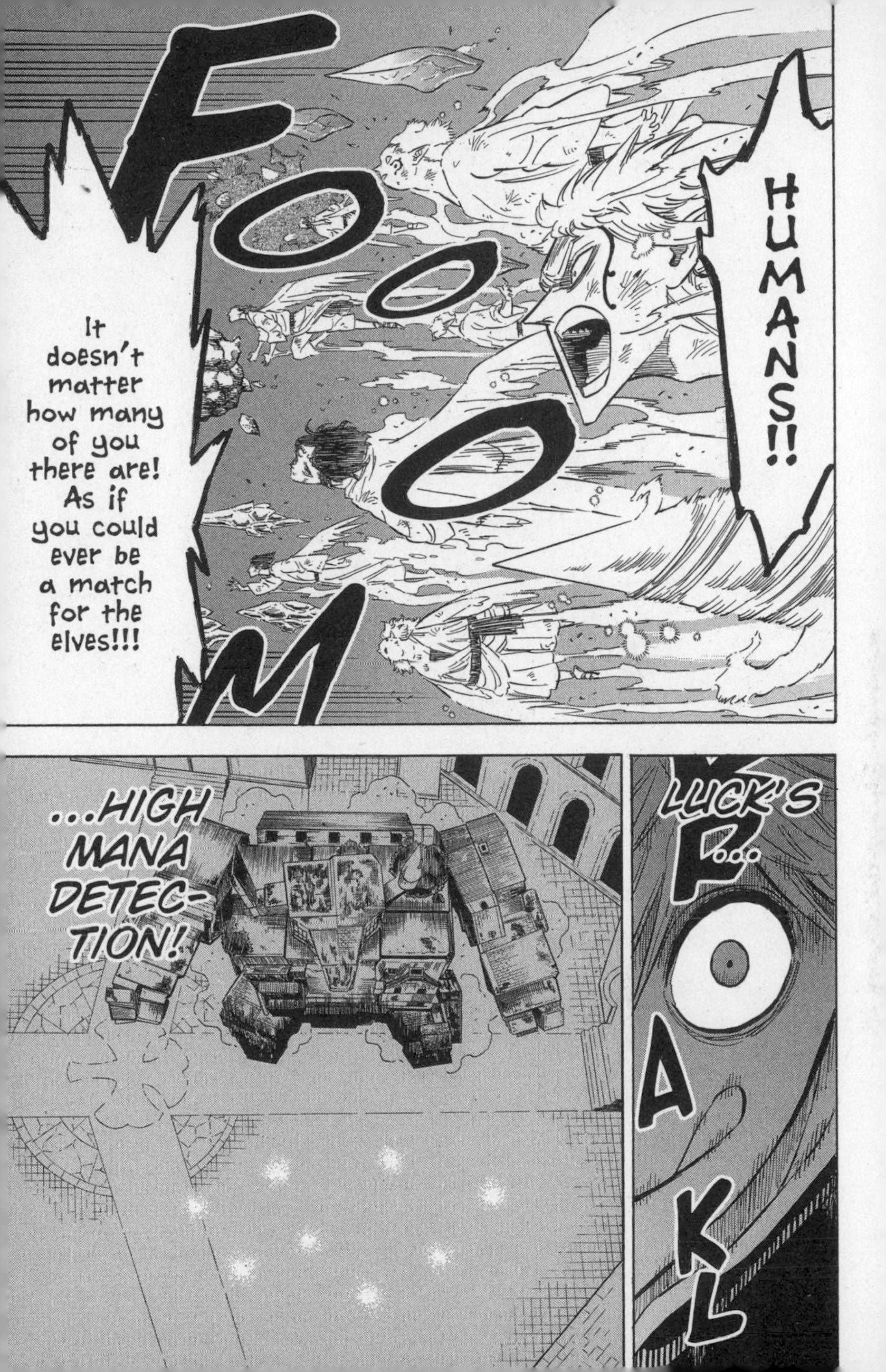
HUMANS!!
FOOOOM
It doesn't matter how many of you there are! As if you could ever be a match for the elves!!!
LUCK'S P...
OAKL
...HIGH MANA DETECTION!

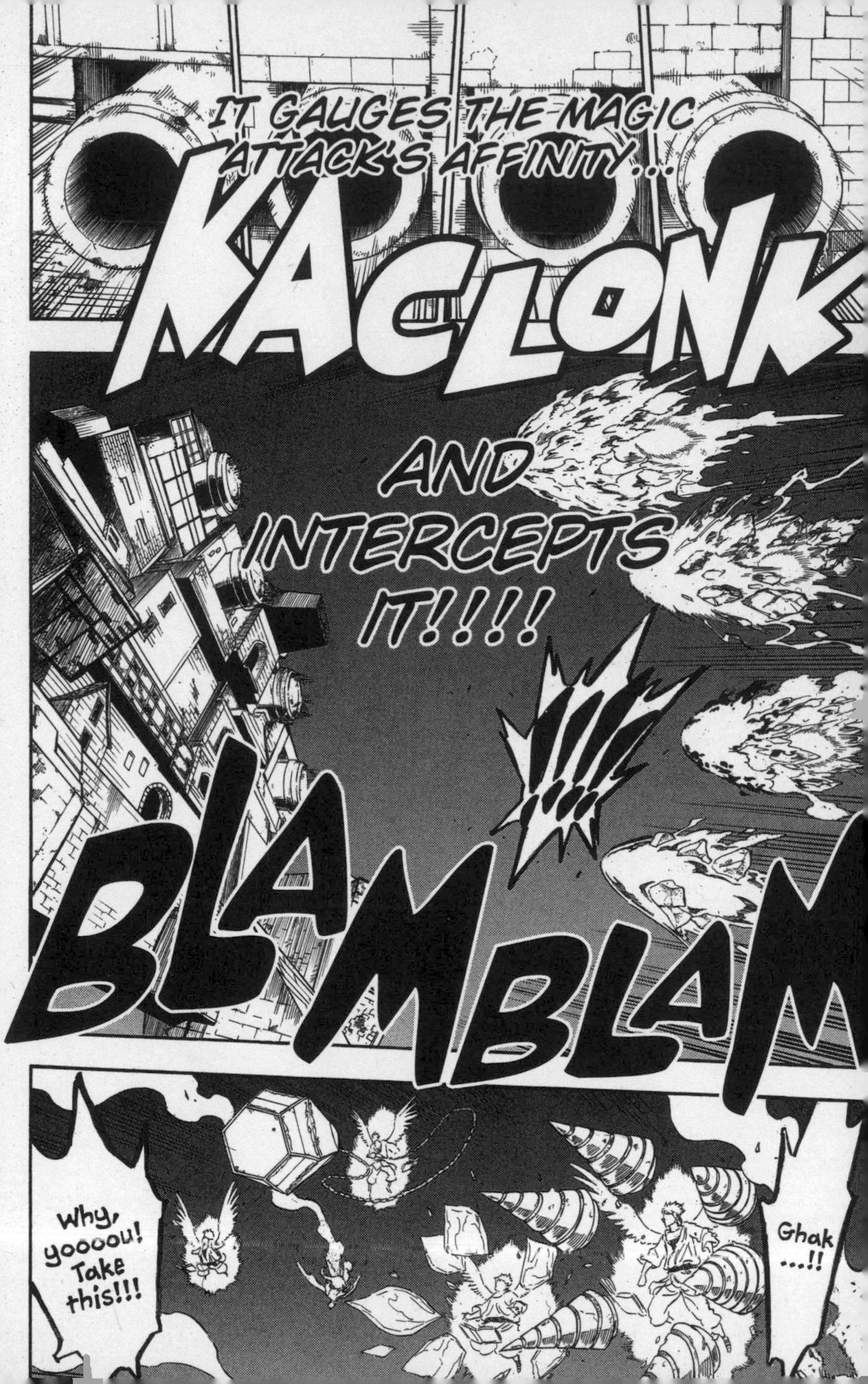
IT GAUGES THE MAGIC ATTACK'S AFFINITY...
KACLONK
AND INTERCEPTS IT!!!!
BLAMBLAM
Ghak ...!!
Why, yoooou! Take this!!!

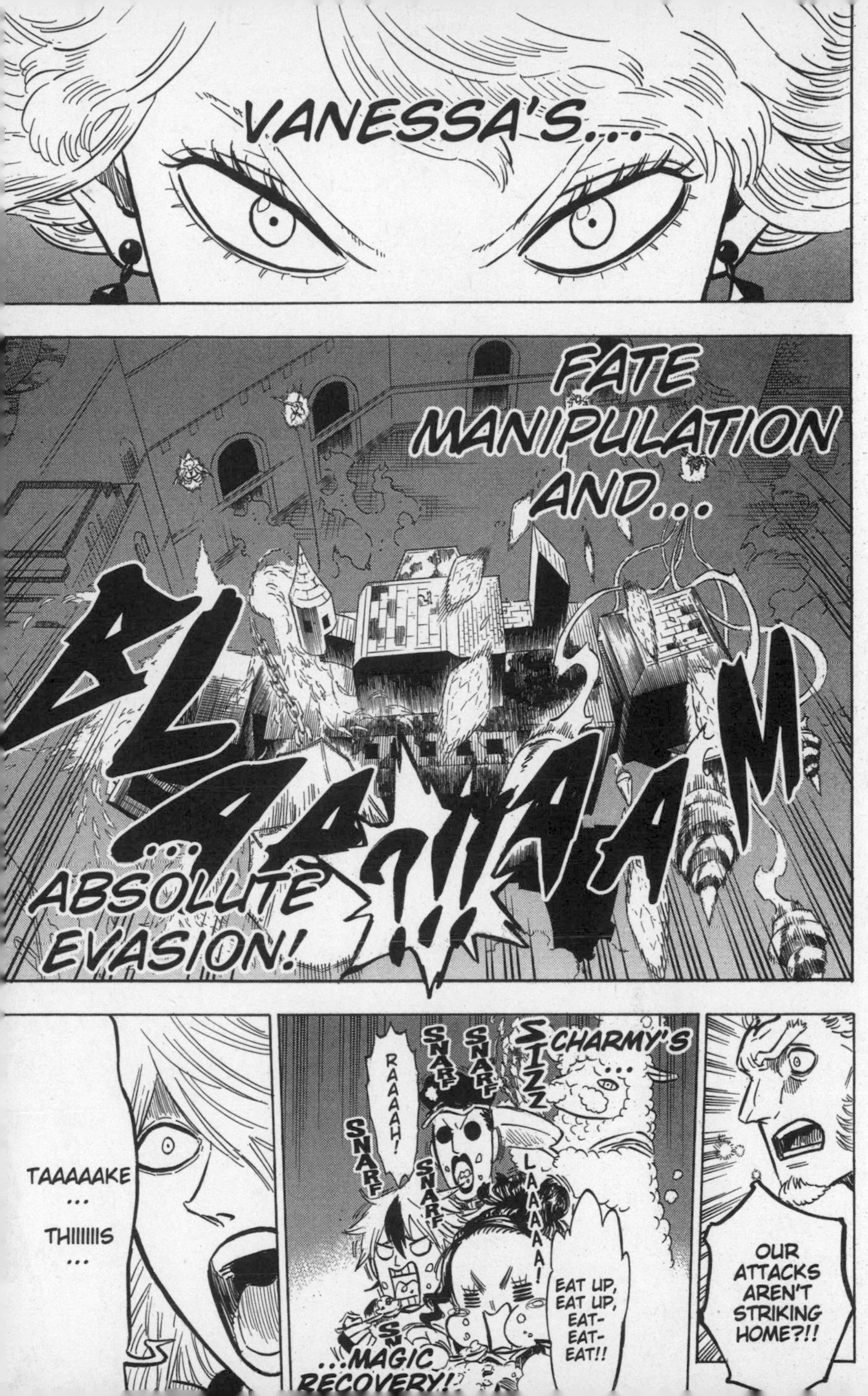
VANESSA'S....
FATE MANIPULATION AND...
BLAAAAAM
...ABSOLUTE EVASION!
?!!
OUR ATTACKS AREN'T STRIKING HOME?!!
CHARMY'S...
SIZZ
SNARF SNARF
RAAAAAH!
SNARF
SNARF SNARF
LAAAAAA!
EAT UP, EAT UP, EAT-EAT-EAT!!
SN
...MAGIC RECOVERY!!
TAAAAAKE... THIIIIIS...

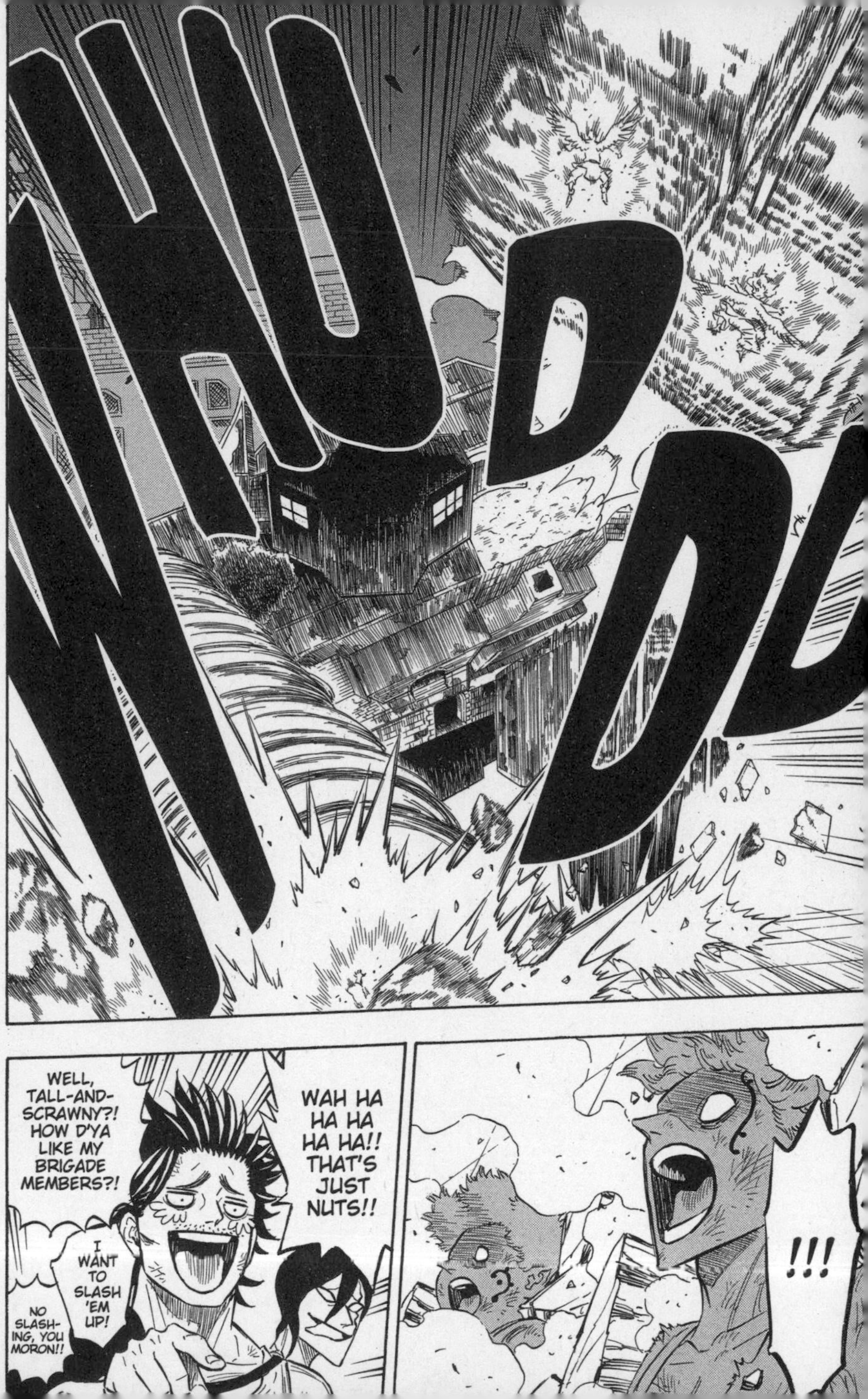
THUDDD
!!!
WAH HA HA HA HA HA!! THAT'S JUST NUTS!!
WELL, TALL-AND-SCRAWNY?! HOW D'YA LIKE MY BRIGADE MEMBERS?!
I WANT TO SLASH 'EM UP!
NO SLASHING, YOU MORON!!

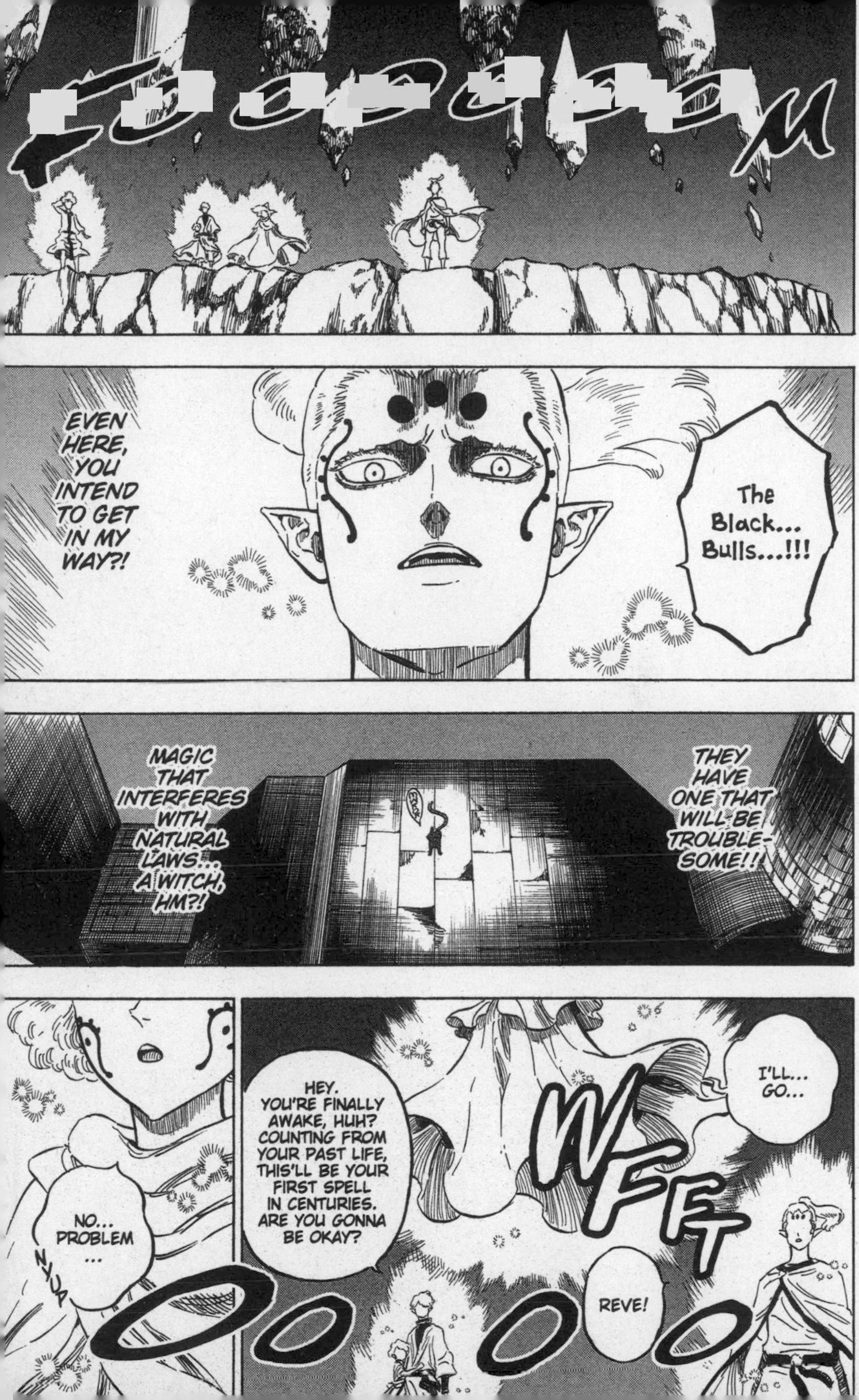
The Black... Bulls...!!!
EVEN HERE, YOU INTEND TO GET IN MY WAY?!
THEY HAVE ONE THAT WILL BE TROUBLE-SOME!!
MAGIC THAT INTERFERES WITH NATURAL LAWS... A WITCH, HM?!
I'LL... GO...
WFFT
HEY. YOU'RE FINALLY AWAKE, HUH? COUNTING FROM YOUR PAST LIFE, THIS'LL BE YOUR FIRST SPELL IN CENTURIES. ARE YOU GONNA BE OKAY?
REVE!
NO... PROBLEM ...
NYUP

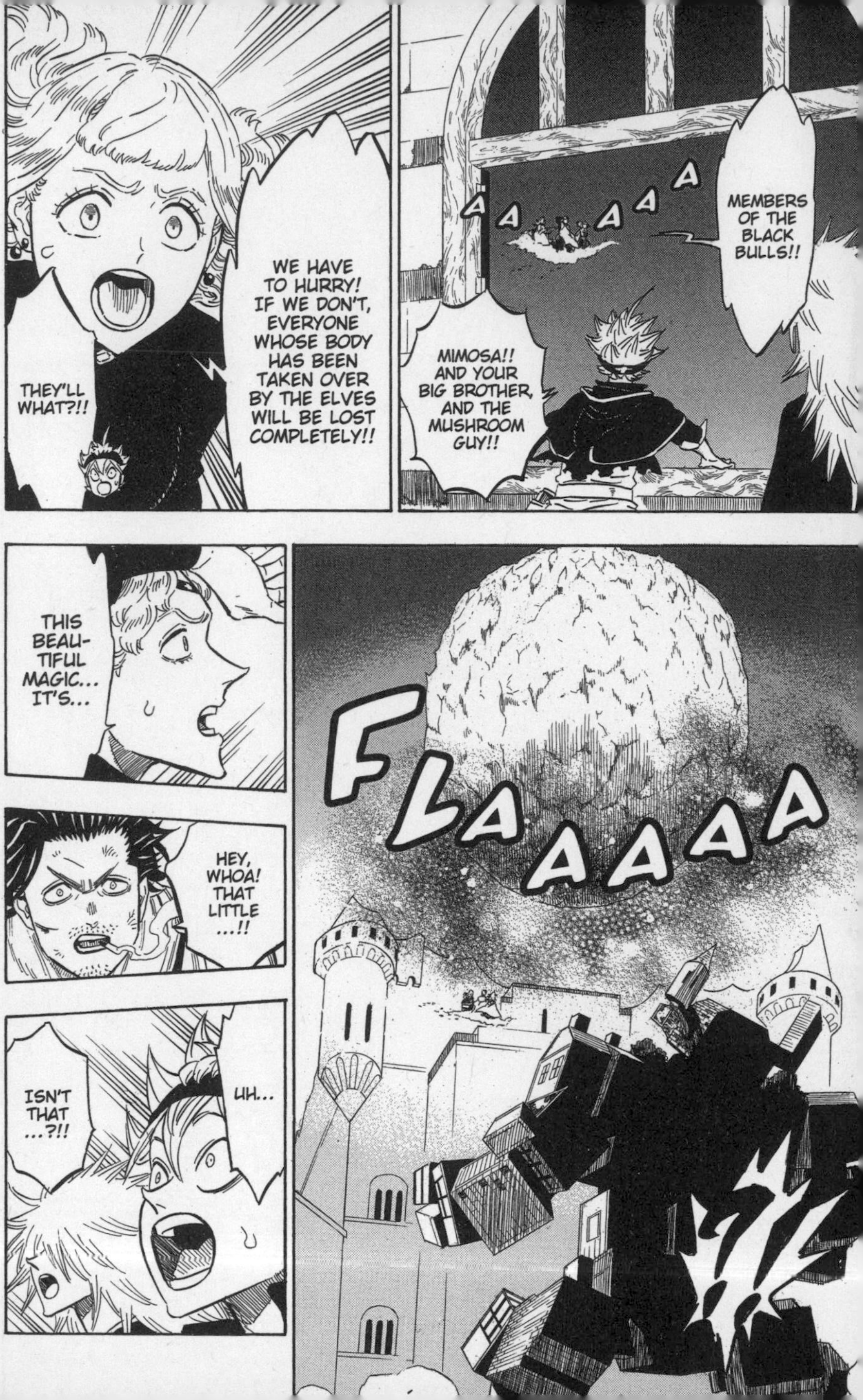
MEMBERS OF THE BLACK BULLS!!
AAAAAA
MIMOSA!! AND YOUR BIG BROTHER, AND THE MUSHROOM GUY!!
WE HAVE TO HURRY! IF WE DON'T, EVERYONE WHOSE BODY HAS BEEN TAKEN OVER BY THE ELVES WILL BE LOST COMPLETELY!!
THEY'LL WHAT?!!
FLAAAAA
THIS BEAUTIFUL MAGIC... IT'S...
HEY, WHOA! THAT LITTLE ...!!
UH...
ISN'T THAT ...?!!

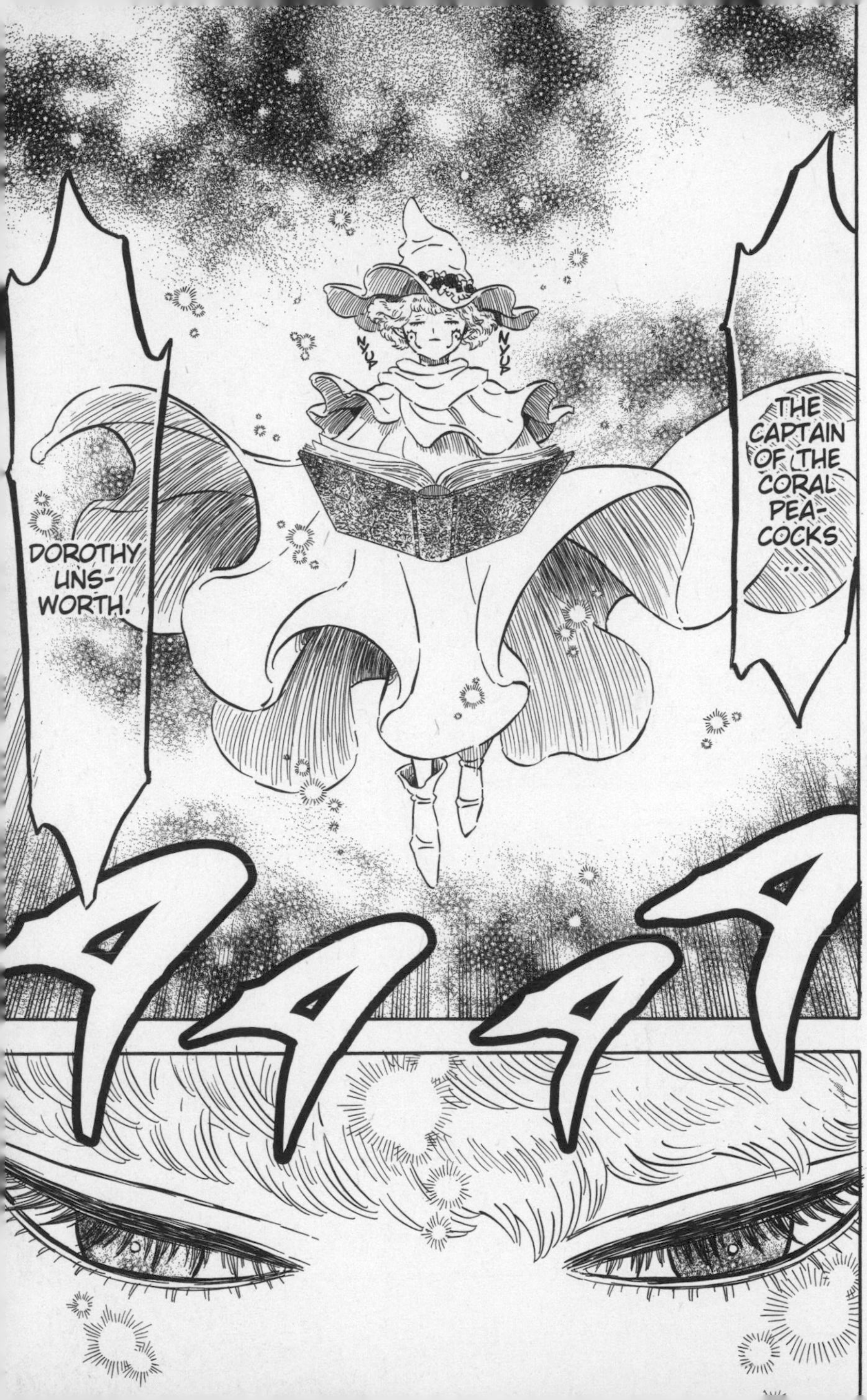
THE CAPTAIN OF THE CORAL PEA-COCKS...
NYUP
NYUP
DOROTHY UNS-WORTH.

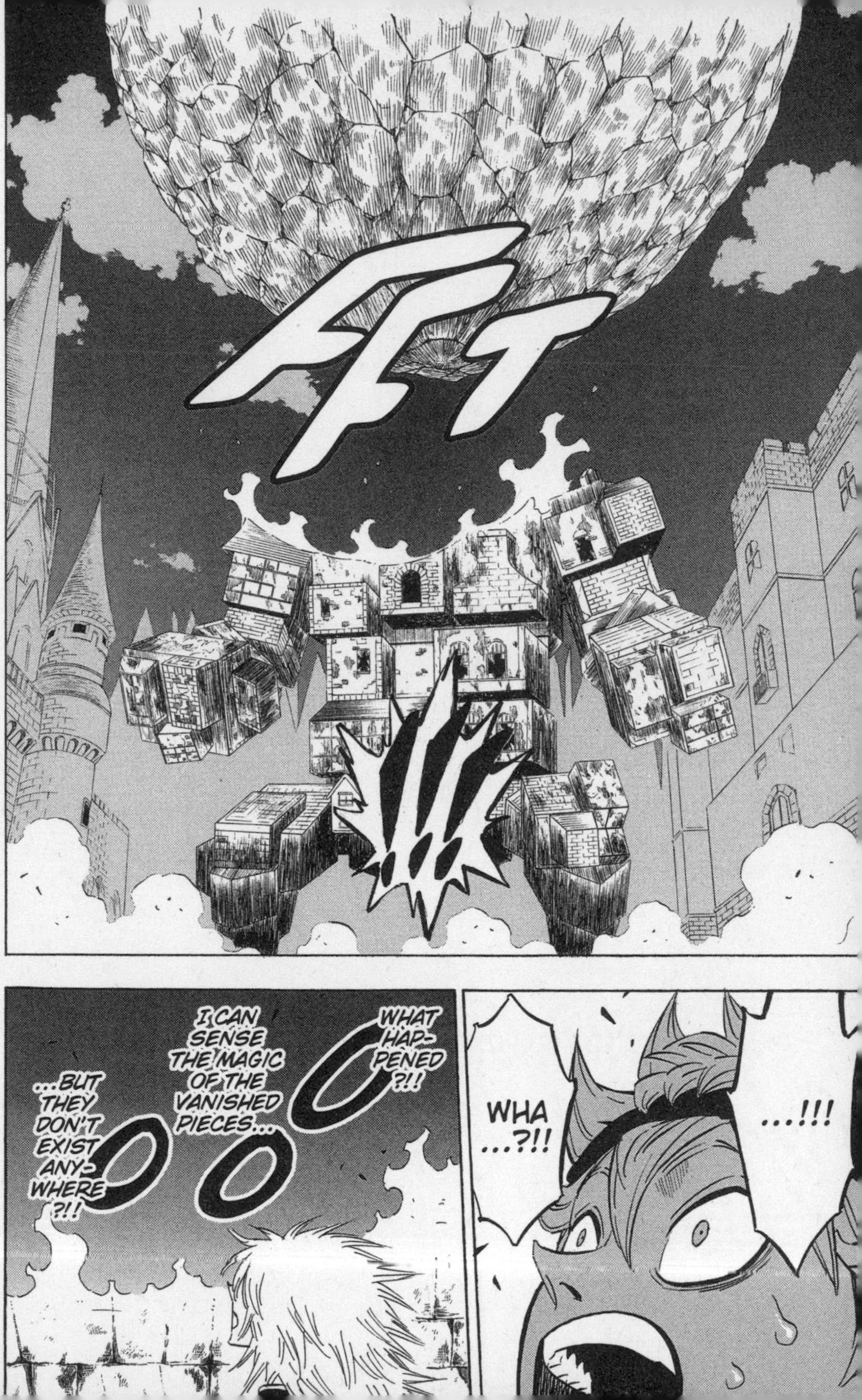
FFT
!!
...!!!
WHA...?!!
WHAT HAPPENED?!!
I CAN SENSE THE MAGIC OF THE VANISHED PIECES...
...BUT THEY DON'T EXIST ANYWHERE?!!

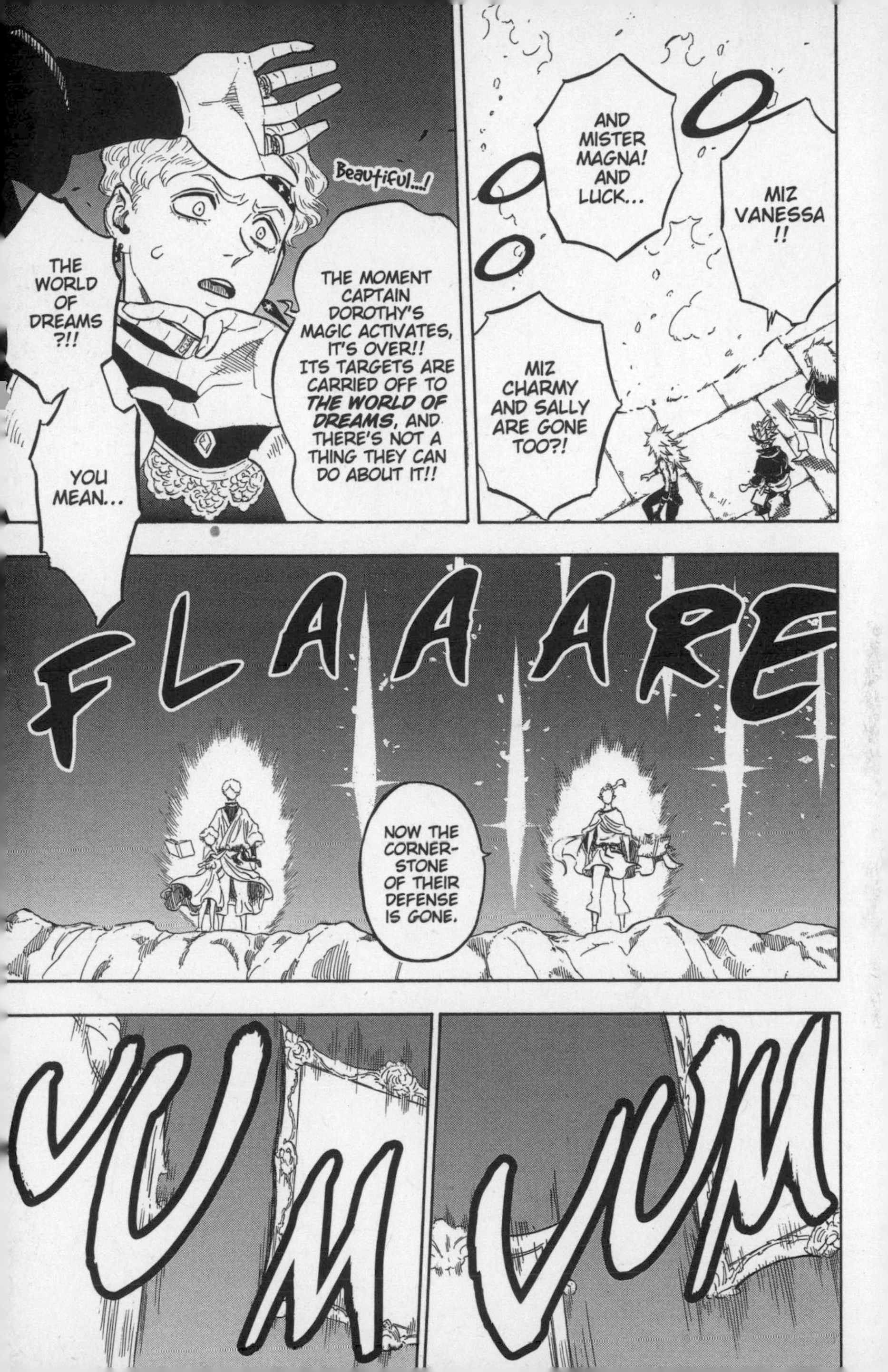
MIZ VANESSA!!
AND MISTER MAGNA! AND LUCK...
MIZ CHARMY AND SALLY ARE GONE TOO?!
Beautiful...!
THE MOMENT CAPTAIN DOROTHY'S MAGIC ACTIVATES, IT'S OVER!! ITS TARGETS ARE CARRIED OFF TO ***THE WORLD OF DREAMS***, AND THERE'S NOT A THING THEY CAN DO ABOUT IT!!
THE WORLD OF DREAMS?!!
YOU MEAN...
FLAAARE
NOW THE CORNER-STONE OF THEIR DEFENSE IS GONE.
VUM
VUM

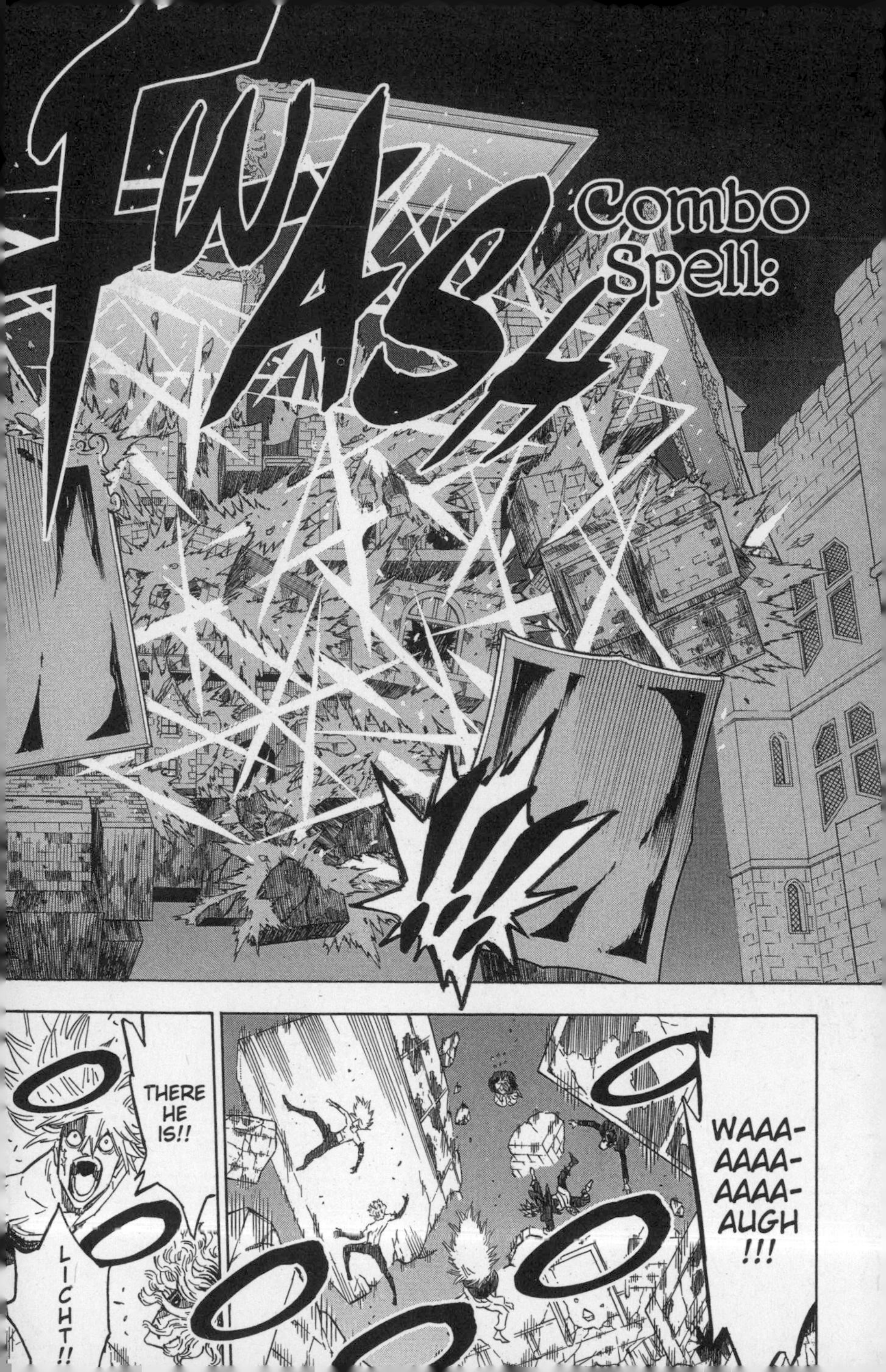
FWASH
Combo Spell:
!!!
WAAA-AAAA-AAAA-AUGH!!!
THERE HE IS!!
LICHT!!

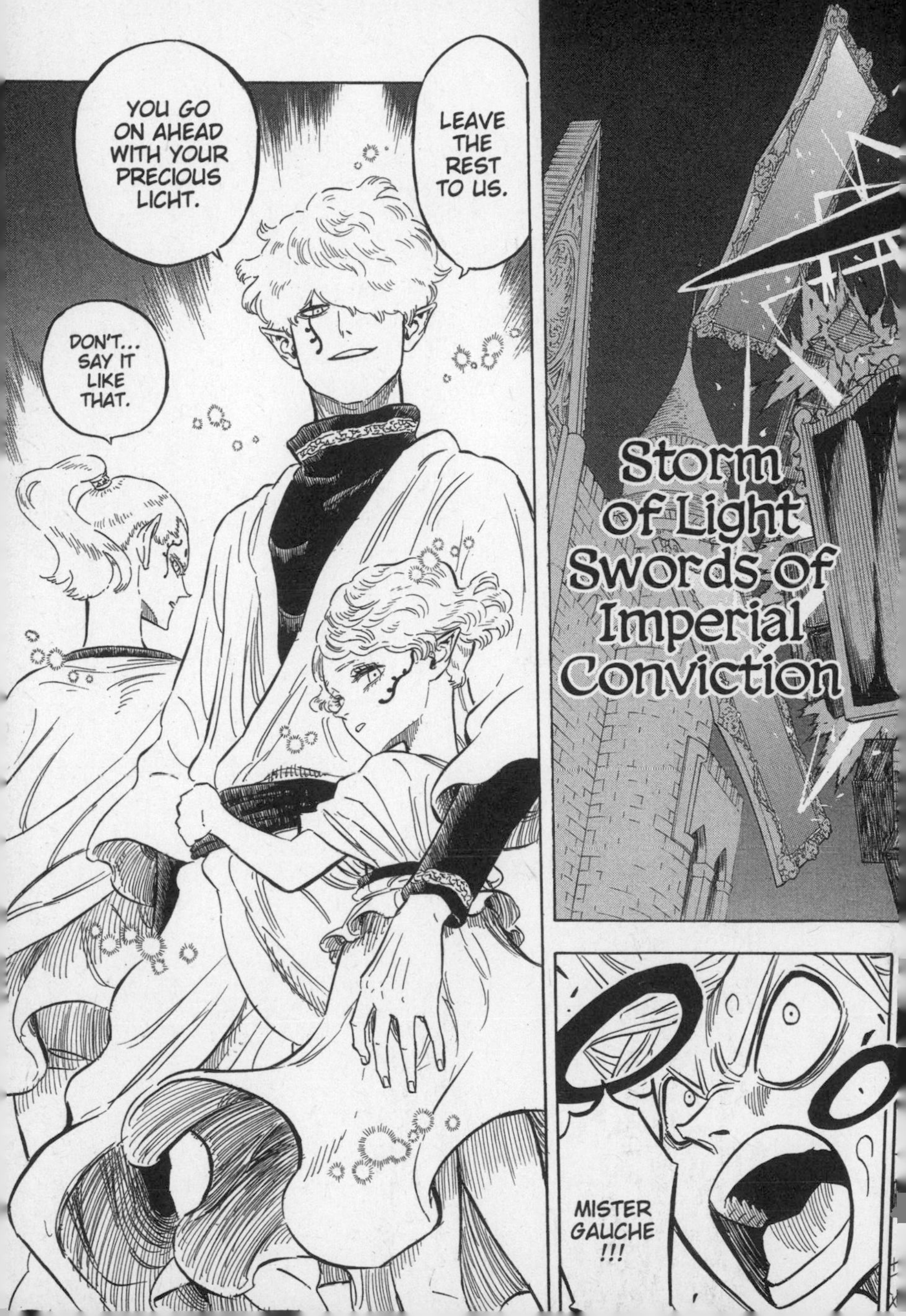
Storm of Light Swords of Imperial Conviction
MISTER GAUCHE !!!
LEAVE THE REST TO US.
YOU GO ON AHEAD WITH YOUR PRECIOUS LICHT.
DON'T... SAY IT LIKE THAT.

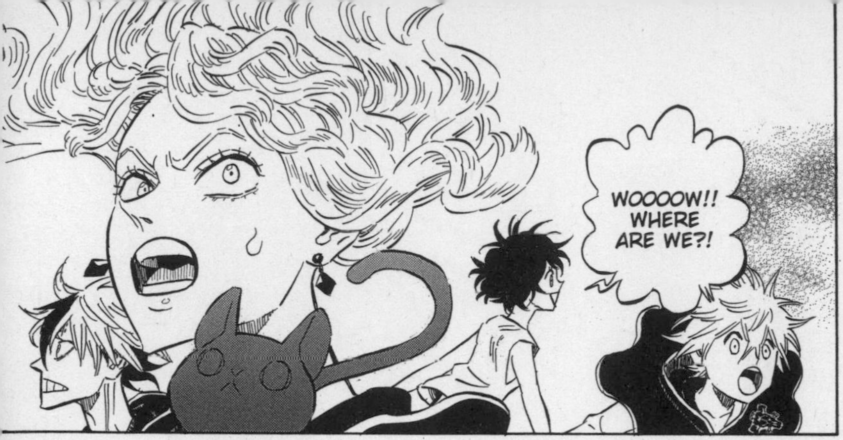
WOOOOW!!
WHERE
ARE WE?!

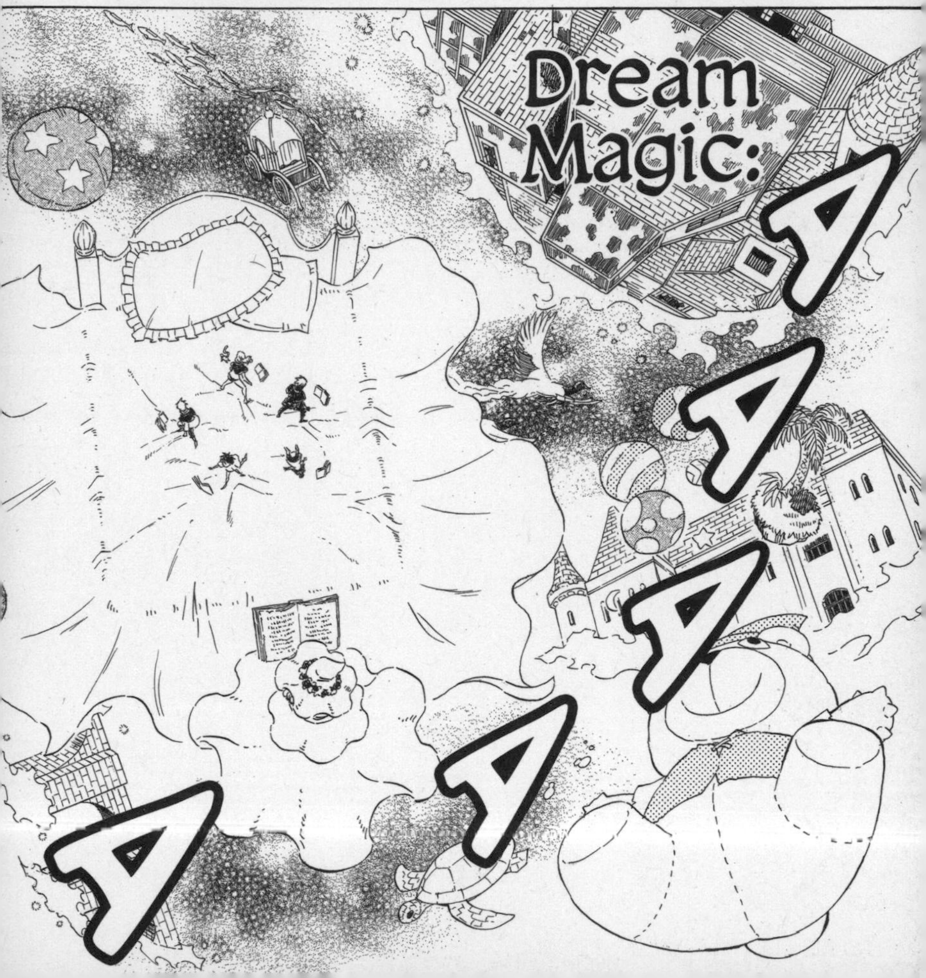
Dream
Magic:
AAAAA

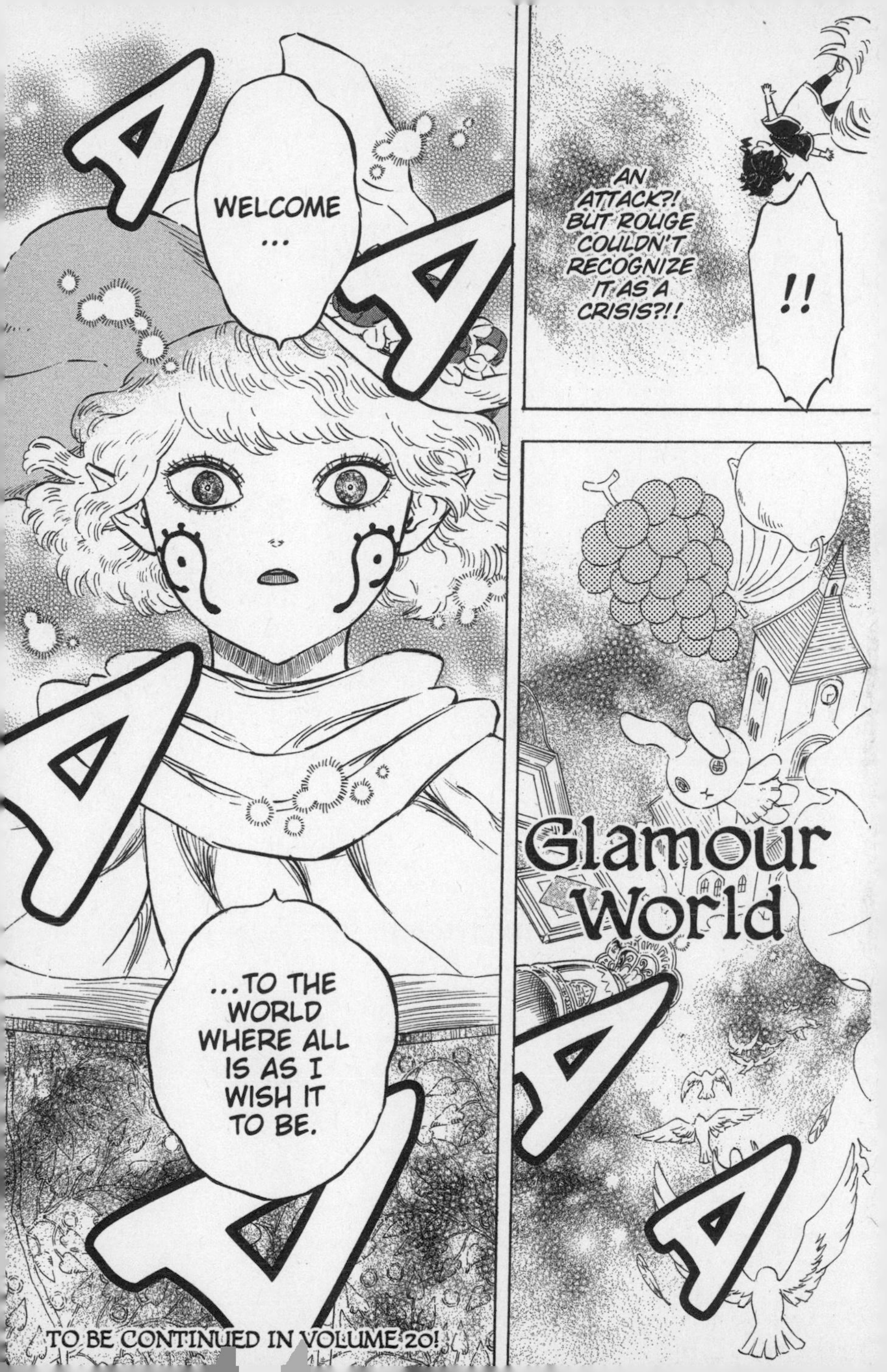
!!
AN ATTACK?! BUT ROUGE COULDN'T RECOGNIZE IT AS A CRISIS?!!
Glamour World
WELCOME ...
...TO THE WORLD WHERE ALL IS AS I WISH IT TO BE.
TO BE CONTINUED IN VOLUME 20!

The Blank Page Brigade

This volume's topic: What are your ambitions for this year?

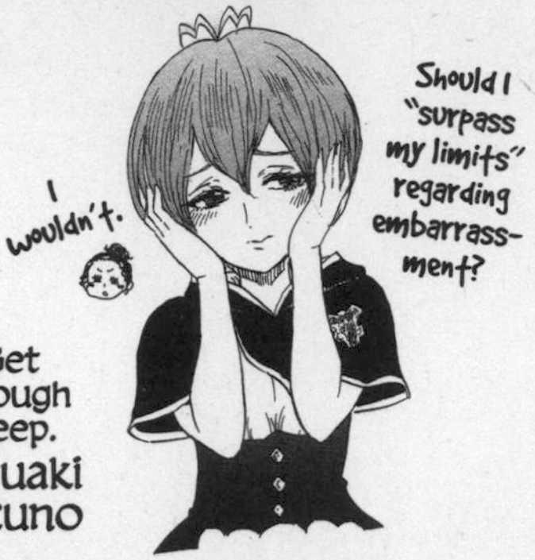

Should I "surpass my limits" regarding embarrassment?
I wouldn't.

Get enough sleep.
Teruaki Mizuno

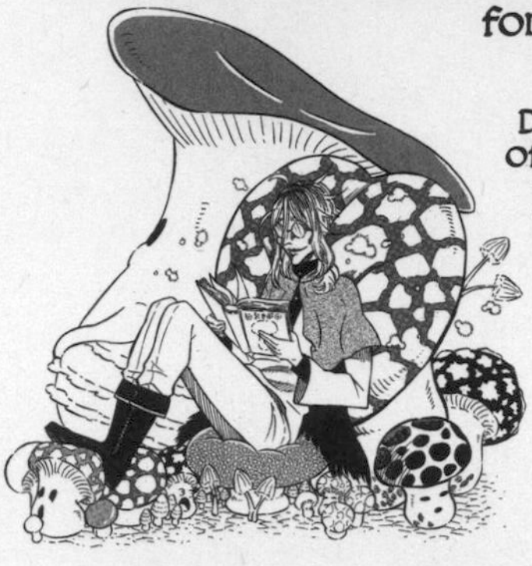

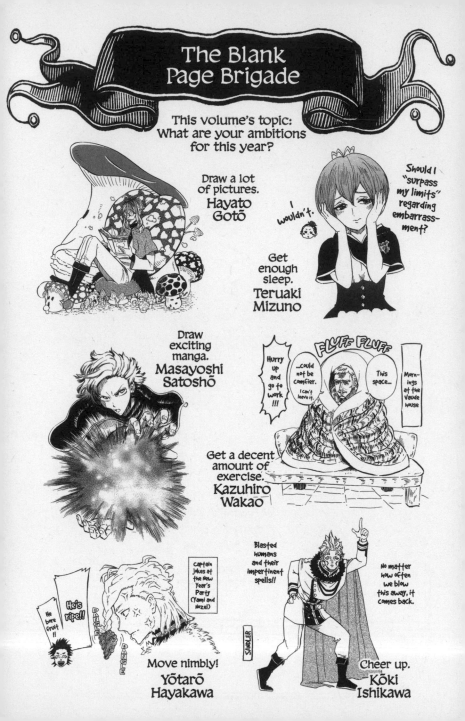

Draw a lot of pictures.
Hayato Gotō

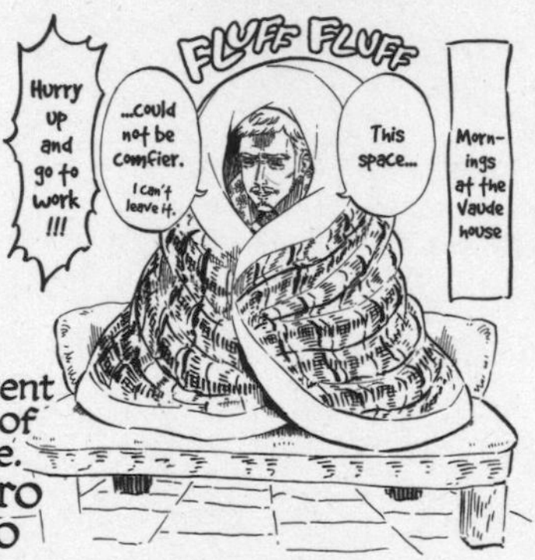

Mornings at the Vaude house
FLUFF FLUFF
This space...
...could not be comfier.
I can't leave it.
Hurry up and go to work!!!

Get a decent amount of exercise.
Kazuhiro Wakao

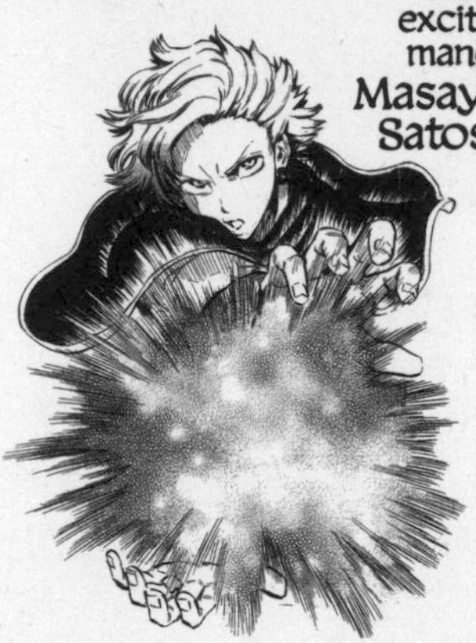

Draw exciting manga.
Masayoshi Satoshō

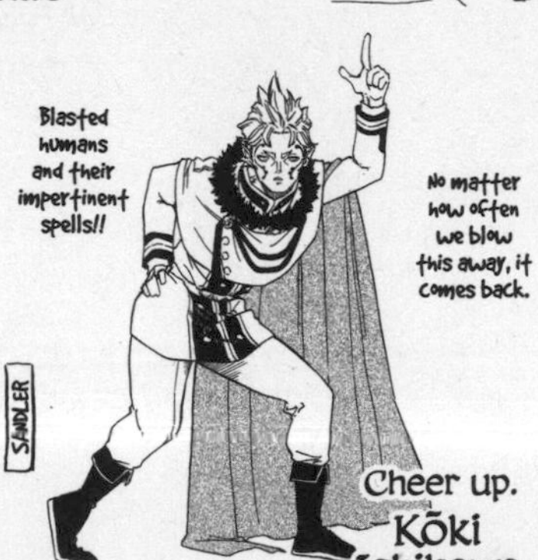

No matter how often we blow this away, it comes back.
Blasted humans and their impertinent spells!!
SANDLER

Cheer up.
Kōki Ishikawa

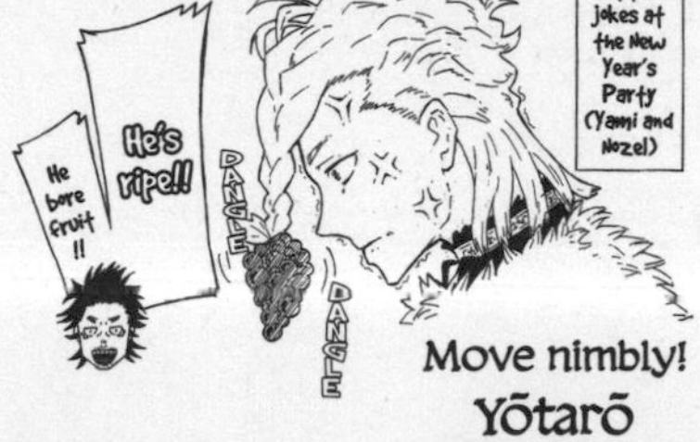

Captain jokes at the New Year's Party (Yami and Nozel)
DANGLE
DANGLE
He's ripe!!
He bore fruit!!

Move nimbly!
Yōtarō Hayakawa

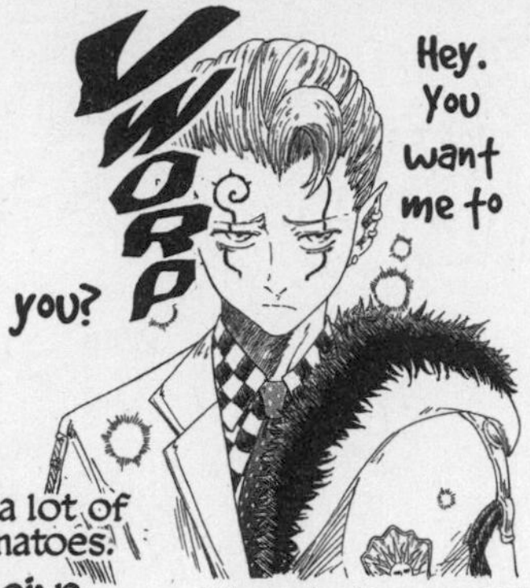
VWORP
Hey. You want me to
you?
*Please make a Line stamp of this.

Eat a lot of tomatoes.
Seiya Miyamoto

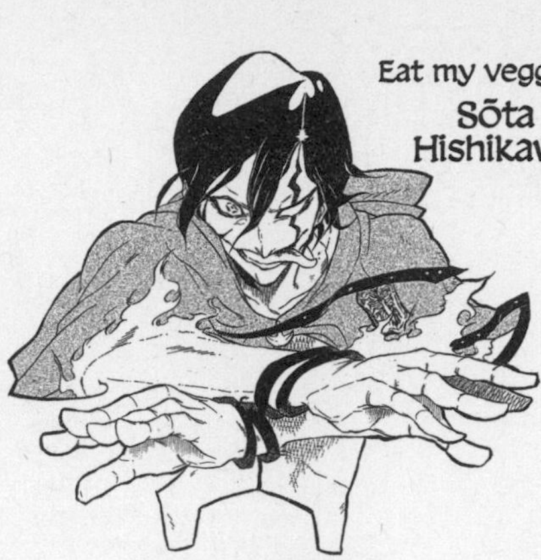

Eat my veggies.
Sōta Hishikawa

Eat in moderation.
©

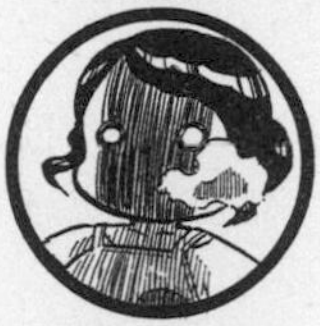

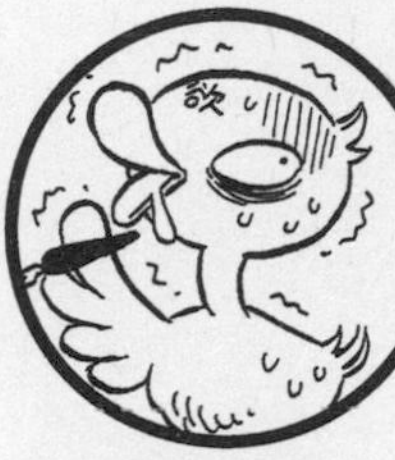

Be insanely healthy.
Captain Tabata

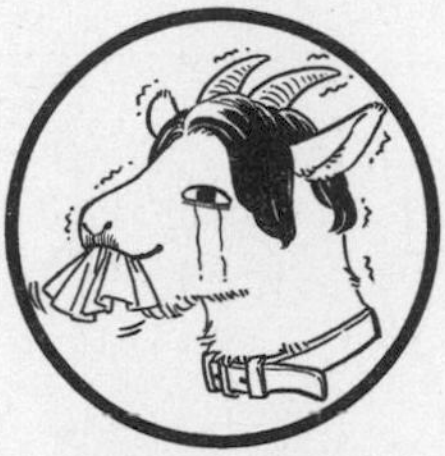

Step up and catch the jobs that come at me!
Editor Toide

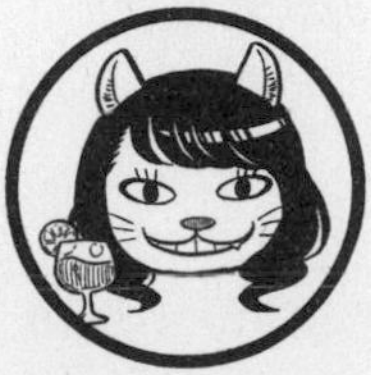

Don't just grin and bear stuff.
Designer Iwai

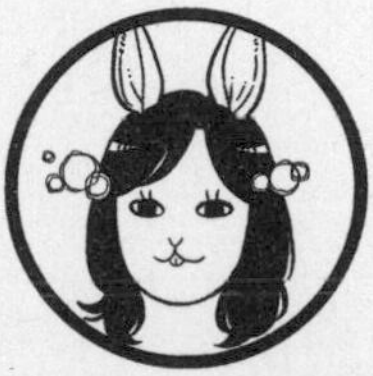

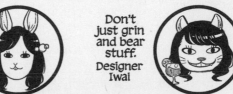

Take proper days off!
Comics Editor Koshimura

AFTERWORD

My shoulders are all busted!! Actually, my whole body's busted!! I used to like exercising quite a bit, so it makes me pretty sad...

That said, I'm getting to do a job that's incredibly worthwhile, and I'm so grateful I could bust, so in exchange for my busted body, I'll bust my butt and work hard!!

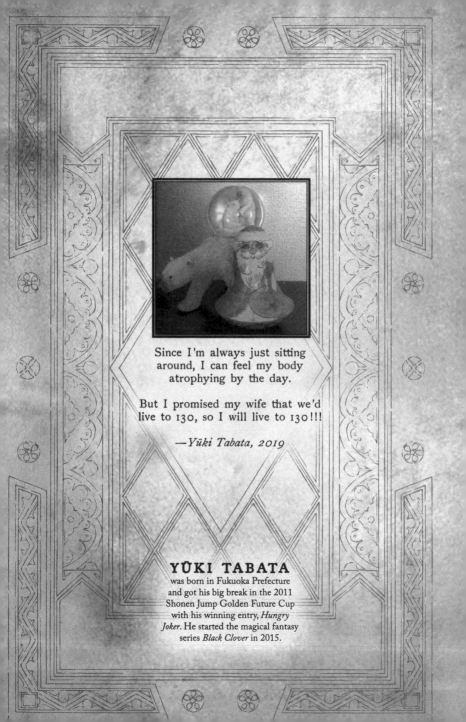

Since I'm always just sitting around, I can feel my body atrophying by the day.

But I promised my wife that we'd live to 130, so I will live to 130!!!

—Yūki Tabata, 2019

YŪKI TABATA
was born in Fukuoka Prefecture and got his big break in the 2011 Shonen Jump Golden Future Cup with his winning entry, *Hungry Joker*. He started the magical fantasy series *Black Clover* in 2015.

BLACK CLOVER
VOLUME 19
SHONEN JUMP Manga Edition

Story and Art by YŪKI TABATA

Translation ✽ TAYLOR ENGEL, HC LANGUAGE SOLUTIONS, INC.

Touch-Up Art & Lettering ✽ ANNALIESE CHRISTMAN

Design ✽ KAM LI

Editor ✽ ALEXIS KIRSCH

Printed in the U.S.A.

Published by VIZ Media, LLC
P.O. Box 77010
San Francisco, CA 94107

10 9 8 7 6 5 4 3 2 1
First printing, January 2020

ratings.viz.com RATED T TEEN

PARENTAL ADVISORY
BLACK CLOVER is rated T for Teen and is recommended for ages 13 and up. This volume contains realistic and fantasy violence.

VIZ MEDIA
viz.com

SHONEN JUMP
shonenjump.com

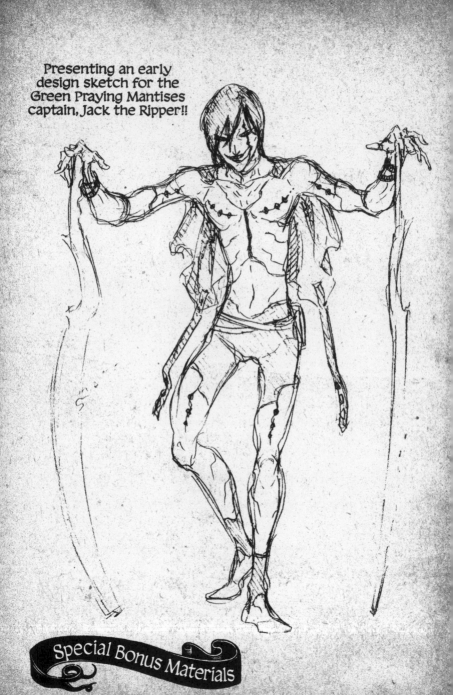

Presenting an early design sketch for the Green Praying Mantises captain, Jack the Ripper!!

Special Bonus Materials

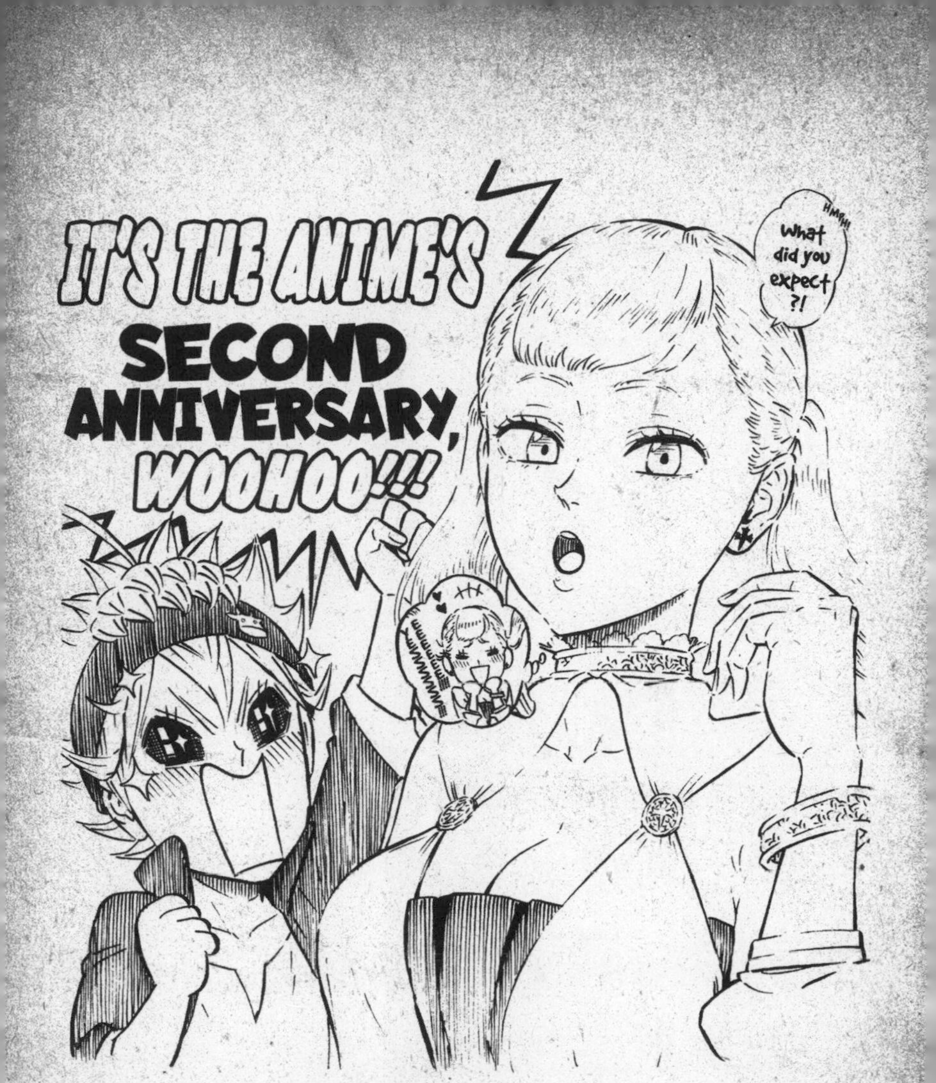
IT'S THE ANIME'S SECOND ANNIVERSARY, WOOHOO!!!
HMPH!
What did you expect?!

This is the art I drew as a reader gift when the anime started its second year. I'm so grateful!! Please keep on supporting it!!!

Story and Art by

KOYOHARU GOTOUGE

In Taisho-era Japan, kindhearted Tanjiro Kamado makes a living selling charcoal. But his peaceful life is shattered when a demon slaughters his entire family. His little sister Nezuko is the only survivor, but she has been transformed into a demon herself! Tanjiro sets out on a dangerous journey to find a way to return his sister to normal and destroy the demon who ruined his life.

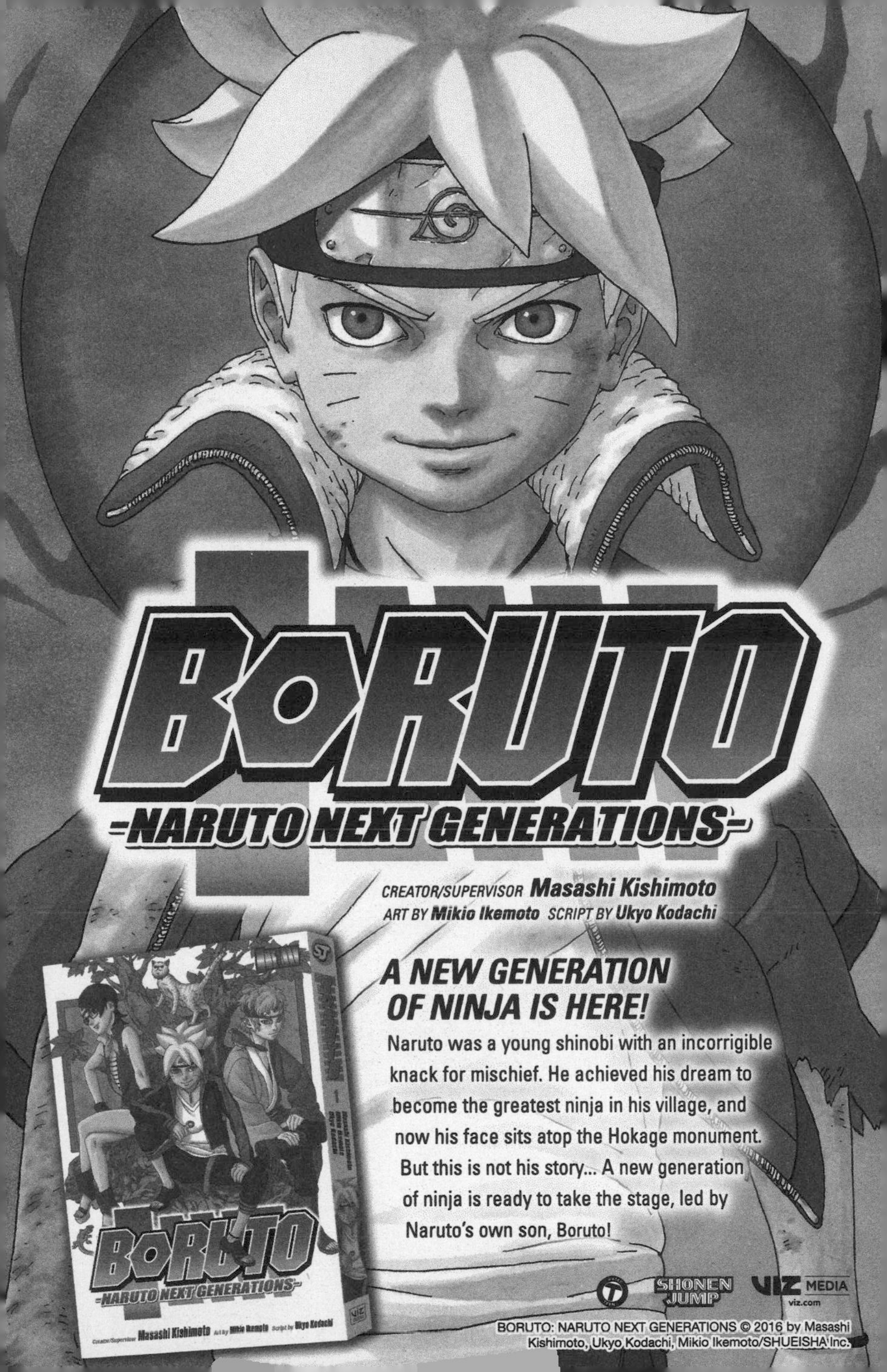
BORUTO
-NARUTO NEXT GENERATIONS-
CREATOR/SUPERVISOR Masashi Kishimoto
ART BY Mikio Ikemoto SCRIPT BY Ukyo Kodachi
A NEW GENERATION OF NINJA IS HERE!
Naruto was a young shinobi with an incorrigible knack for mischief. He achieved his dream to become the greatest ninja in his village, and now his face sits atop the Hokage monument. But this is not his story... A new generation of ninja is ready to take the stage, led by Naruto's own son, Boruto!
SHONEN JUMP
VIZ MEDIA
viz.com
BORUTO: NARUTO NEXT GENERATIONS © 2016 by Masashi Kishimoto, Ukyo Kodachi, Mikio Ikemoto/SHUEISHA Inc.

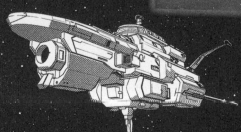

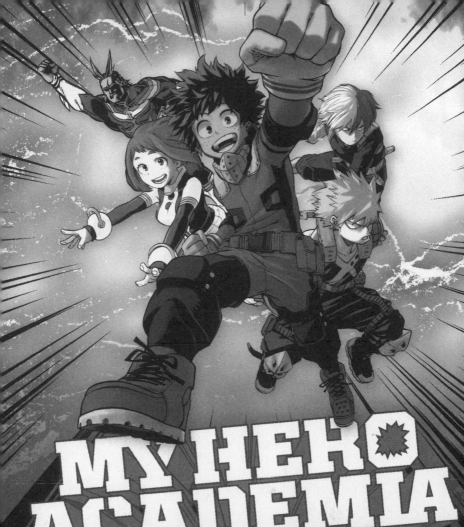

MY HERO ACADEMIA

IZUKU MIDORIYA WANTS TO BE A HERO MORE THAN
ANYTHING, BUT HE HASN'T GOT AN OUNCE OF POWER IN HIM.
WITH NO CHANCE OF GETTING INTO THE U.A. HIGH SCHOOL
FOR HEROES, HIS LIFE IS LOOKING LIKE A DEAD END. THEN
AN ENCOUNTER WITH ALL MIGHT, THE GREATEST HERO OF
ALL, GIVES HIM A CHANCE TO CHANGE HIS DESTINY...

SHONEN JUMP

viz media
www.viz.com

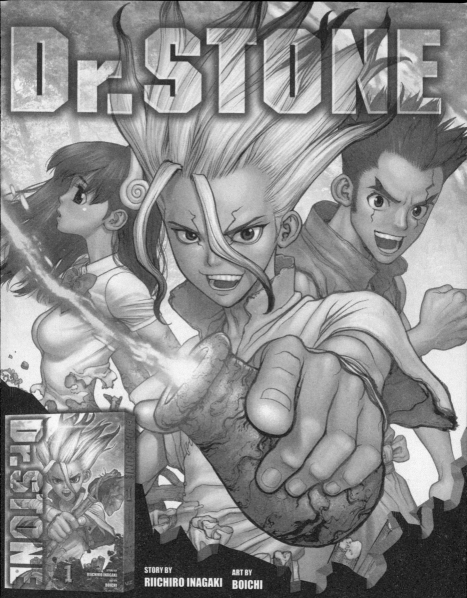

Dr. STONE

STORY BY
RIICHIRO INAGAKI

ART BY
BOICHI

One fateful day, all of humanity turned to stone. Many millennia later, Taiju frees himself from petrification and finds himself surrounded by statues. The situation looks grim—until he runs into his science-loving friend Senku! Together they plan to restart civilization with the power of science!

THE ACTION-PACKED SUPERHERO COMEDY ABOUT ONE MAN'S AMBITION TO BE A HERO FOR FUN!

ONE-PUNCH MAN

STORY BY
ONE

ART BY
YUSUKE MURATA

Nothing about Saitama passes the eyeball test when it comes to superheroes, from his lifeless expression to his bald head to his unimpressive physique. However, this average-looking guy has a not-so-average problem—he just can't seem to find an opponent strong enough to take on!

Can he finally find an opponent who can go toe-to-toe with him and give his life some meaning? Or is he doomed to a life of superpowered boredom?

VIZ MEDIA

www.viz.com

Stop

YOU'RE READING THE WRONG WAY!

1
2
1
3
4
2
5
6
3
7
8
4
9
5
142

BLACK CLOVER
reads from right to left, starting in the upper-right corner. Japanese is read from right to left, meaning that action, sound effects, and word-balloon order are completely reversed from English order.

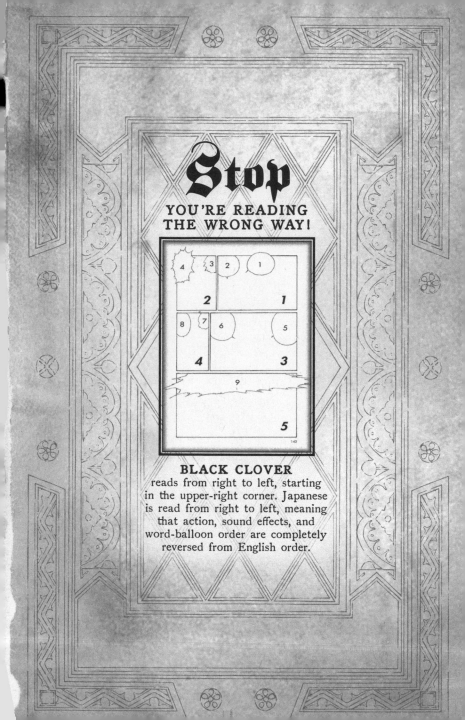